The
AMERICAN CAVALRY
in Vietnam
"First Cav"

Written by Jacques-François de Chaunac
Translated by Lyman C. Duryea

TURNER PUBLISHING COMPANY
Paducah, Kentucky

FOR TRISTAN

Turner®
PUBLISHING COMPANY

412 Broadway • P.O. Box 3101
Paducah, KY 42002-3101
(270) 443-0121
www.turnerpublishing.com

Turner Publishing Company Staff:
Editor/Designer: Herbert C. Banks II

Library of Congress Control No. 2003105699
ISBN: 1-56311-890-4

Printed in the United States of America.
Additional copies may be purchased directly from
Turner Publishing Company.
Limited Edition.

TABLE OF CONTENTS

CHRONOLOGICAL MILESTONES 4
INTRODUCTION 5
TRANSLATOR'S INTRODUCTION 7
PREFACE 8

PART ONE: THE CAV IN THE HIGHLANDS,
CHAPTER I 13   CHAPTER V 68
CHAPTER II 20   CHAPTER VI 77
CHAPTER III 36   CHAPTER VII 86
CHAPTER IV 56   CHAPTER VIII 95

PART TWO: FROM THE COASTAL PLAIN TO THE TET OFFENSIVE: THE COMMUNISTS STOPPED
ON ALL FRONTS, 1966 - 1968
CHAPTER IX 111   CHAPTER XIV 178
CHAPTER X 123   CHAPTER XV 185
CHAPTER XI 130   CHAPTER XVI 191
CHAPTER XII 143   CHAPTER XVII 201
CHAPTER XIII 154

PART THREE: MOVE TO THE SOUTH, 1968 – 1972
CHAPTER XVIII 217   CHAPTER XXII 258
CHAPTER XIX 224   CHAPTER XXIII 272
CHAPTER XX 232   CHAPTER XXIV 281
CHAPTER XXI 248   CHAPTER XXV 291

FINAL ACCOUNT 303
ORGANIZATION OF THE 1ST CAVALRY DIVISION 303
CHRONOLOGY OF THE AMERICAN ENGAGEMENT IN VIETNAM 304
BIBLIOGRAPHY 311
ACKNOWLEDGEMENTS 312

MAPS
THE IA DRANG VALLEY BATTLE, 1965 21
THE COASTAL CAMPAIGN 144
TET AND THE A SHAU VALLEY 202
OPERATION PEGASUS, APRIL 1968 218
THE 1ST CAVALRY DIVISION IN III CORPS, 1969 259
OPERATION TOTAL VICTORY, MAY 1970 THE CAMBODIAN INCURSION 282

CHRONOLOGICAL MILESTONES

<u>7 May 1954:</u> Dien Bien Phu falls and the French garrison is taken captive.

<u>21 July 1954:</u> At Geneva Pierre Mendès France and Ho Chi Minh sign a treaty that divides Vietnam in two at the 17th Parallel. It marks the end of the French Indochinese War.

<u>5 October 1954:</u> The last French soldiers leave Hanoi. One week later the Vietminh officially take control of North Vietnam.

<u>16 May 1955:</u> The South Vietnamese Government formally requests that the United States train the South Vietnamese Armed Forces.

<u>June 1957:</u> The last French training teams leave South Vietnam.

<u>May 1959:</u> The American Commander of the Pacific Theater sends a first contingent of military advisors numbering approximately 320. This is the beginning of a real American military presence in South Vietnam.

<u>8 February 1962:</u> US Army General Paul Harkins organizes and takes command of the American Military Assistance Command Vietnam (MACV). At that time he has four thousand advisors in country. Insidiously, the Vietnam War begins.

INTRODUCTION

This is the story of the 1st Air Cavalry Division in Vietnam. The French author, Jacques-François de Chaunac, lived and worked in Vietnam during the war. He writes from personal observation as well as careful research. The book was originally published in France and found a friendly audience. The translator was a young officer under my command who served in the Garry Owen Brigade at the time of some of the events described in this book. For good measure, the author gives excellent explanations of the tactics and techniques developed by the Division in preparation for taking the war to the enemy through the air as well as on the ground.

When he needs to present some particular aspect of the 1st Cav's operations, of its effectiveness, of the special esprit that characterizes the heroes of his story, the fighting men and the pilots who support them, de Chaunac develops the details in interviews, addresses to the troops, and dialogs between various participants. Journalists at the front interview senior officers of the Division as well as other personnel, both officer and enlisted. Division commanders address their men on special occasions, summarizing operations. Brigade commanders issue orders and guidance to their staffs. Company commanders, platoon leaders, and noncommissioned officers issue operations orders to their soldiers in the field. The men discuss their understanding of the war with each other, sometimes comparing the perceptions of the veterans of several months' combat with those of the new replacements. The topics range from political conflict in the nation's capitol, the evolution of the airmobility concept and the organization of the Division, right along to the choice of girls in a Saigon brothel.

The author has done his research, and there are few departures from accuracy in the book. The present translation has been reviewed by several participants. Their comments have been woven into the narrative as appropriate. The book tells the remarkable saga of the 1st Cav's striking success with the substitution of helicopters for ground-bound vehicles. More significantly, it is the tale of how the officers and men of the Division, in the finest traditions of the cavalry, met the challenge of once again fighting for freedom in a far off land.

This translation of Jacque-François de Chaunac's book paints a vivid tableau. In addition to the fierce battles at the Ia Drang Valley and Khe Sanh and the contest for control of the country during the Tet Offensive, he describes the action in other battles not well known but vicious and fought to bitter conclusions. These include the fighting at *LZs Bird* and *Hereford*, and near the village of Than Son 2 as well as several smaller contacts where cavalry troopers known but to God, their comrades and their families met their end beside their fellows fighting for a cause that was not to be. This book is for them.

Robert F. Litle, Jr.
Colonel, USA, Retired

TRANSLATOR'S INTRODUCTION

This is a book by a very perceptive French author who comes just about as close as you can get to capturing the fighting spirit, dedication, and brotherhood of the men of the First Air Cavalry Division. Jacques-François de Chaunac, an author who sees more clearly than many Americans of the war generation, captures the spirit and the courage of the American fighting man in a fast moving narrative. Those who did not serve can never know. Those who avoided service should know shame.

I had the privilege of serving in that Division from February 1966 to February 1967, the particular honor of serving in the Garry Owen Brigade. For the better part of that year I commanded a company of the 2^d Battalion, 7th Cavalry. Most of the rest of the time I served as air operations officer and for a brief period as the acting Operations Officer. There have never been more courageous fighting men. The challenge was to hold men back, to discourage self sacrifice. The casualties would have been even higher.

There has never been a more finely honed fighting machine or men more devoted to their comrades. Air assaults and all the associated fire support were precise to within seconds. All that was needed for an Operations Order was an LZ time and what to do once on the ground. Helicopters never touched down in an air assault. The men all jumped as the choppers came in on final. It was fun if you made it in one piece and alive.

We could have won the war. We were well the way to doing so in 1969, as I noted with some surprise as I completed a second tour. Why we quit is a shameful story for another book. Much of the blame falls upon the military. We took too long to understand the kind of war we were waging. We won the battles, but lost the informational and political struggle.

We lost the war and abandoned an ally in their hour of need. The Vietnamese people, however, are hard working, courageous, and resourceful. They must wait a bit longer for their political freedom. They will get it.

No soldier fighting for freedom ever dies in vain. The spirits of some fifty-eight thousand Americans linger still above the verdant highlands of Indochina, the South China Sea to the East, magnificent mountains to the West. The world moved a little closer to individual liberty, political freedom and respect for the dignity of the individual because of what they did.

PREFACE

We who know the end of the story.
by François d'Orcival

The first time we met the "First Cav" was at Khe Sanh on 1 April 1968. This American base, located roughly twenty kilometers from the North Vietnamese border, had been under violent siege by two divisions of North Vietnamese regulars for seventy days. Six thousand marines were dug in there behind their sandbags, being resupplied by air. They had no intention of ending up like the French at Dien Bien Phu.

At seven in the morning on the seventieth day of the siege, therefore, General John Tolson decided to send his cavalry to the rescue of "Fort Khe Sanh." He launched three cavalry brigades to break through the circle of enemy troops and force them to lift the siege. It was, once again, the "old army" against the "Indians." But here, the "mounts" of this "old army" were frightening machines that shaved the treetops, hid themselves against the sun, and arrived in your lap with a hellish roar. As for the "Indians," they were real soldiers, hardened and well trained. Their allies equipped them with the most modern weapons.

To destroy the enemy required resistance and force working in conjunction; the anvil of the marines inside the fortified position and the hammer of a force coming from the outside and capable of breaking the back of the besiegers. The operation commanded by General Tolson that thus began on 1 April 1968 employed 250 helicopters, 100 fighter-bombers and reconnaissance aircraft, and 35,000 men. It was not a rescue column, but an army on the march. The pincher movement was accomplished in three days, and on the morning of 8 April, Colonel Hubert Campbell set up the command post (CP) of his 3ᵈ Brigade at Khe Sanh. It was all over. This elegant maneuver had simply overwhelmed the enemy with its unique power. It had been carried out by the "First Cav," the US 1ˢᵗ Air Cavalry Division.

So what was this cavalry? Who were its chiefs? Who were its men? This is the story that the author of this book wanted to tell after poring over the journals of the combatants, the eyewitness accounts, the news reports from a host of sources, and the minute-by-minute, day-by-day accounts of some of the key battles of the American war in Vietnam.

Officially, this war began for the Americans in August of 1965 and ended on 30 April 1975 when the North Vietnamese army surrounded Saigon. But there is another way of looking at it. The first armed helicopters arrived in the South Vietnamese Delta in the spring of 1962 and did not leave until thirteen years later when they carried out the last combat troops.

In fact, this war really lasted only a little more than five years for the Americans, from late 1965 to the beginning of 1971. The expeditionary corps already numbered 500,000 men by 1967. In 1971, the South Vietnamese had taken over from the Americans everywhere. In 1972 they stood up very well to the massive offensive launched by the communists who subsequently had to devote nearly two years to reconstituting their forces. It was only in the summer of 1974 following the resignation of Richard Nixon in August that the North prepared the final offensive, taking advantage of the American retreat from its commitment to the South.

This book thus describes American air cavalry war, the war on the ground and in the cockpits of the assault helicopters, the night fighting, the long hours of watching and waiting, the jungle war in the thick vegetation, where the sun and heat constantly combine with rain and mud. And these continually renewed battles they always won. They were not won because it makes a better story, but because it is true. But they, the combatants, do not know the end of the story. We do. We know that these continually renewed and always won battles ended in total defeat, an unbelievable mess: 58,000 Americans killed, 300,000 wounded, 1,000,000 Vietnamese, civilians and soldiers killed, and how many millions of refugees... .

The 7th Cavalry Regiment, one of the most famous of the American cavalry, and one of the major units of the "First Cav," narrowly escaped annihilation on 25 June 1876 at Little Bighorn, a valley in Montana several miles from the Wyoming border. Sitting Bull and Crazy Horse there assembled their most hardened warriors, ten thousand Sioux and Cheyennes, the best fighters of the Indian nations. At the head of the "7th," Colonel George Armstrong Custer charged into the redskins. The fighting was sharp and furious and lasted about an hour. The morning of the next day the Indians left nothing on the field but naked and mutilated bodies. Custer and his regiment had disappeared in the battle. It was a carnage without survivors other than the Cheyennes and the Sioux to recount what had happened, the last stand of Colonel Custer, surrounded by his officers and cavalrymen... . Custer had made a fatal error. Confronting an enemy with superior numbers, he had divided his forces, dispersing his three battalions rather than uniting them. The result was a massacre.

The Americans never united in the Vietnamese War. They did not cease to bicker among themselves. The administration was divided, Congress was divided, the Chiefs of Staff were divided.

This book opens with the series of battles fought by the 1st Cavalry Division in the highlands in the autumn of 1965 during missions to seek out and destroy enemy forces. In 1966 and 1967, the "First Cav" moved down to the coastal plain to clean out enemy sanctuaries.

At that time Robert McNamara, the American Secretary of Defense, that is to say the Minister of War, was the responsible political chief of operations. This individual so little believed in the successful outcome of the battles he managed that he asked to be relieved of his position. On 27 November 1967 he was named director of the World Bank. It took two months to appoint and obtain Senate ratification of his successor. This was Clark Clifford, whose nomination was approved on 30 January 1968, the same day when the North Vietnamese and Vietcong launched their generalized attacks on all the Vietnamese population centers. This general attack by the communist forces failed. In six weeks, the attackers had been thrown back everywhere. The "Tet Offensive" ended as a defeat for the communists on the ground, but a political success in the domain of American support for the war.

On 25 March 1968, after they had been briefed by senior Pentagon staffers, the Central Intelligence Agency (CIA), and the State Department, several prominent figures who had held high posts in government, including Dean Acheson, McGeorge Bundy, John McCoy, and Henry Cabot Lodge (soon to become Ambassador to Vietnam), and others, came out in favor of withdrawal. For Hanoi, this signified that Washington would not hold out for the long haul. That was in 1968. Washington held out for six more years. But until the very end, the American political and military leadership was torn by dissension.

William Colby, who was at the head of the CIA at the end of the war and who had directed the pacification program on the ground in Vietnam, tells the following story in his account of this period. After the war, an American colonel, Harry Summers, met with one of his North Vietnamese counterparts in Hanoi.

"You know," said the American, "you never defeated us on the battlefield."

"That's quite possible... ," admitted his former adversary. "... but that has nothing to do with the problem. The problem was not in fact to win only on the field of battle, but to have the determination to win the war."

Before shutting down his office the night of 30 April 1975, the

10

CIA Station Chief in Saigon sent off the following message to his superior in Washington:

> It was a long and hard fight, and we lost. The seriousness of the defeat and of the circumstances in which it occurred seem to call for a reassessment of the policies and meager half-measures that have typified most of our involvement, in spite of a generous commitment of men and resources. Those who do not know how to learn the lessons of History are destined to repeat it... .

The battle of the Little Bighorn left the tragic legend of the 7th Cavalry of the "old army." The Vietnam battles have, so far, inscribed neither legends nor traditions in the regimental memories of the units that fought there.[1] And yet, here is the cavalry that enters the scene, announced by bugles blowing, masked by a cloud of dust churned up by rotor blades, as by the horses' hooves of yesteryear...

Translator's Note
[1] While the saga of American fighting units in Vietnam may not yet have captured the imagination of the general public, the battles and campaigns of that war have become a part of the history and traditions of the units that fought it. At this time, thirty-eight years after the arrival of the First Cav in Vietnam, the surviving participants of those far off firefights remember them as clearly as the day they were there. These continue to pass on the spirit and pride of those times to today's cavalrymen. The traditions of individual regiments are alive and well and continue to draw strength from the past.

PART ONE

THE CAV
IN THE HIGHLANDS

1965

CHAPTER I

19 October 1965

The narrow red trail crosses soil composed primarily of laterite. It twines around the knoll on its flank and opens onto a narrow plateau. This open cleared space could pass for an airfield. The runners of thick, coarse grass at ground level contrast with the rough, sharp saw grass and the elephant grass that grows on the slopes and borders the banks of the path. The trail has a tough time maintaining itself as it passes through this aggressive vegetation. In places where there is less erosion it becomes a double track, reflecting the imprint left by passing wagons.

Parallel to the road, a village or just a few roofs of thatch or tin seem to emerge above an enclosure. The palisade of sharpened bamboo rises next to a network of dense barbed wire, everything surrounded by trenches and individual combat foxholes. In the position a signal arrow in the form of a triangle points toward the forest, next to an old French fort of which little remains but crumbling dirt berms.

Plei Me retains but a bit of its Montagnard village character. It is isolated just off trail #5 that connects to Route 14, which leads toward Pleiku. It lies fifty kilometers south south west of Pleiku. The Cambodian border is only twenty kilometers to the west. The terrain is broken and lies against the foothills of the Chu Pong Massif. It is in the heart of *Jaraï* country, a montagnard group of the high plateaus. At this altitude, the temperature is mild. The dry season reduces the humidity. The clay exposed to the sun slowly turns into a mineral and sterile laterite. The sun, red and round like a Japanese flag, returns to its evening quarters in the west while the shadows lengthen.

On the road, some villagers, old for the most part, return from the forest. Stooped, machetes on their shoulders, they are carrying wood they have gathered at the edges of the *ray,* a slash and burn type of cultivation that clears fields which progressively eat away at the surrounding forest. From each coppered and crinkled face emerges a reddish and toothless mouth, colored by the betel nuts that they continuously chew. Behind, in convoy, the women, more numerous, younger, dressed in black, their hair collected in a turban, come back up by the trail. They advance as if suspended by the balance pole that they carry on their shoulders and that bends to the rhythm of their short and jerky strides. As night approaches everyone returns to the compound which lives to the same rhythm as a fortified village reminiscent of the medieval era somewhere in the south of France.

The villagers, in single file, enter the village through a narrow passage reserved for that purpose that wends its way between barbed wire, bamboo punji stakes, ditches, and the minefield. In the middle of these fortifications the village consists of *canhas*, huts of wood, bark, saw grass and coconut palm fronds, occasionally adorned by old traditional sculptures and patched here and there with pieces of tin. The indigenous village has lost much of its charm and the Montagnards are rarely in "loin-cloths."

A tall pole in the village center supporting a few antennas provides the only link with the rest of the world. On the ground, on each side, two round dug-in pits, each surrounded by sandbags look like cut off igloos. In the bottom are 81mm and 60mm mortars. The entrance to the bunkered command post of American and Vietnamese Special Forces is just a few meters away.

The sun is already sinking behind the mountain, facing a bluish horizon across the sky. The village resonates with the cries of children, squawking poultry, and oinking small black pigs. The pigs, fast and surly, solve the village's refuse problem. The *nhos*, the kids, laughing but fascinated, watch the hairy green giants issue orders to the night patrol.

Plei Me is a camp with a Special Forces cadre. In October 1963 the Americans launched the program of establishing Vietnamese military units called Civil Irregular Defense Groups (CIDG), to organize and support ethnic minorities that had already fought the Vietminh. Detachment A225 is posted to the Plei Me camp. Ten Green Berets, including a lieutenant and their commander, Captain Harold Moore, ten South Vietnamese commandos, and 275 Montagnards make up the operational force of the fortified village.[1] Those *Jaraï* and *Nung* tribesmen that remained allergic to the Vietcong and North Vietnamese provide a particularly effective counter-guerrilla force.

The Green Berets are the rare Americans really immersed in the local population. These commandos, trained at Fort Bragg, share the life of the villagers, linked to their headquarters only by the sky: the radio for messages, helicopters for everything else. The Green Berets are without doubt the only American soldiers to take pleasure in sharing the food and customs of the Montagnards. In addition to military training, they work at improving the hygiene and nutrition of the tribes whose lives they share. The mission of the American Special Forces resembles that of the French *Groupement commando mixte aéroporté*, special units integrated with the different Montagnard ethnic groups that practiced counter-guerrilla warfare.

The Green Berets, impeccable in their camouflage uniforms, check the equipment of the Montagnards leaving on patrol. Lined up, more or less, the irregulars present for inspection their US M1 Carbines, the World War II era carbine sometimes carried by officers, small and light, perfectly adapted to their size, but whose .30 caliber cartridge is singularly lacking in stopping power. Fortunately, they all carry M48 hand grenades and two patrol members are armed with .45 caliber M3 submachine guns.

"*Mau len, mau len!*"[2] Shouts a sergeant in Vietnamese to wake up the *Jaraï*, who are in no hurry to spend the night outside the camp. "Hurry up, it's going to get dark," insists the Green Beret Officer.

During this time the half-naked children play around the group. One of their favorite games is to jump in close and pluck a red hair from the sergeant's forearm. Hair is a sign of strength and power to them, the more important since the Vietnamese are beardless. When they have one or two whiskers, Asians take great care to show them off. Ho Chi Minh's sparse goatee is such a symbol.

One child, like a picador trying to snatch the ribbon from the horn of a small cow, in the tradition of a variety of bullfighting practiced in the south of France, dashes at the crossed arms of the green giant. The American sergeant lets himself be approached and, at the last minute turns around, faces the youngster, and shouts "Yeah!" The American's shout and the terrorized look of the *nho* set everyone laughing.[3] The patrol, led by two Vietnamese Special Forces sergeants, takes off at a jog cracking up with laughter.

Calm rapidly returns to the village. The women round up the kids and, without much effort, make them go back inside the *canhas* along with the chickens and ducks.[4] The men on guard go back to their bamboo and sandbag bunkers at each of the four corners to take up their watch behind .50 caliber machine guns. Night settles in, black, interrupted only by buffalo toads. Americans, Vietnamese, and Montagnards on guard have a hard time staying alert as the night wears on.

All at once, heavy silence fills the darkness. The insects and toads fall silent. In the east bunker, a *Nung* instinctively tenses, and coming out of his drowsiness listens to the night. A hissing sound, then a second and a third—there is no time to count the following ones because a violent explosion already lights up an area some fifty meters outside the village perimeter. The noise comes a fraction of a second later and the shock wave shakes the straw and tin of the huts. A series of explosions follows hammering the hill. Sixty millimeter mortar rounds and then 82mm rounds follow one another at an increasingly rapid rhythm.[5] Each detonation shakes the village and lights it up like a photographer's flash.

"They're lighting us up with mortars! Hold your fire, wait until you see them," cries the redheaded sergeant who dives into one of the mortar pits in the center of the camp.

"Minh, come help me! Pass me the illuminating rounds!" The Vietnamese Special Forces sergeant arms and fires rounds, sliding them one after another down the mortar tube. A hiss, then suddenly a flash, and the night gives way to light.

"Minh, keep it up! Fire a round every ten seconds!" The lieutenant scrambles into the command bunker. He finds the radio telephone operator, the RTO, already at work. "This is Alpha 225. The Victor Charlies are attacking the camp. We're receiving 60mm and 82mm mortar fire. We're waiting for them to attack."

"Tell them that this time the VC are throwing everything they've got at us and that it looks serious," yells Moore, already outside the underground shelter.

The two hundred Montagnards have gained their fighting positions in the trenches and bunkers. A Green Beret directs the 81mm counter battery fire. "Watch now, be ready to fire as soon as they break out of the edge of the forest. Sarge, take charge of the Claymores. Fire them when they try to get through the first row of concertina."

"Sir, the RTO wants to talk to you!" The officer descends into the bunker.

"Did you get Pleiku?"

"Affimative! I told them what's happening. For the time being we've got to get ourselves out of this shit. They're keeping the net clear for us. That's not all. The patrol called in. They're trapped between the VC and us. They can't get back!"

"Where are they?"

"Near the stream."

"Okay. Call Van and tell him to break off towards the south entrance! Do it so the VC won't be able to understand. They have our frequencies for sure. Signal 'go' in three minutes. Tell Van and his men to shut their eyes until they move out!"

Captain Moore goes outside again and rejoins Minh who has the role of lighting director for the "American Night." "Minh, double the rate of fire for three minutes, especially towards the east, and after that, cease all fire for five minutes. Follow?"

The rate of fire of the flare rounds, suspended by their small parachutes, increases. The light intensity is almost blinding. Stimulated by the increased visibility, the native soldiers in their foxholes fire with greater accuracy.

"Sarge," cries Moore, running towards the east bunker.

"Yes sir!"

"In two minutes and thirty-five seconds give me a "mad minute" with the .50s and the mortars, the time when the patrol breaks contact! Be aware they're going to cut the illumination."

"Roger!"

The officer leaves again by the central trench towards the south. The enemy shells are now exploding in the first line of defense of the camp. Several mines explode sympathetically. The shrapnel from exploding rounds and Claymore balls rip through the air.

Moore sends five men on a recovery mission to bring back the patrol and provide them cover.

The last parachute flare burns out, swallowed by the forest. Darkness falls again on Plei Me, while the north and east portions of the perimeter are outlined by the raging muzzle bursts of every weapon on line. The minute over, when the redheaded sergeant calls cease fire, a calm seems to return to the Plei Me plateau.

"Reload your magazines, and do *not* light up!"

To the south, the patrol finally reenters the camp. The irregulars step carefully as they trot along the narrow dike that crosses through minefields and punji stakes. Once inside the camp, the very excited Montagnards all speak at once. "Whoa, quiet! Get the wounded to the aid station. You, come with me. I need a quick debriefing for Pleiku! Did you see anything?"

"Affirmative, Captain, They aren't Charlies. They're regulars. We saw helmets and green uniforms, not black pyjamas."

"You're sure?"

"Certain! You'll see tomorrow."

"Okay, come on, let's get to the radio."

Moore goes down into the bunker, grabs the TR20 headset. Pleiku is already in contact with headquarters. "Inform the II Corps Commander that we are under heavy attack by regular troops of the North Vietnamese Army. At this time we estimate their strength to be one company strongly supported by 60mm and 82mm mortar batteries. For right now, we're holding. Over."

The first light of day comes to free the villagers from the anguish of the night. But they have, however, the disagreeable certainty of being under siege. Patrols sent out to locate the enemy positions don't take long to come back. Plei Me is completely encircled by regular North Vietnamese troops. During the night, the enemy dug trenches for the infantry and prepared emplacements for mortars and recoilless rifles. Last night's harassment was nothing but the preliminary to a decisive attack. An unusual silence weighs on the village. The cries of children and poultry are replaced by the hollow sounds of picks digging into the ground, repairing and improving positions.

As the sun descends, tension mounts among the Montagnards. Hissing noises.

"Look out! It's starting again," cries the sergeant.

Explosions. The trajectory of the rounds ends in the middle of the concertina wire and the defensive berm. Direct fire from 57mm recoilless rifles kicks up dirt and bursts the sandbags at the base of the .50 caliber machine gun bunkers. This time the preparation is systematic.

"Minh, get us some light, quick!"

"Sarge! Make sure sappers don't open up any holes with Bangalores!"

The *Jaraï*, instinctive night fighters, repel those sappers that had slipped through the defenses. The bombardment is intense. The North Vietnamese are no longer stingy with their munitions. Suddenly, the explosions are intermittent and then stop. Silence. The night recovers its calm, but in the forest first a murmur, then voices, and finally loud shouting is heard.

"*Chêt! Chêt!*"[6] The first infantry assault wave falls on Plei Me, yelling as they come on. "Fire at will," cries the captain. Clenched fingers squeeze the triggers. All the firearms of the camp fire salvo after salvo to crush the assault. A new light show allows weapons crews and individuals to effectively adjust mortar, machine gun, and carbine fire. Momentarily reassured by the reaction of his CIDG troopers, Moore heads for the radio.

"Tell them that this time they intend to take the camp. At this pace, we'll run out of ammo quickly, same for medical supplies. We have to expect the worst from now on!" The last part of his sentence is lost in the trench; he is already somewhere else.

The survivors of the first North Vietnamese charge turn back, discouraged by the reaction of the defenders. Two huts explode into bits, the broken wood and straw mixing in the air. The bombardment begins again. There are as many shells for the interior of the camp as for the defense perimeter. Blown over banana trees hang sadly on their broken stalks.

"Captain! *Mau len!* The RTO has news from Pleiku."

"That's it. They're reacting. They've decided to send reinforcements, but by road!"

"By road? We're fifty klicks from Pleiku, and the trail is blocked." He disappears into the bunker. The RTO continues: "II Corps is supposed to come and relieve us with South Vietnamese rangers loaded on M113s and with some M41 tanks."

"In how much time?"

"Twenty-four hours at the most according to what they said."

"We won't be able to hold out! Give me the mike!" The bunker resonates, a hollow blow. The ground vibrates.

"The bastards! They must have hit the antenna tower. I've lost radio contact. It's getting interesting," mutters Moore, who decides to play it cool.

Translator's Notes

[1] Captain Harold Moore is not related to Colonel and later General Harold Moore who served in the First Cavalry Division.

[2] "Hurry up! Hurry up!"

[3] Child.

[4] Huts

[5] The 82mm mortar was either the Soviet 82mm mortar M-1937 or a Chinese copy, the Chinese Communist 82mm mortar Type 53. With the munitions in use at that time, it had a range of over three kilometers.

[6] "To the death! To the death!"

CHAPTER II

"Gentlemen, here then is our hunting ground: nineteen hundred of the four thousand square kilometers of mountains and jungle in the high plateaus." Lieutenant Colonel Harlow Clark is the acting commander of the 1st Brigade, filling in for his hospitalized chief, Colonel Elvy Roberts. He has finished his reconnaissance and is back at Camp Holloway to brief his unit commanders. The "All-the-Way" Brigade is organized for this mission with four infantry battalions, a battalion of light artillery, the reconnaissance squadron, and a battalion of assault helicopters.

"The North Vietnamese," continues Clark, "have a presence in this area the equivalent of three divisions, as yet unidentified except for the 33d North Vietnamese Regiment that attacked Plei Me. There is no way to penetrate this area, no major roads or trails leading in that we can identify—just streams and mountainsides. The maps are only approximate. The Charlies are very much at home here. They've cleared a dense network of trails that are well protected from aerial observation by the triple canopy. Right now that's all we know. The North Vietnamese are masters of the ground and we are masters of the sky. We have the advantage of surprise. They don't know what we have or how we fight."

"Stockton," speaking to the Lieutenant Colonel who commands the reconnaissance squadron, "you're the first to be committed. With your squadron you must identify and locate the enemy divisions and find out which way they are moving. After that, we'll take care of them."

John Stockton is the first to rise. He salutes Clark and leaves the tent. His comrades wish him good luck. They watch him leave with an air of both amusement and admiration. Stockton is the caricature of a cavalry officer, British Indian Army style: slender, balding, with a half circle of red hair and a huge handlebar mustache. He has given the 1st of the 9th Cavalry Squadron a striking presence.[1] At Fort Benning he made quite a reputation by making his officers wear the traditional black broad-brimmed hat of the cavalry with golden hat cords, their "Stetsons." His squadron has a wide variety of equipment. Its mission is reconnaissance and it is usually out front. The 1st of the 9th, completely self-contained, is one hundred percent airmobile. Stockton likes to call it "The Cav of the Cav."

Shortly upon his return to Camp Radcliff, Stockton organizes and launches his aerial ballet. The OH-13 reconnaissance helicop-

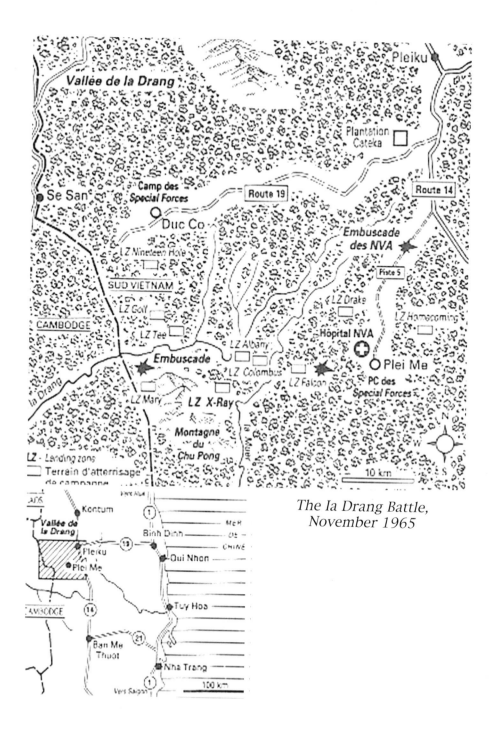

The Ia Drang Battle,
November 1965

21

ters obstinately probe the forest, looking for any indication of enemy presence. Their mission: locate the enemy and pass their positions on to the attack helicopters that can "take care of them."

Clark looks for the best way to optimize the efficiency of his brigade and speed up the systematic search of the jungle. He outlines his plan to Lieutenant Colonel James Nix, commander of the 2d Battalion, 8th Cavalry. "Jim, we can cover the terrain better if we divide our forces. We need to work in company-sized units. We're going to divide up the area in grid squares surrounding the landing zones we've identified plus others we've got to find. We'll put a company in each LZ with enough food and ammo for twelve to twenty-four hours with the mission to thoroughly search its sector."

"Okay, Harlow, but what happens if the company runs into a superior force strong enough to overrun it?"

"This plan requires that the LZs be relatively accessible and enable the simultaneous landing of several slicks."

"Right. During the insertions, as the patrols move into the jungle, we'll have to use engineers to enlarge the LZs. They'll need chainsaws and explosives to do the job in a hurry. That'll also insure the recovery of the patrols."

The brigade becomes a veritable beehive. The helicopters work without letup, spreading out and landing the infantry companies, mounting patrols and ambushes to gather the maximum information of the enemy. Several days pass. Gone is the excitement of the beginning of the hunt. The grunts tire and wonder what they are doing. Clark consults the G2, the division staff officer responsible for intelligence.

"Anything new?"

"Nothing. Even the night ambushes haven't produced any results."

"I'm still sure the enemy is there. I'm continuing with my plan. We'll end up getting them."

Two days later, at division staff again, the G2 tells Clark: "Harlow, a 1st of the 9th patrol has brought us three prisoners."

"You've learned something from them?"

"Yup! The prisoners are Viet Cong, but they've confirmed the presence of North Vietnamese units, at least several regiments."

"Do you have some idea of their morale?"

"We understand they're astonished by the presence of so many helicopters and hampered by our continuous patrols. They give the impression that the initial North Vietnamese dispositions have been disturbed and that they're swarming through the forest like a stirred-up ant hill."

"Excellent! We'll continue the pressure."

Back at the CP Clark confirms: "We're right. The enemy's there," he says as he slaps the map with the palm of his hand. Unmarked a week ago, the map now looks like a pointillist painting, with all the LZs marked with the symbols of the companies that opened them.

"Intensify your reconnaissance of the mountainous area next to the Cambodian border. Keep an Eagle Flight on standby in each unit.[2]

On 1 November 1965, Captain William Gillette, S2 of the 1st of the 9th, conducts a ground skimming reconnaissance by OH-13 the length of the rivers and valleys of the Chu Pong Massif. At water level, he flies below the treetops and gains a fleeting view of the edge of the forest. Between Plei Me and the mountain, about eight kilometers west of the Special Forces camp, he spots a group in uniform that hurriedly moves out of sight.

Gillette transmits the coordinates right away to the CP. Colonel Stockton immediately launches an Eagle Flight. The operation is now under the command of Brigadier General Richard T. Knowles, the Assistant Division Commander under Major General Harry W. O. Kinnard.

Coming from the oldest tradition of the US Cavalry the command "Saddle Up!" electrifies Captain Jack Oliver's aero-rifle platoon, one of three rifle platoons or Blue Teams that make up the Blue Troop, the alert element of the 1st of the 9th Cav. The men leap up, grab their weapons and, in eight-man aircraft loads (ACLs), pile into the four helicopters standing by for that purpose. Gillette has identified a clearing near the place where he spotted the North Vietnamese. He guides the Hueys to this new LZ. The four aircraft with Oliver's platoon land simultaneously. Just as the skids brush the grass, shots come from the woods. The "pang" sound of striking bullets resonates in the helicopters. Surprised by this reception, the grunts surge from the choppers and fire long bursts from their M16s in the direction of the enemy fire. Bent double, running in slalom between clumps of brush and bushes, they quickly move under cover.

"They're in the trees at the edge of the woods," yells Oliver, leading the charge.

The M16 assault rifles pick up the fire again, but with short bursts. You can hear the muffled sound of bodies falling some forty meters away. The Blue Team has cleaned the snipers from the edge of the clearing. "Captain, look over here, the woods are crawling with Charlies!" one of his men calls.

The two remaining Blue Platoons commanded by Captains

Chuck Knowlen and Don Valley arrive on the scene at ten-minute intervals behind Oliver. The Blue Troop, now directed by Major Bob Zion, its commander, circling overhead in a helicopter, shortly discovers a field hospital perfectly camouflaged in the forest.[3] "Pick up the pace, gents!" directs Zion. "Get through those hooches fast. Take weapons, medicine, and whatever else of value you find. Priority in prisoners to senior people." The men of the Blue Troop screen through the "hospital" and systematically destroy the various structures. Picking up the medical supplies, food, and weapons takes up part of the afternoon. To avoid any unpleasant surprise, armed helicopters cruise the forest at treetop level.

"'Blue Team' this is 'White One.' Have in sight a hostile element moving just about south in your direction. It looks like about two companies."

"'White One,' 'Red One,' we're ready to engage," crackles over the PRC25s on the ground as the gunship platoon responds to the information.

The gunships plunge on the enemy who slips along under the canopy. Salvo after salvo the 2.75in rockets tear into the forest. Branches, bark, and leaves are chopped up by the mass of bullets loosed by long bursts of machine gun fire. The wind quickly sweeps away the dust and smoke raised by the explosions. The pilots try to estimate the effects of their fire. The 1st of the 9th troops on the ground have a quick answer. The North Vietnamese fall upon them brutally and with heavy fire. Their pugnacity and aggressiveness have in no way been diminished by the intervention of armed helicopters. On the contrary, the North Vietnamese pressure increases. The Americans hold them off, but to hold the enemy outside the perimeter of the hospital takes the massive intervention of the gunships. Angered by their lack of initial success, the pilots pour in everything they have, to the point of firing within just a few meters of their own friendly positions.

In the meantime, Stockton has managed to join his troops on the ground. General Knowles is following everything as it happens on the radio. Stockton calls him. "Send the 2d of the 12th, make it happen fast! We've stumbled right into the middle of them. The PAVN are at regimental strength."[4] It is about 1400 hours.

The North Vietnamese are amazed that the Americans have surprised them in an area where they considered themselves at home. But the Blue Teams do not have time to complete a search. In less than twenty minutes the North Vietnamese launch a counterattack. The Cav troopers have to abandon the hospital and withdraw. The enemy has carefully cut off their route back to the LZ. The North Vietnamese are completely familiar with the area, and so they are able to get a good grip on the Americans, ten of whom are already wounded. As the men of Blue Troop withdraw they pass through a swampy sunken area and set up a perimeter along its edge. The wounded drop down by the water, half in, half out. The reddish tint of blood discolors the water. Stopped in their advance, the North Vietnamese deploy snipers and zero in on the wounded Americans. Aware of the risk, the Blues evacuate the wounded one by one. Each man hoists a comrade over his shoulder. M16 in one hand, the other holding a wounded soldier, in this manner the men get back on the trail to the LZ. Here, they place the wounded under cover while waiting for evacuation. The able-bodied men are exhausted. Their sweat-soaked uniforms, spotted with blood, stick to their skin. However, they manage to pin down the North Vietnamese and at the same time secure the LZ for the smooth deployment of reinforcements.

At about 1700 hours the slicks of the 227th Assault Helicopter Battalion (AHB) begin inserting the first reinforcing infantry element, a rifle company from the 2[d] Battalion, 12th Cav. Stockton meets them on the LZ and moves them into position. The reinforcements greet the Blue Troop grunts with silence. Those just arriving are going to their baptism of fire. With some anxiety they note the stark expressions that mark the faces of their battle-tested comrades. "Welcome to hell!" remarks a Blue Troop sergeant to break the silence.

A second company from the 2[d] of the 12th begins landing in four-ship flights arriving at ten-minute intervals. Stockton uses the reinforcements to replace his Blue Platoons in the perimeter. The North Vietnamese decide to break contact with the arrival of American reinforcements. The firing stops. The men of the 2[d] of the 12th and the 1st of the 9th sweep the area. They identify ninety-nine North Vietnamese KIA and bring back fifty-four prisoners. They are all regulars, carrying identification cards issued in Hanoi. They recover one hundred cubic meters of penicillin, quinine, morphine, and other medicines as well as the equipment for three mobile operating rooms. Stockton turns the position over to the senior company commander of the 2[d] of the 12th and starts the extraction of his Blue Troop.

The 1st Brigade lost eleven men and suffered twenty-one wounded. Division Headquarters, well satisfied with the results of the operation at the hospital of the 33[d] Regiment of the Peoples' Army, wants to refine its tactics and exploit the new information learned about its adversary.

General Knowles calls Stockton to plan the follow up to this engagement. Tall, thin, forty-four years old, he offers Stockton a cigar. "John, if we put together what we learned at Plei Me with what we learned at the hospital, it all leads me to believe that most of the North Vietnamese units are traipsing around the Chu Pong Massif, maybe along the Ia Drang.[5] What do you think?"

"The nearness of the Cambodian border and the natural access route that the Ia Drang provides ought to cause them to establish a serious logistical route in the area."

"We've got to check that theory. We've identified an LZ in this area. See if you can find any indicators to confirm or deny your suspicions. Be careful, it's not a big LZ. Take steps to make sure you're not trapped there if things get hot." Stockton leaves to set up his CP at the Duc Co Special Forces camp. Here he finds Major Norman Schwarzkopf, adviser to a South Vietnamese airborne battalion. The next day, 2 November, Captain Knowlen and his Blue Troop boss, Major Bob Zion, report to Lieutenant Colonel Stockton.

"So, Knowlen, have your men recovered from their visit to the Vietnamese hospital?"

"Oh, yes *sir*! They know now that the North Vietnamese Army exists."

"I have a job for you tonight. We need to keep finding out more about the presence of the enemy in this area and to harass them so that they feel less secure. We're mounting three abushes tonight, Yours will be on the trail that parallels the Ia Drang, very close to the border." Stockton unrolls the map. "You will be inserted at *LZ Betty*. Be careful, you are very close to Cambodia. The Charlies should be pretty relaxed and not on their guard. There's a major trail right here," he indicates on the map. "I want you to set up an ambush right about here," he indicates on the map again. Pick a spot close by and let us have the exact location when you pick it. Depending on what happens, bring me prisoners or information, both if you can. If you have to clear a new LZ, clear it good! We'll have to get in and out in a hurry. I'm putting an Eagle Flight on alert to extract you if you have a problem. I've given Major Zion OPCON of the Montagnard Company, about fifty *Rhades* the SF guys have loaned us.[6] They'll be about two klicks north north west of you. They know the area well. Jack Oliver will be on ambush too. I'll give you his ambush position later. It's your game, Captain."

Shortly after leaving, Knowlen summons his Platoon Sergeant. "Sarge, pick me twenty-four men. I want volunteers and 'pros.' They'll take five M60s and five M79s. I want three demo men with a double issue of Claymores. Make sure the RTO has a full load of smoke grenades. The rest of the men will carry 12 gauge shotguns with double-ought buck, as well as grenades. Bring me the list in thirty minutes."

Two November, 1700 hours. Three Hueys are on the way loaded with Knowlen's Blue Team of the 1st of the 9th. The slicks are escorted by two gunships. The pilot of the lead slick pushes the intercom button for his radio. "Captain, *LZ Betty* in thirty seconds. I'm making a one-eighty to the right so you can get a good look at the ground."

Touchdown! Knowlen and his Blues empty the choppers and the platoon moves into the shelter of the forest. The flotilla of Iroquois is already gone. At the head of the column, Knowlen organizes the advance with two teams of troopers one on each side of the route of march. Night has now fallen but there is a full moon and it is relatively light. The Blues march for about an hour with the caution of Indians. They are four kilometers from the Cambodian border.

"Captain, we're coming out on a trail that looks like it's regularly used. It goes east-west."

"Okay! Be alert, we're there."

The trail clashes cleanly with the exuberant vegetation through which the Blue Team has been moving since leaving *LZ Betty*. It has been cleared by machete through different types of palm trunks and branches and bamboo. There are fresh and deep footprints and bicycle and wagon tracks. "They're not traveling empty, there's traffic here," concludes Knowlen. "We'll go west. Another fifteen minutes and we'll pick our ambush site." In the same formation, the Blues advance silently on each side of a trail so wide that it seems like a boulevard. "Stop! Pass it back," Knowlen whispers to the sergeant. "This place looks good to me."

The Captain chooses a location that offers the best chance of surprise and protects any withdrawal. He positions all his men on the same side of the trail and carefully emplaces his Claymore mines, some set with trip wires, others to be command detonated. He has his men emplace eight antipersonnel mines. Knowlen checks the positions of his troops and then picks the locations for the machineguns and grenade launchers so that any survivors will be forced to throw themselves on the mines. Then he gives a final briefing. "Drink now, then don't touch your canteens. There can be no noise, even during the fight. Check your skin camouflage.[7] Bug juice for everyone and button up your collars and sleeves. For opening fire, it's simple. I'm in the center of the position at the bend and I'll fire the claymores in the middle of the trail. You fire a Mad Minute when the Claymores go off. Depending on the target that passes I will decide to fire or not. Got it? Any questions?

Get the word out and move to your positions." Knowlen then relays his position in code to the 1st of the 9th CP at Duc Co.

The Blues are lying in the humid vegetation. The mosquitoes and other biting bugs do not miss the rendezvous. This is the hour when they are so voracious that they seek out any millimeter of exposed skin. Since the grunts have taken all possible precautions, the bugs have nothing but ears and hands to bite and sting. The bug juice keeps the insects in stationary flight and it's hard to resist the impulse to slap them.

The forest slips into night. The habitual night noises briefly interrupted by Knowlen and his men pick up their rhythm. The Captain checks his watch: 2130 hours. He shields the lighted dial by force of habit, but then realizes that bugs and vegetation much more phosphorescent than his watch surround him.

Flap, flap, the sound of wings. These are parrots and turtle-doves taking off, disturbed during their sleep. The men, startled, scrunch down closer to the ground. At the same time that they peer into the darkness, their fingers, instinctively, check the position of their weapon stocks. Added to the noise of flocks of birds leaving their perches is the sound of loud voices and bursts of laughter. At first far off, the sounds become clear

The Blues quiet their breathing, searching for the best position by silently slithering closer to the ground. Cramps go away immediately. Each man concentrates on his own field of fire, straining to see, ready to open fire at the signal.

Knowlen grabs his binoculars. Their light collecting characteristics enhance visibility in near darkness. He makes out a fairly heavily loaded down column moving along without any special attention to security. He puts down the glasses and wipes his hands before reaching for the detonator. He starts counting: another fifty meters. Thirty meters. At fifteen meters, a man detaches himself from the column.

"Choï! Choï!"[8]

The soldiers stop, break formation, and begin chattering again as they had been doing on the march. The column leader has called a break. Knowlen concentrates so hard that his RTO reads his lips: "shit, goddammit!"

The Vietnamese, a mix of North Vietnamese regulars and coolies, squatting on their heels, take out their chopsticks and cooking bowls. They pluck a rice ball and a bit of smoked pork from a small, sausage-shaped bit of cloth, the whole soaked in *nuoc-mâm*. The strong fishy odor reaches the Blues' nostrils. Aware of the absurdity of the situation, they exchange grimaces of disgust for this "delicacy" that they have not yet had time to discover since their arrival at An Khe. Some of the NVA soldiers leave the trail and, still bent over, relieve themselves in the dense jungle vegetation.

Knowlen picks up his binoculars. "Eighty-seven, eighty-eight, eighty-nine, ninety, he counts. They're ninety and we're only twenty-five!" The Vietnamese are carrying cases of rations and munitions. They have placed machine-guns, 60mm mortars, and 57mm recoilless rifles in the middle of the column. The inventory done, the Captain is puzzled. Should they take advantage of what will be total surprise and annihilate the convoy, or not budge and let it pass? "But what the hell is going on?" A pause, five nerve wracking minutes. Constrained to immobility, the Blues are soaked by the dampness of both the ground and the air. The effectiveness of the insect repellent wears off and the mosquitoes attack with impunity. The NVA empty their bowls with a clacking of chopsticks, belch, and relieve themselves, sometimes just a few meters from a grunt, now frozen silently in position, muscles beginning to cramp. "Without doubt," ruminates the Captain, "one of these assholes is going to crap on a Claymore or piss on one of the troops." Imagining all the possibilities, he goes from exasperation to barely controlled belly laughter. The break lasts an hour and a half. It is an eternity for the Americans who meet the North Vietnamese in such an intimate way.

"Di, di!"[9]

"Mau len!"

The sharp orders shake the forest. Each soldier takes up his load and place in ranks. The reformed column moves out and advances toward the curve. Knowlen makes his decision. He will pulverize these bastards; these Charlies who have given him so much worry for almost two hours. He lets the convoy advance, waits till the middle of the column with the heavy weapons arrives at the center of the bend in the trail.

"*Okay!*" and he squeezes his detonator. The two Claymores explode at the same time. Thousands of fragments of steel spiral through the air, the ground, and flesh. The explosion liberates the Blues of Bravo Troop. Fingers crush triggers. A storm of fire mows down the two files of the North Vietnamese caterpillar. The survivors try to escape into the forest and catch their feet in the trip wires that set off the other Claymores. The fusillade lasts three minutes. The Vietnamese have not had time to fire a single shot. The Blues are mute, groggy, tired by all the waiting, shocked by the violence of the action.

"Up! Move it gents," yells Knowlen. His order seems out of place. "We can't stay here. No time to count or collect stuff. We're moving out now, back to the LZ. Sarge, set up the security and the point! Keep a watch to the rear. Saddle up!"

Knowlen is sure he has just "zapped" the advance guard of a larger unit, a battalion maybe. No more moving like Indians. The Blues cut a path, force their way through palms and jungle growth, tearing their jungle fatigues on thorns as they pass. They make it back in thirty minutes. They finally come out on *LZ Betty*. Don Valley's Blue Team as well as the mortar platoon on loan from A Company, 1st of the 8th Cav are there to meet them.

"RTO, get me Bullwhip Six."[10]

Hearing Colonel Stockton's call sign, the RTO acts fast. The PRC25 crackles: "This is Bullwhip Six, over."

"We hit the bull's-eye, about ninety Charlies bought it. Over"

"Congratulations. You're breaking contact now? Over"

"Before we lift out, I'd like to check out the area and gather whatever information I can from the bodies. But there's some risk of having a bunch of PAVN on our butts. I need reinforcements. Over"

"You want to conduct a night operation? You're real sure about that? Over."

"Roger. Piece of cake. Over."

"Okay. Make it happen. Big Six may question this, but that's not your worry! Out."

Knowlen knew he could count on Stockton to support him without waiting for a decision from headquarters. The General would probably not agree to launch a night operation without advance planning, and even if he would, it would take too long to get a decision.

The Captain gave the mortar platoon the mission of defending the LZ, and left with his and Valley's Blue Teams to check out the results of the ambush. He finds a confirmation of what he was hoping. The action indeed involved a regular unit: the 8th Battalion of the 66th Regiment of the North Vietnamese Army. With his harvest of documents and maps, Knowlen retraces the route, but the Blues have not yet reached the LZ when, already, mortar rounds begin to fall, seeking them out in the forest. "We've done everything we could to get them on our asses!" an infantryman placidly concludes.

Knowlen is already on the radio. "Bullwhip Six, we're on the way back, but we've stuck our nose in a hornets' nest. It's going to get hot. We need reinforcements. Over."

"Roger. I'm going to send in Danielson with the rest of A Company, 1st of the 8th. Keep me posted. Out."

The situation on the ground is delicate by the time the Red

Team gunships arrive. After the mortar fire, the North Vietnamese send in their infantry to exact revenge. The choppers have the difficult mission of providing supporting fire in the middle of the night. They empty their rocket pods at the shadows moving about on the ground. The pilots adjust their fire in very close and succeed in breaking up the enemy charges barely fifteen meters from the positions of the Blues. The *LZ* is completely surrounded by snipers that force the 1st of the 9th platoons to keep their noses in the dirt. All the while, the NVA mortar gunners adjust their fires.

In the meantime, the Montagnards remain in their ambush position without contact. Oliver, following the action on headphones, decides to move his Blues back to *LZ Betty*. It will be a tricky business getting back inside the perimeter.

The slicks with the men of Alpha Company are on final approach. But the slow tempo and heavy sound of Chinese 12.7mm machine gun fire greets their arrival. The NVA are still there, watchful, ready to make the Americans pay for their incursion. The assault landing takes place under uninterrupted mortar, heavy machine gun, and 57mm recoilless rifle fire. A long burst of 12.7mm direct fire hits a gunship, a UH-IB. The helicopter falls. It crashes just behind the *LZ*. It begins to burn. The four-man crew, unhurt, quickly exits the flaming cockpit and fuselage. Some NVA move out of their positions on the run to capture the Americans who have fallen into their lines. A lift ship from the same unit leaves formation to descend and pick up the crew before the Vietnamese can get there. Another helicopter is hit, a lift ship. Seriously damaged, it manages to fly as far as Duc Co with its load of wounded.

The *LZ* is narrow, but happily there is a full moon. The Hueys can only land three at a time. With an ACL of eight, pushing the limit, the reinforcements arrive at the fight in groups of twenty-four.[11] The train of arriving helicopters continues. The hail of ground fire riddles them all.

Knowlen's men who came through the ambush unharmed now take casualties. Parrot and Sergeant Pascal are killed. Uncounted numbers of other soldiers are wounded, but the presence of the fresh infantry company changes the balance of force. The North Vietnamese can no longer infiltrate the positions of the Cav. The intensity of combat diminishes. The dry crack of SKS semi-automatic rifle fire suddenly replaces bursts of AK47 fire. It is at this point that Captain Oliver and his platoon begin carefully to slip back into the perimeter, avoiding the ever present NVA and calling out to their comrades to identify themselves. The word goes out. A Blue Team is coming back in.

"The PAVN have withdrawn, but they're trying to pin us down

with their snipers. Stay under cover, don't expose yourself!" Knowlen tells his men. "Gary, go round up the platoon leaders for me, but be damn careful, the Charlies are very good at shooting in the dark." One by one officers and non-commissioned offices emerge from the obscurity, arrive at the CP, and report to the Captain.

"It's 0330 hours. We're not going to let ourselves be shot like rabbits. It's clear they're going to mount a large scale attack at dawn. First, make sure the wounded are protected and be ready to move them out as soon as we get some lift ships in. Second, we're going to maintain the security of the LZ and then move the perimeter out so the choppers can get on the ground without drawing fire. Got it? Okay! The maneuver will be simple. Fix bayonets when you get back. At 0615 hours we'll move out. You have two hours and thirty minutes for each man to pick his targets. When I kick this off, charge out and kill your targets. Until then, no movement, no noise. Until tomorrow." Before leaving, everyone does a time check with the Captain's watch. The LZ sinks into a lethargic state sporadically broken by rifle fire. The light slowly gets milkier. Sheets of fog break up on tufts of grass.

"Go! Yeah!" The sudden shout yelled by two hundred grunts echoes back. The Blues spring from their foxholes all at once, bayonets fixed. As soon as they are up, the noise made by bursts of M16 fire and the "pop" of outgoing M79 fire overlays the shouting. The M60s gobble up linked 7.62mm ammo.

The Vietnamese snipers, surprised by the vigor of the charge, are shot full of holes before they can react. They rock in their perches and fall, arms and legs every which way. The troops clean up the perimeter of the LZ. The Blues now turn their attention to their dead and wounded.

Colonel Stockton is waiting for Charles Knowlen when he gets out of the helicopter that brought him back to Duc Co with part of his team. "Good job, Charles! Lots of materiel and some good info! But that was a hot one."

"Thanks sir. I think we counted one hundred and fifty dead PAVN and we're bringing back ten prisoners. But, we have five dead and twenty-five wounded. This time, we've located the 66th NVA Regiment and we've roughed up the 8th Battalion around *Betty*."

"That was a nice piece of work. I'm on my way to the MAAG Compound at Pleiku to see General Kinnard.[12] I know he's been following things closely."

Stockton, anticipating a pat on the back for a successful operation, heads for Pleiku. As it turned out, General Knowles did not at all appreciate Captain Knowlen's initiative, and Stockton had sent the company of 1st of the 8th without authorization. When Stockton reports to General Kinnard, he is advised that he faces charges of insubordination and disobedience to a direct order. The charges are later dropped, but Stockton is transferred to Saigon and a staff job. The troops at ground level think this is a poor move. Division Headquarters does not use the information that the 1st of the 9th collected at such a high cost. General Knowles does not launch a pursuit operation. He prefers to continue with searching the area grid square by grid square.

Six November, Bravo Company, 2d Battalion, 8th Cav is inserted on *LZ Wing* on the upper reaches of the Meur River. The mission is to search along the river valley.

Bravo Company progresses from west to east, heading downstream. The company has gone less than fifteen hundred meters when it enters a maze of trenches, individual fighting holes, and bunkers prepared by the North Vietnamese infantry, a site laid out by the 6th Battalion of the 33d NVA Regiment. The company is immediately taken under fire by a force of about two platoons, part of a larger force that quickly begins a movement to encircle the Americans. As the first rounds are fired, Charlie Company, 1st of the 8th, screening along the other side of the river tries to link up with Bravo Company and come to its aid. The impenetrable vegetation in which it finds itself hampers Charlie Company's progress. When the men break out at the river's edge to cross it, the area is under mortar and sniper fire. The link-up is impossible.

The North Vietnamese cannot be dislodged, thanks to their perfect knowledge of the terrain and their well dug-in positions. They have an advantage over the two companies of the 8th Cav who call in ARA support. The aerial rocket artillery helicopters fire their loads of rockets and force the NVA deep into their holes. Bravo and Charlie Companies take advantage of the diversion to link up and establish a defensive perimeter.

It is night again. It is not a question of conducting a night operation as at *LZ Betty*. The two companies dig in and wait for the next day. Following their normal operational procedure, the NVA conceal their departure and cover their withdrawal with a screen of efficient snipers: their patient, elite sharpshooters. At dawn, Bravo and Charlie Companies are alone in the forest. The grunts carefully search the NVA positions and count seventy-seven bodies. They estimate the actual number of NVA KIA to be one hundred and twenty. For the 2d Battalion of the 8th Cav, the losses are severe: twenty-six killed and fifty-three wounded. Since its arrival in Vietnam on 13 September, the First Cav had not until then sustained such heavy casualties.

Since the North Vietnamese attacked Plei Me on 19 October 1965, the 1ˢᵗ Brigade alone has conducted the hunt for the enemy. The NVA infantry were out to launch a major offensive to cut South Vietnam in two. A month later, off balance, the soldiers of the North are forced to defend their own ground. Now that the 1ˢᵗ Brigade has forced the communist forces into showing themselves, General Kinnard decides to pass the Baton to the 3ᵈ Brigade. Colonel Thomas Brown thus picks up the action where Harlow G. Clark leaves it off.

Translator's Notes

[1] Numbered battalions and squadrons in the United States Army are now either the subordinate units of numbered brigades (a flexible organization with sometimes two, usually three, and sometimes more battalion sized units) or, in the case of reconnaissance squadrons are assigned to divisions. Because the tradition of American battalions and squadrons resides in the regiments to which they originally belonged, every battalion and squadron has a double numerical designation. The first number designates the battalion. The second number indicates the regiment with which the battalion is historically associated. The regimental tradition is something men often prize above life. The 9ᵗʰ Cavalry Regiment, of course, is one of two (the other being the 10ᵗʰ) famous Indian fighting horse cavalry regiments organized at the close of the Civil War. It was composed at that time of black enlisted soldiers, the "Buffalo Soldiers," and white officers.

[2] An Eagle flight usually consisted of a platoon-sized or somewhat smaller reserve unit of riflemen with a lieutenant or noncommissioned officer in charge. The "flight" included a sufficient number of lift ships to move them and either gunships or aerial rocket artillery ships in support, or both. They remained on alert until needed, and could be dispatched immediately to any location to fix an enemy, reinforce a unit in contact, facilitate an extraction under fire, or, as was also the case, to get airborne and follow a White (Reconnaissance) Team when contact was anticipated.

[3] The normal practice for military operations for the 1ˢᵗ of the 9ᵗʰ Cav was to "scramble" Blue Teams (infantry platoons), Red Teams (gun ships), and White Teams (aerial reconnaissance units employing OH-13 observation helicopters) task-organized for a specific mission. It was unusual for the Blue Teams to be employed together as a Blue Troop in an "unscrambled" configuration.

[4] Peoples' Army of Vietnam. The common use of the acronym "PAVN," pronounced "pavin," was later displaced by "NVA" for North Vietnamese Army. The abbreviation "NVA" was unsuitable as an acronym and the letters were spoken, "enveeay." Apparently the use of "people" in "PAVN" was politically unacceptable. The term "PAVN," however, continued to be used for a year or so and evokes memories of the early bloody fighting in the First Cavalry. When either term is used as a noun it may refer either to enemy soldiers or to the North Vietnamese Army, depending upon the context.

[5] The Ia Drang, or Drang River.

[6] Operational control: a relationship of a temporary nature for a particular military operation. The Rhades are a particular Montagnard tribal group.

[7] Skin camouflage was critical to all missions. It gave the soldier an edge when the shooting started as well as reducing the likelihood that he would be seen first. It was used by men of all skin colors.

[8] "Hold up! Hold up!"

[9] Come, come!

[10] The "Six" suffix of a call sign designates a commander.

[11] The aircraft load or ACL is influenced by factors such as heat, altitude, and amount of other gear loaded on the helicopter. An ACL of five or more usually six was common for the UH-1D Huey.

[12] Military Assistance Advisory Group

CHAPTER III

General Kinnard picked the 3^d Brigade to accomplish the Division mission: rid the high plains of North Vietnamese. The two battalions that compose the 3^d Brigade at this time, the 1st and 2^d Battalions of the 7th Cavalry, trace their origin to the 7th Cavalry Regiment, the most famous regiment in the history of the American cavalry. The regimental song of the 7th Cav, "Garry Owen," is the best known symbol of the American cavalry. General Custer, the legendary figure of the Indian Wars who forged the 7th Cavalry Regiment into an elite unit chose the song. The 3^d Brigade is thus the "Garry Owen" Brigade. The commander, Colonel Tim Brown, brings the two 7th Cav battalions and the 2^d Battalion of the 5th Cav as well as two artillery battalions into the game on the ground.

"So, Tim, you've found a more agreeable place than *Homecoming* to put your Garry Owen troopers?" Kinnard asks.[1]

"Yes sir—real colonial décor. I picked the Cateka tea plantation southwest of Pleiku."

"I've flown over it," says Kinnard. "The tea bushes, all the same height, all in line, look very attractive. Nature puts on a better face when it's all lined up. I prefer the well pruned tea bushes to the damn elephant grass on all the LZs."

"The plantation is great. It looks like people in Saigon really like this tea. I'll send you some if you don't come by! I've set up my headquarters at the northern edge of the plantation."

"I don't think the VC will let you have any time to learn about growing tea, Tim."

"Just so, sir! Right now, the 32^d PAVN Regiment worries me a lot more than the care of young tea plants!"

The 3^d Brigade travels light. Colonel Brown's CP operates from three General Purpose Medium Tents. These are pitched at the south end of the Cateka District airstrip. The tents are close by the French planter's tea plantation fields. That, however, does not stop two young women from sunbathing in their bikinis by the pool next to the large white colonial house. This new position is situated but a few minutes by air from the 1st Brigade base, Camp Holloway, on the edge of Pleiku, that the grunts have already christened the "Turkey Farm."

Brown thought it would be a simple matter to find the enemy after all the groundwork done by Lieutenant Colonel Clark. But the North Vietnamese seemed to take advantage of the change of teams to disappear into the terrain and vegetation. Brown must show as much perseverance as Clark in searching through the zone.

On ten November the 3ᵈ Brigade, led by the 1ˢᵗ of the 7ᵗʰ Cav, moves into the Plei Me area. There are three days of routine during which OH-13 and Huey helicopters explore forests, valleys, hills, hillsides, and clearings. The patrols pass like a fine tooth comb through the valleys and hills to the east of Plei Me. Nothing happens. A few minor skirmishes. Brown tells his S2 to mark up a map with the location of all the contact sites and other indicators reported by the patrols. Lieutenant Colonel Bob Lang, the Division G2, marks the Chu Pong Massif on his Intelligence Map with a red star. When Moore asks him what it means he responds, "enemy base area." Brown concludes that the Chu Pong area needs checking out.

In the late afternoon of 12 November Brigadier General Richard T. Knowles, the Assistant Division Commander, flies south out of Pleiku in his command helicopter to see Colonel Brown. The Corps Commander, Major General Stanley Larsen, had just visited the Division. His order was to move the operation to the Ia Drang and Chu Pong area where both Larsen and the Division Commander believe they will have more success. Brown is in the field visiting his 1ˢᵗ of the 7ᵗʰ Commander, Lieutenant Colonel Hal Moore. Knowles and Brown both think the Ia Drang Valley is where the enemy is. General Knowles tells Brown to get in there, and Brown passes the order to Moore. Then Knowles and Brown, each in his own chopper depart, leaving Moore to plan the operation.

Harold Moore is forty-three, West Point class of '45. He belongs to the airborne generation of officers, earned his army aviator wings in 1970, and has solid airmobile credentials. Seventeen years earlier he was already working for General Kinnard. A First Lieutenant at the time, he was a volunteer to test a new parachute. On his first jump, his chute hung up on the tail section of the C-46 from which he had jumped. He got out of that situation using his reserve parachute. He linked up again with General Kinnard in June of 1964 in the 11ᵗʰ Air Assault Division.

At 1123 hours on 12 November incoming mortars rounds shake the tents bordering the plantation. One round lands directly on the tent of the team that runs the refueling site. Seven men die and twenty-three are wounded. The Americans recover six Viet Cong dead among the surrounding tea bushes. The North Vietnamese and their Viet Cong allies could not resist the temptation to show that they were still there. Bayonet Six is both annoyed and relieved.

"We look everywhere for them and they come to our house and leave their calling card. *Okay*, the game begins again!" he comments to his S3. A 229ᵗʰ lift ship pilot barges into the tent. "Sir, excuse me for cutting in. The French planter wants to see you."

"What's he want?"

"He told me he wants to complain about tonight's attack."

"He wants to complain about the Charlies?"

"No, he says that it's our fault, that our CP is too close to his plantation and that that causes him problems."

"That asshole doesn't give a shit about us! He pays a million piastres a year to the VC to leave him alone! He better not complain to me. He bills us fifty dollars apiece for any tea bushes that get damaged. I'll give his tea plants a dose of napalm! Tell him to come back later when I've calmed down."

In the late afternoon of Saturday, 13 November, Brown again joins Moore in the field. Moore is with his Alpha Company. "Hal, you're going to move your battalion toward the west tomorrow morning! That will be your AO, the northern part of the Chu Pong Massif, in the Ia Drang Valley.[2] Your mission is unchanged: find and destroy the enemy. They're there, Hal, but we have no good intelligence on their number or location. The only way left is to latch on to them directly and pretty much by chance. Doing it this way, the results may be a surprise. You can just as well stumble on a battalion as on a patrol. The morning of Sunday, 14 November, Brown goes to see Hal at the Plei Me landing strip to go over his plans.

"Sir, I've picked *X-Ray*. It's the best of the LZs."

"*Okay*, but stay together. Don't let your companies get separated."

The 1ˢᵗ Battalion of the 7ᵗʰ Regiment of cavalry has three companies—Alpha, Bravo, Charlie—each with an authorized strength of 164 men led by six officers. Each company breaks down into three infantry platoons and a weapons platoon. The fourth company, Delta Company, authorized 118 men and five officers, is a support company with mortars, machine guns, and the Battalion Reconnaissance Platoon. The field strength of the Battalion is significantly less than its authorized strength.[3]

The artillery is on another *LZ, Falcon,* further to the east on the other side of the Meur River. The Chinooks of the 228ᵗʰ Assault Support Helicopter Battalion sling in 105mm howitzers along with their ammunition. As soon as two batteries of the 1ˢᵗ Battalion of the 21ˢᵗ Regiment of field artillery are on the ground they open an intense artillery preparation on *LZ X-Ray*. It starts exactly at 1017 hours.

Overhead Moore's S3, Captain Matt Dillon, orchestrates the *LZ* prep. Once the 105s finish firing on preselected targets, the ARA ships come in to clean out the edges of the *LZ*. They expend half their munitions in thirty seconds of fire. The gunships make a final pass just before the assault landing. Drowned in thick smoke, the forest is punctuated with orange explosions and lacerated with flying lead and steel.

In the meantime Bravo Company, 1st of the 7th Cav, has lifted off from Plei Me in 229th AHB choppers. In formations of four flying in a "heavy left V formation" the Hueys, at one hundred and ten miles per hour, head for *LZ X-Ray*. Major Bruce Crandall, callsign "Ancient Serpent Six," also known as "Old Snake" and "Snakeshit Six," commander of Alpha Company, 229th AHB, pilots the lead ship. In this chopper are Hal Moore, two RTOs, Sergeant Major Basil Plumley, the S2 Captain Tom Metsker, the Vietnamese interpreter Mr. Nik, and the aircrew. Captain John Herren, twenty-nine, is in the helicopter right behind Moore's with the first lift of Bravo Company. In the uproar of the chopper's turbine and the wind that howls through the open doors, the infantrymen chew gum and watch the leafy tops of the jungle vegetation pass under the skids of the slick, a view from two thousand feet up. The door gunners adjust their position. The aircraft descends to an assault altitude, treetop level, about twenty-five meters.

Eight machine guns simultaneously open fire. The tracer fire outlines the perimeter of the *LZ*. The gunships have returned now to protect the flanks of the flight of lift ships. The pilot announces to Herren: "Captain, we're thirty seconds out." Herren turns back to his men and gives them a thumbs up. Four men ride the skids, front and rear, and fire along with the door gunners. They and their buddies in the chopper prepare to leap as the aircraft nears the ground.

Crandall picks his spot, leaving room for the three slicks in formation behind him. Momentarily, with a perfect flare, the four helicopters, in a movement at once awkward and precise, slow to a near hover three or four feet over the *LZ*. The door gunners hold their fire as the men jump from the skids. Before the choppers get much closer to the ground, the remaining four infantrymen in each aircraft have jumped clear.

Hal Moore followed by the rest of the of the men in the lead slick all leap from the chopper and run for the trees at the western edge of the clearing, firing on the go. Everything is calm. In Herren's aircraft, the last man out is a machine gunner, his torso wrapped with linked 7.62mm ammunition. With the added weight of his eleven-kilo machine gun as well as the linked ammunition, he rebounds from his heavy landing on well-conditioned legs, ready to cover his comrades who are already running to secure their piece of the *LZ*. It is 1048 hours.

Suddenly relieved of their loads, the helicopters regain altitude. The elephant grass returns to its natural upright posture. The first flight has already left the *LZ*. The ballet continues. The next flight of the first lift is coming in on final.

Herren with his company moves to the north of the *LZ*. The men relax, reassured by the presence of their "patron" at their side on the operation. Moore tells Herren to check out the perimeter in depth, pushing to the west. Herren gives the task to Lieutenant Devney's 1st Platoon. Devney sends a squad out and across a dry creek bed. It advances a hundred and fifty meters. Sergeant Mingo, a Korean War veteran, takes the lead with two or three men. At the top of the slope he spots an enemy soldier observing them. "Hey, you! Don't move, I've got you."

After a brief game of hide-and-seek, Mingo returns with a young, haggard North Vietnamese at gunpoint, a lookout. Barefoot with neither weapon nor ammunition the man has only an empty canteen. Informed of the catch, Moore is pleased. Nik interrogates the first prisoner of the Battalion.

"How many of you are there? Where are they?"

After a brief pause the young prisoner answers and Nik translates. "He says there are three battalions in the mountain and that they want to kill Americans but that they haven't found any yet."

At 1120 hours the sixteen helicopters of the 229th are back with a second lift and the rest of Bravo Company as well as the 3d Platoon of Alpha Company with the Company Commander, Captain Tony Nadal.

Crandall brings in the third lift to deliver Nadal's remaining platoons. Captain Ramon Nadal, called Tony, is twenty-nine. He comes from an assignment in intelligence. His prior position was as S2. A West Point graduate of the same class as his friend Herren, he has already completed a Vietnam tour with the Special Forces. It is 1210 hours when Tony has all his men on the ground.

Suddenly, at 1215 hours, gunfire erupts from the place where Mingo had taken his prisoner. This time it is Sergeant Gilreath who makes contact. Moore radios Herren right away: "Jolly Roger Six, deploy the rest of your company and develop the situation! Hurry!"

Turning to Nadal: "Tony, take over LZ security and be prepared to move up on Herren's left on order."

Lieutenant Al Devney with the 1st Platoon is now about one hundred and fifty meters beyond the dry creek bed to the west.

Lieutenant Henry Herrick with the 2^d Platoon protects the rear of the lead platoon and crosses the dry streambed. Sergeant Gilreath calls Al. "*Sir*, Sergeant Burton of the 3^d Squad has visual contact of an enemy column. They're in single file and haven't spotted us. They've still got their weapons slung."

It is 1300 hours. About forty helmeted NVA infantry armed with assault rifles fiercely attack the 1st Platoon, which is leading.[4] The platoon is caught in their fire. The intensity of the shooting increases. One man is wounded, hit both in the neck and hip, the first casualty of the day. He continues to advance, M16 at the ready. Lieutenant Deal goes to find him and bring him to the rear.

Al radios Captain Herren. "Six I'm getting hit from two sides. I can't move, over!"

"Roger One Six, Two Six is coming to help you from the right side and reestablish contact. Keep me posted. Out." The redheaded lieutenant leads his platoon with spirit, eager to get his hands on the enemy. He catches up with Devney and, in his enthusiasm, charges after the NVA who disappear into the bush. Sergeant Savage realizes that by advancing this way the platoon has lost contact with the rest of the company. Herrick and his men charge into the flank of some fifty NVA. M16s on full automatic ravage the enemy. An NVA machine gun crew tries to get into the act but is cut down reloading a new belt of ammunition. Herrick discovers that he has bitten off more than he can chew and informs his captain.

"Two Six, get back to the 1st Platoon. You're too far up. Come back this way!"

But it is too late. The enemy has closed in. He is caught in an intense fire, up against more than five hundred enemy infantrymen. Moore, now at the creek bed with his RTOs, can hear the firing. As he monitors the Bravo Company net he can hear the explosions of mortars and rockets as background to the company traffic. "Shit! I've got one platoon cut off and don't have all my people on the ground yet!"

The last few men of Nadal's Alpha Company arrive at 1332 hours. Moore orders: "I want you to loan Herren a platoon to help him get his cut off platoon. You'll have the support of Charlie Company that is coming in behind you with Bob Edwards. Go! Have at it!"

Nadal orders Lieutenants Joe Marm and Bob Taft to link up with Deal's 3^d Platoon of Bravo Company that has already moved out to bring back the survivors of Bravo Company. Progress is difficult, the vegetation almost impassable. The Americans wade into the NVA trying to take Deal's platoon in the rear. A space opens between the two relieving platoons and Deal's platoon. The Americans and NVA exchange bursts of fire at pointblank range. Many NVA, previously hidden, show themselves and open fire. The two platoons are separated. Lieutenant Bob Taft and his RTO are hit at the same time. Taft is killed, the RTO wounded. The NVA mount a frontal attack on Joe Marm and his platoon, attempt to encircle their prey, fail, and withdraw. To keep from being over-run, Joe takes advantage of a ravine as a defensive position. His platoon faces the Chu Pong and thus covers the western side of the *LZ*. In Herrick's still isolated platoon Sergeant Savage fights with a fierce intensity. He has already killed twenty NVA.

In the meantime, the next lift brings in the last few men of Alpha Company and the lead elements of Captain Edwards's Charlie Company. Hal Moore; his Command Sergeant Major Plumley; the interpreter; his RTO on the battalion command net, Bob Ouellette; and Captain Tom Metsker, become the target of enemy fire. Tom empties several magazines at the NVA that surge from the bushes at less than one hundred meters. He is wounded in the shoulder. "*Sir*," the Sergeant Major announces, "if we don't find a better po-sition, we're going to get killed. If you go down, we all go down! Over there, Colonel, there's a big termite hill with trees around it."

Hal Moore and his command group bound across the thirty meters through a hail of bullets. The Lieutenant Colonel is dead set that the Ia Drang not become another Little Big Horn where George Custer, eighty-nine years earlier, let himself be trapped by the Indians.

Hal is confident. He has something that Custer did not have—fire support. Moore now has a several complex responsibilities: lead the fight on the ground, confront an ever increasing enemy, coordinate fire support, keep the *LZ* secure, and care for the wounded, among other related tasks. He is going to juggle artil-lery, air strikes, and ARA. In a few minutes the mountain disap-pears in a great cloud of smoke and red dust.

Seeing that the enemy was moving to his left (south), Moore sends Captain Robert Edwards off at a run with so much of Charlie Company that has landed to hold the southern part of the clear-ing. The North Vietnamese infantry attack just as Edward's com-pany arrives. Well situated on the ground the Americans stop the assault, but a second wave of NVA falls upon their position, yell-ing as they come. The enemy tries to penetrate between the two American companies.

At about 1430 hours, a flight of Hueys comes in on final to offload Delta Company. A machine gun opens fire from the edge of the *LZ*. Several helicopters are hit in flight. Captain Ray Lefebvre is wounded by the bullet that kills his RTO. The lead chopper is damaged. Amidst the whine of turbines, the slicks lift away from the *LZ*. It had gotten very hot!

In the meantime Moore has committed all his reserves. He recovers the survivors of Delta Company who were with Captain Lefebvre (now gravely wounded) when their chopper was hit by ground fire. Staff Sergeant Gonzales has taken his place in command of what remains of Delta Company.

The *LZ*, better protected, can now accept reinforcements. In spite of the heavy ground fire, only two helicopters are disabled. They remain on the ground. At 1630 hours Alpha and Bravo Companies launch a counterattack to reach the 2^d Platoon, still isolated to the west.

Marm and his men abandon their ravine and scramble up the slope. They receive heavy fire from directly to their front. Grenades explode close by, machine guns fire long bursts. They all return to the shelter of the ravine. Lieutenant Marm's RTO passes the handset to him. Captain Nadal orders, "Two Six, don't take useless risks. I'm going to have them pound the hillside again. There'll be a lot of flying metal. Keep your guys down. Over"

"Wilco!" responds Marm.

Turning to his men he commands, "Get down, get whatever cover you can find. Be ready to move on my signal!" The Garry Owen troopers hunker down into whatever cover the ravine provides, their M16s aimed toward the top of the hill. Hugging the earth, they feel the ground shake as the 105mm rounds explode in the NVA positions. The artillery of the 1st of the 21st Artillery at *LZ Falcon* unloads directly on target now that the enemy positions are correctly designated. The ground stops shaking, the sky starts to rumble. Joe catches the eye of several men close by. Pointing upward he tells them, "Skyraiders, be ready to move out!" The fighter-bomber dives at the hillside, recovers at the last moment, and releases two five hundred-pound bombs. It makes a second rocket-firing pass and then yields position to the ARA. A UH-IB empties its rocket pods and finishes off with a machine gun run.

Thick smoke and a cloud of red laterite rise from the ground. The forest crackles as bullets strike, slapping into tree trunks and chopping up branches. Clumps of bamboo are blown about and entangled like a game of "pick-up-sticks."

"Go! Go! Go!" Marm shouts, as he bounds up the hill leading the assault, followed by his men who fire short bursts on the run. The NVA snipers, stunned by the bombardment, do not have time to react. The company moves out of their fields of fire. Marm catches his breath behind a stump and reloads with a full magazine. He moves out on the run, firing a short burst with each bound. On his right flank the fire intensifies. He angles in that direction. Carried along by the sound and rhythmic firing of his assault rifle, he heads for his next covered spot. Three enemy soldiers break from the woods right in his face. Joe is the first to fire. One of the soldiers goes down. He empties his magazine at the remaining two. They crumple under the impact of the high velocity 5.56mm rounds. Marm and his platoon are in the middle of the North Vietnamese position. The situation is reversed.

"Be careful," Marm warns. "They're dug in good." The NVA 7.62mm machine gun opens up again and stops them from moving up the hill. "Okay gents, let's dig in. Keep your butts down! Don't let them get behind us. Where's Toliver?"

"Present *sir*!" Sergeant Charles Toliver answers, dodging fire as he closes on Marm's position.

"Charles, take four men and move the seriously wounded back to the *LZ*! Go!" Marm then tries to pinpoint the NVA strong points blocking their advance. Ten minutes later he comes face to face with Sergeant Tolliver. "What are you doing here?"

"Sir, I couldn't get through."

"Get the wounded under cover where the snipers can't hit them. We're going to take care of their machine guns. Get me a LAW."[5]

"Yes Sir."

Marm crawls forward to get a fix on an NVA position concealed behind a thick clump of bamboo up against an anthill. Sporadic bursts of machine gun fire erupt from this position. He takes the M72 and extends it to its firing configuration. The rear sight pops up. He aims and fires. An orange flame flares at the rear of the firing tube. The explosion lights up the left corner of the position. The smoke and dust thrown up by the blast rapidly disperse in the breeze.

"You got 'em sir." Before Joe could answer the NVA machine gun fires a long burst that forces the grunts to flatten themselves to the ground, noses in the dirt. Exasperated, the Americans fire away, emptying their magazines at where they think the enemy is. "The only sure way is to get a grenade right on them," Marm muses aloud. Sergeant Toliver, flat on the ground next to his lieutenant, heaves a grenade, trying to fulfill his chief's command. It falls short and explodes without effect.

"Hold your fire!" Marm commands. Surprised, the 7th Cav troopers stop shooting. Marm leaps immediately from his hole, M16 in one hand, grenade in the other. He charges the NVA position, reaching over with his left hand to pull the pin on the run. He lets the safety handle spring away activating the fuse and tosses the dirt-brown fist-sized explosive directly into the NVA position. Three seconds and the mud, bamboo, and anthill are blown in all directions. Marm is already at the edge of the dug in position. M16 at arm's length he empties two magazines, one after the other, into the hole. Pleased with himself, standing at the lip of the trench he concludes: "A double! I *zapped* at least two of them!" Marm smiles and signals to his men to come on up. A bullet strikes him in the face shattering his jaw. The smile is gone. The sniper was paying attention. Groggy, his face bloody, Marm seeks cover at the base of the still smoking position. Sergeant Keeton goes to his position and binds his gaping jaw with several layers of gauze. One of his men helps him back to the LZ where a 229th helicopter evacuates him. The next day, in the entrenched position cleared by Lieutenant Marm, the Americans discover the body of one officer and eleven North Vietnamese soldiers. Thanks to Marm's charge the troops of the Alpha and Bravo Company platoons are able to break the grip of the North Vietnamese.[6]

If the operational tempo had continued unabated, it would have been possible to assault the hill and throw the NVA into disorder. But the artillery support waned and with it the momentum of the attack. The fire support provided by the 1st Battalion of the 21st Artillery is hampered by the loss of many of the forward observers. The precise coordinates of targets to attack no longer come over the fire direction net. The NVA marksmen choose their targets with care. They look for antennas and officers in an attempt to cut off communications and command.

In the confusion of combat, radio communications with the artillery get confused and sometimes frantic. The calls for fire support multiply, tainted by panic and imprecision. Many forward observers and RTOs are out of the fight, dead or seriously wounded. At his CP in the center of the *LZ* Lieutenant Colonel Moore realizes that the attack is running out of wind. He calls the Brigade CP at the Tea Plantation.

"Bayonet Six. I need reinforcements right away to maintain the balance of force. All my reserves are committed. Over"

"Roger. All Bayonet elements are engaged. I'll send you the only company I've got at this time! Over."

Brown can only send Moore Bravo Company of the 2d Battalion, 7th Cav. All the others are on operation. Bravo Company, under the command of Myron Diduryk, is at Cateka to provide base security. At 1700 hours thirteen choppers of the 229th arrive on final at *LZ X-Ray*. On the ground, enemy infantrymen climb quickly into trees to provide a hot reception for the helicopters. Captain Diduryk's troops leap from the flaring helicopters. They fire on full automatic directly to their front, running like madmen as they seek shelter at the edge of the *LZ*.

All out of breath the Captain arrives at Moore's CP. "Garry Owen, *sir*! Captain Diduryk and Bravo Company, 2ᵈ Battalion, 7ᵗʰ Cavalry, a hundred and twenty men strong reporting for duty!" Diduryk is excited by the challenge. Moore sends him to occupy a position to the northwest of the CP and act as the battalion reserve.

During this time two sergeants of the army Public Affairs Office film the battle with their 16mm camera. Moore had not been informed of their arrival and is not aware of their presence.

At about 1740 hours daylight begins to wane. Moore orders Nadal and Herren to pull back. "Pull back just to the edge of the creek bed. Use artillery to cover your move. Night's approaching. That's the best choice." For the two captains, the biggest problem is to break contact and disengage without getting badly hurt. Nadal's RTOs and forward observers are dead.[7] He has to switch frequencies on his PRC25 between his company command channel, the battalion command channel, and then the fire support channel when he needs to adjust artillery fire. He calls Moore. "Trojan Six, we could use some smoke to cover our move. Over"

"Roger, Fire Chief Six. It's on the way. Out." The Battalion Fire Support Coordinator (FSC), Captain Jerry Whitside, is monitoring the battalion command net in the Charlie-Charlie in the air over *X-Ray*. Moore's RTO passes his boss the radio handset of the radio on the Fire Direction Net. Moore addresses the FSC: "You monitored! Give them a heavy smoke screen one hundred meters in front of their position. He's got commo problems so come up on his company push for adjustment. Over." Whitside rogers the request. A few moments pass when the fire support radio breaks the silence. "We don't have any smoke, over."

Moore is speechless. "Roger. You have Willy Peter, over?"[8]

"Roger that, Over."

"Roger. You're going to fire the mission with Willy Peter. Get with my unit on his net for adjustment. Out."

At the firing battery the Fire Direction Officer rogers the request from Captain Whitside. The Fire Direction Center team makes the calculations in seconds and just as quickly passes the data to the gun crews. A veteran sergeant comments: "If the PAVN haven't seen White Phosphorous before it'll surprise the crap out of 'em. They'll either stop shooting to watch the spectacle or crawl under something to keep from being roasted alive." One minute later the rounds whistle over the heads of the Americans. All at once, blindingly white flashes—a real fireworks display, tear up the already black sky.

"Fuck! What the hell are they doing? They're crazy! The assholes have that shit coming in awfully close!" Nadal is just as surprised as the NVA. Thanks, however, to the dazzling brightness, his men are able to quickly gather the dead and wounded.

The NVA, stupefied, stop shooting. The sergeant was right. Surprised, the NVA are cut down by bursts from M16s. They seem almost indifferent to the losses they suffer. Sometimes they charge with their weapons at sling arms.

As soon as they have pulled back, Alpha and Bravo Companies dig in their defensive positions for the night. Moore is satisfied with the move. He is waiting, however, for another company from the 2^d of the 7th Cav and wonders why it has not yet arrived. "*Okay, we'll get out of this shit by ourselves tonight while we wait for any support to get here. We'll see what happens tomorrow. Have Diduryk send a platoon to reinforce Bob Edwards and his Charlie Company to the south and have him attach his mortars to Delta Company for centralized fire support.*"

Around 1930 hours the Charlie-Charlie puts down on the *LZ* and Dillon, the S3; Whitside, the FSC; and Lieutenant Charlie Hastings, the Forward Air Controller or FAC, the Air Force officer charged with coordinating close air support join their boss on the ground. United Press International reporter Joe Galloway is with them.

There is no sleep for the troops hunkered down in their foxholes. Their eyes burn from the effort of trying to pierce the obscurity to identify suspect shadows and to make sense of the tufts of tall grass undulating in the breeze. Sergeant Keeton cares for the wounded through the night in a "standard" grunt "tent" consisting of two ponchos snapped together. He has managed to get thirty syrettes of morphine. Moore spends the night with his weapons at the ready: an M16, his .45 semi-auto pistol, and two fragmentation grenades.

Dawn finally arrives. "Watch out, they're coming, Sarge!" one of the Charlie Company men yells. "There's a bunch of 'em. Get ready!" The patrol sent out by Bob Edwards has saved Charlie Company from an unpleasant surprise. At 0630 hours, Monday, 15 November, the 7th Battalion of the 66th NVA Regiment, bayonets fixed, yelling, charges out of the south. The enemy infantry roll down through the high grass and fall on Charlie Company. The Garry Owen soldiers instantly open fire. They are supported by 105s and mortars. Despite the vigor of the response, the NVA manage to get into the cavalry troopers' positions. The fighting continues hand-to-hand. Soldiers empty AK47s and M16s at each other in face-to-face confrontations, simultaneously cutting each other down with their bursts of fire. Killed or wounded they collapse in the dust. Those who fight skillfully and instinctively have a chance to survive, but the natural law of superior numbers makes the difference.

The Platoon Leader of the First Platoon is found dead in his hole surrounded by five dead enemy soldiers. In the next foxhole one of his men, also dead, grips the throat of a North Vietnamese regular. Shotguns, pistols and Bowie knives are better suited to this kind of fighting than assault rifles or grenade launchers.

Moore radios Brigade: "Bayonet Six this is Trojan Six, we need help, over!"

"Roger Trojan Six. I can't help you right now. Keep me posted and hang on. Out."

The FAC urgently sends over his radio a cry for help: "*Broken Arrow! Broken Arrow!*" His message unleashes all available close air support in South Vietnam on a priority basis.

"Ah! I'm hit!" Bob reports by radio while giving an account of the desperate situation of his company. He is wounded in the left arm and chest. He takes cover in a foxhole with his sergeant.

At about 0715 hours Delta Company in turn comes under frontal attack. It defends the mortar platoon that the NVA are trying to isolate and destroy. The situation gets "iffy." The air support arrives about forty minutes later. The jets raise the hopes and expectations of the men on the *LZ*. Moore orders all his units to mark the front of their positions with colored smoke so the pilots will know where to unload their ordinance. Plumes of yellow smoke hiss slowly from can-sized metal smoke grenades. An indistinctly colored haze forms over the *LZ*.

Skyraiders, Phantoms, and Super Sabers circle in vain, unable to identify a target. North Vietnamese and Americans are thoroughly intermixed. Lieutenant Colonel Moore in his CP in the center of the *LZ* keeps calm in the midst of the confusion that reigns about him. Two F-100 Super Sabers dive down the long axis of *X-Ray*. Moore, one knee on the ground, juggles several radio handsets. He sees the two jets overhead. All at once, the first looses two drums of napalm. A half second later the drums barely miss the CP and the LZ erupts in roiling flames. Moore has already yelled to Hastings. "Tell that stupid bastard to break off!"

"*Pull up! Pull up!*" Hastings is already shouting over his radio. "Sir, get some cover! The napalm fell very close to our spare ammo and grenades. They may blow." Moore calmly turns to his FAC: "Don't sweat it Charlie! Tell them to keep coming."

The F-4-C Phantoms and the F-100s have disappeared behind the hills. Twenty seconds later, the jets, like sharks, shoot out again to loose their bombs with surgical precision. The aircraft slip noiselessly as they precede the roar of their engines and the thunder of the explosions. The bombing lasts an hour.

This time the five hundred-pound bombs break up the concentrations of North Vietnamese infantry. About 1000 hours, the NVA give up their attack. The pressure lessons on Charlie Company, which has lost half of its men and all its officers. The Garry Owen troopers take advantage of the letup to catch their breath and tighten up the perimeter.

Moore orders Myron Diduryk to go recover the survivors of Charlie Company, 1st of the 7th and to bring back Bob Edwards, bleeding his life away in a hole somewhere. Diduryk finds them surrounding Sergeant Kennedy, the highest ranking survivor. American and North Vietnamese dead are strewn about the ground, often intertwined. An Hispanic and a Black, linked together as if trying to help one another, were killed by the same burst. Bob Edwards's Charlie Company, in four hours, lost all its officers and sixty-two of a total of 106 men. The wounded and dead are placed near the CP, beside the termite hill. The First Platoon of Joël Sudginis's Alpha Company replaces Charlie Company, 1st of the 7th on the southern flank of the perimeter.

Profiting from a break in the action, a Huey lands next to Moore's CP. Tim Brown gets out. Moore goes to meet him and salutes. "Sir, I asked you not to come. It's not secure around here yet." Brown waggles the eagle on his collar indicating that he is senior to Moore and can land wherever he wants. "Sorry to bother you Hal! You've done a super job!"

About 1145 hours Lieutenant Colonel Bob Tully with the lead elements of his battalion, the 2d on the 5th Cav, nears the perimeter from the southeast. Captain Dillon orders the elements manning the eastern and southern parts of the perimeter to hold their fire. The relief column had been landed the evening before on *LZ Victor* and advanced without much resistance. Tully and his men discover, incredulous, the condition of their comrades of the 1st of the 7th.

At noon Tully shakes Moore's hand. "I'm glad to see you Bob. The Black Horses are welcome at *X-Ray*. Come on, we've got to set up the rescue of the lost platoon!" Moore thinks that the most logical solution is to keep Tully's fresh battalion moving with Captain Herren's company leading as guide. Herren knows just about where to find his platoon and is in a hurry to rescue his men. Tully opts for an intense artillery preparation, given the size of the NVA troop concentrations in the area.

Movement begins at 1315 hours. The operation progresses without incident. ARA helicopters and 105s have cleared the way. The Black Knights advance using grenades to systematically clear every break in terrain, each termite mound, and every tree stump so as to reduce the likelihood of any surprise encounter. But nothing happens—no snipers, no ambush, and no mortar attack. Nothing more than a land covered with North Vietnamese cadavers with their weapons.

In the meantime, back at *X-Ray*, Bravo Company, 2^d of the 7th Cav sweeps forward of the perimeter to improve the security of the *LZ*. As they advance a group of NVA soldiers tries to get behind them. One of them throws a grenade. Staff Sergeant Charles McManus pushes two men out of harm's way, throws himself on the grenade and smothers the blast with his own body. He is dead.

At the isolated platoon's position Sergeant Ernie Savage and his men have not been able to do so much as stick their noses out of their holes since dawn. The NVA riflemen are intent on getting them and have decided to take them out, one by one. Lieutenant Dennis Deal, Bravo Company, 1st of the 7th Cav, moves at the front of his troops and calls out as he approaches the survivors: "Are you guys still there?" Finally a voice responds, "Yes, we're here!"

"Ah! There's still someone here!" Deal advances. He finds the body of his friend Herrick. It is already so hot that the smell of death is pervasive. Deal is strongly affected as he looks around the area. He finally spots Savage and his men. They are very hard to pick out, covered with red dust. "Hey, Lieutenant! Looks like the dirt and dust from all the shit that's fallen around here has hidden us pretty good!" His men stay in their holes, too shocked to move.

Lieutenant Ken Duncan, Bravo Company Executive Officer, looks at them. They do not budge from their positions, staying seated or prone. "It's okay, come on, let's go." They cannot believe it. A few meters away, leaning against a tree, a seriously wounded NVA soldier expends his last ounce of energy. The Americans observe him, impressed by his determination as he dies attempting to pull a grenade from his ammo pouch.

Back at X-Ray, Moore makes sure the dead are evacuated. The Hueys come and go, one after the other, an unbroken cycle, their cargo the dead, wrapped in ponchos, the shroud of the fallen soldier. The pilots do not look back anymore. They have been flying non-stop for two days. On the way out, they carry live soldiers, on the way back, a mixed cargo of wounded and dead. Their machines smell of death and are impregnated with the flat odor of blood.

That night Captain Myron Diduryk's Bravo Company, 2^d Battalion, 7th Cavalry, occupies the perimeter position previously held by Edward's Charlie Company, 1st of the 7th. The Mad Cossack expects a serious attack. His platoons dig in deep, tie in with each other and with the units on their flanks. Lieutenant Rick Rescorla, First Platoon Leader, ties in with his friend Lieutenant Bill Sisson, a platoon leader in Alpha Company on his right.[9] They promised each other to tie in their sectors "tight as a duck's ass." Rescorla tells his men: "They will come at us fast and low. No neat targets. Keep your fire at the height of a crawling man. Make them pass through a wall of steel. That's the only thing that will keep them out of your foxholes."

The Bravo Company platoons clear out fields of fire to at least two hundred meters, plan interlocking final protective fires, set out trip flares and anti-intrusion devices as far as three hundred meters. They place trip flares and booby-trapped grenades on possible avenues of approach. Every man has at least double the basic load of ammunition. Ammo resupply points are set up. Radios are checked.

Diduryk then gets with his FO, Lieutenant Bill Lund, and they register targets all across the company front. There are no safety factors here. Lund fires in the targets forty to fifty meters out. Further away and they would not stop a ground assault. Much closer and some of the rounds would fall directly on friendly positions. As it is it is, the men have to get down in their holes when the targets are registered. Flying steel whangs over friendly foxholes. Lund has four batteries of 105s registered and available on call.

Around midnight Moore receives a bizarre order over the radio to get to Saigon in the morning to brief General William Westmoreland's staff on the battle. While this message is coming in, the NVA test the perimeter of Bravo Company, 2d of the 7th with automatic weapons. About an hour later a five-man sapper team tries to get through the perimeter of Bravo Company, 1st of the 7th. Two are killed; the others slip back into the night.

Finally, after these episodes, about 0130 hours, Moore gets on the radio and off the hook. He can stay until the fight is over. The rear echelon mentality, born of comfort, security, and a sense of urgency for administration is an often sour puzzle for front line soldiers.

At 0422 hours the enemy strikes Bravo Company, 2d of the 7th in waves. Lund calls in his fires: point detonating high explosive, variable time fused air bursting high explosive, white phosphorous, and illumination rounds. Many of the M16s jam. The men use the weapons of earlier casualties while down in most of the foxholes one man clears the jammed weapons with a cleaning rod.[10] This first attack lasts only ten minutes.

Twenty minutes later, the NVA attack again with screams, shouts, and whistles. The battalion's 81mm mortars join in the fray. An Air Force C-123 flare ship *Smoky the Bear* now throws out flares nonstop. The 105 batteries conserve their illumination rounds. This attack fails and at 0503 hours the NVA shift their forces and launch a third on Bravo Company's right. This effort too fails. Thirty minutes later they attack again, this time with bugles and whistles blowing. Some of the burning Willy Peter falls on friendly positions slightly burning Sergeant John Setelin. He picks the still burning phosphorous from his arm with the point of his bayonet. The attack lasts a half hour but fails. *Smoky* runs out of flares. The final attack kicks off at 0627 hours, again in Bravo Company, 2^d of the 7th's sector. It too fails. Hundreds of brave North Vietnamese die against the iron defenses of Bravo Company which suffers just six men lightly wounded.

Surprisingly, the rest of the perimeter is quiet. Moore orders two minutes of free firing at 0655 hours. The shooting blasts the early morning calm scrubbing trees, raking hillsides, and shredding bushes and every place where an enemy might hide. This two minutes of noisy violence has a liberating psychological effect that erases the tension of the night. Several snipers, hit by the fire, fall from trees. The suddenness of the fire surprises some forty North Vietnamese who surge from the tall grass and brush one hundred and fifty meters in front of Captain Sugdinis's Alpha Company, 2^d of the 7th. The shooting apparently triggered their attack. They are stopped in their tracks by intense rifle, machine gun, and artillery fire.

About 0930 hours the rest of the 2^d of the 7th begins to close on *X-Ray*. Moore regroups his forces and begins a thorough cleanup operation in depth beyond the perimeter of the *LZ*. He wants to have the best security possible for the coming and going of the choppers that are going to extract his men. Finally, when his search teams recover the bodies of three missing men, Moore agrees to leave *X-Ray*.

At 1115 hours the first lift of troops loads out. At 1830 hours all the effectives are back together at Camp Holloway. Moore leaves the defense of *X-Ray* to Tully's 2^d of the 5th and McDade's 2^d of the 7th. General Kinnard, in accord with General Westmoreland, unleashes a B-52 strike on the Chu Pong Massif to complete the work largely accomplished by the 1st of the 7th Cav.

Hal Moore is promoted to Colonel on 23 November. He replaces Colonel Brown as commander of the 3^d Brigade at the beginning of December. The results of the battle at X-Ray are eloquent. The North Vietnamese leave 643 soldiers dead on the field. The KIA are estimated at one thousand. Six are captured. A large quantity of weapons and matériel are recovered. The 1st Battalion of the 7th Cavalry and attached units lost seventy-nine killed, including three lieutenants and many noncommissioned officers. There are no missing.

Translator's Notes

[1] A base area.

[2] Area of operations.

[3] Due to Malaria, soldiers that had completed their tours of duty in Vietnam or time in service but had not yet been replaced, three to five men on duty at base camp, ill soldiers, soldiers on administrative retention, a few men on base camp development detail, eight to ten men going, on, or returning from Rest and Recuperative leave, the field strengths were: A Company, 5 officers and 115 men; B Company, 5 officers and 114 men; C Company, 6 officers and 106 men; and D Company, 4 officers and seventy-six men. Following major engagements, it was not unusual for a rifle company's field strength to dip another twenty to twenty-five men, to eighty or ninety officers and men as it awaited replacements for its KIA and those too seriously wounded to return to their units, and for men due to return from the hospital when sufficiently recovered from their wounds.

[4] By definition, an assault rifle is capable of both semi-automatic and automatic (or fully automatic) fire. Selection of either mode of fire is by a selector switch. The assault rifle carried by the NVA was the AK47 of either Soviet or Chinese Communist manufacture. It fired a 7.62mm (.30 caliber) cartridge slightly shorter and less powerful than the NATO 7.62mm round. The weapon accepted a magazine of thirty rounds. The North Vietnamese rifleman wore a khaki-colored bandolier containing three extra magazines, a small two-section can with both oil and solvent, and other cleaning accessories.

[5] The M72 Light Anti-Tank Weapon is employed by an individual rifleman. It is a hand held, extendible anti-tank, anti-bunker recoilless rifle that is fired once and then discarded.

[6] Marm is awarded the Congressional Medal of Honor.

[7] The Direct Support Artillery Battalion provides each rifle company with a three-man forward observer team. The senior member of the team is the Forward Observer or FO, a lieutenant, usually a second lieutenant. He is provided with an RTO. The third member of the team in the Reconnaissance Sergeant, or Recon

Sergeant. He packs his own radio. The FO and the Recon Sergeant operate on the Artillery Direct Support (DS) Battery's Fire Direction Net. The mortar platoon of Delta Company (the batallion's 4.2inch mortar platoon) also provides a non-commissioned officer forward observer to each rifle company. This individual is on the fire direction net of the battalion mortar platoon. When operating beyond the range of the battalion mortar platoon this individual operates on the DS Battery's Fire Direction Net. The Company Commander thus has a fire direction element to accompany each rifle platoon. The FO usually stays with the company commander who, generally, accompanies one of his rifle platoons. Each company maneuver element thus has an FO of its own. Ideally, every single infantryman, officer and enlisted, understands the basics of calling for and adjusting fires and also knows the frequency of the Fire Direction Net.

[8] White Phosphorous. The name "Willy Peter," from the phonetic alphabet in use prior to 1956, continues in use today to designate a type of munition that serves several possible purposes: anti-personnel, incendiary, marking, illumination, smoke, or some combination of them.

[9] Rick Rescorla died a hero's death on 11 September 2001 when, as the chief of security for a corporation with offices in the World Trade Center, he went back into the burning building to search for more survivors and the tower collapsed.

[10] From early 1964 to early 1965 I was a test officer in the Small Arms Test Division of the US Army Infantry Board at Fort Benning, Georgia. The principal problem we identified and reported with the then XM16E1 rifle was a malfunction rate ten times that of the standard M14 rifle, overwhelmingly consisting of a failure to extract. This was caused by an engineering design defect. The extractor stripped a piece of the cartridge case rim from the expended cartridge, leaving the expended cartridge case in the chamber. This type of malfunction could not be cleared by "immediate action." Although the Infantry Board carefully documented the problem, the M16 went to Vietnam without an engineering fix. The only way to clear the rifle was to employ the cleaning rod to force the expended cartridge case from the chamber. Compounding the problem was the fact that this cleaning rod, consisting of several sections that had to be screwed together, was made of aluminum to save weight. It was not strong enough to stand up to field use. The female ends of each section flared. The sections could not be screwed together. Loose sections tended to get stuck in the bore and had to be shaken out. The M16 jamming problem was serious, often occurring after a single shot was fired, when

54

the rifleman was counting on a burst of fire or being able to employ all twenty rounds in his magazine. When the malfunction occurred, the M16 was as useful as a muzzle-loader. Commanders were often unaware of the cause of the malfunction and attributed it to improper cleaning. Many men died due to this malfunction before the problem was corrected a few years later.

CHAPTER IV

At Camp Holloway Moore's Brigade catches its breath. The units that participated in all the fighting at *X-Ray* are granted a period of rest and reorganization. But the terrain was not abandoned. Part of the 2[d] Battalion of the 5th Cavalry under the command of Lieutenant Colonel Robert Tully spent the night of 17 November there with the men of the 2[d] of the 7th that came from *LZ Columbus* with Lieutenant Colonel Robert McDade. At dawn each must move out with his men to his respective LZ where they will be picked up by helicopter. Tully thus will leave for *Columbus* and McDade for *Albany*, ten kilometers to the northeast of *X-Ray*, just beside a meander of the Ia Drang.

Captain Edward Boyt of Charlie Company, 2[d] of the 5th, recounts to McDade the adventures he experienced during the course of the last thirty-six hours: "Sir, you see my men aren't too excited about digging in. Frankly, last night was a bitch. We didn't get into a fight with the PAVN but it was a real ball-buster. Colonel Tully had decided to advance in two columns, so I split off with Charlie Company with the plan of linking back up near *X-Ray*. The idea was to take the PAVN in the rear if possible. Bayonet Six was persuaded we could surprise them. After a couple hours on the march, we found ourselves in really shitty terrain—a thicket of brambles, palms, and bamboo. It's almost impossible to follow a compass azimuth in that crap."

"We had to hack a path through the stuff just to takes a compass sighting and not get stuck in one place. We made a hell of a racket! We got started slowly, first with Bowie knives, and then with machetes. We had a couple of engineers with us, and finally, when the men had had it, I told them to fire up their chain-saws."

"But I was watching the time slip by and I was late. At about 1700 I get a radio call to hold in place, make an LZ, and get ready to be extracted. Bayonet Six had finally got hold of some choppers at the Plantation and he was worried about leaving a company isolated in the middle of the forest overnight."

"There was no clearing near you for an extraction?"

"You got it sir. There was one hour before dark to cut a hole in the jungle big enough for one lift ship to get in and out. I'll skip over the details of the defense perimeter where we put out trip flares and other early warning devices to warn of any approaching Charlies. I used all my men like engineers. We used fifteen kilos of C4 to blow down the biggest trees. Then the men, naked to the waist and sweating like animals, chopped the branches off the trees and cut down the clumps of bamboo. We busted up a bunch of machetes and entrenching tools, one after the other, some seventeen! The men were pooped. Fortunately, the 229th pilots are real pros. As night fell the slicks dropped down one after the other into the green hole we had cut through the canopy, hovered, and lifted us out."

"I was in for a surprise. Just as soon as we got out of that green hell, everybody really beat, we could see just how wide the valley was. Then, in the fading light, we could see explosions, tracers, and illumination rounds a few klicks off. The pilot told me, 'That's X-Ray.' I knew right then inside the chopper, listening to the engine whine and the rotor blades whapping through the air—damn, asshole, you want hell—there it is!"

"Two minutes later we landed at *Victor*. You know now why my men are a bit slack with their digging in. With their stiff backs and blisters they're not all that charged up for pick and shovel work right now!"[1]

The next morning the men of Garry Owen and the Black Horse troopers each form a column. Tully leaves with the 2[d] of the 5th for *Columbus*, less Captain Boyt's Charlie Company attached to McDades's Battalion. McDade heads out for *Albany*. The Battalion Scout Platoon from Delta Company 2[d] of the 7th heads up the column followed by Boyt's company. Lieutenant Colonel McDade and his command group are in the middle of the column. Alpha Company, 1st of the 5th, just arrived and attached to the 2[d] of the 7th, brings up the rear.

Lieutenant Colonel Frederick Ackerson's 1st Battalion, 5th Cavalry had been sent by General Kinnard to assure the security of the 3[d] Brigade at the Plantation. Colonel Brown had stripped Cateka, sending all his reserves into the fight at *X-Ray*. Alpha Company, 1st of the 5th had been landed at *X-Ray* to relieve the severely tried and tested Bravo company of its own Battalion, coming in on the same lift ships that extracted Moore and the 1st of the 7th soldiers.

The column crosses clearings and tongues of forest. The point element of Charlie Company, 1st of the 5th, now leading the column, arrives at the edge of *LZ Albany*. Everything is calm. The men are glad to get there. It is 1700 hours. The men have been marching in the sun for three hours.

"Okay, good, the *LZ's* in sight!"

"Yup, there's nothing more except to wait for pickup."

"In an hour I'll have washed my butt and be settled down with a cold beer." The rustic comfort of Camp Holloway takes on a whole other aspect after two days of hell in the bush.

"The break comes later!" comments Boyd.

"Sarge! Get patrols out to check out the areas to the east, north, and south of this place before the rest of the column closes in. Get some trip flares out! Get back with me in twenty minutes please."

The Sergeant issues his orders to the troops. Ten minutes later he is back. "Sir, we've spotted some PAVN moving around out there."

"Where exactly?"

He is answered directly by the North Vietnamese themselves who fire several sporadic bursts.

"Take the second platoon and reinforce the perimeter. The column is way stretched out. We've got to keep the *LZ* open."

A deluge of mortar rounds, AK47 bursts, grenade detonations, and heavy machine-gun fire follow the initial bursts of fire. Boyt looks back. "Shit! They're attacking the middle of the column."

The 8th Battalion of the 66th North Vietnamese Regiment unleashes its ambush at the heart of the American battalion. Snipers prioritize their targets and take out officers and their RTOs. The NVA infantry charge into the stretched out American line, throwing it into disorder. In the middle of this column, shocked by the violence of the attack and stripped of its leaders, the survivors give ground and disperse. The column is cut in two.

Caught up in their élan and eager for revenge, the NVA look for wounded to kill. The survivors, able bodied or crippled, find refuge in the forest. Often in a state of shock and isolated, the Americans fire at anything that moves. The air is saturated with metal. At point blank range, from behind tree trunks and clumps of bamboo, the adversaries shoot each other up with singular effectiveness. Colt 45s in hand, the surviving leaders try to gather their men and organize a defense. Intense small arms fire holds back the enemy soldiers that try to pursue them.

The melee is general, any notion of tactical order gone. The men fight so as not to die, index fingers curled around triggers. There is constant small arms fire in every direction. Each man looks for a path in the direction of the *LZ*, both to get out of the thick forest and see beyond two meters and to get closer to the helicopters.

The North Vietnamese commit their own reserves. They do not have time to ground their packs. Loaded down with all their "stuff;" packs, blankets, pots, and boots, they charge into the fight. In the violence of the clash, everything gets scattered about over the ground. They did not have time to put on their boots. They attacked wearing sandals, the famous Ho Chi Min sandals with soles cut from old tires and held on the feet with thongs. In theory, the North Vietnamese soldiers march in sandals and charge in boots.

The Americans trying to link up with the *LZ* get lost and turned around. They butt up against the NVA. Some of the isolated troopers freeze in place as if locked to the ground, others thrash through the undergrowth as if whipped along, sometimes the hunters, sometimes the game. Added to the noise of exploding munitions are the cries of the wounded, the groans of the dying, and the calls for help. The medics are overwhelmed and unable to respond.

Direct support by the artillery is impossible, the two forces are thoroughly intermixed. Little by little, the Americans regroup in two pockets and get themselves organized. The survivors of Charlie Company link up with McDade's command group. In the heat of the action, Delta Company and part of Alpha Company have been pushed to the east of the *LZ*. The gunships that have had the time to arrive circle at treetop level, impatient to get into the fight. From their position they see things a bit more clearly. They dive on the NVA who are pursuing the Americans and slow them down. The Skyraiders finally arrive. Slow and awkward, they unload canisters of napalm on the NVA. North Vietnamese and Americans are so close to each other that some of them die, carbonized, on opposite sides of the same clump of brush. Then the jets return, launching two hundred and fifty-pounders. With each bombing run, the infantrymen, their spirits up, shout their approval. A final run raises the pucker factor way up when the planes strafe one of their own platoons. A hail of fire sweeps through the underbrush.

McDade manages to get through to Brown at Cateka. Bayonet Six has no reserves at his disposal. All the units of the 3d Brigade have left X-Ray and returned to Camp Holloway. He calls back Bravo Company, 1st of the 5th that had been attached to McDade's battalion earlier and had just closed in on Holloway. At nightfall, the slicks unload Bravo Company near the main pocket of resistance.

In the meantime, the company of Ackerson's battalion that had headed off toward *Columbus* changes course. These troopers move out to go to the aid of the other isolated pocket of resistance: Delta Company and the debris of Alpha Company pushed off to the east of *LZ Albany*. It soon turns out that Bravo Company, 1st of the 5th, is best placed to assist her separated comrades.

At about 2300 hours a powerful light pierces the night sky. "Flap, flap, flap," the Hueys, searchlights on, plunge like flying night predators on the NVA caught in the beams of light. Rockets disperse their ranks and dim their ardor. Their rockets expended, the Hueys come back and work the perimeters with 7.62mm fire. The bullets stream from the choppers to the ground, the tracers describing a cascade of glowing worms that strike the ground and ricochet in every direction like drops of splattering water. The artillery is able to get into the act as soon as the lines of contact are defined and the elements in contact are able to communicate their coordinates.

Held up where they confront organized resistance, the NVA begin an unmerciful hunt for isolated and wounded Americans. Sporadic explosions and noisy bursts of fire signal desperate confrontations in the night forest. Oscillating flares from illumination rounds describe moving shadows as they descend at the end of their parachutes.

Volunteers move out to look for their comrades. Their weapon of choice is the 12-gauge pump shotgun and hand grenades. A shotgun loaded with double O buckshot is the weapon-ammunition combination best adapted for this type of close-in, low visibility fighting. The patterns of flying lead unleashed at any suspicious noise or movement finish off any North Vietnamese waiting in ambush. Under the pale light of illumination rounds and the beams of the helicopter searchlights, the Americans and NVA race to be the first to find the missing or wounded Americans. Sometimes two men from the same unit barely avoid disemboweling each other as they detour by some obstacle or round a tree trunk and come face to face. The medics home in on the wounded's cries for help, often arriving too late, the NVA having gotten there first and finished them off. The luckiest are those who have lost consciousness and are left for dead.[2] The whole night of 17 November passes in this nightmare.

At first light, the North Vietnamese decide to disengage. McDade reaches *LZ Albany* and establishes a perimeter to guard the access in and out. The men of the 1st of the 5th link back up with Ackerson at *LZ Columbus.*

McDade and his men begin the day of 18 November combing through the area adjacent to *Albany* and the different places where the fighting raged to recover the dead and wounded. They also amass a considerable and varied collection of matériel abandoned by North Vietnamese units surprised on the move.

The slicks come and land in the clearing among the scattered and stunted trees. They lift out the dead. Aligned in the shadow of the trees, they are carried in their ponchos to the helicopters that come and go on their sinister task in dismal rotation. The losses of the night of 17 to 18 November at *Albany* are heavy: 151 dead, 121 wounded, and four missing. McDade had less luck than Moore.

In addition to his known dead and wounded, some men are still missing when he is extracted. On the North Vietnamese side, the Americans count 403 dead. The estimated enemy losses are much higher in view of the many signs left on the field of battle.

Seven days later an OH-13 of the 1st of the 9th spots a blood-spattered T-shirt floating in the breeze in a narrow clearing. The scoutship pilot sees a man frenetically waving his fatigue shirt. Toby Braveboy, Private First Class, Alpha Company of the 2^{d} of the 7th has spent a week in the jungle, seriously wounded in the arm, with just a canteen of water. The fifth day he narrowly escaped capture by two young North Vietnamese, then an American airstrike almost blew him away. Taken to Duc Co for initial treatment, he is then lifted to Camp Holloway. His Captain, Joël Sudginis, receives him. He finds Toby wounded, shaken, and dehydrated, but otherwise in good shape.

On twenty November General Kinnard decides to give the 3^{d} Brigade a break. It has provided the major effort since the beginning of the month. The bulk of its forces have endured fire under very demanding and sometimes dramatic conditions. He thus orders Colonel William R. Lynch to take the baton from the 3^{d} Brigade.

The Black Horse Brigade takes over the pursuit of the North Vietnamese from the Garry Owen Brigade. Up until then, the 2^{d} Brigade had been carrying out a security mission, keeping Route 19 open from Pleiku to the sea, the only line of communications linking the high plains with the coast.

The 2^{d} Brigade must chase the North Vietnamese forces still present in the Chu Pong region. The operation will be conducted jointly with a South Vietnamese airmobile brigade following a B-52 strike.

Around the Duc Co Special Forces Camp the allied troops, led by Major Norman Schwarzkopf, make contact with some isolated elements of the NVA Regiments back from the battles of *X-Ray* and *Albany*. In a few days, it is clear that the North Vietnamese have withdrawn into Cambodia. They appear to have abandoned their major highlands plateau offensive.

The 2^{d} Brigade leaves the Duc Co and Pleiku region for the Bong Son plain. Colonel Lynch establishes his Brigade at *LZs Two Bits* and *Brass*.

General Kinnard decides to draw up an account of the trimester's actions. The First Cav has been in country only three months. The American press, on the lookout for reports of the fighting and details on the lives of the young American soldiers, arrive at An Khe to learn about the new "spearhead" of the American army in Vietnam. Kinnard orders his PIO to gather the journalists at Camp Radcliff in order to give them a summary of the activities of the First Cavalry Division during the three first months in the Highlands.[3]

"Gentlemen, good morning, welcome to An Khe. The First Cavalry Division Base is open to you. I recognize some among you for having seen you in the field. I salute Charlie Black of the *Columbus Enquirer*, whom I have also seen as much at ease with a shotgun in his hands as with a typewriter. I hope Sam Castan's photos come out. I see Joe Galloway of UPI. He knows about as much about what's going on as I do. He was there for much of the fight at *X-Ray*. His article in the *Enquirer* has already made us out to be heroes."

"I think it might be useful to outline for you what we have been doing the last three months." The first month, we set ourselves up here at An Khe, site of our 1st Cavalry Division headquarters and the base from which the three Brigades move out on their operations. First of all we set up our security, then we went about reopening Route 19."

The serious stuff began on the 19th of October with the North Vietnamese attack on Plei Me. From the 19th of October to the 26th of November we conducted two operations with the code names *Long Reach* and *Silver Bayonet.*

"The successive intervention of the three brigades has enabled us to defeat a major offensive that had been planned for several months by the communist forces. The types of fortifications we discovered and the extent of the stocks of military equipment, rations, and munitions we intercepted testify to the careful organization with which the North Vietnamese had prepared this offensive. They committed their 32^{d}, 33^{d}, and 66th Regiments to this offensive. The simultaneous intervention of the 1st Brigade at Plei Me at the side of South Vietnamese Rangers prevented our Special Forces camp from being overrun."

"Next, our mission was to seek out the communist forces hidden in the forest, to pinpoint their location and destroy them. That's the mission General Westmorland gave our Division once he had a clear indication of the offensive intentions of the North Vietnamese. The principal confrontations occurred, as you know, around *LZs X-Ray* and *Albany.*"

General Kinnard concludes his briefing and answers questions.

"We have succeeded in fixing the enemy, we have obliged him to fight and, as the statistics testify, the shock of our combined arms has whipped him. Here are some numbers for the period from 19 October to 26 November. The Division has identified 3,561 North Vietnamese and Vietcong dead and taken 157 prisoners in the whole of Pleiku Province. Two thousand and forty-nine communists were killed in the Battle of *X-Ray* alone.[4] The matériel recovered amounts to 900 hundred individual weapons and 129 crew-served weapons. You'll find a detailed summary by unit in your handout."

"But, sir, what has been the price paid in men by your Division?"

"I'm coming to that! Our statistics are even more precise on our own situation. In effect, as you know, the enemy does everything possible to conceal his losses, and whenever he can, he carries off his dead and wounded, which does him justice. To come to our own losses, they may be listed as follows. We have lost 305 killed in action. Seven hundred and thirty-six men have been wounded. Three hundred and sixty-four men have been injured in accidents and 2,828 have suffered one or another form of serious illness."

"The balance favors the First Cavalry Division if you only compare the number of dead, but if you take the total figure it still amounts to twenty-five percent of the Division strength out of action from one thing or another in this campaign. What lets you say that you've won?"

"First, the fact that you're here to ask me the question! In effect, if the First Cav had not intervened, the 32[d], 33[d], and 66th Regiments of the North Vietnamese Army would surely be in Pleiku and An Khe too. Then there would not have been a press conference but just a victory announcement. In short, they have gone back to Cambodia with, without doubt, five thousand fewer men, a large part of their logistic infrastructure destroyed, and their high plains sanctuary penetrated. This military setback has a direct impact on their propaganda."

"What are the technical or tactical reasons for your success?"

"Thank you for asking that question. Up to now I've given you the figures. Unfortunately there isn't any other way to present the situation, whether of an army or of a business. We can, however, analyze these results. We owe this success first of all to a concept—airmobility. I plan to give you a short lesson on that subject at another time. It will be well worth the effort."

"It's my conviction that the North Vietnamese could never be stopped using classic means. In short, the 1st Cavalry Division represents a new concept that completely integrates air and ground mobility. The real winners of the battle are the helicopters. We call the men 'skysoldiers.' We've traded our 'mounts,' our trucks or armored vehicles, for helicopters. We have in this manner gained mastery of the third dimension—the air."

"Let's go back to the numbers for some facts. In thirty-five hours of fighting, with our own logistical means, we moved 5,048 tons of freight directly to where it was needed by the operational units. More than that, we took 8,205 tons to Pleiku from the storage depots in Qui Nhon and Nha Trang. In the tactical arena, all the infantry and artillery units were moved by air. We evacuated 2,700 refugees to get them out of the combat zone."

"In counterpoint to this activity that represents several thousands of flight hours, we've recorded fifty-nine aircraft in flight hit by ground fire and three hit on the ground. Only four were shot down and we recovered three of them. We have totally disoriented the North Vietnamese with our mobility, our ability to operate over such extended terrain, and to respond almost instantly to any initiative."

"Firepower is our second trump card. On the ground, we have highly motivated infantry armed with automatic rifles supported by helicopter mounted aerial rocket artillery."

"General, I understand your enthusiasm with respect to your division which really is very impressive. But Colonel Moore at *X-Ray* needed the Air Force, and he would indeed have preferred to avoid the napalm that hit his CP. Have too many risks been taken? What lessons have you drawn from your first one hundred days in Vietnam?"

"There are many questions. You will permit me to reserve the results of the analysis of these techniques for my command. However, on the question of risk, I'm going to try to give you my personal impression. I, myself, and the commanders of the 1st and 3^{d} Brigades have taken calculated risks by dividing their forces and dispersing them on the ground. The principal objective was to force the enemy from his lair. We had very little information about his forces and where they were. And the risks turned out to be very real. When Colonel Moore set up at *X-Ray*, he didn't know he would stumble on a regiment, but in fact that was the objective. We came a bit close to the edge in the execution. This Division must, without fail, be ready to instantly dispatch the necessary reinforcements to quickly crush the adversary."

"A perfect logistical system, powerful and reliable communications, a maintenance program that assures the availability of the entire fleet of aircraft—that's where we're looking now for potential improvements. As to the concept, it's still excellent."

"General, you've been in several wars. Have you made comparisons between the types of fighting you've been in now and yesterday, including Korea?"

"I'm not going to share my memories with you and play the

role of 'old soldier.' I'd rather give you the figures. For the Ia Drang Campaign the ratio of dead to wounded is one to two point two. During the Second World War and also in Korea, the ratio was one to four. In the fighting we've just been through, the majority of wounds were from small arms fire. The majority of hits were in the head and chest. The dead were generally hit several times. We recorded very few shrapnel wounds. That should describe for you without a long-winded explanation just how determined and pugnacious this enemy is. It explains the violence of the fighting."

"The lesson that we draw from this is that the quality of the fighting man still depends on his personal courage. This cannot be separated from the firepower we bring to the fight that compensates us for inferior numbers. Gentlemen, I thank you for your attention."

Kinnard raises his hand in a salute to the group and leaves the room. He leaves the correspondents, the cameramen, and the sound technicians in the smoke-filled tent and goes back to the CP. The CP had been established in an old French colonial building, in the shadow of a magnificent Poinciana tree. In contrast to the plantation homes, this one is a large cube without a veranda. Its only adornment is a stairway in front with a few steps, but in the middle of a tent city it is striking.

"So, sir—the journalists have let you go?"

"With a warning! We haven't gotten them off our backs. The war as it happens apparently gets more of an audience than news releases. I told it like it is, as spelled out in my orders."

"So, let's get on with an analysis of our shortcomings! We've noted some commo problems. At *X-Ray* we found that our radio communications weren't very good. The relief and the weather screwed up our commo over the relatively extended distances to Pleiku or here, or even with *Falcon* where the artillery was located. The commo people think the solution is to set up a relay, a CV2 in an aircraft that orbits above the theater of operations. We'll have to try it with the 2^d Brigade in *Operation Clean House* that's getting underway."

"For logistical requirements and setting up alternate stockpiles of fuel and spare parts, have our Support Command folks get together and come up with some solutions. If we need more men or matériel to make it happen, get back with me."

"I'll take advantage of our all being together to tell you that Secretary of Defense McNamara has already received a report on *Operation Shiny Bayonet.* You know how much he was personally involved in the creation of the Division. I'll repeat for you his comments when he was briefed on the after action report:" 'It was,' he said, 'a result without precedent, ... ' and he added, 'Unique in its display of valor and courage, the Air Cavalry Division has established a record that will long remain hard to beat by the other divisions.' So, I've forwarded a memorandum in which I write, ' ... the only distinction appropriate for the Division is the *Presidential Unit Citation!*'"

At first silent, the officers break into applause.

To calm the emotion the General adds: "Don't get all worked up, it's not a done deal yet, it'll take time. But since we're at the point of citing awards, the Vietnamese high command has advised me that they are going to award the Vietnamese Gallantry Cross with Palm to the 1st of the 7th for its heroic conduct at the Ia Drang. A final note, Captain Ramon Nadal, Alpha Company Commander in the 1st of the 7th has recommended the Medal of Honor for Lieutenant Walter Marm for his exemplary conduct under fire. Colonel Moore and I support this recommendation and I have approved and forwarded it. 'Joe' Marm will be the first American soldier to earn this distinction in Vietnam."[5]

Kinnard produced a glass and filled it with bourbon. He intoned alone the first line of "Garry Owen:" "Let Bacchus' son be not dismayed ... " and the other officers joined in, "But join with me each Jovial Blade ..." They followed with the chorus of "Garry Owen" in the guise of a toast for Bayonet Six, and for Colonel Moore to inaugurate his advancement to "Bird Colonel."

Each officer congratulated the two architects of the success of the 7th Cavalry.

"Gentlemen," interrupts Kinnard, "I propose that we continue this celebration at the club at 1800 hours. To conclude, here is what General Westmoreland said, and I quote: "The Americans have proven once again and in an incontestable manner their ability to take their own measure and to defeat the best troops the enemy has to offer on the ground, as well as the validity of the airmobile concept.'"

"Gentlemen, I believe we have made some progress, certainly with respect to our own military. It remains to convince the North Vietnamese, but, for that, I have confidence in you."

Translator's Notes
[1] Properly "digging in" is one of the keys to survival. Once ingrained as a standard practice, soldiers dig proper positions no matter how exhausted they may be or how long it takes.

[2] A lucky few, literally in the midst of the North Vietnamese, successfully feigned death and survived.

[3] Public Information Officer.

[4] This is a new and more precise estimate than that made at the time of the battle and cited in Chapter 3.

[5] Actually the second.

CHAPTER V

"Hey, hello! I'm a journalist. My name is Sam Castan."

The trooper reassembling his M16, seated at the entrance of a tent, raises his eyes. "Hi, Sam."

"What is it that upsets you the most here?"

"D'you mean off the top of my head?"

"Yes, Sergeant Mitchell," Castan adds, reading his nametag.

"Ah, it's 'Mitch.' Well, look, it's night! It's six fifteen and you can't see anything."

"Yeah, but in the States it gets dark even earlier. It's December."

"There, ya, it's December! But here? Me, I left Georgia in August. Since then it always gets dark at the same time. You soak in the same high humidity and heat."

"But how is the sudden coming of the dark important?"

"Because the night here is terrible and it lasts twelve hours."

While he listens to Mitch Sam slaps a mosquito and scratches his forearm.

"Look, Sam, the night has started. All the damn bugs wake up and bite the crap out of you. From six to six thirty it's the mosquitoes and other flying bugs, later on it's ants, other unknown stinging fuckers, spiders, black creatures. You light a kerosene lamp and the ephemeral little bastards come and fill the air over it. There are so many of 'em they get in your mouth. You want to sleep, you've got bunches of beetles in your hooch. I don't want to give you nightmares so I won't mention the scorpions and snakes. That's why I don't like the night!"

"But in Base Camp, haven't you got your tents?"

"Negative!" An Khe by night is Broadway and Disneyland both together. Go to the CP in a quarter of an hour and Donald Duck'll meet you in person. There's a big screen and it's like a drive in. There's a refreshment tent right by it. It's a new addition. In addition to the Blue Ribbon beer from the rations, now you can find a *Ba Muoi Ba,* the local *Bière 33*, souvenir of the French. The dark is like soup. It's not any better in your tent. If you're tired enough, you sleep, but haunted by bad dreams. And then you discover the fear that you didn't have time to feel under fire. If you lie awake, you get the shakes, and that's worse. The Charlies are like the insects; they always attack at night. Me, I prefer to be wide-awake for an Eagle Flight. You wait with your buddies. You clean your weapons, you play cards, you listen to the radio. But you're always under pressure. I don't like the night."

"In three months you haven't had a single night when you felt different?"

"Yeah, at Pleiku! I went into town once with an SF guy. He took me to a shantytown. The walls were made of beer cans. Bad! We went to a restaurant, a room with tables and stools and a dim neon light. There were a few South Vietnamese soldiers and us. We sat down and some girls came over. Each of us had a girl; very pretty, small, light brown. They wore the traditional *cái quân,* the trousers they wear in the country. They were smiling. My SF buddy ordered beer. The girls brought glasses, ice and the beer, in cans. Mine gently poured the beer into an inclined glass. I watched the blond liquid fill the glass with fascination. The girl handed me the glass with just two fingers of foam. I drank that beer, don't know what kind it was, and felt the foam make a mustache on my upper lip. All of a sudden, things seemed to change."

"The girls sat down with us and observed us, smiling, very sweet, not at all vulgar. There, I felt like I was someplace else. I won't tell you what happened after that, you, coming from Saigon. You know all that by heart. They talked about Tu Do Street and the road to Tan Son Nhut."

"You want some addresses for when if you get to Saigon?"

"Nah, it's too late for that. What do you really want to know?"

"Do you know how the First Cav landed at An Khe, in this valley?"

"No idea. Better ask the General. He was the first one here. You'll see, he's the man. Tomorrow there's a bunch of FNGs coming in. For sure he'll be giving them his welcome speech."

"FNGs?"

"*Fucking New Guys*, recruits, whatever! Call them *fresh meat* if you want. We're in a period of rotation. There's a bunch of old guys finishing their tour. They're going back to the "world," they're leaving, their replacements are on the way."

"Thanks for the word! I don't dare say 'goodnight,' so, see you tomorrow!"

The next day a bunch of FNGs emerge from the bush. They come out haggard having spent the night rolled up in poncho liners among clumps of elephant grass. For them, the first night at An Khe was not a winner! At first light a mess sergeant woke them with runny powdered eggs and bread. The journalist joins them.

They have been assembled in a large tent to eat and fill out some forms. There, they warm up a bit after their Spartan night in the chill outdoors. "Up! Get in ranks and stand at attention," commands a Sergeant Major. From zombies the FNGs turn into soldiers standing impeccably at attention. A one-star general appears behind the Sergeant Major.

"At ease! Be at ease gentlemen. You may sit. Open the tent flaps a little so we can breath. Thanks … Good morning, I'm General John Wright, the Assistant Division Commander. General Kinnard couldn't be here today to welcome you. He gave me the mission. In the name of the officers and men of the First Cav, I welcome you to the best American Division in Vietnam. Most of you have already read about many of the things we do here."

"We've cut this base camp out of the bush. We did it with machetes, axes, and saws. It's the biggest heliport in the world. We're a high spirited super-hardworking team here. That's what I expect from you."

"It's been two months now, well, everybody was working on clearing the area. A group of Viet Cong in black pajamas came down off Hon Cong, the mountain just beside the base, and opened fire on the camp. The men put down the machetes, picked up their M16s, and returned fire. It was the VC who were scared shitless. We kept our cool and reacted with determination and firmness. That's the spirit that rules here."

"We've latched onto and beaten the enemy every time he's shown himself. Our problem is to find him so we can fight him. We can do what we want when we want. Our Division has over four hundred helicopters at its disposal. It's completely airmobile. Contrary to what you have heard, our individual weapons have shown themselves to be perfect.[1] In the Ia Drang Valley the PAVN learned first-hand about the M16. Its trajectory is so flat they couldn't crawl under grazing fire. We've all got a tough job to do here. All I ask of you when you join your units is to do your part. I'm counting on you. Thank you." "Ten hut!" commands the Sergeant Major.

Wright leaves the tent as the sounds of shuffling people and chairs fill the air. Sam Castan catches up with him. "Nice to meet you sir!" he says as he presents himself.

"Hi Sam," Wright responds. "How may I help you? You know everything about the Cav if you heard my welcome talk, not to mention yesterday's press conference."

"General, I'd like to know why you picked An Khe for your headquarters?"

"Come with me to the CP. I'll put you with the PIO so he can explain the reason we set up here. Come see me at ten hundred and I'll fill you in with some more details." The two men walk together back up onto Route 19. The First Cav tent city is set up along each side of the road. They pass in front of village hooches stretched along footpaths, then take an alley bordered by magnificent Poinciana trees.

"Have you seen these flowers? They're beautiful, left over from the French like this big building that serves as headquarters." The General takes in the six steps at the entryway in three strides. "Lieutenant, Sam's a journalist. Brief him on our setup here. At ten hundred bring him to my office."

"Right sir!" Turning toward Castan, the lieutenant adds: "We'll begin by looking at a map. We're here, in the CP on the north side of Route 19. The road on the An Khe plateau is oriented east-west. Toward the west Route 19 goes toward Pleiku, and toward the east, Binh Dinh and Qui Nhon. An Khe is at an elevation of 462 meters. The plateau is situated between two passes: Deo Mang Yang or the Mang Yang Pass to the west, and Deo Anh Khe or the Anh Khe Pass to the east. It extends about five kilometers from Hon Cong mountain to the northwest that you can see easily, and Nui Nhon mountain to the northeast. The troops call Hon Cong 'Hong Cong.' Remember that. It'll help you to understand. The Song Ba, or Ba River crosses the Anh Khe basin. This river flows in a north-west-southeast direction. It cuts Route 19 two hundred meters from the CP. You had to cross the bridge."

"This place already has a well-known military past. The French had set up a major fortified military position here. It was to control this high plains road. In April 1954, *Groupement Mobile 100*, a mobile force made up mostly of the French battalion of the UN Korean forces, had replaced a lighter unit, *Groupement Mobile 11*, which had previously occupied Anh Khe."

"This Mobile Force 100 improved the defenses of Anh Khe and rebuilt the air strip. They had to lengthen it so the twin engine Dakotas and Bristols could use it. The French set up here to resist and if possible to protect Pleiku from the Vietminh advance. It was just eleven years ago. Dien Bien Phu fell 7 May 1954."

"The soldiers of Mobile Group 100 learned of the defeat of their comrades in the Tonkin area barely a month after their arrival in Anh Khe. They thought of themselves a little bit as the Dien Bien Phu of the South. They defended their valley with strong points here and there, with some artillery batteries in the north and another in the southwest at An Cu. They emplaced additional minefields. We inherited them," the Cav Lieutenant explained, "but it was not a gift. We would have much preferred it if they had been removed. When we first arrived with General Wright, the mines were a real pain in the ass. We had to systematically probe the whole area for mines and remove them."

"Well, how did it end for the French at Anh Khe?"

"Yeah, well, General Salin came in mid June to tell the Korean

War vets that the forces assigned to the high plateau needed to be reduced, and therefore it was necessary to evacuate Anh Khe.

"Was it a big position?"

"Oh yes! Ten units and a fleet of some two hundred vehicles of different kinds. Some of the matériel was backhauled by air, but all the heavy equipment, the artillery and the ammunition, had to be moved by road. About two hundred Vietnamese civilians who the French had not been able to dissuade from leaving with them followed the convoy. All those people left on 24 June 1954. The Vietminh were waiting for them. They sprang a major ambush at kilometer stone 15, fifteen klicks west of Anh Khe. Vehicles and equipment were abandoned and destroyed. Those who survived the ambush regrouped at kilometer stone 22 and retreated toward Mang Yang Mountain through the forest, fighting all the way with the Vietminh." Using a pointer, the Lieutenant points out on the map the different positions of the Vietminh trap.

"A monument was erected at kilometer stone 15 after the cease fire, a simple plaque engraved in Vietnamese and French: 'Here, the 24th of June 1954, French and Vietnamese soldiers gave their lives for their country.' When you convoy through this sector your spine tingles."

Having finished his story on the history of Anh Khe, the young officer accompanies the reporter through the broad tiled corridors of the headquarters building. "The large colonial houses are extraordinary, they stay cool just as if they were air-conditioned," the Lieutenant comments to make conversation. They enter the General's office.

"Hello Sam! You know everything about this valley! But if you want us to stay friends, stay away from drawing parallels between Mobile Force 100 and the First Cav in your articles. The temptation is great but we only have Korea in common. Here, we've just shown the NVA the difference. We're the ones that lay the ambushes. There's a real difference in scale. Look, the First Cav has 15,000 men, 7,100 vehicles, and 470 aircraft. We are the first airmobile unit in the world. So, we've nothing in common with two hundred mobile group troopers in retreat. We, ... we're winners!"

"I tell you that so you can avoid making table talk type analyses with your reporter colleagues, cognac and soda in hand, on the terrace of the Hotel Continental in Saigon. You know, the drink before the massage, how to relax for supper."

"Thanks sir. I've made a mental note of that. But why is the First Cav at Anh Khe?"

"Your question concerns me directly since I'm the one who chose this location. General Kinnard gave me the mission to locate the site to establish the Division Base. I left Fort Benning on 2 August 1965 with thirty-one officers and men on a regularly scheduled flight for Vietnam. To be precise, general order number 185 issued by III^d Army Headquarters on 1 July activated the 1st Cavalry Division, Airmobile. I therefore left a month and a day after the official birth of the Division."

"It thus took only eight weeks to put the First Cav on the ground, but ten years to firm up the concept! On that subject, go see the man who put the idea together, at least one of those who designed this surprising war machine."

"But you, you're the one who built the base!"

"If you wish. General Kinnard's first idea was to set up the Division in Thailand, in Cambodia, or in Laos, so as to be able to cut off the North Vietnamese from their logistical bases. From one of these three countries, we would have been able easily to cut the Ho Chi Minh Trail. The North Vietnamese would have been strangled in their South Vietnamese sanctuaries and forced out of their bases in Cambodia and Laos. Our government didn't select this option because it wanted to keep American military action inside the borders of South Vietnam."

"When I arrive in Saigon I go directly and report to General Westmoreland at MACV, Military Assistance Command Vietnam. Westmoreland had it in his head to give the First Cav the mission of keeping order, of providing security for the principal lines of communication over the whole of the country, each Brigade having its own assigned area of operations. Suffice it to say that General Kinnard was upset. Divide the First Cav; that would dilute his forces and lose all the advantage of the airmobile concept. He had battled ten years to forge this tool and the high command wanted to convert his unit into a security force!"

"So, I leave for Qui Nhon with my thirty-one folks. Kinnard himself arrives in Saigon on 16 August to talk directly with Westmoreland who receives him in his large office and takes him over to the map."

"I'm describing this scene to you just like Kinnard gave it to me. Westmoreland mounts a frontal attack."

"There it is!" he says to Kinnard. That's how I'm going to deploy your Brigades. I'm going to put one there, the second here, and the third over here so as to cover the whole country."

Kinnard, very calm, replies: "With your permission, General, let's talk about that."

Kinnard presents his case at length. "The Chief of Staff instructed me that the principal mission of the Division would be to prevent the North Vietnamese and Vietcong forces from splitting

Vietnam in two. The critical axis goes from the Cambodian border to the coast. Route 19 represents this axis from Qui Nhon to Pleiku."

"I need total mobility, but also all my forces. Visualize this: if you spread out the change in your pocket over the whole country, you have no buying power anywhere!"

"Westmoreland had the courtesy to listen to Kinnard. He understood him too and decided to keep the Division together, giving it the mission of securing the major axes of communication in the high plateaus."

"The mission thus clearly defined led to the current divisional disposition. The 3^d Brigade was sent to Binh Dinh province along the coast, the 2^d to Kontum province, and the 1st to Pleiku province in the high plateaus, including Chu Pong Mountain."

"The 1st Squadron, 9th Cavalry, the mobile squadron, must provide reconnaissance for the whole operational area, an area with several strong points, the Plei Me, Duc Co, Plei Djerang, Plei Mrong and Dak To Special Forces camps. These camps are placed along a line stretching the length of the border to the west of the high plateaus."

"So much for the infighting at headquarters." After a pause, Wright adds: "During this time I'm in Qui Nhon with my thirty-one guys and I get the mission to find the center of gravity of this operational area to set up the Division Headquarters. This site must be the real pivot point of the airmobile division in order to respond to the demands for logistical support, maintenance, radio communications, and all the many specific aspects of support for a completely heliborne division."

"MAVC gave me the support I needed. My problem was to find a location between the sea and the Cambodian border able to accommodate all our helicopters as well as the infantry units and Division Artillery. You remember the numbers!"

"Don't forget that we also had to find the necessary space for a good perimeter defense and secure the Division from any ground or air attacks. When I arrived, I was very worried about the vulnerability of our units to an aerial attack that might come from North Vietnamese or even Chinese bombers. I was afraid of 'Kamikaze' type attacks. When I talk about this with General William Depuy, MACV Operations Officer, he laughs. He told me: 'Don't concern yourself about air attacks on your base. If that happens all we need to do is wipe Peking off the map, and they know it!'"

"Looked at like that, I was more comfortable with my search. My intentions needed to be kept hidden. My team wore civvies, as if they were technical types. We crisscrossed the area. Given our pretty hard-core looks, I don't think we went completely unnoticed, but we stood out less. I visited the Green Beret camps on the high plateaus, the positions held by the Vietnamese Army, and also the hamlets along Routes 19, 14, 6c, and other remote trails."

"So, all said and done, you picked Anh Khe?" Castan asked.

"That's right! Yes! The French didn't make such a bad choice. There are very few places in the area so open and with an existing landing strip, and with meteorological conditions that meet our needs for airmobile operations. In addition, there was already a Special Forces camp with montagnards that patrolled the two passes vulnerable to ambushes: the Anh Khe Pass and Mang Yang Pass. Anh Khe is in the middle."

"Moreover, this area has a bad reputation. The SF were heavily attacked in February. Since Anh Khe was in VC controlled territory, Route 19 was always closed. The South Vietnamese Army didn't try to open the road till July. If one were to put the Cav in the heart of enemy territory, the only choice would be to clean up the area, and fast. That's what we're doing."

Castan tries to pick up the chain of events: "So, by the end of August, there are only thirty-two of you at Qui Nhon, and you're waiting for the Division to get here so you can get it set up at Anh Khe."

"Exactly. I get the green light for Anh Khe. While we're looking around, a contingent of 1,030 men is getting ready to come to Vietnam. They lift off on 14 August from Warner Robbins Air Force Base in Macon, Georgia, and land at Cam Ranh Bay. On 27 August Hercules C-130s borrowed from the Special Forces land them on the reinforced landing strip at Anh Khe."

"The one thousand troops unload their gear and line up their tents along the road. I'm there and I'm waiting. I had some simple ideas for the organization of the base area and I had to get the word out fast. I let the different units set up their tents then, when I see that they've finished, I move between the lines of shelters and point out, without speaking, at random, twenty-five officers and NCOs from among the most experienced.

"I take them onto the plain covered with elephant and saw grass, with bushes, facing the line of tents. Seeing twenty-five senior people grouped together, the rest draw up out of curiosity and make a half circle around me."

Then Wright continues his story. "I took off my fatigue shirt, yanked off an old tee-shirt that I knotted around my head, then I unsheathed my machete and, without a word, I began to cut the vegetation around me while being careful to cut it close to the ground, without uprooting the clumps of grass."

The men were watching me, disconcerted. Most of them knew

that I had been a prisoner of the Japanese during the Pacific War, and that I was a specialist in mass manual labor. I cleared a circle of about seven meters fast enough and, seeing the group of spectators was growing large, I ceased work, running with sweat. I told them: 'If each of you swings your machete for as long as I have and clears a circle of this size, altogether we can clear a rectangle two by three kilometers. There won't be anything left on the ground but this superb green grass. You've been selected to prepare the First Cav Base Camp. We've got to be ready, with the least delay possible, to receive four hundred thirty-five helicopters. All the work must be done. But we have no bulldozers, no earth moving equipment. It's not a question of plowing under this rampant vegetation, the bushes, the grass. For the well being of the helicopters, we can't have either dust or mud, so your best tool is the machete. And the base area must be as well clipped as a golf course.' In fact, the name 'golf course' stuck, and that's what we call the airfield!"

"At first, we had to clear the brush and bushes out of the valley without disturbing the ground. The dry season dust is the turbine engine's worst enemy. The monsoon mud is no better for other reasons. We laid out steel plates, PSP, on the French landing strip, and reserved it for air traffic.[2] Priority goes now to camp defense. To protect people and matériel from mortar and rocket attacks we're digging trenches and fighting positions, filling sandbags. It's a permanent, daily task, shitty but necessary. That's why I personally undertake to get the word out. Mister Castan, is your curiosity about Anh Khe satisfied?"

"Yes sir, but you've just told me that the name of the base is the Golf Course. The official name is Camp Radcliff, isn't it?"

"Donald G. Radcliff belonged to my advance party. Radcliff was the first officer of the Division to be killed here. On 17 August, he was on a reconnaissance mission over the Anh Khe valley. When he flew over Mang Yang Mountain, at about three thousand feet, his helicopter was hit by a burst of 12.7mm fire. He was posthumously awarded the Distinguished Flying Cross and so this base is called Camp Radcliff."

Translator's Notes
[1] See Translator's note 10, Chapter 3. In fact, the problem with the M16 Rifle went largely unrecognized by commanders above company level, and were attributed to poor maintenance.

[2] Perforated Steel Planking that may be used to provide an aircraft landing strip on unstable terrain such as sand. It may also be used to construct bunkers.

CHAPTER VI

"Thank you, General, but if you could set me up to see the Major General, I would like to know more about the famous airmobility concept."

"Don't tell you're passionately interested in military tactics. You're going to bore the shit out of your subscribers."

"You can't say that till after the fact."

"If you insist, with pleasure. You know that, in the American Army, we're open, we talk to each other and to the public."

"Precisely, I'll take advantage of that before things change!" Sam takes his leave and exits the CP. In the time it takes him to get his bearings, his shirt is soaked in sweat and sticks to his back.

"We're lucky. We've got some elevation here. It's cooler," the guard, amused, watching him says.

"Where can I find some helicopter pilots?" Sam asks.

"What unit?"

"Don't know. The ones that were at Ia Drang."

"Pilots—there's all kinds: scout pilots, cargo chopper pilots, gunship pilots, Chinook ... there's a choice."

"Okay, I've got a lot to learn. I'm going on down to the landing zone." Along the way, Sam runs into Mitch, the man who hates the night. "So, you've seen the wheels? Wright told you how he turned us into brush cutters and bag filling machines?"

"Yup, he mentioned that."

"It's day, I'm in a good mood, come on and share some of this garbage they feed us.[1] I'll tell you the way I see things."

"Thanks for the invitation. I'll go see the pilots afterwards."

"At this hour, they're eating, or recuperating from the night or the morning. When it's hot, it's not ideal for flying. There's got to be an operation before they'll fly in this heat. Me, I'm going to tell you about the life of a grunt who keeps this damn golf course cleared. As he told you, it's all done by hand, but you've got to see the vegetation we had to cut, dry as an old rice paddy. Elephant grass, that too, but the saw grass, what a pain in the ass, the blades are razor sharp."

In the bamboo thickets there are poisonous snakes. But, when you find one, the most dangerous thing is the twenty-five guys who all go after it with their machetes at the same time, trying to kill it. The termite hills are hard as concrete; you bust your entrenching tool on them. The ant hills, not little ants, but big fuckers. The sneaky bastards climb up inside your trousers and only start to bite when they're on your ass or your balls, with pinchers like a stapler. Just a little bit less apocalyptic than the night, huh!"

"It was hard to understand. We're in the biggest army in the world, the first airmobile division ever created, and we work like in the early days of the West. And for motivation, a real treat—two packs of cigarettes a day, two cans of beer a week! For chow, C-Rations, and when the mess tent's finally set up, powdered shit: powdered eggs, powdered milk, powdered coffee, everything powdered."

"You don't get anything locally?"

"Yeah, onions. They're something here. They grow in eighteen days. Onions with Tabasco sauce, it's like medicine."

"Comfort and hygiene in the Army, it's a myth then?"

"For those of us who made like pioneers, that's a roge! We bathed when it rained. Look at the bare-assed guys washing like kids, in the river, or in the rain. But there are plenty of razor blades and soap. It's like the Middle Ages, but clean."

"We built everything. There was nothing, no tents, no mess, no water, no crappers. We built two-holer latrines with half 55-gallon drums. We got by the first ten days like that. To go with the twice a day C-Rations, we got our water directly from the river. It went from the river to water tanks. We filled our canteens from them. We shaved out of our steel pots!"

"And you're well equipped now?"

"Yes, for sure. At the edge of the river there's a water treatment plant. The river water's filtered, heated, and chemically treated and they've set up tents for a shower point. There's at least six tents just for that. We're maniacs for keeping clean in the Cav. The latrines haven't changed though."

"You're not real happy, Mitch?"

"Hell no, Sam! Haven't you figured it out? I'm a grunt. We're all grunts. We complain, grouse about everything. It's our second nature. That's why we're called 'grunts'! The Marines call themselves 'grunts' too."

"Ah! Okay. You complain on general principal."

"Yeah, you've got it."

"Good, but before getting into this situation you were trained, weren't you?"

"For sure! Training and drill up the ass. I was twenty-three when I was finally drafted. They'd exempted me for a while. I had a bad knee from football. At my second physical, the doctor said I was no good for the infantry, excused from long foot marches. I was sent to Fort Gordon for a five-month course in electronics. I was supposed to be assigned to Europe. I was already dreaming about it. I got travel orders for something I'd never heard of, the 11th Air Assault Division. To me, air assault, that sounded like airmobile or airborne—some kind of shit like that, huh? I went by bus to Fort Benning, a place with red clay dust, already like Vietnam. The only difference: pine trees. There aren't any here."

"Maybe at Dalat!"

"Where's that?"

"I'll show you on a map. Go on!"

"I was assigned to Charlie Company, 3d of the 17th Cavalry. Fort Benning was huge. There weren't many people where we were. The classroom, if you can call it that, was as big as a football field. It looked like a cow pasture. There were three B-Model Hueys on it, at least a dozen H-13s, and lots of other aviation stuff. Though there were just a few of us at first, people were arriving every day. Then more helicopters, and a bunch of officers. The Engineers went to work. They laid out a new airfield with laagering areas and a taxiway. People come in from everywhere. There are more than seven thousand five hundred families that discretely set up housekeeping in the Fort Benning area. What a Hell of a logistics operation!"

"We were issued new gear, olive green jungle fatigues, super. But all the tee shirts and skivvies were an immaculate white. What a joke! They tell us: 'There's only one color, olive drab, do it!' For a whole week we became dyers. We took all the laundries by assault and grabbed up the supplies of green and black dye. The green party! With our green underwear, we were already different from the rest of the Army."

"The second difference was much easier to see. We were issued M16s, the new assault rifle. So, we were the first to be armed with it. The Marines were still dragging the M14 around."

"I remember the sergeant who was instructing us on the firing range. 'The M16 produced by Colt Industries Firearms Division,' he said, 'is an individual weapon of the new generation!' It's true, everything's new. The 5.56mm or .223 caliber Remington round has a muzzle velocity of 988 meters per second. In fact, the bullet fired by the M16 will explode a drum of water when it hits it. The 7.62mm round of the M14 rifle makes a hole in the same target, that's all."[2]

"With respect to usability, the rear sight is an integral part of the carrying handle. Most important, in addition to safe, the fire selection switch has two positions: semiautomatic and fully automatic. The fully automatic rate of fire is eight hundred rounds per minute. You've got to watch how much ammo you use. The magazines hold twenty rounds."[3]

"With respect to performance, a high hit probability and good stopping power. Very concentrated fire, yup! In short, the rifle of the century, except you can't let it get dirty. So, you clean it all the time. I'll disassemble and assemble it for you blindfolded."

"They also invented the M79 grenade launcher, a funny single fire gun that breaks open like a shotgun. You load in a fat 40mm cartridge and it'll lob an anti-personnel grenade one hundred and fifty to two hundred meters."

"We all burned several belts of linked 7.62mm ammo in the M60 machine gun. Here, we call it the *pig*, it's so voracious it guzzles ammo. During training everybody fired it: cooks, mechanics, drivers, and admin and logistic types. For conditioning, a daily run through the lazy Georgia countryside. No exceptions, everybody out for the run."

"To see if everyone understood, Kinnard conducted a training exercise: Operation *Sky Soldier*, in North and South Carolina—seventy days of living like animals in the field. We got our fill of it there. Just like it was at first here: nothing. No tents or barracks, no showers, no beds. The steel pot was used for washing. We ate C-Rations morning and evening. He threw the 101st Airborne at us as Aggressors. Well, for all that, we pretty much won. Only a storm just about got us. The choppers were grounded by a hurricane."

"Then we left for a jungle training phase, a ranger training exercise at Fort Gordon, and finally for live fire exercises in south Georgia under real demanding conditions. At the risk of repeating myself, we were ready for action. But there were so many rumors about our final destination that we weren't even sure if we were being trained for Vietnam."

"Three July 1965 was an exciting day. In our impeccable jungle fatigues we were assembled on *Infantry Field* at Fort Benning. A huge review, great weather. The staff and colors of the 11th Air Assault Division were front and center, in full view."

"Ten Hut!"

"Several thousands of men snap to attention and present arms. The Color Sergeant lowers the staff with the colors of the 11th Air Assault Division. A noncommissioned officer of the Color Guard folds the material and attaches a new flag. The band strikes off with *Garry Owen* and the rousing martial music salutes the new Division colors as the Color Sergeant raises the staff.[4] The first airmobile division is born. It was pretty emotional. We were proud."

"General Kinnard moved to the mike and announced: 'You are now sky soldiers, thanks to those among you who, with me have not spared your efforts in the 11th Air Assault Division. From now on, the soldier is freed forever from the tyranny of the terrain!'"

"While he was speaking, we all looked at the new Division Colors: the yellow shield, crossed with a diagonal black bar with a horse's head on the right. That was really something. It had been twenty-two years since those colors had floated in an American breeze."

"Starting the next day we had a real sewing contest. We had to sew all the new patches on our uniforms. To be ready in time, Kinnard had ordered the patches from Japan. Funny, huh?"

"From the 3^d Battalion of the 17th Infantry Regiment of the 11th Air Assault Division, I find myself in the 1st Squadron of the 9th Cavalry Regiment of the First Air Cavalry Division. It's a recon unit, the eyes of the Division, its mission: provoke the enemy into exposing himself. We stir up shit."

"The officers really busted their tails to build esprit de corps in each unit. Bullwhip Six frankly spoiled us. To build perfect solidarity in the front-line units, he dumped all the troublemakers, pussies, and fuckups into base camp type outfits. At least twelve guys got the boot. Stockton didn't screw around. It wasn't all that noticeable because we were at least twenty percent short of our full Division TO&E.[5] A lot of draftees had served their time, even though they had gone through all the training with the 11th Air Assault Division. They did everything they could there to get them to extend or re-up. There were two choices: extend for ninety or one hundred and eighty days. There weren't too many volunteers. There were those with no more than thirty days to go. Those, they let go. Those who had less than sixty days were given admin jobs. All the rest were scheduled for the trip to 'Nam.'"

"The 16th of June, I heard in the news, like everybody else, that Robert McNamara, the Secretary of Defense, authorized the creation of an airmobile division for the Army. We were less surprised than the journalists and happy to learn that we hadn't worked our asses off for nothing for all those many months."

"McNamara added in his sober style that the Division must be ready for combat in the next eight weeks. Then, on 28 July, President Johnson declared in an address to the nation: 'I have today ordered the Airmobile Division to leave for Vietnam.' This announcement electrifies the press. The journalists head directly for Division Headquarters at Harmony Church."

"Kinnard gave them a very straightforward and unembellished statement: 'I have no doubt about the ability of our Division to successfully accomplish whatever missions might be given to us in Vietnam. I believe the Army and the nation will be proud of us.'"

"From then on, everything was clear, any misconceptions dispelled. To hurry the replacements along to their units, eight hundred and fifty troops a day are gathered in a big tent at Harmony Church. The organization of it all was intimidating. Completely centralized at the command level, the operation was totally decentralized in its execution."

"Did you continue your training during this time?"

"For sure, more than ever, in as much as we now knew what we were getting ready for and where we were going. The people under the most pressure were the chopper crews. They were training at Fort Rucker, Alabama. They had to train pilots and door gunners at the same time."

"The last few days are clearly less amusing. We were always behind. We worked fourteen to sixteen hours a day packing gear, filling out admin poopsheets, updating insurance coverage, drafting wills, and composing the last letters to friends, sweethearts, and family. Finally, we moved out in mid August."

"The 1st Brigade leaves first on the 15th. The movement of the Division mobilizes a veritable armada: six troop transports, four aircraft carriers, and eleven cargo vessels. Me, I was among the last to leave with the second wave of the 3d Brigade."

"We leave on a Sunday morning. It's hot and humid, a good beginning. We clamber into buses with our gear. We are nine hours on the road to Charleston, South Carolina. Many of our buddies had gone by train. They had gone to Jacksonville, Florida. There's lots of confusion and even the threat of a dock workers' strike."

"When we get to the port, we embark on the *USS Darby*, a troop transport left over from the Second World War. It had been redeployed from transporting officers and their families to Europe. It was perfect for officers, but no provisions had been made for transporting troops. We were packed into the passageways. They bunked six to ten of us in spaces intended for four. We passed the day loading stuff on this boat and settling in as well as possible."

"The ship slowly left the quay. The atmosphere was great. There was cheering and singing. The ship pulled out to sea. The lights from the shore grew dim. The laughing stopped. We were on the way to Vietnam."

"The crossing was supposed to take a month. We organized ourselves fast, finding people with similar interests. The trick was to find doers, people with a good sense of humor and, above all, lucky. We went through the Panama Canal and had a stopover at Long Beach, California to take on fuel. I was lucky, because those who left on the aircraft carrier *USS Boxer* went by the long route, through the Suez Canal!"

"Why that detour?"

"Naval Headquarters refused to refit it so it could go through the Panama Canal. The first few days on the *Darby* were horrible. With all the troops seasick, you can imagine the smell that was everywhere. Also, you almost had to fight to get into a latrine. There weren't enough for all the troops."

"I found a job as a butcher's helper. I worked from six in the morning to four in the afternoon. Other people had tasks to do or studied Vietnamese. Most of them played cards, usually poker. The Colonel got a bright idea, stop the card playing. Three days later, revolt. Everybody got out their cards. How are you going to keep thousands of guys crammed onto a boat occupied?"

"We started a market in live ammo. There were grunts that wanted to off-load with all the ammo they could carry. We had been issued just two magazines of M16 ammo. It's crazy, but the price of M16 ammo reached ten bucks for twenty rounds! Nobody wanted to debark in Vietnam just to get killed. The Colonel knew about it but didn't say anything."

"On the other ships, the crossing went better. My buddies have better memories. On the aircraft carriers they were able to continue their training: tactics, counterguerrilla warfare, survival, map reading, and first aid. On the *Buckner*, thanks to a Navy Chief, the 2d Brigade was able to conduct live-fire marksmanship training. The Chief jerry-rigged a target that was towed behind the ship—a floating firing range, funny huh?"

"On the *Croatan*, which was supposed to be the first to leave about the 11th of August with the 229th Assault Helicopter Battalion, the pilots memorized their checklists and flight procedures by heart. You're making me tell you my life story. I have one Hell of a thirst! D'you want a coke or a cold one. I've got some '33.'"

"A '33,' thanks. Better yet, a 'Larue'? Larue, the beer that kills!"

"How's that?"

"It's a saying that makes me laugh each time I drink a local beer. The brewery that makes "33" brews a low-end beer destined for the locals. Because there are some pretty dangerous types in that group, the Vietnamese call it '*La bière Larue, la bière qui tue.*' Just an anecdote to make you thirsty."

"Thanks! While some guys, the serious students, studied hard on the courses they were taking, the rest of us were killing time. Our only diversion was the Hawaiian coast. We spotted a small sailboat, it drew closer, we signaled it. We almost hit it: no sign of life. A real mystery. We continued on our way, but that was the topic of conversation for at least three days. We didn't run into a single living soul on the whole voyage. Lonesome."

"Thirteen September 1965, about midnight, we came into the

port of Qui Nhon. No one was sleeping; everybody was at the rails. You couldn't see anything in the dark; we tried to pick out shapes. Dawn came and then—we were dumbstruck! On the water, beside us, four aircraft carriers and a whole fleet of ships: supply ships, destroyers, and barges. On the shore, a small village surrounded by palm trees, a white beach, all seen in the rose-colored light of the rising sun. A real post card scene. Where's Hell?"

"Kinnard took advantage of the occasion anyway. He managed to reassemble the whole Division before Qui Nhon, shipboard, for the forty-fourth anniversary of the First Cav. With his sense of how to say the right thing, with loudspeakers on each ship, he gave us a welcome speech. But we didn't need any stimulation, we were so happy to arrive. He couldn't let the occasion pass. He concluded: 'The eyes of the world are fixed on our Division. We are the incarnation of a new tactical doctrine. Whatever happens, we'll handle it. *We are the First Team.* We're number one.'"

"At 1100 hours the back and forth relay of boats is in full swing. Naval landing craft, LMCs and LCVs, come and tie up against the sides of the ships to take the troops to shore. There was a real welcoming committee: Westmoreland, MACV Commander, with Henry Cabot Lodge, the US Ambassador to Vietnam."

"Someone told me that Lodge was a veteran of the Cav, that he'd been a cavalryman around 1925. It was kind of funny, as 'sky soldiers,' to arrive by boat. For us, that was the longest day. An incredible goat-screw: choppers everywhere, truck convoys, armored vehicles, monster traffic jams. I rode all the way to An Khe in the back of a deuce and a half, not by Chinook, like everybody else. I got here, pooped, sweaty, covered with dust, and thirsty as Hell. We off-loaded the trucks and there was—nothing. We had to start from scratch. General Wright's team was mostly working at the helipad to receive the swarm of choppers. We were on our own."

"You're not called 'grunts' for nothing, Mitch."

"But me, I'm making out good, three more days! I'm going back to the world, but I won't forget those who stay in country. I'll never forget. Anyhow, give me your 'hot' Saigon addresses, just in case I decide to extend and do a second tour. Then they'd be useful. Take care of yourself!"

Castan jots down some addresses on a card and finishes off his beer. He folds his wallet back up, warmly shakes Mitch's hand, and salutes the group of friends now gathered about them.

"If you want, check out the pilots, some of them are off duty now. Go to the 229th AHB, the *Preachers* or the *Snakes*. There's some hard core types there."

"Thanks. Have a safe trip home!"

84

Translator's Notes

[1] Actually, the rations provided the American soldier were superb, providing the basic nutrition needed for good health under demanding conditions and for sustained physical exertion. Three C-Ration meals per day, however, were insufficient for infantry soldiers on operation. In the field, I ordered and served four rations per day per man, and still, after a few months, we were all thin as rails.

[2] The 5.56mm (nominally .223 caliber) round (the M193 ball cartridge) has a muzzle velocity of approximately 3,250 feet per second (991 meters per second). The 7.62mm (.30 caliber) round (the M80 ball cartridge) has a muzzle velocity of approximately 2,600 feet per second (792 meters per second). The weight of the former is 55 grains, of the latter 147 grains. The tracer cartridges in each caliber weigh slightly less. Kinetic energy (KE) equals the mass (M) times the velocity (V) squared. For the mathematically inclined, KE is in ergs, M is in grams, and V is in cm/sec. Lethality depends principally upon the amount of KE expended in tissue damage upon striking a target. The 5.56mm bullet tends to tumble after striking flesh or liquid and so dissipate KE. The 7.62mm bullet tends to punch through, retaining (wasting) more of its KE. The greater velocity of the 5.56mm cartridge at combat ranges (historically an effective maximum of roughly 300 meters but much, much less in Vietnam) means a flatter trajectory that both enhances accuracy and reduces dead space under grazing fire.

[3] Filling the magazine to capacity increased the probability of a malfunction. Soldiers generally loaded their magazines with eighteen or nineteen rounds.

[4] *Garry Owen* is to a cavalryman what the *Marine Hymn* is to a marine. It lights the spirit with the vision of an unbroken chain of men, linking past and present, who laughed in the face of very poor odds, and often sacrificed themselves for a greater cause. The rousing, haunting notes of *Garry Owen* electrify the spirit.

[5] Table of Organization and Equipment.

85

CHAPTER VII

A jeep, with a Lieutenant at the wheel, whips around Sam Castan. The driver slams on the brakes. Sam disappears in a cloud of red laterite dust. "Excuse me sir, for the dust. General Wright sent me after you to give you a press packet about Major General Kinnard. What's more, he's set you up with an appointment with the General."

"Oh! Right?" Castan answers, surprised.

"He's agreed in principal. He's still got to find a good time. Can I drop you off somewhere?"

"If you could give me a lift to the 229th pilots...?"

"Hop in back!" The driver hits the gas and the jeep leaps off, trailing a red cloud.

"Do you always drive like this?"

"Yup! The VC snipers really like to shoot at vehicles. They always figure there's important people in them. They don't pay as much attention to men on foot. To wrap up what I was telling you this morning, let's make a quick tour. The camp still doesn't have a well-defined perimeter, which makes defending it a little bit harder. You don't have to worry if you hear shooting at night. A few days ago, a returning patrol lit itself up on the way in. Five of them were killed. You're at the mercy of a nervous grunt on guard duty. You can't get mad at 'em. Half the time they're shooting at a VC. Three days ago, we were roused by a lot of shooting, over a hundred shots. The same sort of thing—Maggie, the mascot mule of the 1st of the 9th, got blown away. She couldn't give the password to the guard, an engineer type. The next day, it was the turn of a water buffalo!"

"You still manage to get some sleep?"

"You get used to anything—even to snipers."

The jeep heads north. "They're huge, those helicopters."

"Yeah, they're like enormous prehistoric skeletons. The CH-54 Skycranes can lift ten tons. Look at those big containers next to them. They're mobile surgical suites, completely equipped in mobile home-type units ready for transport. The CH-54 can also sling-load a 155mm artillery piece with its ammunition."

The jeep pulls up in front of a tent. "So, I'm going to drop you off here. This is Preacher's operations tent, 229th Assault Helicopter Battalion. I'll link you up with Captain Owens, the 'ops' officer."

Operations are set up in a "General Purpose" or GP tent. It is roughly seven by fourteen meters. Part of the space is set up as a briefing room with map and butcher boards set up on easels. Several officers share the rear of the tent as their living area. Sam waits for the Lieutenant who comes back with Captain Owens.

"Captain Owens can give you a few minutes then take you to the crew tent."

"Come on in! Our CP's still a little primitive but that doesn't affect how we get the job done. Where do you want to start?"

"How about with your Coat of Arms," Castan suggests, "pointing to the unit guidon hanging over the maps.

"The Coat of Arms, yeah! Why not? The motto is simple: 'Winged Assault.' A lightening bolt, showing how fast we strike, dominates the shield. As you look at it, it goes from the upper left to the lower right which shows that what we do is for the guys on the ground. The background of the lower left is blue with a silver sword, which means combat. In the upper right there's a wing, because we fly. It's on a background of red. So much for heraldry."

"The father of this outfit is Lieutenant Colonel Robert Keller. He's been the Battalion Commander since July. In few words, the 229th was activated in March 1964 as a part of the 11th Air Assault Division, Test. On 3 July 1965 it was integrated into the 1st Air Cavalry Division. We left for Vietnam on 13 September."

"We didn't waste any time. On 18 September we put thirteen Huey UH-1Ds and two UH-1Bs into action. They left to support the 101st Airborne Division and the 1st Brigade in an operation northwest of Qui Nhon. We had to do that right away. The flight crews and support people on the ground didn't have their unit assignments or billets yet."

"Our baptism of fire happened on 18 and 19 September. We were lucky, in spite of the lack of preparation and training. We didn't lose a single helicopter. Afterwards, we developed a rhythm of operations: support operations around the clock with limited visibility and lousy weather. Starting in October, the 229th participated in brigade-level operations, mostly for the 3d Brigade during operation *Shiny Bayonet*. We flew 2,405 sorties to transport 3,655 infantrymen and eighty-one tons of supplies."

"For the Pleiku campaign that ran from 23 October to 26 November, we transported the equivalent of one hundred and twenty-eight infantry companies, that is, a total of 10,840 sorties. Fourteen of our aircraft were hit by enemy fire, two were shot down, but none was lost. During the toughest of the fighting in November, our choppers provided the basic medical evacuation while accepting the highest risks. But go ahead on over to the next tent where Bravo Company's crews live — 'Preacher,' for those in the know."

"And the 'Snakes'?"

"Ah! You already know the Companies by their surnames? Congratulations. Charlie Company is further away."

"Okay, thanks for tying things together for me. I'm going to try and find what's happening at company level." Castan enters another GP tent. The era of hammocks is over; the men now have cots. Lined up in rows of ten, the cots are only a few tens of centimeters apart.

He spots a pilot in flight uniform, seated on his cot, carefully cleaning his revolver. "Smith and Wesson?"

The pilot looks up while continuing to push a cleaning rod into the muzzle of his gun. "Thirty-eight special, two inch barrel."

"Your personal weapon?"

"Affirmative. I prefer it to the issue .45. It's less heavy and there's no risk of it jamming. I also have a Derringer, very thin, hidden in the holster, a .22 magnum. Here, it's better to be prepared, able to resist until help arrives if you get shot down, or able to blow your brains out if nobody comes to look for you."

"I'm a journalist accredited to *Look Magazine*. Having seen the war machine at work at Ia Drang, and having had the official briefings, I wanted to get to know the individuals who make the machine go. For two days now I've been wandering around Anh Khe trying to understand how you live your daily lives and how you were prepared for this fight. To get right to the point, what were you doing before you started to clean up your six-shooter?"

"My six-shooter, as you call it, is a tool of the trade, a matter of life and death! It deserves more respect than your pen."

"Okay, you're right."

"Good! Before you walked in, I was writing a letter to my wife. That's what I was doing. I haven't closed the envelope yet."

"Is it too indiscreet to know what you were telling her?"

"Last night, I was a little down. It was pouring rain. The downpour was pounding like a drum on the tent. I was in lying on my cot and I started a stupid enough letter to my wife and kid. In the background you could hear the out-going artillery. Well, I told my wife that I had run into a buddy in the States who had come back from Vietnam and who had told me that Vietnam was really great. He told me about his villa overlooking the South China Sea, of his houseboys who did all the work, of the cook who fixed his food, of the nights at the casino, and the trips to the PX, a real tax-free supermarket. I really thought that my buddy had tried to BS me, or that he was just full of crap, or being an asshole. This morning, with its beautiful weather, I was less pissed off. So, I added as an afterthought that in fact I *had* been thinking wishfully. When I don't fly, I play in the sand. I fill sandbags, and that it's child's play. So, that was my message for the day."

"A little bitter, a little hacked off. Since you're here, I expect it's not just by chance?"

"Just so. I wanted to be a helicopter pilot. As a little kid, it was already my dream. I got my pilot's license when I was seventeen, but my objective was to become a helicopter pilot. That kind of license cost a lot, so I joined the army last year to get it. As an NCO, I went to Fort Rucker, Alabama for training."

"That's all?"

"Before teaching us to fly, the army wanted to be sure that we would be able to command. The selection was hard from the first part of preflight training. The tests, however, were pretty much my kind of thing. This phase lasted two months! Everything changed when I saw my flight suit, helmet, gloves, glasses, and flight manuals."

"From the hands of the sergeants, we were passed to those of the IPs, the instructor pilots. I was turned loose on a Hiller H-23, a two-place training helicopter with an internal combustion engine. It was a capricious beast. I graduated last May."

"More than sixty percent of my graduating class was sent directly to Vietnam. That time I was lucky. I was among the minority that stayed there. I was assigned to the 3d Transportation Company in Virginia to fly a two-rotor banana, a Piasecki."

"I settle in. After a month, I get orders for Fort Benning. All I knew was that it was the Infantry Center. The rumor was that a new division was being formed. I get to Benning and am assigned to the 11th Air Assault Division, Test. In June hundreds of pilots like me arrive. We are going to familiarize ourselves with new flying techniques: air assault, close formation flying, low altitude flying—the whole bit. We alternate flying hours with hours of flight simulation. We're cadred, monitored, by old troops—Vietnam vets with mustaches. They teach us nap-of-the-earth flying, and have us practice autorotations that sometimes were scary."

"These IPs are real cowboys.[1] They don't resist any opportunity to make our hair stand on end. The one with my group of student pilots is Bill. He invents a 'confidence course' for us to test our young pilots' nerves. 'You've got to reduce to a minimum your exposure to enemy fire. The best solution: nap-of-the-earth flying.' It was his refrain."

"One day he put three of us in a chopper, an H-19. Bill takes off and puts the helicopter in normal flight. He picks out some train tracks on the ground and follows them. He accelerates. I note the air speed indicator at one hundred knots. He comes down to ground level and races along just over the gravel rail bed in a place where the tracks are bordered by poplar trees. In the cockpit, you've got a sensation of lightening-like speed as the crossties pass by on the ground and the trees blaze by on each side. The poplars seem to move out of the way at the last possible moment. Anxiety takes over. The chopper is rushing through a green canal. We too, we were all green inside."

"To spice up the exercise, Bill eased the helicopter against the foliage. The leaves and branches brushed the fuselage and the rotor blades clipped the tops of the trees. In the chopper, we're petrified. As if nothing out of the ordinary were happening, Bill continues to raise the collective and balance the cyclic, pushing the airspeed up to one hundred and twenty knots. The helicopter seems to be slipping through a green fog. I had closed my eyes."

"Back on the ground our pretentiousness as pilots was reduced. The method is brutal but efficient. Day after day, he jangles our nerves. We had to master new flight procedures that contradicted existing regulations. For example, in the Air Force, helicopters are not permitted to fly in formation. It's considered too dangerous. In the First Cav, it's basic. Our job, it's to put ten helicopters on an LZ at the same time. Our mission is simple: take off, fly, land together, and as close together as possible."

"In the beginning, the regulation distance between choppers for formation flying was three rotor blade diameters. For Bill, his standard was just barely one rotor blade diameter. That's awfully close!"

"When I heard over television on 28 July that President Johnson was sending us to Vietnam, I believed I was ready. When I get here, after a month on an aircraft carrier, I feel like I don't know how to fly anymore. When I was assigned to fly Hueys, I lit up."

"Several days earlier I walked around the Iroquois. I opened the door of number 879, mine, and slipped into the left-hand seat. My hands fell into place on the collective and the cyclic, and I recited my checklists. That had to become just as instinctive as lighting my 'Zippo.'"

"One morning we finally come in sight of land, in Lang Mai Bay, to the south of Qui Nhon. We have a neighbor, the *Iwo Jima*, a Marine helicopter carrier. We cast anchor at 1100 hours, 13 September. We were thirty-one days in the crossing since we left Florida."

"Our helicopters were already reassembled and, from the flight deck, we watched the big Marine H-34 helicopters a bit mockingly but with some anxiety."

"The H-34s seemed to you outmoded compared to the Hueys?"

"Yes, in the first place, but above all the Marines had not integrated their helicopters into their combat units. Every evening, the USMC choppers returned tranquilly to their base for the night. From there, we saw them leave again to provide logistical support for the fight at Chu Lai."

"For our arrival, headquarters had kicked off a regimental-sized operation—the first since the Korean War. There were about five thousand men on the American side, plus the Navy, and some Vietnamese Army units. The results were announced as seven hundred Vietcong killed at a cost of fifty Marines. For the Vietnamese side, they didn't give us any numbers. We were there as spectators to the round of fighting marked by a background of explosions and columns of black smoke—they used lots of napalm."

"*Time* spoke of Vietcong losses on the order of two thousand killed," Castan notes. "The coordination between the Marines and ARVN as well as the artillery and the Navy seemed to work well."

"Yeah, but we weren't sure that all the dead were Vietcong. Among ourselves, we really questioned that! The Captain insisted that 'If you want to win the war for the Vietnamese, you've got to prepare yourself to see the war as it is—clear, simple, and dirty. We'll either do it or we won't. The Cav's there now and so are we!' Since the debate was turning on issues of common sense, we let it go at that, as well as because a briefing was about to begin in the ops center. The major was waiting for us in front of a map. He swept over a huge area with the back of his hand. 'Gentlemen, we're going there, right into the middle of things!'"

"This whole zone is supposed to be VC territory. Our base camp is right next to the village of An Khe, here, about half way between Pleiku and Qui Nhon, on Route 19. The road was just reopened in July by the South Vietnamese Army. The Cav is going to be the first unit based in the middle of a VC zone. The idea: clean it up, good and quick. We'll get there following the road, but flying up high! The little villages that you see all along the route are under VC control. There are snipers in them that amuse themselves taking pot shots at targets of opportunity."

"About sixty-five clicks from the coast there's a hill, the beginning of the Central Plateau region. The base is fifteen klicks from there. You've got some altitude there; ideal it seams as far as climate is concerned. The nights are cool. The heliport there is one by one point two kilometers. In a few days, there'll be almost twenty thousand men in the base camp. I can't tell you any more about it. I'll find out what it's like the same time as you."

"The call sign of Bravo Company is 'Preacher,' and that of Charlie Company 'Snake,'" continues the Major. "Write down the

FM frequencies, UHF and VHF. Watch out, they're changed frequently. These are the ones in use for your next flight. Good, you have your mission, your maps, your frequencies. Everything's clear. We don't have H-Hour yet, but companies will lift off at twenty-minute intervals. The aircraft carrier will be empty in two days."

"One more thing. The Navy folks are complaining that a lot of stuff has disappeared. I cannot imagine that anyone from this company would be capable of stealing any material that didn't belong to him. I don't want to know what you've got loaded on your aircraft. Got it?"

"We exchanged knowing winks. We had in fact scavenged as much stuff as we could to better confront the unknown at our new base camp at An Khe. So, that was the final briefing we received aboard the *Croaton*. The next morning at 1100 hours we were ready to lift off. The 'let's go' shouted by the lead pilot ended the thirty-two hours of waiting."

"You went directly to An Khe?"

"No. After takeoff we went to Qui Nhon to top off; two hundred gallons. We didn't get to arrive over the Vietnamese beach with its fine sand. We landed at the base of Qui Nhon in a place surrounded by barbed wire—a mountain of concertina. Moreover, the place stank. Apparently it served as a latrine for part of the city. The barbed wire was caught up with with toilet paper blown into it by the wind. We didn't waste any time there. We took off again, climbed to three thousand feet, and headed for An Khe. From up there you could see little villages, jungle like parsley, and clearings on the hills filled with groves of bananas. The road wended its tortuous way through them from one hill to the next."

"All at once the countryside changes. We come up on a large basin covered with grass and stunted trees with, to the north, in relief, Hon Cong Mountain. I tune to the radio frequency and the pilot depresses the push to talk button on the cyclic."

"Base, this is Preacher 879."

"Roger, Preacher 879."

"This is Preacher 879. Where do we put down?"

"Preacher 879 this is Base. Switch to Golf Course flight control push. They'll take you down. You're on the southern part of the field, row three. We'll send somebody over to pick you up, Okay?"

"This is Preacher 879, Roger, over."

"This is Base, out."

"We reduced speed. Due north we saw the mountain with, on the side, Camp Radcliff and the Golf Course. We called flight control."

"Golf Course, this is Preacher 879. We're in-bound from eight klicks to your east requesting landing instructions."

"Preacher 879, this Is Golf Course. You're cleared for a direct approach to row three on the south side. A pathfinder on the ground will guide you down, over."

"'This is Preacher 879, roger.' We flew over the Song Ba River that crossed the eastern part of the perimeter. We passed the village of An Khe. There, near the river, between the village and the camp, was the old landing strip. 'This is Preacher 879. We're on short final, over.'"

"Roger 879, you're cleared to land."

"Below, you could see six rows of helicopters separated by vehicle access paths. There was a mix of olive green tents, POL trucks, jeeps, various other vehicles, and soldiers—impressive. We had arrived, at least almost ... ! In the intercom the pilot commands, 'to you.' Instinctively I respond, 'I've got it.' I have the controls."

"I over-fly the northern part of the perimeter where our infantry is assembled. Close to the ground, the terrain looks less friendly, less clear than from fifteen hundred feet. At two hundred feet I slow the Huey and work to stabilize it. I have my eyes glued to the instruments and at the same time aim for row three to the south. Finally I spot a guy on the ground waving his arms."

"'You see 'im?' The pilot asks in a neutral voice."

"'Roge, got him,' I answer, sounding a bit strained. Sweat's starting to run down my back."

"I bring the chopper to a hover above the other helicopters, watching my ground guide and the narrow space I'm supposed to put down in. I'm worried about my tail rotor hitting something. The soldier on the ground points out my spot between two other helicopters. I can't quite control the rotor balance and almost whack into a tree trunk. I jerk the nose up and try again. My movements are too sharp, and I have to overcompensate for each one."

"'Relax, no sweat,' the pilot, who doesn't touch the controls, tells me, while watching my discomfort as I try to regain control."

"I pull back the stick to make an end of it, pitching the nose up again. One skid hits the ground hard, then the other, and the chopper comes to rest."

"'You've got to work a bit on getting down the last few feet,' the Senior Pilot concludes. In front of us, the ground guide crosses his arms in an 'X.' It's finally over. That's how I landed the first time in Vietnam, at An Khe—hard."

"Me, I arrived by fixed wing. I didn't have as good a view of the area coming in. Your story fills in the description that I received this morning at the CP."

"Robert, there's a driver from headquarters looking for a journalist," comes a voice from the entrance to the tent."

"Okay, he's with me. He's coming!"

"If you want to give me your mail, I'll be happy to get it sent for you."

"Thanks. For the moment, the mail system's working well, but let me know when you leave."

The journalist goes back outside to the trail where waits the jeep, motor idling. "You're Sam Castan?"

"Yup."

"Major General Kinnard asked me to pick you up."

"Perfect. I'm with you."

As soon as he climbed aboard, Sam scanned through the dossier on General Kinnard that the Lieutenant had given him. The journalist tried to read the biographical profile as the jeep bounced and rocked its way through ditches and over potholes.

> Henry William Osborn Kinnard, born in Dallas, Texas, in May 1915. Age: fifty. Graduated from West Point in 1939 and commissioned as a Second Lieutenant of Infantry. After a tour in the Pacific, he was assigned to Fort Benning, graduating from Airborne School in 1942. He was then assigned to the 501st Airborne Infantry Regiment. On 6 June 1944 he parachuted behind the Normandy beaches, in France. In September, he jumped into Belgium, and received his Colonel's eagles. He is only twenty-nine. He fights at Bastogne during the Ardennes Forest Battle. After the War, he stays with airborne forces where he occupies a series of staff positions. Next, he commands the First Airborne Group of the 501st Infantry Regiment. On 21 July 1962 he is named Assistant Division Commander of the 101st Airborne Division at Fort Campbell.

"We're there, sir!"

Sam Castan again mounts the steps of the CP. He spots a Captain there to meet him. "Sorry sir, but the General had to leave in a hurry. The 3ᵈ Brigade has gone back out on an operation. He went to see Colonel Moore to coordinate *operation Clean House.*

Translator's Notes
[1] Instructor pilots.

CHAPTER VIII

"Sorry to have skipped out on you the other day, Sam, but *Operation Clean House,* being a combined operation with the South Vietnamese and the South Koreans, I went to see Hal Moore who just took command of the 3ᵈ Brigade."

"But he commanded the 1ˢᵗ of the 7ᵗʰ Cavalry at *X-Ray,*" Castan notes, surprised."

"Yes. He was just promoted and has replaced Tim Brown at the head of the Brigade. He hasn't even had time to catch his breath, nor have his troops. *Clean House* kicked off with great haste, a clean-up operation of four days, drums beating. The score sheet is not in yet, but there should be about one hundred and fifty enemy KIA. According to the G2, Division also recovered a lot of information that is now being evaluated."

"Where did the 3ᵈ Brigade get into the act, if it's not confidential?"

"No! The action is over. They were deployed in a valley to the northeast of Binh Khe. Come over here, if you want to see it on the map. It's in Binh Dinh Province."

"Good troops, the Koreans?"

"The very best! The Korean division deserves its name: the Tigers, of the Korean Capital Division. We also call them ROKs, for the Republic of Korea. Moreover, they quickly carved out a reputation for themselves, and the VC and NVA seem to be afraid of them. Asians have no conscience dealing with each other. They speak the same language: cruelty."

"How so? They employ particular methods?"

"First, they let it be known that they don't take prisoners. Next, they're real professionals at close combat and anti-guerrilla fighting. When they're not fighting Charlies, they practice by fighting among themselves to keep in shape. When you visit their base, they're all in shorts and T-shirts. They spend their time practicing at *Tae Kwon Do.* Their arms work like small windmills, they look like jugglers. Their specialty is killing silently. They whip out their butterfly knives with lightening speed, locking the blade faster than a switchblade."

"They're based up in this area?"

"We agreed that they would have an important mission, one for which they're well suited: provide security for Route 19 and keep it open from Qui Nhon west. I think if they set up some ROK platoons along the road, particularly on Mang Yang Mountain and

Mang Yang Pass, they can reduce infiltration by the Sao Vang or Yellow Star Division. The Koreans are the kinds of troops to set up very effective ambushes in their area of operations, their AO."

"But you didn't agree to see me to talk about the Koreans."

"General Wright told me you are interested in some of the special tactics we use. Is that right?"

"Yes sir, for sure. It's easy to see that the First Cav is different from other units, and also from other services, such as the Marines. What's more, you are known to be one of the architects of the new tactical doctrine. I wanted to learn more about airmobility and air assault. I would like you to recount to me how you succeeded in putting the Division together."

"As you may imagine, it's a subject that's important to me, so you assume some risk in asking me to expand on it. Okay, let's begin with a snapshot. I like the way I put it on 3 July at Fort Benning in Doughboy Stadium, at the ceremony where the 11th Air Assault Division became the First Air Cav Division. What I said was, 'The soldier is from this day forth freed from the tyranny of the terrain.' Don't think that quote's a scoop. Your colleague from Newsweek's already used it."

"Here's the main idea. The age-old dream of general staffs has been to find a way to employ all the energy of fighting men in combat. Since the dawn of history, the soldier has always been a beast of burden carrying weapons, ammunition, and all his other gear, like a nomad.[1] Use of the horse marked the first major advance and to that we owe all of our traditions. The internal combustion engine marked a revolution, but we were still tied to the ground. More recently, the airplane and the helicopter have changed things, have marked a new advance. But an airborne division or one flown to distant fields by air transport is still dependent. To move, they have to get their transport from somewhere. Airmobility is the capability of a unit to move itself by air with its own resources. It thus is the master of any tactical situation. I'm going to quickly spell them out for you."

Kinnard, as he begins his exposition, punctuates the discussion by introducing each item on the fingers of his left hand. He starts by attacking his upraised thumb. "The ultimate objective of airmobility is, first, to conduct high-intensity sustained operations while retaining complete flexibility to respond to rapidly changing tactical situations. Second, to withdraw from one engagement and rapidly move in another direction to engage in another fight, whatever the distance between the two areas of contact. Third, to operate on the enemy's turf with nothing but 'vertical flanks' for entry and withdrawal. Fourth point, to rapidly seize whatever initiative the enemy may offer, and to exploit any advantage gained by friendly forces. Next point, to cross over all types of terrain features and obstacles, and any devastated or contaminated zones, without slowing or halting the progression of ground forces. Finally, to have our own logistical support thanks to our own divisional support structure and organic aviation assets. There you have it, the six specific characteristics of airmobility. Do you see it more clearly now?"

"Yes and no, because there are other units besides the First Cav that are largely autonomous, and have very considerable organic logistical support capabilities."

"You're quite right there. One can say that the Marines are for example, overall, airmobile, but they are a separate, completely integrated force. The 173^d Airborne Brigade and the 101st Airborne Division are also airmobile. The classic definition of airmobility may be summarized as the capability of a military unit to make tactical moves by helicopter."

"You mean to say that the First Cavalry Division is really more than just airmobile?"

"Exactly, it's *Air Assault*. That means it integrates helicopters into all phases of combat: command, fire support, reconnaissance, infantry transport, artillery transport, logistical support, and medical evacuation. The helicopter is the prime mover for them all. It becomes the vehicle for everything, or just about."

"The difficulty, then, was to adapt the helicopter to this diversity of roles?"

"Yes! To get there, it took us almost ten years. Ten years to convince the brass anyway. General Staffs are very attached to the classic service divisions: land, air, sea. The air power advocates didn't see any reason at all to provide the army with an independent air capability, except for observation."

"The easiest way to answer your question is to do a quick flash back on the evolution of the tactics and materiel. Air mobility clearly goes back to the airborne operations of the Second World War. Airplanes and gliders were the principal means used to put infantrymen on the battlefield. But, once on the ground, they stayed there. An important step was taken in 1952 when our army created, during the Korean War, twelve helicopter battalions. The nature of the terrain and the hostile topography led us to quickly employ helicopters to transport troops, for medical evacuation, and for tactical reconnaissance. Already the Marines were thinking of using helicopters to insert small units with heavy firepower directly into combat."

"Larry Bell, the rotary wing designer, came to Korea himself in

1953. What's more he declared that 'Korea has advanced the development of helicopters by ten years.' The first armed helicopter saw the light of day in Korea; an OH-13 armed with a bazooka. In parallel with the experience that we had in Korea, our allies also familiarized themselves with the use of helicopters. The French, after having left Indochina, where they too had jerry-rigged an OH-13 with a machine gun, and even an H-21 with a 20mm canon, mostly employed helicopters in Algeria to move their parachute units and provide fire support. The results on the ground in counter-guerrilla operations were conclusive. In like manner, the Brits in Malaysia married up helicopters and commandos."

"After the Korean War, the military authorities encouraged consideration of how to further develop helicopters. They received a welcome reception from the engineers in the aircraft industry who were very interested in rotary wing machines. A significant part of the military budget was dedicated to research in this area. This collaboration with the aircraft industry was fruitful."

"At the conceptual level, a few officers had a determining role in the evolution of the tactical doctrine; Tolson for example. In 1955 John Tolson was named commander of the Airborne Department of the Infantry School at Fort Benning. One of his missions was to work out the role of helicopters in various phases of combat. Tolsen began by changing the name of his Department. From the 'Airborne Department' he created the 'Aviation and Airborne Department.' That meant that from then on the Army wanted to develop its own aviation arm and no longer be dependent on the Air Force to provide air transport at the operational level."

"Tolsen got the project off the ground. The task was confided to Major William C. Howel, a veteran. He had been Eisenhower's pilot. From the results of tests conducted with Sikorsky H-19 and H-34 helicopters, Howel and his team produced a manual: *Army Transport Aviation Combat Operations.* Howel's work is full of pertinent observations and enabled the army to establish the required characteristics of future army helicopters as well as their capabilities. Myself, I was largely inspired by the results of his study as I developed the 11th Air Assault Division."

"During this time, he proposed to arm transport helicopters with a turret to enable them to return fire during the final approach to a hostile LZ. With respect to this, many tests were conducted on the 'light turret' proposed by Howel. In fact, we'll find it again later on on the gunship. Nothing is lost."

"Colonel Jay Vanderpool arrived in 1956 to head up the US Army Combat Aviation School at Fort Rucker, Alabama. Vanderpool is a 'doer' and a tonic. He formed a platoon with twenty-seven officers and noncommissioned officers that he called 'The Sky Cav.' A year later it became the 'Air Combat Reconnaissance Platoon.' Vanderpool was not short of ideas. He tinkered with his aircraft: some H-25s and H-21s or H-19s. He tried all possible types of weaponry: rocket launchers, machine-guns, canons, grenade launchers, and missiles. He transformed his helicopters into veritable flying fortresses. At the same time, his team was quickly nicknamed 'Vanderpool's fools.'"

"After having his fun with various experiments, Vanderpool took on a more theoretical task. He came up with a proposal of the principals for the organization of a whole ground-air division that he called an 'Armair Division.' His Division was built around troops, squadrons, and brigades. He submitted his project to the US Army Director of Aviation, Major General Hamilton H. Howze, the key player for the acceptance of the idea."

"During the summer of 1957 Lieutenant General James Gavin, the US Army Chief of Research and Development, published an article where he described his vision for a new cavalry: 'Cavalry! I don't mean horses. I mean helicopters, light aircraft to insert soldiers armed with automatic and anti-tank weapons as well as light reconnaissance vehicles.'"

"In 1958 our aircraft needs were estimated at 6,400 machines, and we only had 5,500, most of them assigned to reconnaissance and observation missions. The US Army's aircraft inventory was no longer a minor issue. The topic needing a thorough study was just exactly what were the Army's specific aircraft needs. What it amounted to was to address the requirements 'gap' that existed between what the US Air Force provided and what the Army needed."

"The first clear requirement: conceive and develop aircraft specifically for army use. The US Army of Research and Development folks created an ad hoc commission headed by General Gordon Rogers. The Commission defined three essential tasks for the new helicopters: light observation, armed reconnaissance, and air transport."

Kinnard interrupts himself to down a cup of tea. "Would you like some? It's from Cateka!"

"Thanks, no, but since you enjoy local products, I would like a beer."

"You like *Ba Moui Ba*, you too? Thank God the breweries aren't out in the sticks. I can just about imagine a brigade setting up near a brewery like we did at the Tea Plantation. The French planter was so happy to see us leave that he sent me a stock of his best tea leaves. It's stronger than the mess hall tea."

"Do you still want to know more about the evolution of our tactical doctrine?"

"That's why I'm here, sir."

"Okay, the Famous Rogers Commission got together in December of 1959 at Fort Monroe, Virginia, with the principal contractors interested in submitting bids. Barely two months later, fifty-five companies presented 119 projects. You can see how the industrial guys got thoroughly involved. Rogers linked up ten specialists like Hamilton Howze. He had five major generals on his commission, but also Tolson, at that time Assistant Director of Aviation for the Army. He was a member of the Board, but without vote. This tribunal had the task of drafting the list of requirements to accomplish the three different missions. I'll spare you the details on the choices regarding observation and reconnaissance."

"Regarding transport, the Commission recommended an aircraft able to take off vertically or from a short runway, capable of long range flights, and that could replace the Chinook and the Caribou. It was to be in service by the beginning of the '70s. The conclusions indicated that each model of aircraft needed to be replaced every ten years, sooner if possible, depending on operational requirements and technical advances. A very ambitious program, as you can see."

"The Commission decided to begin a systematic study to evaluate the feasibility and usefulness of an air combat unit. Their recommendations were approved in March 1960. While the specialists were conducting these studies, the engineers were very productive and made real progress. Bell produced the prototype XH-40, a transport helicopter powered by a turbine. Originally conceived for medivac, the XH-40 proved an excellent base for further developments. The prototype made its first flight in October, 1956, with a seven hundred horsepower Lycoming turbine."

"In 1958 Bell received an order from the US Army for nine prototype models of the UH-1A Utility Helicopter Number 1, with a 770 horsepower engine. The next year, the order was for one hundred UH-1A helicopters with turbine engines developing 960 horsepower. The first operational aircraft were delivered in June 1961. They were destined for the 82^d and 101st Airborne Divisions, as well as the 57th Medical Detachment. The UH-1s of the 57th were the first to leave for Vietnam in March of 1962."

"Things were moving on the ground too. There was no lack of initiatives rich with lessons learned. We were on the ground in Vietnam from the beginning of the '60s. Military advisors had wide latitude of action. Anecdotally, there's the story of a pilot of an H-21 flying over a clearing in his 'banana.' He sees a group of Vietcong moving out from cover. He does a three-sixty and makes as if to land in the middle of the clearing—just like that, just to see how the Charlies would react. The Vietcong open fire on the helicopter right away. It makes a great target. The pilot holds his chopper at hover, moving away slowly, and with an amazing *sang-froid* observes how the Vietcong shoot at him. He notes that the rounds impact several meters to his front, kicking up clumps of dirt and grass. When he got back to Tan Son Nhut, he recounted his experience to his astonished buddies. As he told it: 'All the rounds hit more than twenty meters in front of me. It looks like their training cadre screwed them up when they trained them how far to lead the target!' He was, moreover, correct. We discovered training ranges with wooden helicopter mockups arranged in column. The political commissars also gave classes in ballistics."

"In the universe of pilots, this type of story greatly contributed to evolving mental attitudes. The helicopter appeared to be less vulnerable than one would have thought. Other lessons learned in Vietnam were fundamental as far as adapting the materials to the climatic conditions: the humidity, the corrosion, the dust. The knowledge of the problems caused by these conditions enabled us to harden the circuitry and also to protect the turbines and rotor blades."

"In December 1961 the aircraft carrier *USS Card* off-loaded thirty-two H-21 helicopters and four hundred men at the Saigon dock. The men were a contingent formed from the 57th Transport Company coming from Fort Lewis and the 8th and 9th Transport Companies from Fort Bragg. Twelve days after their arrival, the helicopters participated in a big operation coordinated with the South Vietnamese Army. They lifted one thousand ARVN airborne troops fifteen kilometers out of Saigon and completely surprised the enemy. They surrounded a Vietcong Headquarters and destroyed an important radio station. There's an example of a successful air movement in Vietnam."

"In June of 1962 some UH-1s equipped with Browning M2 machine guns and rocket pods arrived in Vietnam. They belonged to the Utility and Tactical Transport Helicopter Company (UTTHC). Their mission was to protect the H-21 Shawnee transport helicopters of the 57th, 33[d], and 93[d] Helicopter Companies. At that time, our attitude was very cautious regarding the protection of cargo helicopters. The armed helicopters were only authorized to return fire when fired upon, a very defensive concept. Six months later, the rules had evolved. Escort helicopters could open fire on a clearly identified enemy who threatened the security of the movement."

"To establish doctrine, we needed to be sure about things, so we asked our military statisticians to run some tests to measure the efficiency of armed aerial escort. Very creative, they invented a measure: the number of hits received per flight hour. In the reputably dangerous zones, they counted .11 hits per hour on unescorted cargo helicopters. In the same areas, when escorted by armed choppers, the hits per hour fell to .0074. We thus confirmed that the Vietcong fired more heavily and aggressively on unescorted helicopters because they feared the riposte from the gunships. These figures were confirmed by the cargo chopper pilots who felt much more secure when they had an escort on their flanks."

"This wasn't enough. We also had to determine the vulnerability of the escort helicopters. The gunships are very exposed during the final phase of an air assault into an LZ because they are then flying at low altitude, about one hundred feet, and quite vulnerable to small and mid-caliber weapons. The UTTHC drafted a report covering five month's of operations, some eighteen hundred flight hours of escort missions. During this period, their return fires accounted for 246 enemy KIA. On their side, no gunship was shot down, only one being seriously damaged. The risk seemed quite acceptable."

"Brigadier General Anthis, US Air Force, CG of the 2[d] Air Wing added his contribution in a paper titled *The Escort Helicopter.* He contended that gunships should fire for a period of one minute before the first troop-carrying helicopter touches down, and for one minute after the last lifts off, to clear the LZ of enemy. There was still a serious problem to solve. Who would have the authority to give permission to open fire? This was an issue between the Army and the Air Force, and was not easy to resolve."

A UTTHC initiative in June 1963 pushed this issue toward a solution. The Company participated in an operation with the Marines and attached itself to them. The UTTHC accepted their authority, and put itself under the operational control of the ground commander. It took its turn at providing fire support, after the artillery and the air strike, just before the infantry off-loaded. As the action developed, the different actors coordinated with each other and integrated their efforts according to logic and efficiency rather than hierarchical protocol."

"The studies conducted during this time demonstrated that six or seven gunships could efficiently protect a flight of twenty to twenty-five lift ships. An offensive doctrine began to see the light of day. In Vietnam, MACV had, during 1964, created several rapid reaction task forces called 'Eagle Flights,' highly trained autonomous heliborne platoons. The mission of an Eagle Flight is to find and engage an enemy force in order to fix it until allied reinforcements arrive to destroy it. An Eagle Flight at that time generally consisted of five gunships and seven lift helicopters, but sometimes less. This arrangement saw rapid development and reinforced the coordination between the South Vietnamese Rangers and US Army Aviation."

"By the end of 1964 all the helicopter companies employed Eagle Flights and kept one Flight on alert twenty-fours hours a day. As you see, things were moving ahead rapidly on the ground. The art of war is the art of adapting. With the North Vietnamese and Vietcong, it's a matter of keeping ahead of the curve. Vietnam offers the ideal environment in which to test an abundance of new ideas. On the other hand, decisions are slow in coming from headquarters. There was little evidence of the political interest in this matter. The intervention of Secretary of Defense McNamara was going to change the course of events. He first demanded a report on the aircraft needs of the Army and above all precise conclusions on the evolution of tactical doctrine. His request was simple: 'Put together a cost and benefit analysis for proposed specific missions.'"

"The military continued to poke along at its own pace with committee meetings. At this point McNamara abruptly intervened, because during this period American military involvement in Vietnam was accelerating. On 19 April 1962, he addressed a memorandum to the Secretary of the Army that could not be ignored:

> I am not satisfied by the Army's recommendations regarding tactical mobility. I don't believe the Army has completely explored the opportunities available today using available aeronautical technology. This technology offers a revolutionary advance compared to traditional means of ground transport. The machines now being developed for flight above but close to the ground seem to me to offer new possibilities for unleashing efficiency."

"He took the side of the helicopter right away. His memorandum continued with financial considerations. 'I am convinced that air transport is less expensive than travel by rail or ship, even in times of peace.' In conclusion, he asked for a complete reexamination of the question. He personally designated the composition of the committee that he wanted to see study the question. He cited by name Major General Hamilton Howze, Brigadier General Delk

Oden, Brigadier General Walter Richardson, Colonel Robert William, Colonel John Norton, Colonel A. J. Rankin, as well as civilians such as Frank Parker, Edwin Paxon, and Edward Heinemann."

"His memorandum had the effect of an electrical shock. Political authority interfered directly in the military field of competence. The impact was immediate. Less than one week later Major General Hamilton Howze was named president of a commission charged with studying the tactical mobility needs of the Army."

"The fact that McNamara was personally involved in this matter meant that it short-circuited several levels of military hierarchy that would, certainly, have complicated and held up the process. This time the planning was compressed. Howze had to submit his findings by mid-August. His Commission was composed of thirteen officers and five civilians. He focused their concentration on the concept of airmobility by studying all its aspects. Howze and his assistants did a study in depth. They had no desire to have their report kicked back by McNamara."

"They tackled the entirety of the problems of organization, of operations, of research, of testing. They increased the numbers of experiments by several orders of magnitude. Three thousand two hundred military personnel and ninety civilians were mobilized for the different tests and studies. The 82^d Airborne Division provided soldiers on a part-time basis and the 6th Aviation Squadron put 150 aircraft at their disposal for eleven weeks. Fifty live-fire exercises were conducted."

"Howze submitted his report on 20 August 1962. The awaited tactical innovation was presented under the name of an 'Air Assault Division.' The number of aircraft principally characterized this new type division. A regular division had one hundred aircraft. The Air Assault Division was to have 459, of which 316 would be helicopters. On the other hand, the number of ground vehicles was greatly reduced. It decreased from 1,100 to 345. The artillery was also modified. The report proposed to retain only 105mm howitzers and Little John Rocket Batteries, both air-transportable by Chinook. The other novelty was aerial rocket artillery that gave the Division solid close air support. It consisted of twenty-four Mohawks and thirty-five Hueys armed with rockets."

"The Howze Commission took advantage of all the earlier studies and used some of the results of previous tests. The report represented a lot of work. 'Believe me, an enormous task!'" interjects, Kinnard, completely carried away by his subject.

"This time there was major tactical innovation. This follows, since the project contemplated that the Division would have the means simultaneously to move one third of its combat strength by air. It's organized into three brigades, as you see it working here. Howze proposed that the Army's conventional divisions be progressively replaced by airmobile units. To defend his conclusions, he wrote at the end of his report: 'The adoption by the army of the airmobility concept is necessary and desirable. This evolution is just as inevitable as that which intervened to move us from animal to machine power.'

"Howze concluded thus this report of 3,500 pages put together in ninety days. In the vast program of reorganization, he recommended the creation of five air assault divisions and anticipated basing one in Korea, one in Hawaii, and three in the States."

"But these recommendations, did they know what it would cost? Had they calculated the impact on the national budget?"

"Of course, the Commission had calculated the cost of its recommendations. The cost of one of these divisions was estimated at 980 million dollars, compared to 742 million for a conventional division. An important indirect effect concerned the training of flight personnel. The project required that 8,900 pilots be trained for 1963, and 20,600 by 1968. The most amazing thing in all this is that the Howze report was not deep-sixed, but it came very close."

"In effect, General Howze, shortly after he submitted his report, was recalled to head up an airborne unit to confront serious racial troubles that exploded in Mississippi. Fifteen days later the Cuban Missile crisis took center stage."

"In spite of the international crisis and budgetary debates, in January 1963 the plan for the reorganization of the Army was published. The plan prescribed the organization, the training, and the testing for an air assault division and its transport brigade."

"This 'test' division was established at Fort Benning, Georgia on 15 January 1963. It was organized under the colors of the 11th Airborne Division, a unit that had distinguished itself in World War Two as the 'Blue Angels of the Pacific.' Its new designation was '11th Air Assault Division (Test).'"

"And you were named to head up the Division!"

"Right, exactly. I received Alpha and Bravo Companies of the 227th Assault Helicopter Battalion. You've just seen them. They were there since the beginning of this adventure. I picked up the 1st Battalion of the 187th Infantry, Alpha Company of the 127th Engineers, and Bravo Battery of the 6th Battalion of the 81st Artillery. Such was the initial nucleus, sized for the first phase of tests."

"Your mission thus consisted in showing that the proposals of the Howze Commission were realizable?"

"Yes, I had to prove their feasibility and above all their effectiveness. I took advantage of my airborne experience to outline and define the various aspects of mobility and assault tactics. Then, we had to come up with the equipment we would need, work out procedures, choose communications systems, and above all, develop the right mental attitude. In effect, we had to unleash a real cultural revolution and believe me, in the Army that's not easy. For example, until then, it was forbidden in the Air Force to fly helicopters in formation. With us, it's a necessity. For artillerymen, to be deployed like infantry on the battlefield, was something new."

"And you can see what we've had to invent in the areas of coordination and logistics—a veritable new art of war. For example, to communicate and recognize each other in combat, we created the famous color and number code that allows immediate identification on the radio and by sight."

"On the moral level, I have instilled an esprit de corps similar to that of the airborne. I've struggled to keep the men on jump status. For the rest, I had to innovate. To be efficient, I had to decentralize innovation. Also, at the beginning of 1964, I created an 'Idea Center,' so that individually officers and men from the ranks might contribute to proposing innovations that would contribute to our efficiency."

"I gathered a first class team around me with John Wright as my second in command, a veteran of Corregidor, whom I sought out in the 7th Army in Germany. He took in hand the logistics and aviation of the Division. He's the one who solved the problem with the Chinooks. Several CH-47s had lost a rotor blade in flight. We got off on the wrong foot with this helicopter. Wright called in Bob Therrington of Boeing, and they got that problem under control. To better understand pilots, he went to flight school and earned his wings. I got Dick Knowles as my assistant for operations and tactics, Bob William for the follow-on tests, etc."

"I sought to develop an attitude of technological watchfulness and of creativity. I must say that it worked well. In February 1964 the 11th Air Assault Division received the Bell Foundation Award for research in the domain of rotary flight. We also received other recognition. Everybody came to see us. Civilians and military wanted to visit this new tactical laboratory."

"In July of 1964 the Division was reinforced. I received three battalions of Infantry from the 2d Infantry Division, as well as two battalions of artillery. I then had about four thousand men and 175 aircraft. So we entered into the second phase of testing: Air Assault II. We went through a period of intensive exercises with the 82d Airborne Division as the aggressor."

"We were really beginning to put the whole thing together, but the program just about came apart when the economists working on the budget decide to get involved. To reduce the budget deficit, the reduction of the military budget was the order of the day again. The solution that seemed easiest was to stop the development of the new Division. Do you know how the project was saved?"

"By lobbying by the companies building the helicopters maybe?"

"Not at all. By the North Vietnamese! The Pentagon received information proving that the communists were keeping very active and were infiltrating south of the 17th Parallel. They concluded that the North Vietnamese Army was preparing a big offensive to cut South Vietnam in two."

"The South Vietnamese Government believed itself seriously threatened and insisted that the United States help them to resist the growing aggression. In March 1965 the Pentagon made the decision to transform the 11th Air Assault Division (Test) into a combat unit. So we picked up the pace of the exercises without the men really knowing that they were preparing themselves for Vietnam. McNamara officially announced the creation of a new division on 16 June. After that, as you know, things happened fast because the Secretary of State gave us eight weeks to be ready for combat. There, in short form, is how the unit you saw at work in the Ia Drang came into being."

"Thanks, sir, for the whole story. I better understand what I have been able to see on the ground. But I would like to know if you already have information on the enemy's reaction to such massive use of helicopters? Have they found some way to counter your tactics?"

"The North Vietnamese and the Vietcong reacted quickly to the allied use of an increasing number of helicopters. In early '63 we recovered documents in which we found their analysis of the evolution of our mobility. They already recognized that helicopter raids were causing them many losses. They state the advantages of airmobility with great objectivity. I had it translated, because it had many lessons for us."

"For them, there are three strong points in our tactics. First, the perfect coordination that can be established between the means of attack, of support, and of reinforcement. Second, the ability to penetrate deep into their territory with a strong offensive capability and the capability to withdraw just as quickly. Finally, they also recognized that we had sufficient and appropriate means to destroy their forces while they were still weak and before their reinforcements had the time to arrive."

"On the other hand, they think that these tactical advantages have their own limits. They evidently mix objective elements with ideological considerations unique to their system. Moreover, that's where they start so as to be sure not to lose sight of their own dogma. 'The population being on our side, it will resist with all its means.' That said, the observations that they make are very pertinent. 'Relatively limited forces being used for deep attacks, it is possible to organize counterattacks that lead to the withdrawal of the intruder.' They explain that airmobile operations need up-to-the minute intelligence that must be validated. The time it takes to confirm the information is sufficient for the situation to change, and the operation becomes futile."

"They develop four other arguments that are quite perceptive: 'Enemy forces are generally little familiar with the terrain upon which they embark. They can also easily be encircled and rapidly defeated.' There's a reality that we've directly confronted on several operations last month. They add: 'The capacity to bring in reinforcements is limited by the availability of helicopters.' That's perfectly true!

"The North Vietnamese also try to reassure themselves. They think that the nature of the terrain—the jungle and the relief—constitute real protection and considerably limit the effectiveness of airmobile operations. They also believe that terrain evaluation conducted from the sky is very incomplete, that LZ landings hold many surprises, and that it is easy to set ambushes."

"The last point of their analysis concerns more precisely the mode of transport, the helicopter itself. For them, It has two weak points. First, it flies slowly, and is therefore vulnerable to ground fire. But above all, its use is limited by its down time. It takes three hours of maintenance on the ground for each hour of flight, and ten hours of scheduled maintenance every two or three days, thus its availability is limited. Its fuel consumption is also a limit on its radius of action."

"You can see that one may have confidence in the North Vietnamese to formulate a lucid critique of our strong points and of our weak points. Our task is not an easy one, because our adversaries are cunning, tenacious, and intelligent. But, up to that point, they had only come up against *air movement* operations. Today, we are serving them a new version: *air assault*."

Translator's Notes
[1] There is still an element at work in the Army trying to make a beast of burden of the infantrymen by developing load-carrying equipment designed to carry ever-heavier loads. In the 7th Cavalry in Vietnam we traveled and fought as light as possible, just as did our enemy. I recall only a single instance, on road convoy,

when we wore flack jackets. We wore only soft hats for many operations. Marching for ten or more hours in steep mountainous terrain, in hot and humid weather, with scarcely a break and the prospect of digging in when we halted, thirty or forty pounds was the maximum load for a pack. Weapons, ammo, radios, rations (in socks tied to web gear) added much more weight to the load. Many of us used captured North Vietnamese packs because they were lighter and, not attached to the web gear, simpler to shuck when the shooting started.

PART TWO
1966 - 1968

FROM THE COASTAL PLAIN TO THE TET OFFENSIVE:

THE COMMUNISTS STOPPED ON ALL FRONTS

CHAPTER IX

McNamara was largely responsible for the Air Cav becoming rapidly operational and being sent to Vietnam. There had been four years of work since Secretary of the Army Cyrus Vance, on 15 December 1962, presented him with the conclusions of the Howze Report, with which he was in complete agreement.

Also, when Moore's 450 men confronted and defeated the 1,700 North Vietnamese in the Ia Drang Valley, he characterized the operation as an "exploit without precedent." However, the fact that in four days of fighting the First Cav lost 230 men killed and 4 missing troubled him.

Westmoreland, in order to deal with the massive infiltration of North Vietnamese into the central part of Vietnam, asked the Secretary of Defense for a supplementary contingent of 41,500 men. Taking this request into account, the American forces reached a strength of 375,000 men by the end of 1965.

McNamara wanted to draw his own conclusions about the situation. He left Paris where he was attending a NATO conference for a quick visit to Saigon. He spent thirty hours in Vietnam and drafted a memorandum to President Johnson. His report of 30 November opened certain questions regarding an appropriate strategy. He was no longer convinced, as were Westmoreland and Depuy, that the solution was in a war of attrition that depended upon always increasing American ground forces. "Four hundred thousand men may not guarantee success," he wrote in his report. He concluded, however, that it was necessary to "hold fast to the objectives established for this war and provide whatever is necessary in the way of men and matériel."

He recommended a three-part plan. First, provide Hanoi an opening for negotiations. If Ho Chi Minh failed to take advantage of that, intensify the air war and provide Westmoreland with a force of 400,000 men. The opening would be expressed by a three or four-week suspension of the bombing in the North. McNamara thought that the May 1965 experiment of a five-day suspension of bombing was not meaningful, that Hanoi needed more time to react.

McNamara advocated using this month-long truce to undertake an intensive diplomatic initiative and to prepare American public opinion for the eventuality of an intensification of the war. "We must prepare the American public and world opinion to accept such an enlargement of the conflict ... while offering the North

Vietnamese Army the opportunity to cease their aggression without losing face." President Johnson let himself be convinced and ordered the McNamara plan implemented.

The bombing of North Vietnam was suspended beginning on 24 December, in time for Christmas Eve, but thirty-six days later, Hanoi had not changed its position or demands one iota. On 31 January 1966, Johnson therefore gave the order to restart the bombing. The strategy of attrition again became the official doctrine. Westmoreland now needed 459,000 men.

On the ground, despite the approach of Tet, operations had not ceased. The 1ˢᵗ and 2ᵈ Brigades had participated in *Operation Matador* between Pleiku and Kontum. Communist logistics were profoundly disrupted.

Westmoreland then asked Kinnard to support II Corps, the tactical headquarters that was responsible for the area running from the South China Sea to the Cambodian border. The 4ᵗʰ Infantry Division had settled in at Pleiku. The area was markedly calmer after the Ia Drang fight and *Operation Matador*. The Cav thus changed its theater of operations. Its new mission is in Central Vietnam: the borders of the Bong Son plain, the length of the coast to the north of Qui Nhon. This region is one of the most densely populated in Vietnam with almost 500,000 inhabitants. It is a vast rice granary that already had been a Vietminh sanctuary at the time of the war against the French.

During the preceding months, the 3ᵈ Sao Vang North Vietnamese Army Division had infiltrated the region. After coming down the Ho Chi Minh trail all the way into the Bong Son Plain, The Yellow Star Division had linked up with the 2ᵈ Vietcong Regiment and, together, they had eliminated all trace of the Saigon government's authority in the region. From then on, the 3ᵈ NVA Division included the 18ᵗʰ and 22ᵈ NVA Regiments and the 2ᵈ VC Regiment.

The geographic configuration of the region, consisting of alternating mountains and rice producing valleys, all terminating on the shores of the South China Sea, offered the Vietcong and their allies zones of refuge perfectly adapted to their actions. They had established a network of fortified hamlets and of protected tunnels very difficult to locate in the jungle. From there, they launched guerrilla actions to destabilize the weak governmental presence.

The Sao Vang soldiers, with the VC, enlisted the villagers to transform each hamlet into a fortified village. They turned access to the rice fields, in open terrain, into a firetrap covered by fields of crossed fire from machine gun emplacements in camouflaged bunkers made of mud, bamboo, and coconut tree trunks. The communists had gathered the crossties and rails of the old colonial railway that ran along the coast for use in building their fortifications. The individual fighting holes dug into the dikes and the canals were equipped with shelters capable of withstanding bombs from the air and artillery fire. A vast network of zigzagging trenches facilitated the movement of munitions and reinforcements.

The South Vietnamese authorities and the allied general staffs judge it essential to reestablish their presence and clean out this enemy sanctuary. This is the objective of *Operation Masher. Masher* is a vast operation planned for forty-five days and mobilizing twenty thousand American, South Vietnamese, and Korean soldiers of the ROK Division. Since *Operation Atlante* conducted by the French in 1954, there had been no operation of this magnitude in central Vietnam.

The First Cav is allocated the southern wing of the troop dispositions, right where the enemy is most prepared. The targets are a recruitment center near Bong Son, and above all, major stocks of rice. The operation should also allow Route 1, insecure for a long time, to be reopened, most importantly between Qui Nhon and Bong Son. The allied forces mobilize the 22^d South Vietnamese Infantry Division and the Korean Tigers for *Masher*, and on the American side, the III^d Marine Amphibious Corps and the 3^d Brigade of the First Cav.

Once again Hal Moore is on the front lines. After having born the shock of *LZ X-Ray*, just promoted to Full Colonel, he had replaced Tim Brown at the head of the Brigade. In the meantime he had conducted *Operation Clean House*, which had allowed him to familiarize himself with the coastal region and the new countryside. From the sky, after the jungle canopy, he spots the flooded rice paddies that, like little mirrors surrounded by their dikes, reflect the light. The spectacle becomes unreal when, at sunset, the reflections turn pink. The paddies send thousands of salmon colored beams skyward as if reflected from a cut diamond. The soldiers, packed on their helicopters, enjoy the view from the gaping open doorways. Intrigued, they forget the noise that surrounds them and the violence to come.

In a few days the Monsoon arrives, early and in force. The rice paddies overflow, all of them flooded. The ground is spongy, the darkened sky low overhead. It is humid and cold. Fairy-like, the countryside takes on a sinister aspect.

On 26 January, a C-123 Fairchild prepares to takeoff from the An Khe runway. In its fuselage are forty-two men of the 2^d Battalion, 7th Cavalry. The C-123, its twin engines at takeoff power, props at full thrust, rolls noisily down the metal covered runway. Flaps up, it devours the takeoff distance. The Fairchild tears itself from the ground at An Khe and drives into the foggy ceiling. It turns in the direction of Bong Son. Five minutes later, radio contact is lost. The aircraft has plowed into the mountainside. Soldiers and aircrew perish in the crash. *Masher* has not even begun and the toll is already heavy. Hal Moore, who had refused to leave *LZ X-Ray* until he had recovered his three missing sergeants, looks with concern at the wreckage of the Fairchild, his eyes filled with emotion. He looks at the line of pancho-covered bodies awaiting evacuation. Lieutenant Colonel McDade is at his side. "One could end up thinking that the 2^d of the 7th is a bad-luck outfit. Just put back together after the losses from *LZ Albany* and bang! forty-two men lost in this crash. Tomorrow I'll start the action at Cu Nghi. I cross my fingers that nothing bad happens."

The next day begins, still with a heavy fog. The countryside is bathed in this thick, humid mist that clings to the ground and trees. A hundred Hueys fly just over the top of the milky bank of fog: an impressive charge. The approach to Bong Son is along the seacoast. The village is eight kilometers further up the shore, to the north of Cay Giep, on high ground rising from the plain.

McDade, standing behind the pilot, follows their progress on his map. The villages pass below like green patches in the middle of the long stretch of rice paddies. It has been difficult to pick a landing zone because everything is flooded. McDade wound up choosing another alternative, a large sandy area surrounded by coconut palms. The lift ships fly along the shoreline, surfing over the trees, flanked by gunships at a slightly higher level.

The first lift of four Hueys approaches the *LZ*. There is no tube artillery preparation, no ARA, and no gunship escort. The intent is to catch the NVA by surprise. But the movement was late getting off the ground, and it is already 0700 hours. Suddenly, framed by the helicopter doorways, the horizon rocks. Tracers zebra through the sky. *LZ 4* is hot. The sky turns unhealthy. Twelve point seven-millimeter machine guns have opened fire. Well camouflaged and hidden by the fog, they have escaped damage from the naval gunfire preparation of the VIIth Fleet.

The choppers, each carrying six troopers, roar in. Two men on each side ride the skids coming in on the assault as the door gunners fire into the trees surrounding the *LZ*. The lift ships abruptly flare, slowing to about five miles an hour in a moving hover, twelve feet over the *LZ*. The men riding the skids leap, their comrades bounding out behind them. The Charlie Company Commander, Captain John Fesmire, is in chopper number four of the first lift, the rear chopper in the diamond formation. Four of the six men in his Huey are wounded almost as soon as they hit the ground. The man carrying the radio communicating with Brigade breaks his ankle when he lands, something rare for the well-conditioned infantrymen, although with the radio, weapon, ammo, rations, and other gear, he is packing about a hundred pounds and the landing is hard. Jumping in from a high hover is the next best thing to a malfunctioning parachute. Among the wounded is the RTO whose radio is on the Battalion push. PFC Gerry Skelly packs the radio on the Company frequency. The Hueys take light fire on the ascent. The men spread out to make room for the second lift.

The second lift is on final approach right behind the first, but pulls up short. The men leap out some fifty meters behind the first lift. These helicopters draw even more fire on the way out and the men on the ground take heavier casualties. Both lifts go back to pick up the rest of Charlie Company. The Hueys return with the third lift and put the troops down another fifty meters back. Six men are killed in the choppers during the assault. These four helicopters draw heavy fire. They are unable to land and pick up wounded. Behind them the fourth lift, bringing in the company 81mm mortar platoon, unloads its troopers a hundred meters further back. This lift loses twelve more killed and nine wounded during the assault. They are separated from the rest of the company. SP5 Charles Kinney, "Doc," the senior aidman for Charlie Company, comes in on this lift. He drags some of the wounded further off the *LZ*, dresses their wounds, and starts to dig in.

This *LZ*, an area designated by McDade, located to the east of Cu Nghi, is hot. Charlie Company is spread out. Fesmire has no radio contact with the Mortar Platoon; its RTO killed in the assault landing. The RTO of the Third Platoon is wounded, his radio destroyed by fire. Fesmire decides to move to the center of mass of Charlie Company. With Skelly he makes a wild two hundred-meter dash back toward the Mortar Platoon. These men from the fourth lift are now widely scattered in what proves to be a cemetery, their dead and wounded spread out among and behind the mounded graves. He orders everyone within hearing to take cover. "Quick, get down behind those little mounds," yells Fesmire to the grunts scrunched down in the wet gray sand. The order is unnecessary. They have long since taken cover to avoid the heavy fire.

"Shit, these are graves! We're in a cemetery!" remarks a sergeant who had just noticed that small shrines here and there surmount the raised mounds. There is no time to worry about the choice of locations. Machine guns and mortars lash the area with heavy fire. The men call back and forth to each other to check on status.

The intensity of fire coming from all directions causes the lift ship pilots to put A and C Companies on the ground some distance from each other. Captain Joël Sudginis's Alpha Company offloads a little more to the south than Charlie Company. The two groups are separated by a few hamlets. For them, it is vital to link up.

Alpha Company progresses rapidly toward Cu Nghi. Just when the troopers think they are about there, tens of automatic weapons begin to fire just at ground level. The well dug-in North Vietnamese positions had hardly been touched by the naval gunfire. Fesmire and his troops remain cornered in the cemetery. A cold, penetrating rain follows the chilly morning shower. His men slip into their panchos. Awkward in their wet rain gear and aggravated by the sand that gets into everything, they wait for artillery support.

"Sir, the artillery can't fire. Alpha Company is too close to the NVA. They're working their way toward us."

"That's just our luck. I hope Joe can get through! Okay, call him and tell him we're tossing yellow smoke—and get the smoke out."

A few kilometers away flies a Chinook with a 105mm howitzer in sling load. Enemy 12.7mm machine guns zero in on it. The sound of the rounds striking the chopper resonates in the cockpit. The pilot feels his aircraft begin to shake. He immediately ceases forward movement and begins an emergency descent. The CH-47 gunners lean into their M60s, ready to protect the chopper during its tricky landing. The 105 touches the ground. The pilot releases the sling and sets down next to the howitzer. He sends out a call for help, giving his coordinates, but he is pretty pessimistic because he has put down very close to an NVA position.

The radio crackles: "Hook this is Serpent Three.[1] Hang in there. We're not too far away but the place is crawling with Charlies. Hold on, we're coming."

"Okay guys, don't be stingy with the ammo. Some Garry Owen troops are close by. They're coming for us," the pilot announces on the intercom. Reassured, the crew repulses the NVA assault. The cockpit is lacerated with bullet holes. A race begins between the North Vietnamese who had just shot down the huge Chinook, and the grunts of the 1st of the 7th. For the NVA, it is a matter of a real prize: the 105 on the ground and its ammo as well as three M60 machine guns in the Chinook. The Garry Owen troopers, covered by accurate fire from the Chinook, arrive before the NVA.

Lieutenant Colonel Kampe's men establish a security perimeter around the helicopter.

A sergeant sizes up the situation. "You five come with me, we're going to set up the 105. Get that thing pointed toward the NVA and break out some ammo." Moving quickly, the men drag the howitzer around and point it toward the North Vietnamese positions. The place gets unhealthy in a hurry because the North Vietnamese, furious over losing their trophies, are just that much more aggressive. From their positions can be heard cries of "Tien Len! Tien Len!"[2] The little men leave their holes and rush toward the helicopter, bayonets fixed on AK47s.

"Fire!" The 105, muzzle pointed at the enemy, fires its first round. "If you find any canister rounds, bring them here first," shouts the sergeant who ejects the smoking 105 case from the breech. The sergeant fires directly into the NVA ranks, where the rounds detonate. The fire discourages the North Vietnamese, all the more so since fire from M16 rifles, M60 machine guns, and M79 grenade launchers accompany it. Frustrated, the NVA retreat to their fortified positions.

The North Vietnamese machine guns have been diabolically effective. In the first hour, four CH-47s have been shot down and twelve Huey lift ships seriously damaged. By midday, the Brigade counts twenty-eight aircraft out of action.

During this time, in the rice fields at Cu Nghi: "Look, yellow smoke! Charlie Company is just on the other side. We're almost there," Sudginis tells his lead platoon leader and his RTO. "We're going to go around the village behind the paddy dikes. It'll be good cover. We ought to be able to link up just behind it, don't you think? Let's do it. Keep your intervals. This could get nasty!" No sooner do the Garry Owen Troopers of Alpha Company, 2d of the 7th arrive at the first dike than they have to plunge into the muddy rice paddy to take cover from the embankment. Automatic weapons sweep with precision and thoroughness any area in the open. McDade orders Sudginis to hold on to the paddy. "We have to hold it and use it for an LZ to bring in reinforcements."

About 1600 hours Captain Fesmire decides to move from the Mortar Platoon area to join the main body of Charlie Company that has now fought its way into the edge of Cu Nghi. It is another two hundred-meter dash across mostly open terrain. Fesmire, lightly wounded earlier, races through the graveyard. Skelly watches his company commander speed across the open terrain, knowing he must follow. He is loaded down with his PRC25, six grenades, an M79 with a double basic load of thirty-six rounds, two canteens, a pancho, a .45 caliber pistol and ammo, rations, and assorted other gear. He is packing well over a hundred pounds. Fesmire makes it safely. Skelly hoists his heavy load and begins the long dash. From the edge of the village the Second Platoon cheers and yells encouragement. The Platoon Leader, First Lieutenant Byron Scoggins shouts, "You can make it!" But Skelly, bobbing and weaving over the wet sand as NVA automatic rifle fire tracks him, does not hear a word of this, intent only on the run of his life. He makes it safely. After that run they call him "Legs." What is left of the Mortar Platoon follows suit. The men work their way to the edge of Cu Nghi and rejoin the rest of Charlie Company.

The two companies are, for the moment, well positioned. Friendly artillery resumes pounding enemy positions. A curtain of fire isolates the eastern side of the paddy allowing lift ships to come in. In spite of all the artillery, the first six choppers are hit by ground fire. Some of the NVA machine guns are still in action. McDade decides to wait for nightfall to move Charlie Company to a more defensible position. He orders them to move away from the village back across LZ 4 to a trench line about three hundred meters away.

Skip Fesmire gets a final status report prior to the move. He thinks some men may still be alive in the graveyard, but does not know their exact location. He plans to pick them up on the way to the new position. Confusing the issue, four men, Doc and three others, are reported to him as killed. Fesmire organizes the relocation in the wet and pitch black night. The men move out in single file, carrying their wounded, at about 2200 hours. The move, conducted in silence, draws fire. The men respond with grenades. They do not find any Charlie Company soldiers during the move, which takes over an hour.

Doc Kinney and a small group of men had been separated from the main body of the Company during the initial assault landing. Kinney early on had scraped out a one-man foxhole in the sand and mud next to a grave. He was soon wounded in both hands, the fire shattering the stock of his still functional M16. Shards from the stock embedded themselves in his face. Shortly thereafter another of the men in this small group was hit twice and killed and Doc recovered his M79. He dragged another trooper, wounded earlier in both legs, close by and lying low, to his position. After dark, two more men who, exposed to machine gun fire in the open had survived by playing dead, scramble to the now cramped foxhole. They enlarge it to accommodate the four of them. Shortly after that they hear movement. Charlie Company was on the move, but it is a dark night, overcast, and they do not know until daybreak that they are alone on the LZ.

The ambiance at the Cu Nghi cemetery for these men is gloomy, a real horror story. They stand off repeated enemy probes with rifle fire, M79 grenade fire, and hand grenades. By this time the loud and very visible ruckus on *LZ 4* confirms for Fesmire that there are still a handful of troopers left in the graveyard. The artillery fires illuminating parachute flares for the rest of the night. The men hunker down in their foxhole, taking turns to peer over the top to listen and look for the NVA infantrymen and sappers. They defend their position, killing at least one NVA soldier. One grenade lands just at the lip of their hole and roles back before it explodes. Numb with cold, under their panchos, dripping with rain, soaking wet; they defend their position. The sand gets into their rifles, and into their rations when they try to eat, making a fine grit between their teeth. The weather is lousy. The wind does not stop blowing and successive blasts howl in the still standing coconut palms. They pass a bad night among the mounded graves.

At daybreak, the ceiling rises a little bit. A FAC flying over the area spots the Americans. A medevac helicopter is heavily damaged by ground fire when it attempts to pick them up and must abort the rescue. US Air Force Phantoms and Skyraiders follow one another coming in over the tops of the palms. They work over the trenches, fortified positions, and hamlets surrounding the cemetery, dropping Napalm, White Phosphorous, and High Explosive bombs to keep the NVA off the Garry Owen troopers. They hit ammo dumps, and the noise of secondary explosions resonates and echoes off the hills. SP5 Kinney gets a direct hit with his grenade launcher on an enemy soldier who momentarily presents a target while shooting at the American aircraft. One of the Skyraiders drops a White Phosphorous bomb short of his target. It falls in the Charlie Company area, giving rise to several interesting comments.

The next morning Hal Moore lands with Lieutenant Colonel Ingram's 2^d of the 12th. They put down north of the village in a perimeter held by Lieutenant Colonel Kampe's 1st of the 7th. As the lift ships move out, four of them open fire on the trench now occupied by Charlie Company. There are more casualties. Some of the men return fire.

Colonel Moore, not wanting to risk the life of his men, does not hold back any available supporting firepower. The 2^d of the 12th infantrymen move forward toward *LZ 4* behind a wall of flame and flying steel, systematically clearing hooches and bunkers alike. Each tunnel, each hole is treated to a grenade. The VC and North Vietnamese, like Indians, refuse to surrender. They would rather die in their bunkers than come out with hands raised.

"Son-of-a-bitch, shit!" shouts a noncom, who sees an M26 come flying back out of a hole to explode under the nose of a surprised trooper. "Hold your grenades for a short two-count after you arm 'em, or they'll come back in your face." In spite of all the artillery and air support, it is by pistol, knife, and hand grenade that the infantrymen impose their will. At 1700 hundred hours Charlie Company, 2^d of the 12th finally links up with the four men left behind in the graveyard.

The 7th, 9th, and 22^d NVA Regiments, under this ultimate pressure, are forced to abandon Cu Nghi and its environs. These three days of fighting, however, leave Hal Moore perplexed. The combination of poor weather, the pugnacity of the communists, and mediocre coordination of allied units limited the success of the operation from the beginning. The Brigade counts 121 dead and 220 wounded. The enemy leaves 660 dead on the field and abandons fifty-five heavy weapons. The Brigade takes 215 VC and NVA prisoners. The survivors retreat down the An Lao Valley toward the Central Highlands.

"It's not a question of stopping now. We've got to continue. We've just stirred up an anthill. We don't want to miss the return on our investment!" says Kinnard. Before going on, they have to change the name of the operation. President Johnson is furious that they had code-named it "*Masher.*" " '*White Wing*,' that ought to make him happy," Kinnard concludes as he picks a new name for the ongoing operation.

"Hal, you're going to follow the Sao Vang southwest toward the An Lao Valley. You'll have Colonel Lynch's 2^d Brigade to back you up. Don't forget, '*White Wing*!' But pay attention, the NVA don't give a crap that we've changed the name of the operation. It's an unhealthy area. The SF have tried several times to clean up the Valley. In the course of *Operation Delta*, they sent elite detachments into the area, in particular Detachment B-52. It didn't work out. The NVA sent back the bodies of their Green Beret infiltrators. Do you have the latest weather info?"

"Yes sir. The weather's still bad. It really limits our helicopters. Frankly, we've had crummy luck with the weather. Right now, the monsoon is the enemy's best ally."

"Happily the Charlies don't have anti-aircraft weapons, otherwise, there wouldn't be a single chopper in the air," adds Kinnard. "We've got to be very vigilant since several unfavorable factors are working at once. The weather seriously restricts our mobility and our ARA. Our infantry on the ground, in the rice paddies, or in the jungle is at a disadvantage with respect to the North Vietnamese who have prepared the terrain and know it by heart. We can't permit ourselves to relieve the pressure now that we've attacked. We have to prove to the population that we're the strongest. Otherwise, from their perspective, we'd 'lose face.' Here's how I see what we've got to do to clean up central Vietnam," continues Kinnard, addressing himself to the two Colonels.

"Hal, with your Brigade, you're going to go after them in the Kim Son Valley, in the area known as the Crow's Foot. I don't know who picked that name but it was well chosen. These seven steep-sided ravines feed into an eighth bigger one giving the impression of a crow's foot. I think the NVA are as well dug in in the Crow's Foot Valley as in that of An Lao. They make two excellent fall back areas for the NVA who've had plenty of time to set up their rear areas. Block all escape routes well and harass them until they try to escape. Use the same technique as in the Ia Drang: aerial reconnaissance and, when you find them, hold them with an Eagle Flight. Don't engage them with a large infantry force. Use ARA and 105s. Get enough disruptive aerial activity going to deceive them about our intent, which is to wait for them at the mouth of the Valley."

"Bill! Do the same thing in the Kim Son. But watch out, you could be pushing NVA into each other's AO. You could find yourself facing the rest of the units that have fled An Lao, chased by Hal, but that managed to slip past the 3^d Brigade screen. We're solid along the coast. You have the ARVN 22^d Infantry Division and the Korean Tiger Division. To the North of Bong Son, along the coast, Marines from III Corps seal off the area. We're the most mobile and need to be ready to intervene at any moment depending on the reaction of the enemy. We've got to be ready to move with all speed on several fronts to take full advantage of any information we get."

"There are some restrictions. The An Lao and Kim Son areas are considered hostile zones but, before you bring in B-52 strikes on them, we've got to let the people know and evacuate anyone that wants out. Don't ignore the psychological dimension of the mission. Headquarters wants to put the emphasis on pacification. Do that as best you can without putting your men at risk. It's your game! Above all, keep me posted on any indications of NVA presence or movement so that we back here at Base Camp can do our best to coordinate everything and do it in the most timely way."

On 4 February, *White Wing* takes the baton from *Masher*. Moore, with the 3^d Brigade, makes the first move in the An Lao Valley. The weather is terrible and the monsoon storms slow down the kickoff of the operation. The 3^d Brigade loses two days of planning time. The fog and a particularly low ceiling cling to the jungle hiding the broken terrain. The NVA and VC profit from the Cavalry's delay and the dismal weather to disappear. The Garry

Owen troopers arrive only to discover freshly abandoned base camps and empty trenches. They are, however, astonished by the number of caches they discover with food and ammunition, stocks of supplies and rice intended for withdrawal hidden in the forest. It constituted a whole self-sufficient, isolated region beyond the control of the South Vietnamese Government.

The 3ᵈ Brigade links up with the 2ᵈ Brigade in the Crow's Foot. Lynch and Moore don't want to let the NVA outwit them again. Gunships and scout choppers streak through the valleys looking for any indication or trace of NVA withdrawal. Moore maintains intense aerial activity to hide its futility. On 11 February, taking advantage of the traffic launched the evening before, companies of Garry Owen troopers, after two days of preparation, are landed on the hilltops. Other infantry units hold the exits at the ends of the valleys. The artillery covers the hillsides, ravines, and trails. The batteries of 105s strike obstinately at the mountain like a steam hammer. The troopers of the 7ᵗʰ descend progressively along the slopes to check out the damage inflicted by the shelling. The grunts, as they advance, note the number of enemy struck down by the hail of shells.

The night descends quickly. Moore does not want the NVA to be able to profit by the darkness and slip away. He sends in ARA choppers from the 2ᵈ Battalion, 20ᵗʰ Artillery. These helicopters, equipped with powerful searchlights that pierce the obscurity, saturate with rockets and bursts of machine gun fire any area that reveals some indication of enemy movement. The ARA choppers put the lie to the adage that "the night belongs to the Charlies."

The tally for the two-day sweep amounts to 249 NVA killed. The Cav only laments a loss of six KIA this time.

Translator's Notes
[1] The "three" suffix to a call sign designates the unit operations officer.
[2] "Kill! Kill!"

CHAPTER X

A young Sergeant carefully searches through the backpack of a dead VC. "Sir," he informs his platoon leader, "we found a map and some documents on a VC body. There's some interesting stuff." The platoon leader passes this find up the chain. Colonel Moore orders an immediate follow-up. South Vietnamese interpreters and intelligence officers chopper into the area right away. They analyze the documents. An hour later the S2 excitedly reports to Colonel Moore, "Sir, the map shows the location of the headquarters of a unit of at least battalion size. We've got to act fast."

"Where is it?" Moore asks, very interested.

"Here, near the Soui Run," the S2 answers, pointing out the spot on the map.

"Okay, we'll close the trap on them before they can get away. They'll try and split up. MacDade, here's a job for Diduryk. Lift him with his Company close to the Soui Run. He's got to fix them so they can't get away, like they just did at An Lao."

Diduryk's Company is inserted on 15 February along the bank of the Run River. The vegetation is dense, tough to penetrate. The intelligence is precise. The NVA react as soon as the Americans move into the jungle. They stop the Company's progress from their well dug-in positions. Two platoons are violently engaged and held up on the far bank. Their situation is critical. The Captain reports to McDade. "Hold on!" he tells them. "Reinforcements are on the way. Don't let them get away. While you're waiting, we're sending you the Pink Team."

About noon fighter-bombers and gunships erupt above the valley. The pilots easily locate Diduryk's platoons wedged in along one side of the Run River. The aircraft rock as they drop their high explosive and napalm bombs and launch their rockets on the far bank and surrounding area.

"Fix bayonets! Get ready to cross as they make their final run. Let's do it," the 3^d Platoon Leader says to his sergeants. "Go." The troopers of the 3^d Platoon leave their position and wade into the river, quietly, without noise. They climb over the bank, silent and determined. The NVA are surprised in their foxholes, still deafened by the noise of the bombs and somewhat scorched by the napalm. Stimulated by their initial success, Diduryk's men take on the enemy soldiers in the position, supported by the Huey gunships that open the way. Quickly, the Company occupies the position and defeats a force twice its size.

General Kinnard is pleased. He calls Hal Moore to his CP on top of Hon Cong. An enormous First Cavalry Patch has been painted on the side of the mountain that overlooks An Khe. "Congratulations Hal. Your Brigade has done a super job. I'm very happy for McDade. He and his men are ending this operation with a bang, a real victory. After the string of bad luck these guys suffered, the courage and combativeness they demonstrated at the Run River shows that their morale was in no way affected. They've just written a new page in the story of the Cav! Hal, I've decided to relieve your Brigade and give it a rest. It needs one. The First Brigade will take it from here."

Responsibility switches as between runners in a relay. Kinnard turns to Colonel Elvy B. Roberts, First Brigade Commander: "Elvy, you've got to keep up the same rhythm and pressure on the NVA. The objective is to get down into the Kim Son Valley. You know the reputation of the place, inaccessible and inviolate, another sanctuary that's got to go. Who will you send?"

"Lieutenant Colonel Edward Meyer, Second of the Fifth."

The 18th Regiment of the North Vietnamese Army is effectively at home in the lower Kim Son Valley where it has constructed bunkers for its 57mm recoilless rifles and its 82mm mortars. They have set up the area as a private preserve. No sooner does the 2d of the 5th offload than they are hosed down by heavy automatic weapons fire. Bravo Company is hit by heavy weapons fire coming from somewhere upstream. Meyer turns to his Fire Support Coordinator, but commo with the FDC is momentarily lost. He orders his FSC to "fix the problem, get up counterbattery fire, and blow the bastards away." He turns to one of his RTOs. "Get me Brigade. We'll need reinforcements to get behind them."

Meanwhile, the rest of the First Brigade is getting ready to mount up. At the Division CP, Kinnard is following the action blow by blow. "Sir," a G3 staffer gets his attention, " the G2 informs me that the Second Brigade has captured an important prisoner, a battalion commander of the 22d North Vietnamese Regiment. Under interrogation, he revealed the location of the Regiment."

"Where's that?" demands Kinnard stepping up to the map.

"In the eastern part of the Crow's Foot."

"Good. Get Colonel Lynch on the horn for me ... Bill, great, what a prize. How do you figure to exploit it? Over."

"I'm sending Ackerson now with the 1st of the 5th to verify the info and fix the NVA if the 22d is really there.[1] Over."

"Right, but be careful. The NVA may be there in force. I already have the 1st Brigade up north and it's hot there. Bob had to

124

send reinforcements to Meyer. He's got his fangs into some heavy stuff! Have at it. Out."

17 February 1966, the 1st Battalion of the 5th Cavalry leaps to the attack along the steep mountainsides to the east of the Crow's Foot. The welcoming committee is waiting. The 22d Regiment has perfectly fortified its perimeter and will not let the Black Hawks approach. The jungle hides earthworks that protect both light and heavy machine guns. They repulse all attempts at frontal attack. Cav troopers and NVA infantrymen alternately stand off each other's frontal assaults. The 1st of the 5th companies cannot get at the fortified NVA positions that cannot even be seen until the soldiers are right on top of them. The North Vietnamese attempt several time to break the American vise.

Three days later, the 20th, the NVA attack Alpha Company's CP three times. They come very close to overrunning it.

At Kinnard's CP on Hon Cong: "Sir, MACV's on your direct line. It's Westmoreland."

"Harry? What's happening at the Triangle and the Crow's Foot?"

"Everything's under control sir, but the NVA are fighting hard to defend their bases, and those bases are pretty well fortified."

"The hardest part is over. The NVA Regiments are clearly identified and located. It would be a waste to lose more Infantrymen and Marines. Pull your people back onto the surrounding hilltops. I've decided to finish the job off with an Arc Light, like at Ia Drang. But, after the B-52 strike, comb carefully through the area to get a final count for the results. In fact, did you get hit by a serious mortar attack yesterday?"

"Right sir, but everything's okay. The NVA are just trying to impress us."

The next day, 21 February, the 1st and 2d Brigades break contact to open the area for a high altitude bomb strike. Suddenly the earth trembles and the air vibrates to the rhythm of a giant and invisible drum. The grunts wait quietly for the strike to end. An FO lights up a smoke with his Zippo. The smoke gets in his eyes, which water up, giving his face a wet look. "If the God Damn NVA haven't understood our leaflets telling how many bombs a B-52 carries... now they'll get the message five by five." With respect to the information war—the Division is getting better. This year, 1966, is the Chinese Year of the Horse. First Cav leaflets, real greeting cards, point this out. A great idea!

"Saddle up! We're going back." The 1st of the 5th retraces its route. As they move, no one recognizes the countryside they left a few hours earlier. Enormous craters gut the land and forest. The relief is inside out. The Battalion finds the bunkers and trenches they had taken by assault the previous evening broken and collapsed. The partly caved-in tunnel network glares at the sky.

The Brigade occupies the terrain and screens through the area around Kim Son. The North Vietnamese no longer have any doubt about the means the allies can mobilize to drive them from their zone. Thereafter, they only think about getting away while they wait for the Americans to leave the area. But they abandon 710 dead after three days of combat. It is difficult to guess at the number of dead they carried off, or the number of wounded, traumatized by the shock effect of the bombs. Colonel Lynch's Brigade itself has taken a severe blow: 107 killed and 561 wounded. But it continues on the enemy's trail so as to give no respite to the Sao Vang Division.

The Brigade then returns to the seacoast on the eastern side of Cay Giep Mountain. This mountain resembles a big stone in the middle of the Bong Son Plain. It is another good refuge for the NVA with vegetation that provides natural protection in among the bamboo trees and vines. "Impossible to find a single LZ in this damn jungle," grouses Lynch.

"No problem sir. We'll use Jacob's Ladders with Chinooks," his S3 proposes.

"Yup! Clark pulled it off with hooks from the 228th. Double up on the ladders. We've got to empty the Chinooks as fast as possible."

At dawn, Skyraider fighter aircraft dive on Cay Giep and launch 350 kilo bombs, set to detonate two meters above the ground. The blasts clear the forest over several tens of meters—instantaneous LZs. The Chinooks come in just following the bombs and hover. The Black Horse Troopers rappel down the long ropes to the ground, like ants. They pull off this spectacular maneuver without a hitch and without opposition. The NVA have already abandoned the mountain. The whole area has gotten too unhealthy for them.

6 March 1966 *Operation White Wing* ends. Kinnard takes advantage of the break to hold a press conference and announce the results of an operation that lasted forty-one days.

"Before making any analysis, I'm going to give you the dry statistics. The First Cav employed two brigades, a third being in reserve. The total operational count directly attributable to our unit is 2,150 KIA for the communists. Our losses amount to 228 killed and 718 wounded."

"Of the nine enemy battalions concentrated in Binh Dinh Province, five have been just about destroyed. The famous Yellow Star Division has lost its luster. Its entire logistical and defensive organization has been torn to shreds. We have attacked and dispersed the 7th, 9th, 18th, and 22[d] NVA Regiments, as well as the 2[d] VC Regiment,"

"On the operational side, the First Cav deployed four battalions of infantry at an average distance of sixty kilometers from its bases while providing them with all necessary support. For those of you who like statistics, in forty-one days our helicopters executed 77,627 sorties and lifted the equivalent of 120,585 troops."

"At the beginning of the operation, the weather conditions seemed to be a problem. Didn't you find this to be a limiting factor for air assault tactics?" asks one of the journalists.

"I think your question is not without malice but I'll answer it willingly. Effectively, during this operation, our worst enemies have not been the North Vietnamese and Viet Cong but the monsoon. The visibility and ceiling have often been below minimal norms. Our pilots have proven their excellent technical mastery. They also demonstrated their courage and spirit of sacrifice to go out and find their wounded infantry comrades in the rice fields or on the mountain sides, without hesitating to take enormous risks."

"We're always moved to speak of the infantry but, in the First Cav, the helicopter pilots play a major role, whether they're at the controls of lift ships, gunships, or scouts. For example, between twenty-six and thirty-one January, the ceiling was so low that the choppers had to fly below fifty feet. At this altitude they're very vulnerable. In spite of this vulnerability, the Huey gunships responsible for providing supporting fire did not hold back in their mission of seeking out and engaging the enemy."

"Near Bong Son, Major Roger Bartholomew, 'black Bart,' the 'Ace' of the 2[d] of the 20th ARA, discovered a 12.7mm that was harassing the grunts. He neutralized it with rockets and killed six crewmembers. He could have left. But no! He lands next to the bunker and goes to recover the 12.7 so that the NVA can't put it back in service. That's the spirit of the Cav!"

"But what kind of special role did the First Cav play using air assault tactics in this operation that mobilized twenty thousand men?"

"In fact, there were five maneuver phases during these forty-one days. To summarize, the South Vietnamese, the Koreans, and the Marines closed off the seacoast and we attacked and cleaned up five different places, successively or simultaneously. We used intelligence in real time that was gained in action to launch one or several other successful engagements. That's what pushed the NVA to throw in the sponge."

"General, did you have any opportunity to try anything new, with respect to Ia Drang for example?"

"Certainly. DIVARTY, Division Artillery, played a big role. For example, we used CH-47 Sky Cranes to move 155mm Howitzers into the operational area, from Camp Radcliff to the Bong Son Special Forces Camp. We also loaned our Skycranes to the Marines for them to lift their heavy guns. You know that I'm very attentive to innovation. I can tell you that for the ARA, the aerial rocket artillery, we've adapted the Huey to mount the SS11 wire-guided missile, twin to the 2.75in rocket but more accurate. We've also turned the Chinook into a bomber to take care of enemy tunnels and bunkers. The CH-47 can drop napalm and CS gas. Using CS, which is more effective than tear gas, we can save a lot of civilian lives and police up more of the NVA as prisoners."

"President Johnson ordered you to change the name of the operation. *Masher* was too out of sync with an image of pacification. Did *White Wing* have some dimension other than searching for and destroying VC and NVA?"

"The objective of the operation, whatever it was called, was to drive out the North Vietnamese, who had massively infiltrated the area, and to try to reestablish government authority in this region of half a million inhabitants."

"The First Cav has gotten into psychological warfare. We've saturated the An Lao Valley with leaflets to convince the people to leave. We've over-flown the area with helicopters equipped with loudspeakers with messages in Vietnamese and we've moved people who want to get out by Chinook, with their baggage, chickens, pigs, and even buffaloes."

"But do you believe that by bombing and destroying tens of hamlets, like you've done along the coast, and by burning out their coconut trees, you've made any friends among the villagers?"

"It's true, sir, that we're not using kid gloves. Could we do it any other way as long as the hamlets shelter machine gun nests camouflaged in their huts? Thank you gentlemen. We'll talk again!"

"General! Excuse me. One last question. The VC have directly attacked you at home in An Khe by mortaring your headquarters. Are you going to react?"

"Go on back to your regular sources. I'm reserving the 'exclusives' for Charlie."

Kinnard did not at all appreciate the attack on his headquarters on top of Hon Cong. Right after *Operation Masher/White Wing* ended, he prepared his response. Intelligence led him to believe that the VC had sent three thousand sappers into the area to attack An Khe again. During the month of March, he is going to have the 1st and 3d Brigades minutely comb through the area around base camp. The terrain presents difficult access problems with very few suitable LZs.

Kinnard kicks off *Operation Jim Bowie* using many resources. He gives the mission of opening the way into the otherwise difficult to penetrate area to Lieutenant Colonel Robert Malley, commanding the 8th Engineer Battalion. The engineers chopper small bulldozers onto the hilltops and the crest lines to prepare LZs. At the same time, tens of patrols penetrate the forest daily to set up ambushes and gather information on the two VC brigades.

But the results are very disappointing when measured by the effort. The Vietcong have had enough time to get out in good order without being found or fixed. *Operation Jim Bowie* costs the 1st and 3d Brigades 380 wounded, many among them from cuts and punctures from the famous pungi stakes, hidden bamboo stakes, sharpened and usually the cause of potentially serious infection. Other troopers suffered burns from brush fires lit by rockets or artillery. All of that for twenty-seven VC killed.

Kinnard is frustrated. The terrain has bogged down the Cav. Its companies have futilely thrashed through the jungle chasing a faster enemy. He has been working to refine the tactics and adapt them better to this war, and so stay master of the game. But for him, the game is over. His tour of duty is at an end. On 6 April 1966, another paratrooper, General John Norton, takes command of the First Cavalry Division.

Translator's Notes

[1] The term "fix" in a military context means to so engage an enemy force that it is unable to break contact and thus is incapable of initiating some other activity and is itself subject to destruction when a sufficient force superiority is mustered.

CHAPTER XI

"Jack" Norton, the new patron of the First Cav, arrives at a good time. He inherits a perfectly polished tool. The Major General, girded as always in jungle fatigues and web gear, receives Moore and Litle. Norton is tall and strongly built. He has a John Wayne-like face with chiseled nose and chin. He has the looks and presence that go with command of the elite Air Cavalry Division. He is the son of an officer, born at Fort Monroe in April 1918, a 1941 West Point graduate where he was First Captain. He has spent his entire career in airborne units, first in Europe in the 82^d Airborne Division, then in Korea where he commanded the 2^d Combat Group of the 4th Regiment of the First Cav.

Jack Norton is thus a Cav veteran and an accomplished sky soldier: a paratrooper and pilot, both fixed-wing and rotary. A Brigadier General since 1963, he was the Assistant Commandant of the Infantry School at Fort Benning. Westmoreland selected him as the successor to Kinnard. It took a heavyweight to fill the boots of the soldier who created the air cavalry concept.

Five days after the end of *Operation Davy Crockett*, on 15 May, the 3^d Brigade S2 receives a report. A Special Forces patrol out of the Vinh Thanh SF Camp intercepted a small group of VC a few kilometers to the east of their base. They recovered a 120mm mortar sight, firing tables, and a plotting board from the bodies. Decoded and translated documents revealed a plan for an attack on the Green Beret Camp and the hamlets in the valley.

"Do you really believe this, this attack plan? They would be taking a really big chance in an area so close to us!" Norton, perplexed, asks Moore.

"Sir, Ho Chi Minh's birthday is in four days. It's completely possible that they want to show that they're still able to take the initiative."

"If you're right, we've got to dig into the area right away to see what's up."

The next day, at 1000 hours, Bravo Company of the 2^d of the 8th lands at *LZ Hereford*. It is a narrow clearing covered with elephant grass, pinched between wooded hillsides above the Green Beret Camp located to the East. The LZ accommodates just one slick at a time. The first chopper arrives on final. An SF Sergeant guides it in. By his side is his Vietnamese counterpart and an interpreter. In Indian File the Iroquois come in, one after the other, to land their troops. Captain John Coleman quickly assembles his company in a covered position and issues his orders.

"We'll move out in column up to the crest line, third, first, fourth, and second, in that order. Watch your intervals—keep spaced out."

The column moves out. The sun is high. It is swelteringly hot. Aside from two cases of heat exhaustion and a punji stake wound, all is quiet.

"Three-six, keep the lead. Get security down along both sides of the slope," Coleman orders when they reach the crest line. The men move out again, sweat soaked, wearing soft caps. It is too hot for helmets.[1]

Up front, the infantrymen move out cautiously, watching for suspect movement in the grass and bushes. The point man suddenly freezes, raising his hand. The column halts. He shoulders his rifle and fires. A short 5.56mm burst of fire resounds off the hillsides.

"What goes?"

"I saw, like, someone running. I'm going to see if I got him!"

As he moves forward, intense fire answers the short M16 burst. The 3ᵈ Platoon dives to the ground. The noise of explosions rolls over the hills. The Captain moves quickly to his RTO and takes the handset. "Meany, what's goin' on?"

"We're held up by some dug in VC. They're hidden good."

"Hold on, we'll break you loose. I'll get one six to send one of his elements around their flank. They'll be coming up on your right. Watch out for 'em." The 1ˢᵗ Platoon Leader sends his first squad off to flank the Charlies on their left. The squad moves down off the right side of the crest a way and then forward, coming up well off the right flank of the lead platoon. The Americans do not even reach a point even with the 3ᵈ Platoon before a squad of VC moves out of concealment and cuts them down. They are all killed but one. Seriously wounded, he plays dead, and so avoids a *coup de grace.*

Meany and his men are not able to help their comrades. They are nailed down by automatic weapons fire. His radio is hit and destroyed. He is out of contact with Coleman. "Fuck! We're not going to let ourselves get screwed by these assholes!" yells Meany, to fire up his troops. He initiates several probes to show the VC his determination, but each time he suffers additional losses. He has the disagreeable impression of getting surrounded. Very much at home in the high grass and thick vegetation the Charlies crawl and deploy easily.

One VC sapper, AK47 in the crook of his elbow, snakes along

through the grass. He rises up slightly and, crouching, moves forward on flat feet, duck-like. He comes up to a tree, shoulders his assault rifle and gently parts the greenery with the barrel of his weapon. He seems to smile. He has successfully slipped up on his enemy. "It's full of *My*" he muses to himself.[2] No more than ten meters distant, clustered together, large helmeted men move about around a radio. He closes one eye and squeezes the trigger. The AK47 jumps, and the burst downs three men. The Charlie flattens himself behind the tree trunk, moves around behind it, and looks for another target. He hears a flat sound behind him, like a falling stone, and instinctively turns to look. On the ground, a round, green object hisses. As soon as he sees it, the grenade explodes. The M26 lacerates his flesh and knocks him, lifeless, on his back. He had had just enough time to kill the RTO and two sergeants in the 3[d] Platoon before the grenade neutralized him.

Coleman divides his 2[d] Platoon in an attempt to link up with Meany. RPD and AK47 fire hit the men who move out on the right.[3] They have to mount two counterattacks to recover their dead and wounded. They are not able to get to all of them. Finally, they are pushed back inside their own original perimeter.

Brusquely, lightening tears open the sky. Thunder adds its crashing to the clash of arms. The heat of the day nourished enormous clouds that all at once unleash their moisture in a stormy downpour, a deluge! A curtain of water falls on the hill transforming the ground into a gluey and slippery trap. "You can't see a fucking thing through all this green shit. All we need now is a flood. I can't believe the noise this fucking rain makes!" grouses a pissed off grunt. The Charlies take advantage of the rain and noise to infiltrate more of their people in closer and increase their advantage over the isolated platoon.

Coleman elects to go on the defense and to strengthen his position in a clearing at the top of the hill. He regroups his company minus around the clearing with the 1st Platoon at six O'clock and the 2[d] Platoon at twelve O'clock relative to the direction of their settling in on the summit. The men listen to the close by firefight between the 3[d] Platoon and the VC. The Americans dig in. Their two-man foxholes fill with water as they dig. They cover their positions with panchos in a futile attempt to keep from floundering in positions that quickly resemble earthen bathtubs.

The sky darkens with the heavy overcast. The enemy takes advantage of the obscurity to harass Coleman's Company. In their holes, the nerves of the men are on edge, their senses sharp. They empty their magazines at shadows that surge malevolently from behind a bush or around a clump of grass.

132

"*Sir*, look, those aren't just VC out there. They aren't all in black pajamas. There! Those are NVA regulars."

"Yup, you're right!" exclaims Coleman. "We're too close to them and to the 3ᵈ Platoon to call in artillery unless things get worse. We need to do this one on our own. It's 1630. We've an hour and a half of daylight left. We've got to take advantage of it to get to the rest of our dead and wounded."

He calls his 1ˢᵗ Platoon Leader over. "Take two squads out to the east to bring back our guys. Make sure you get 'em all. Keep me posted. Move out right away while we have daylight." An hour later, when the patrol brings the wounded into the perimeter, his medics check the field dressings and bind untreated wounds. The dead rest under panchos.

Coleman calls his officers and platoon sergeants to the CP. "In my opinion, the Charlies have an accurate count of our strength. They know we're isolated and are goin' to want to finish ..."

"Watch out! Incoming!" Explosions seed the edge of the clearing—60mm mortar rounds and B40 Recoilless Rifle rounds, one after another. "*Tien Len! Tien Len!*" An attack by the book, with an artillery prep followed by charging infantry—one wave, then others.

Bravo Company resists, but with each assault they repulse Coleman loses men. Cloud cover darkens the sky. The ceiling is low, night approaches. The medics can do little more to put the wounded at ease. The wounded themselves no longer dare to ask if they have a chance of being lifted out. Three of the medics are wounded.[4]

The silence is heavy and just as sticky as the air. "*Listen,*" comments a trooper. A collective murmur can be heard coming from the wounded. The rain drums without stop on the leaves and drowns out other sounds. "Flap, Flap." The familiar sound finally gets the upper hand. "Yeah, I'm sure. That's a chopper," a medic announces. Before the grunts can take stock of their own impressions two Hueys surge over the bare crest line.

"Hey!" From the hillside a shout of joy salutes the passage of the two helicopters. Coleman's radio crackles. The Captain dashes for the radio. "Sir," announces his RTO," it's Colonel Brady himself, from the 2ᵈ of the 20ᵗʰ." Coleman grabs the handset. "Welcome! It's good to see you. What have you got for us? Over."

"I'm heading south. I'll come back along the axis of the crest line. Tell me where I need to make my rocket run. Over."

The two aircraft disappear into the night. The NVA, who sense their prey escaping, lance a violent assault. They are just a few meters from Bravo Company, in the open. The rockets reap through the wave of enemy infantrymen. The ARA ships make several passes that break the NVA vise.

On the ground the grunts are galvanized. "Get ready," shouts Coleman. "We're goin' to unass our holes after the final ARA pass and charge. Get ready … ten seconds … *Go!*" As the final 2.75in rockets detonate, the survivors of Bravo Company drive into the enemy lines and burn their last cartridges. The VC, surprised, break contact and vanish into the forest. The noise of fire becomes sporadic and the fighting ends. Coleman reflexively looks at his watch: 2000 hours. The hill is calm again.

Coleman calls his Platoon Leaders over to his CP, a soggy as yet incomplete hole in the ground. "Okay guys, good show! We'll stay around our clearing for the night. Battalion's goin' to bring in Alpha Company, 1st of the 12th, back at *LZ Hereford*. Keep workin' on your positions. Don't quit 'til they're deep, even if the water's up to your chest. I want one LP per platoon.[5] Keep at least a fifty-percent alert and get your Claymores and trip flares out." Turning to his FO: "I want a target plotted up front and behind us along the crest and one down each side. Don't fire them in until Alpha closes. Make sure every platoon has your push and those targets." To his leaders again: "I need a casualty report from everybody in fifteen minutes. And be God damn careful. We've got friendlies coming in along the crest behind us. Make sure all your guys know that, One-Six."

Casualty reports come in to Coleman's RTO. "*Sir*, we've got twenty KIA and forty wounded." Bravo Company is down to an effective strength of forty-five men.[6]

"Damn! Well, we'll hang in here until Alpha Company gets here. They're coming in on *Hereford* now. I'm counting on Captain Cummings to move up smartly!"

Later: "It's almost 2200. They ought to close in soon. We haven't heard any shooting. I hope they didn't get lost."

"Sir, Alpha Company's got contact with One-Six's LP."

"Good. We can breathe easy now. Put the word out to everybody—friendlies moving in. Let's go find their CO." Coleman and his RTO leave their position to find Captain John Cummings.[7]

"Hey Jack! Am I glad to see you!"

"Next time pick a less shitty place to start a fight."

The two Captains decide to stay in the same perimeter and double its strength. Alpha Company occupies a little over half of the position and Cummings puts out his own LPs. The night passes without incident. About 0600 the sky behind the hill turns a dirty gray. Everyone and everything is soaked by the early morning humidity. The men, cold and long immobile, move slowly. Numb and stiff, the Americans peer through the haze. They greet the new day with a mad minute that shatters the quiet dawn. Exploding mortar and B40 rounds respond. The Americans, just stretching their limbs, quickly duck deeper into their foxholes. The NVA are back. They have also been reinforced.

"They're giving it everything they've got. Seeing as how they've got mortar support, there's at least a battalion," Coleman notes to Cummings. Alpha and Bravo Companies aggressively throw back charge after charge of enemy infantry. Every fighting position is the object of a fight to the finish. With bayonet, knife, pistol, or grenade, the Americans, with the enemy on top of them, finally halt the obstinate assaults of the men in green. The troopers are amazed by the wild NVA attacks.

"Go easy with your ammo. We haven't got much left. Use your bayonets. Finish them off with cold steel!" yells an Alpha Company Sergeant, Bowie knife in hand. Most of the grunts are on their last magazine, their M16s on semi-auto mode.

"Good show, guys! Don't let up yet. We've got another company coming up from the 1st of the 12th that landed at *Hereford* just a while ago." Charlie Company, 1st of the 12th, arriving by forced march from the *LZ*, falls on the NVA flanks. Aware of the danger, the enemy prefers to break contact. The sound of gunfire slackens, then ceases.

Coleman rejoins Cummings and gives him a friendly slap on the back. "Jack, that's the second time in twenty-four hours that my Company pulled its ass out of the fire. You bring me luck!" The grunts, tired and worn, climb out of their holes, their faces marked with powder burns, and spattered with dirt and gore. Scattered about in green uniforms of different shades lie the still bodies of the dead.

Coleman and Cummings quickly assemble their Companies. Platoons take a head and casualty count. Bravo Company has twenty-five killed and sixty-two wounded: Alpha; three dead and thirty-seven wounded. The commanders immediately organize the evacuation of their casualties.

"We can't let them get a head start on us, or any break at all," interjects Cummings who wants to go after the VC. Charlie Company, with the remaining able-bodied men of Alpha and Bravo Companies, forms on line to comb through the hillsides from where the North Vietnamese attacked. They find only thirty-eight enemy bodies.

"Shit! Those bastards have hauled their dead off! It can't be that we zapped less than forty," grumbles a big sergeant with a knife.

"We can be sure now they belong to the 2^d VC Regiment. They're equipped like NVA regulars, but they're even crueler, nastier bastards," an RTO, who only got through the fight thanks to his .45, answers back.

"Hey, look! The grass and the ground are all bloody. There's some field dressings over there! Yea, we kicked their ass, and they moved out with their dead and wounded." The Sergeant checks out the area, like a bloodhound, trying to figure out what happened.

Bravo Company finishes evacuating its wounded and stays on the position during the day of 17 May. Two days later, a prisoner captured on the other side of Vinh Thanh reveals that the 2^d VC Regiment to which he belonged lost between 130 and 200 men in its fight with Bravo Company."

Coleman and his men get a break while they wait for replacements. The same day the Division kicks off a big operation, *Operation Crazy Horse*, in conjunction with the South Vietnamese and the Korean Tigers. Crazy Horse was one of the great Indian Chiefs after whom the 5th and 7th Cavalry Regiments long chased during the Indian Wars.

Norton orders Colonel John Hennessy of the 1st Brigade to intercept and destroy the 2^d VC Regiment that has already lost a company at Vinh Thanh, and to find and fix the 12th NVA Regiment that is preparing to attack the Special Forces Camp to commemorate the birthday of Ho Chi Minh on 19 May. Lieutenant Colonels William Roy, with the 1st of the 5th, and Otis Lynn, with the 2^d of the 12th make unopposed assault landings to the east of Vinh Thanh Valley and of Soui Ca.

The region is fairy-like. Under a triple canopy the almost virgin land is in perpetual twilight under a thick green roof. Here and there rays of sunlight pierce the canopy creating spots of magical illumination. The ground is completely overgrown with aggressive vines, spiny rattan trees, sharp palm fronds, and impenetrable bamboo thickets. The actual lay of the land only appears at the last minute, revealed by wet and clinging moss and rushing water. The Americans are both fascinated and oppressed by this natural exuberance, lovely and threatening all at once.

Moving through the thick jungle is hell. Not only is it impossible to find any LZs, but the enemy is invisible. On foot, there is the constant worry about booby traps: poisoned punji stakes, trip-wired grenades. The 2^d of the 12th inserts at *LZ Horse*, near Hill 766. The moveout thus begins into a landscape that evokes both dreams and nightmares.

"Sergeant, take five men and break a trail to the top of this hill, Hill 766, got it? Do it!" Staff Sergeant Jimmy Stewart and his team attack the hill, slipping silently into the vegetation. Stewart takes a compass reading and follows the slope of the ground. He can see neither horizon nor sky, nothing but tree trunks and leaves. He makes sure his men maintain a proper interval while keeping in sight of each other, a paradoxical and difficult exercise.

The men regroup to climb over a huge fallen tree, overgrown with moss and ferns, that holds them up. The men step out along the trunk, the bark slippery in the wet jungle. Behind them, Stewart sees his men bunch up. "Hey! Spread out!" A long burst is the response. Fired from higher up the slope, the rounds cut through the curtain of greenery and hit his five men. "The fuckers," the Sergeant impotently curses just under his breath as he ducks down behind the trunk on which he had been leaning. The NVA machine gun stops firing. The only noise comes from wounded soldiers struggling to control pain. Stewart freezes in place, quiet, listening. He hears the sound of approaching voices over the rustling of disturbed leaves and branches, then dialog. "Those aren't Americans, they're Charlies," he muses, "coming to check out the results."

Stewart carefully lines up his M16 in the direction of the voices. Ten meters away the outline of two NVA pith helmets appear. He looses a short burst. The silhouettes drop from sight. The Sergeant moves quickly to a new covered position and uses the moment to let his men know that he is still there. "Don't move at all if you are under cover. I'll stay here until the rest of the unit gets here. He crawls to a large Kapoc tree whose buttressing roots provide good concealment. From there, he slips between stumps and fallen trees to where his men lie to collect the ammo from the dead and stock it behind his tree. He faces the enemy, alone.

He drives back three assaults, emptying magazine after magazine as he holds off the increasingly enraged enemy infantrymen. There are already eight bodies around his tree, all dead Charlies. The metallic clack of his bolt locking to the rear announces another empty magazine. It was his last. He removes the bolt and buries it. He still has some grenades, and keeps the enemy at bay. They cannot close and finish off his buddies. By now they have Steward located. A machine gun works diligently over his general location. The rounds strike ever closer. He leaps up to find a better position. A burst cuts him down in mid-stride. Limbs askew, Stewart collapses, lifeless.[8]

His solitary combat lasted four hours. Staff Sergeant Stewart kept his promise; his wounded comrades are evacuated. Twenty-three North Vietnamese are sprawled in death around the body of the Sergeant. The slopes of Hill 766 are swept clean by other Companies of the 2^d of the 12th, which move outward from *LZ Horse.*

Further to the North, the five Companies of the 1st of the 8th move out from *LZ Hereford* and comb through "Happy Valley." The Americans have rebaptized all of the local topography. The Vietnamese names are unpronounceable and the GIs cannot resist an opportunity to inject a bit of humor and derision into the situation.

"Lieutenant Crum, take the recon platoon and lead out. If you come on anything at all suspicious, hold up and check it out." Ray Martin, Captain of Charlie Company, wants to advance with care. Abandoned trenches and tunnels are everywhere. Robert Crum and his Platoon plunge into the forest. On his right, a listening post notes his passing. Its leader stands, raising an arm. Crum moves to his location.

"Lots of luck sir! All these old NVA positions really suck."

"Yeah! You could hide a whole shit-load of people in 'em." Crum beckons to his RTO, some distance off to the side, who then heads toward his Lieutenant. Geysers of dirt erupt as 12.7mm and 7.62mm rounds rain down upon the ground all around them. Mortally wounded, Crum collapses. He has just enough time to see his men scythed down by the same salvo of fire. Alone, David Dolby, the machine gunner, comes through unscathed. He dives to the ground, prone behind his M60. He returns fire immediately to try and cover his Lieutenant. Joined to his weapon as a single entity he furiously feeds it belt after belt of linked ammo. In two bounds, he arrives at Crum's side.

"Break contact! Get away!" orders the Lieutenant who musters his last forces to vocalize the order. "Get out of here, get the men out!" Dolby binds his wounds, but Crum is already glassy-eyed. Dolby moves away, in a crouch, to gather up the survivors and the rest of the Platoon. From here on he is the senior man. But the NVA are lying in wait. Bursts of fire force him to take cover.

"Crum's dead. Pass it up," Dolby orders the RTO, who had not closed on the Lieutenant before the shooting started. Dolby spots the position of the 12.7mm machine gun. Carefully, he fires at it with short well-aimed bursts. A duel begins between the dull-sounding slow pounding of the heavy machine gun and the dry nervous cough of the M60. The rounds from the 12.7mm work over the ground and vegetation around Dolby. Thanks to its more rapid rate of fire, the M60 gives Dolby a slight edge as burst responds to burst. Dolby is tenacious, and an expert with his M60. Each time the NVA fire at him, he looks for the muzzle flashes. Concentrating on them as his targets he succeeds in cleaning up several enemy positions that support the machine gunner. His bursts slam right through the firing apertures of the NVA bunkers. Some of them hit the machine gun crew. Dolby is indefatigable, constantly changing position to throw off the enemy fire, while at the same time caring for and reassuring the wounded.

Heavy rain joins the party. The ground becomes slippery, but the falling water muffles other sounds and hampers enemy visibility. He chooses this moment to move the wounded away from the enemy fire. This done, he goes back on the offensive. Dolby has spotted other automatic weapons emplacements. With a series of leaps and low crawls, the M60 always at the ready, he gets up to within thirty meters of the line of NVA positions. A large deadfall gives him cover. Winded, he crouches low behind his cover while catching his breath, all the while observing the enemy positions through the thick branches of the fallen tree.

With the M60 mounted on its bipod, he removes a smoke grenade from his web gear. After pulling the pin, he gets up carefully from the ground, gets in a good balanced stance, and throws it to within a few feet of the NVA's dug-in positions. Hidden behind the trunk of the fallen tree, Dolby watches with the trace of a smile as a plume of yellow smoke rises from the canister. In a few seconds, an ARA chopper falls like a shark toward the smoke and looses a volley of rockets. The NVA trench and bunker disappear in the explosion.

Dolby bounds out looking for another target, pursuing the common unspoken objective he shares with the chopper crew. He conducts his one-man war for several hours, marking targets for the gunship. Often he uses his M60 to clean up a bunker already hit with rockets. The enemy, still spoiling for a fight, bring up fresh fodder to crew their machine guns and fight on. Dolby has to go back four times to one of the bunkers, firing away with his M60, surrounded by enemy dead. He occupies and dominates the ground until all his buddies are medivacked and, still alive, is the last to leave.[9]

While David Dolby is fighting his war, the 1st Brigade continues *Operation Crazy Horse*, with an operational radius of twenty kilometers, working in liaison with a South Vietnamese unit and the Koreans. Despite the losses it has already suffered, the 2d Vietcong Regiment is not out of action. The hard core of its forces is located in the mountains between the Ca River and the Vinh Tanh Valley.

"It's all well and good to search through the jungle, but it's stupid," says Norton during a staff meeting. "You've got to keep from playing their game. On the ground, they're strong. They have well-prepared positions, and they know the terrain. Everything's booby-trapped. We've got more casualties from cuts, bites, leaches, and Malaria than from gunshot wounds. The zone we have to cover is very extensive. In this very nasty piece of ground the 2^d VC Regiment is very well positioned. Block all the routes of egress and we'll use our air power to get the bastards on the move."

"Sir, we're going to have a hard time closing off this area. There are going to be holes through our positions," objects John Hennessey, 1st Brigade Commander.

"Maybe, but this time, we're going to go all out to close off all avenues of escape. The Chinooks of the 228th are equipped to lay down CS. That'll make them get out of their holes. Then, three days of B-52 strikes along with all the artillery we can dump on them."

Norton's program gets under way according to plan. The coordination between the Air Force and the 1st Cav artillery is careful and close. Norton, in his command chopper, circles carefully around the area to check out the effect of the ongoing bombardment. The fires are so heavy that one of the helicopters following his is hit by friendly fire.

The bombs, the projectiles, and the gas oblige the enemy to flee their hideouts. But some of the survivors once again know how to take advantage of their knowledge of the land and escape from the mousetrap set by the Americans and their allies. *Operation Crazy Horse* ends on 5 June. Three hundred and fifty Vietcong bodies are identified, to which G2 adds an additional estimated three hundred and thirty VC KIA. The Division lost nineteen dead, one missing, and three hundred and fifty-six wounded.

General Norton convenes the press at Camp Radcliff to provide an account of the operation. "Even beyond the personnel losses inflicted on the enemy, this operation was a success. On the tactical level, we cut the Yellow Star Division to pieces with our different attacks. We forced its principal units to disperse and withdraw northward. Also, we've recovered many documents that will help us, in turn, disrupt the organization of the political and terrorist apparatus they had in Binh Dinh Province. On the logistical level, we've broken their back. We seized forty-five tons of rice and ten tons of salt. To that we can add large stocks of munitions that we destroyed."

"In the preparation, and above all the execution of *Crazy Horse*, the allied forces demonstrated their ability to operate in a coordinated manner, and each of them with perfect efficiency. In this regard, I would like to point out the Korean Tigers who, in the final phase, themselves killed 120 VC."

"Still, this operation leaves me with a bit of regret. First off, because we didn't succeed in finishing off the Sao Vang. Although we chopped them up badly, some of their elements managed to disperse in the mountain and forest."

"One other thing particularly affects me. One of you was mortally wounded while he was with us on operation. Sam Castan, who had become a familiar friend of the First Team, is the first journalist killed while covering our units in combat. I hope he'll be the last. I salute him now and all of you who have the courage to share our risks."

Translator's Notes
[1] First Cav troops, when possible, on many operations wore patrol caps instead of steel helmets. To have any chance of keeping up with the lightly equipped, unencumbered, elusive, and swift moving NVA and VC it was necessary to travel as light as possible. The need to avoid heat injuries in the very hot and humid climate encouraged this practice. For the same reasons, First Cav fighting troops never wore flack jackets unless they were in a motorized convoy, which is to say very infrequently.

[2] Americans.

[3] The RPD is the Soviet 7.62mm light machine gun RPD or a version produced in China, the Chinese Communist light machine gun Type 56. It fires the same 7.62mm cartridge as the AK47 Assault Rifle. The cartridge itself is shorter and less powerful than NATO 7.62mm cartridges and not compatible with weapons firing those cartridges.

[4] Combat medics are heroes among heroes. They suffer the highest casualties of all, moving out into hostile fire to care for the wounded. In these early Vietnam years, in the First Cavalry Division, combat medics, if they were very lucky, had about a fifty-percent chance of surviving their tour. Virtually all of those who were not killed sustained one or more wounds.

[5] Listening Post. LPs provide early warning of enemy approach. Coming back into the perimeter in the middle of the night in such an event is particularly risky.

[6] The ratio of two wounded to one killed was pretty much standard for a sharp firefight. The numbers do not add up to the strength prescribed in Tables of Organization and Equipment (TO&E) for a rifle company (about one hundred and sixty men). This is because a handful of men remain fulfilling duties at Base Camp in An Khe, another handful are either on rest and recreational leave (R&R) or regular leave and out of country for a few days. Most absences represent men hospitalized for illness or

141

wounds that will return to their unit and so are not replaced. Some shortages also reflect KIA for whom replacements have not yet arrived. During this period in Vietnam, company field strength was usually between eighty and one hundred men.

[7] Moving around inside a perimeter after dark is risky. After a good fight fingers are light on triggers, and exhausted men often become disoriented in their foxholes in the dark.

[8] Stewart is awarded the Congressional Medal of Honor.

[9] Dolby is awarded the Congressional Medal of Honor.

CHAPTER XII

Since 4 May, the 1st and 2^d of the 7th, the 1st of the 9th Cav, as well as South Vietnamese units have been in contact with the 9th Battalion of the Quyet Tam Regiment near the village of Tuy An.

Observing from his command chopper, Hal Moore overflies the coast, heading toward Bong Son. He is at an altitude of fifteen hundred feet. It is 5 May 1966. He hits the intercom button and addresses the pilot. "Look at that light. You'd think we were in an add for a tour operator. It's got everything: sun, sea, sand, mountains, coconut palms. Just a month ago the ceiling was only fifty feet and it was cold. What a contrast! What's the temperature?"

"One hundred and thirteen on the ground with ninety-eight percent humidity, a sauna."

"But the visibility's super. Charlie's going to have to hide. Get Bullwhip Six for me, and head for Tuy An." Colonel Moore, his S3, and the pilot are all monitoring the 3^d Brigade push. Third Brigade units are still in contact with the elements of the 9th NVA Battalion, a part of the Queyt Tam Regiment. The 1st and 2^d Battalions, 7th Cav as well as the 9th Cav and an ARVN recon unit have surrounded a village and are pounding the place with artillery before they move in. Moore warns his ground commanders not to let the enemy slip away.

His pilot inquires: "Who's Bullwhip Six now?"

"It's Lieutenant Colonel Jim Smith. He got in last night. He replaces Bob Shoemaker in this operation. *Operation Davy Crockett*, there's a name that won't upset President Johnson."

"For me, sir, Bullwhip Six will always be Lieutenant Colonel Stockton—a fine officer! When did he leave Vietnam?"

"In December."

"Right! That was a ceremony. He reviewed his troops on a horse, leading his mule, Maggie, packing an M79 and a rocket pod. The mule was named after his wife. She didn't survive his departure by much—got blown away by a nervous guy on perimeter guard. But you sir, you're still here."

"Yeah. They asked me to extend—so I did. Look, head over by those Hooks that are just offloading 105s.[1] Fly over that Battery of the 1st of the 21st. It should be about ready to fire itself in."[2]

The Huey flies around the chain of CH-47s that have just offloaded their cargoes. They leave the LZ with a strong rotor wash. The artillerymen, bare from the waist up, work with alacrity to set up their guns, sandbagging the trails down in the laterite. Very

The Coastal Campaign, 1966

144

quickly, around each howitzer, each man takes his place, ready to fire.

"Good. They're going to start the prep. Head for Tuy An, over to the right so you don't get in the way of the artillery," Moore orders. With his gaunt face, his prominent cheekbones, his deep eyes, Hal Moore is one of the major figures of the First Cav. He has the appearance as well as the spirit of a warrior-monk. Veteran of the Korean War, he is the victor of Ia Drang. He has forged his reputation thanks not only to his tactical sense but also to the attention he gives his Garry Owen troopers. No missing in action. He leaves no one behind. On board in September 1965, he has had two commands, the 1st of the 7th in the Ia Drang, and keeps the 3d Brigade through June of 1966. According to the journalists, he is the champion hunter of VC and NVA. This is how the *Chicago Daily News* presents him. It is true, out of 4,500 North Vietnamese killed during the first six months of 1966, 3,200 are attributable to his Brigade.

"Fire!" The 105 batteries of the 1st of the 21st Artillery recoil into their shock absorbers, the blasts from their muzzles thundering through the hills. A fifteen-minute fire for effect is underway. The Red Legs manhandle projectiles, powder charges, and expended canisters at a hellish pace, indifferent to the heat and noise. A few kilometers away, an observer in an OH-13 directs their fire. The continuous pounding destruction is impressive.

The pressure is such that it ought to force the Vietcong to abandon their positions. The rolling fire should throw them back into the passes held by the 7th Cav and the 1st of the 9th Cav.

"Cease fire!" Silence descends upon the cannoneers. In the fire pits the men, dripping sweat, clear away the expended shell casings. They freeze in place, groggy, as though recovering from some physical struggle.

"How many did we get?" the artillerymen ask, as they recover their breath, interested in their score, like athletes, eager to do well. Word comes over the radio from an airborne observer: "sixty-one KIA. Out."

"Yeah!" the Red Legs yell in unison, satisfied with the score.

But the VC, aware of the danger, have not moved. They have suffered through the deluge without leaving their holes, despite their losses. For them, only one solution: wait for night to slip out of the net. Hal Moore had the choppers patrolling all night, rummaging through the darkness with their searchlights.

The 1st Battalion of the 7th Cav, sent as reinforcement, marches toward the south of Tuy An village. In the early morning hours the 1st of the 7th attacks. They move carefully forward, but all the living have disappeared, gone, vanished into the jungle. The VC have left 104 dead on the field, then taken advantage of the steep terrain to slip between the 1st of the 7th and the South Vietnamese Company. Hal Moore, accompanying the 1st of the 7th on this operation, is struck with the thought: "These bastards have put one over on us again. With the 1st of the 7th and the 1st of the 9th we bust our tails raking through the valley looking for them. Let's put all our folks to the south of Tuy An and search the villages along the hillside. They have to have water and food, more than ever with the wounded they're carrying." Moore dispatches his two Battalions of the 7th Cavalry along with the 1st Battalion, 9th Cavalry after them.

An RTO interrupts Moore with a message, passing him a handset. "What? A scout ship is receiving ground fire? Where? At Thanh Son? Where's that? Show me on the map! There's a Thanh Son three klicks south of Tuy An! Just now, I heard of a Thanh Son much further away. Damn! With all their screwed up names, these villages were mixed up. Over."

"That's what happened! Wirth has gone down there. He's latched on to what's left of the 9th PAVN battalion. We just got his report at 1100. He's getting in position to block all the exits out of the village and box 'em in. Over."

"I'm on it. I'll get back with you. Out."

Hal Moore sends Delta Troop, 1st of the 9th to block the roads out of the village. He orders a Vietnamese mechanized unit with M113s along as support. Moore turns to his S3: "Pass on to Colonel Litle to take positions with the 2d of the 7th to the south of Thanh Son to block the PAVN escape routes." At this moment, Litle is in place with his companies sixteen kilometers north of the contact getting ready for an air assault. "Have Litle wait for me. I'll be there shortly. We'll pick the LZ together."

Bravo Company, 2d of the 7th is the first to lift off. The rest follow in stride to the rhythm of the following lifts. Before the troop carrying helicopters make their assault landing, Moore and Litle, in the Charlie-Charlie, coordinate the LZ prep. They begin with artillery followed by Phantom F-4C jets that make twelve passes dropping high explosives and napalm. Next, ARA ships of the 2d Squadron of the 20th Artillery finish off the job with 2.75-inch rockets. The troop carrying Hueys loaded with Bravo Company come in on final approach escorted by the 229th's gunships. Scarcely forty-five minutes have elapsed from the first alert of Bravo Company and its assault. Fifteen minutes later, the whole of the 2d of the 7th is on the ground, in position. While Delta Troop intercepts the NVA with jeep-mounted machine gun and 105mm recoilless rifle fire, the 2^d of the 7th executes an aerial envelopment.

Moore seems to be in the process of making quick work of an NVA battalion, in perhaps eight hours. But the North Vietnamese soldiers won't give up. They try to escape to the east. ARA helicopters are watching. Major "Black Bart" Bartholomew and his Charlie Battery of the 20th ARA battalion strike and strike again. "Enemy in the open!" The message crackles over the unit radios. On the ground, the grunts watch the helicopter sweep in fascination, listening to the echo of rockets that explode in the midst of the North Vietnamese. Thanh Son is surrounded by the following day. The battle has been going on for twenty-four hours. The enemy leaves 231 dead on the field. Moore's troops capture twenty-two North Vietnamese, among them the 9th NVA battalion's political officer. About fifty North Vietnamese seem to have escaped the net. Friendly losses are twenty-seven KIA.

This operation passes into the annals of the First Cavalry as the perfect example of a successful airmobile envelopment. *Operation Davy Crocket* has lasted only six days, but the 3^d Brigade, thanks to careful coordination between aviation, artillery, infantry, and allied units has killed 374 enemy soldiers.

In June and July 1966, The First Cav mounts *Operations Deckhouse* and *Nathan Hale* in the Tuy Hoa area, in Phu Yen province. *Nathan Hale* is the last operation in which Hal Moore participates as 3^d Brigade commander. Once again, the exercise is to find, fix, and destroy the enemy. The First Brigade is in on this operation.

On 20 June the 1st Battalion, 8th Cavalry heads for Tuy Hoa to reinforce the 2^d battalion, 327th Infantry of the 101st Airborne Division. The American soldiers link up near Trung Luong village at the top of an unnamed hill, Hill 258 on the map, where the 101st has established firebase Eagle. At dawn two days later North Vietnamese infantry mount an attack on the base now defended by Bravo Company, 1st of the 8th Cavalry. They catch the defenders in a crossfire. The company fights for four hours and, in a hand-to-hand struggle, defends its perimeter. The position holds and the Americans force the enemy to quit the field, leaving behind 134 dead on the slopes of Hill 258. For this exceptional action B Company of the 1st of the 8th receives the *Presidential Unit Citation*.

The 1st Brigade regroups during *Operation Henry Clay*. This allows it to put a new technique of penetration and reconnaissance to the test: reconnaissance by saturating an area with fire team-sized elements. The objective is to occupy the most terrain possible with the fewest number of soldiers. The battalion is divided into fifty-four teams of six men each. These reconnaissance elements are sent on patrols in Phu Bon and Dar Lac Provinces to cover an area of approximately 160 square kilometers. On this occasion the Cav returns to the Ia Drang valley and the Chu Pong Massif. It is an initiation rite for the young replacements. The names are already charged with history.

The 7th Cav had been back for the first time in April to emplace two batteries of artillery and to prepare an air assault into the Chu Pong. The 1st of the 7th had already replaced most of its casualties. Veterans of the Ia Drang fight were rare. Sergeant Steven Hansen was one of them. He had been a forward observer with Captain Nadal's Alpha Company. Without a word Steven looked over the area, incredulous. The vegetation had already covered the most visible traces of the violence of the struggle. Under the grass, however, one found all the left over bits and pieces of both sides: ammunition boxes, cartridge cases, badges, and bones. Since the fight, Steven had been promoted to sergeant in Delta Company. "Well Sarge, what's it feel like to come back?" Captain Coleman, his CO asks. "It feels very funny to walk over an area where so many people were killed. In a way I'm glad to be back, but I would rather have forgotten it all!" he answered, looking at the knoll where Colonel Moore had set up his command post. The termite hill was still there. This time only friendly artillery fire could be heard.

The 32^{d}, 33^{d}, and 66th NVA regiments had taken advantage of the absence of the Americans to reestablish a presence in the zone. General Norton, informed of their return, decided to move in, and initiated Operation *Paul Revere*. The 2^{d} of the 7th headed off for Pleiku and Kontum. Alpha and Bravo Companies occupy a perimeter in preparation for the operation. In the early morning hours they are attacked by the equivalent of a battalion of regulars. The grunts repulse three successive assault waves, their positions almost overrun. The following day Charlie Company is airlifted to the *LZ*. That night the NVA attack the position again but fail to make any penetration and retreat with losses.

For the next few days the 2^{d} of the 7th conducts platoon sized air assaults that then conducts patrols within the protective umbrella of friendly artillery. One morning the weather is so overcast that it is impossible to mount an airmobile operation. At about 1400 hours the weather clears enough to send out the 3^{d} Platoon of Alpha Company, but the twenty-six men are rapidly surrounded by at least an NVA company. The ceiling almost simultaneously closes back in. The platoon leaders and RTOs are early casualties, radio contact is lost, both with battalion and with the Fire Direc-

148

tion Center. The fighting is very violent. Aerial reinforcement is impossible; the helicopters cannot fly or navigate in the now soupy weather. The Platoon is on its own. It is soon overrun. Out of twenty-six men, eighteen are killed; some of them bayoneted by NVA soldiers as they lay wounded. Of the remaining eight, a few, including the Vietnamese interpreter, barely escape into the bush at the last minute. The others, already immobilized by wounds, play dead and survive the random NVA *coups de grace*. The North Vietnamese strip the dead and those feigning death of their weapons, uniforms, and boots, then depart, carrying off their own dead and wounded. The following day another Cav company arrives on foot at the site of the combat. The survivors are airlifted back to their unit or into medical channels, the dead, to graves registration. The NVA casualties are unknown, but estimated to be at least sixteen KIA.

A week later, it is the turn of the 1st of the 7th to deploy to the same area of operations. On one of their platoon-sized air assault and patrol operations, the 3d Platoon of their Alpha Company makes contact with a few enemy soldiers who withdraw. The Americans, eager to tangle with their NVA counterparts, charge right off on their trail. But the handful of North Vietnamese infantrymen are bait. The trap snaps shut as the NVA soldiers close back on terrain they have prepared and turn on the Americans with a heavy machine gun and automatic rifles. The 3d Platoon, too far from Alpha Company for support, calls for assistance. Bravo and Charley Companies are airlifted to an LZ just to the east of the contact. Sergeant Richard Schaaf is killed during the withdrawal while protecting the wounded. Francis Roig takes command of the platoon, and organizes several counterattacks to break contact. The 3d platoon, under his command, breaks loose of the enemy and moves back toward Alpha Company and the security of its perimeter. But the NVA, though under increasingly effective artillery fire, do not want to abandon prey within their reach. They follow closely on the heels of the 3d Platoon as it withdraws. David Frederick and George Hamilton, a machine gun team of the 3d Platoon, position themselves as a rear guard and use their M60 with marvelous efficiency until they exhaust their linked belts of ammunition. They then abandon the red hot and useless weapon and rejoin the moving platoon. At about this time Alpha Company is drawn directly into the action. The Company Commander, Captain Wands, is wounded. Second Lieutenant Jeffrey White replaces him. White, wounded in turn, keeps command of Alpha Company and takes charge of the defense. The Company repels repeated NVA assaults. During the fight, one of the medics, Elwin Polk, takes care of the wounded. He runs from one to the other providing medical assistance, sometimes venturing outside the perimeter to help and comfort those who had been unable to make it back within the company defenses.[3]

At about three in the afternoon, Bravo and Charlie Companies link up with Alpha Company. The three companies together now have the edge and establish a strong position for the night. At this point the NVA are at a severe disadvantage and are very roughly handled by the Cav. The next day the Americans take stock of enemy casualties. For the entirety of operation *Paul Revere*, jointly conducted by the 2[d] and 3[d] Brigades, the number of NVA dead counted on the field is 809. After this particularly hot pilgrimage the 1st of the 7th is assigned to defend Camp Radcliff to provide some breathing space to recover from their Ia Drang and Chu Pong adventures.

The massive replacement of troops who have completed their one-year tour occurs in mid June. The infantrymen whose tour has reached twelve months have their return "ticket" to the "world." The veterans pack their gear and return to the states. Their hard-earned skills and experience will be costly in blood to replace. The last fifteen days run out with the fear of wounds or death that could strike right up to the moment of departure. But nostalgia for the country and for their buddies is so strong that some of them extend in country, or reenlist after a short Stateside leave and volunteer to return for a second tour. The Fucking New Guys, the FNG, the draftees, offload the aircraft, proud to be joining such an outfit and anxious to be accepted and earn the friendship and esteem of the veterans.

From June to September the rotation involves 12,000 men. Starlifter C-141 aircraft of the US Air Force shuttle between Travis Air Force Base in California and Pleiku. This aerial bridge replaces the normal route that uses commercial flights landing at Tan Son Nhut and the waiting at the dismal Camp Alpha Army depot. The liaison office at Travis is a veritable travel agency that takes charge of those on orders to go as well as returning the veterans. Thereafter the aircraft are charter flights uniquely destined for Camp Radcliff. From Pleiku, the Caribou, just like busses, transport the FNG to the "Golf Course." They plunge directly into the thick of things. As soon as they offload, they find themselves bathing in sweat-soaked uniforms. Dazzled by the bright sunlight, they take refuge behind sunglasses. From the moment of their arrival, they discover a Vietnam with its own profound daily rhythm: the Vietnamese children, laughing and begging, the scrawny chickens, and the little black pigs. The longhaired emaciated old women pass in sad dignity, heedless of the American presence, without giving them a glance, their carrying poles bent under the weight of loads at each end.

In mid September, that is, barely six months after *Operation Masher/White Wing*, General Norton again leaves the high plateaus and the Cambodian border to return to Binh Dinh Province. He has good intelligence that the 3^d North Vietnamese Division is back in An Lao Valley, near Soui Ca, and in Kim Son Valley. He organizes *Operation Thayer* to pacify the whole Central Vietnam littoral. *Thayer* is scheduled to kick off on 13 September 1966.

At Division Headquarters one of the officers comes to see Norton. "Sir, there's a problem with our plans."

"Really? What is it?"

"Well, 13 September is *Organization Day* of the Division, the forty-fifth anniversary of the 1st Cav, and it marks a year that we've been in Vietnam."

"You're right. It isn't possible to change the planning for *Thayer*, that's for sure! We'll move our celebration ahead ten days."

The Division mounts a parade on the "Golf Course." Several thousand soldiers participate. All the units of the Cav are present with their colors. They march onto the metallic runway, saluted by Norton. He steps out alone before his soldiers. Facing them he recounts the history of Division and renders homage to the officers, noncommissioned officers, and soldiers already fallen in Vietnam. The soldiers, for the most part in country for only three months, are deeply moved as they hear recounted the exploits of their comrades who came over with the Division. They ask themselves what awaits them and if they will be able to live up to the reputation of the unit to which they now belong. The sun is already above Noui Nhon Hill. It is hot. The companies are perfectly aligned at "Parade Rest," facing the General. "Atten-shun," he orders. The command seems out of place, but in a single movement they respond, six thousand heels come together with a loud "clack." "Present-Arms!" In three quick movements accompanied by the sharp sound of hands on rifles, the M16s snap in position before the soldiers' chests. A heavy silence follows.

Then, as if calling them to duty, an officer reads off the names of the fallen. The names have a particularly American ring: Puerto-Rican, Italian, Irish, German, a sad litany. These are the names of the men killed in *Operation Revere II*. The ceremony pays homage to the sacrifice of all those fallen during the year past.

Thayer I is the largest air assault operation launched by the 1st Cav since its arrival in Vietnam. A three-day B-52 bombardment precedes the action. It is intended to push the North Vietnamese toward the Crow's Foot area and to oblige them to flee an area of steep terrain and heavy vegetation where they are inaccessible. Norton confides the aerial surveillance to the 1st of the 9th. Colonel Smith is to evaluate the effects of the successive air and artillery strikes before finalizing the plans. Airmobile intervention is still impossible because there are no accessible LZs. The North Vietnamese continue to move, sheltered from surveillance by the terrain and vegetation.

On 13 September, the sky is black with helicopters. One hundred and twenty Hueys and Chinooks take to the air to deliver five battalions of infantry on fourteen LZs spread about in Kim Son Valley. Their mission: eliminate the North Vietnamese and Viet Cong soldiers from Binh Dinh Province and break the communist political infrastructure.

The 1st Brigade, commanded by Colonel Archie Hyle, and the 2[d], under the command of Colonel Berenzweig, take position in a half-circle in the Valley. Also on the ground, two airmobile battalions of South Vietnamese are in position to block the northern end of the Valley and prevent the escape of the 18th NVA Regiment. Once again the enemy is well informed. He anticipates the maneuver and fades into the terrain. There is nothing left for the grunts to do but beat about in the forest and on the slopes of the hills. They conduct careful patrols stopping at the slightest noise— the cry of monkeys or flight of wild hogs. As they screen the area they progressively discover the size of the enemy infrastructure and confirm that they have recently and precipitously moved out.

The search turns into a treasure hunt. One platoon finds a hospital, others an abandoned base camp and a grenade factory. Very often what they find only amounts to a couple of cases of supplies, some linked ammunition hidden under baskets, or a pair of bloodstained black pajamas hidden in the brush.

The Chinooks unload platoons to beat through the brush and search for some indication of the enemy in the hopes of catching the Viet Cong on the move. The only notable capture is an ambulatory orchestra with a repertoire of communist music that normally tours from village to village as a part of the recruiting and propaganda effort. The searches bog down. Just like General Kinnard a year earlier in the Chu Pong, General Norton begins to have doubts.

Translator's Notes

[1] CH-47 Chinook cargo helicopters, more commonly known as "shithooks."

[2] An artillery battery "fires itself in" to verify precisely its own

position and so assure accurate supporting fire. This is especially critical because FOs routinely plot and fire in targets fifty meters from the perimeter. The troops get down in their holes when these targets are fired in, and shrapnel blasts over their heads. A mistake can mean steel in your position, not over it.

[3] The combat medics are real heroes. They suffer higher casualties than the infantrymen, exposing themselves to enemy fire as they treat the wounded under fire and move them to covered positions. See translator's note 4, Chapter 11.

CHAPTER XIII

In the Annamite Cordillera Bravo Company of the 1ˢᵗ of the 12ᵗʰ, commanded by Captain Mayer, has guests: a French television crew. Pierre Schoendoerffer, journalist; Dominique Merlin, cameraman; and Raymond Adam, soundman have come to spend four weeks with Lieutenant Joe Anderson's platoon. Anderson, twenty-four, black, is a West Point graduate.

Schoendoerffer, who knew the French Indo-Chinese war well and lived through the Battle of Dien Bien Phu, has returned to rediscover the Vietnam War, the American one. Pierre Desgraupes sent him for a special edition of the magazine *Cinq Colonnes a la Une*. The French crew arrives with two hundred kilos of materiel and, for one month will share the life of Sergeant Owens, of Lawson, of Morgan the barber, of Reese, of Bruce, of Avila, and of others.

They follow them everywhere, sleep in the hills, in the support bases where the artillery fires the whole night through. With the gathered troopers they attend chapel services conducted by a chaplain who arrives by chopper. They film the Huey that comes to bring them a hot breakfast and crashes on takeoff when it hits the trunk of a Coconut Palm, breaking in two when it hits the ground.

They film the rain and the grunts that march, eat, and sleep in the downpour, huddled under their panchos like snails. They endure the same jungle maladies as the troops, and share a grilled pig purchased from villagers. The days pass in searching villages and looking for caches of food and weapons. In the evening, some of the men sing, another plays guitar.

General Norton's perseverance finally pays off. The VC are kept very far away from their base areas by constant pressure. Also, the 7ᵗʰ, 8ᵗʰ, and 18ᵗʰ North Vietnamese Regiments are forced to fight to open themselves a path out. Intelligence indicates that these units are going to attempt to escape to the East, toward the coast.

During the night of 23 September they attack *Hammond*, a support base held by the South Vietnamese. The attack fails. Then they resolutely turn their attention to the coastal plain. By doing this, they draw attention to their location. Norton maintains the rhythm of the pursuit and establishes a large trap to corner two battalions. He decides to block them between the coast to the East, Phu Cat Mountain to the South, and the Nui Mieu hills to the North. All the escape routes are covered.

To make sure they cannot get away, he replaces the 2ᵈ Brigade with the 3ᵈ Brigade, which had been standing down. The 22ᵈ South Vietnamese Division and the Korean Tigers close the circle at Phu Cat. Division announces the end of *Operation Thayer I. Operation Irving* takes up the baton. Five battalions chopper into the operational area.

The Operation gets off to a smooth start. The scouts, the White Team from the 1st of the 9th, spot men in olive green uniforms on the beaches of the Hon Lac peninsula. They call for Red Team gunships of Alpha Troop to engage them. The gunships come in and provide fire support for the Blue Team, the infantry element, to make an assault landing. The mission of the Blues is to gather information on the ground about the enemy.

With his 1st Brigade, Colonel Archie R. Hyle is already in position in front of Hoa Hoi village. The Blue Team confirms that the NVA are well dug-in in the village behind dikes and in the shelter of reinforced sand dunes. The 1st Brigade attacks. Hyle notes that the North Vietnamese resist with great violence.

In the meantime, Captain Mayer and his Bravo Company are in the mountains. They are getting ready to attack a mountaintop. At day's end, the Captain gathers his Company, including Anderson's Platoon, around him. "Good evening! I'm pleased to have us all together; we don't get to do it very often. I'm taking this opportunity to talk to you about your part in the war, and also to explain tomorrow's mission. You see the mountain over there, covered with clouds. There's a village up there, and it's our objective. It may get exciting, but if there's resistance, whoever's there will be sorry to be fighting B Company."

Mayer sets up three cartons of C-rations as a makeshift easel. On them, with a felt-tip pen, he outlines the peak and the LZ. He unsheathes a large knife that he uses as a pointer. "I'm really not an artist, but there's a crude picture that shows what we've got to do tomorrow. We air assault into *LZ JJ* at 0700, secure the perimeter, then search the village. Okay? Well, tomorrow'll be a busy day, get some rest!"

At 0630 hours Bravo Company is up, fed, and ready to lift for their mission around *JJ*. At 0650 they are up and on the way. A few minutes before the scheduled landing, Lieutenant Colonel James Root, 1st of the 12th CO, raises Mayer on FM in his chopper. "Your mission has changed. You're not going to *LZ JJ*. We need your element to support the 1st of the 9th. The NVA have just shot down two choppers. We've got their location. The 1st Brigade is already there. We figure the NVA at two battalions. The Blues can use some help. The objective is Hoa Hoi. Your *LZ* is located between the village and the coast. Be careful. They're in well-prepared positions. It'll probably be hot going in." Hoa Hoi is about fifteen kilometers to the east of *LZ JJ*. The slicks change course and head toward the sea.

Fifteen minutes later the grunts bail off the skids and out of the slowing Hueys, shooting as they move out to secure the *LZ*. They run across sandy terrain and take cover behind paddy dikes and hedgerows. A salvo of mortar rounds lands among them as they move. Mayer is caught between two explosions. He is wounded. Rapidly losing blood, he continues to lead his Company in the assault. His men charge directly at the bunkers and trenches, the latter prepared with glacis to provide for grazing fire that covers access to the village. The other Companies of the 1st of the 12th land in turn and arrive to reinforce Mayer, now in somewhat of a tight spot.

Anderson's Platoon, at first grouped behind a clump of cactus and Mango trees, spreads out. Covered by Avila, the machine gunner, Sergeant Owens, packing a PRC25, bounds out in the open across a rice paddy to link up with the 3d Platoon. The black Sergeant, wounded in the head, groggy, nevertheless tries to keep radio contact with Company. "We can't get him out right now!" Anderson comments. "Thorn, go give him a hand and take over the radio!"

In there with the rest of the Platoon, indifferent to the "snap" of passing rounds, the strike of bullets around them, and the detonations of bursting projectiles, the French TV crew; Schoendoerfer, Merlin, and Adam film the action. The striking depiction of this bit of combat will shock American viewers.

His head hastily bandaged, Colt .45 in hand, Owens waits with other wounded to see if a Medevac ship can get in. Small arms and mortar fire seem to be coming in from all around them. After a moment's hesitation, Anderson's men regroup and with a yell assault the first trenchline.

ARA ships hose down the village with rockets as, behind the explosions, the platoons advance. Lieutenant Grigg leads the Third Platoon of Alpha Company over the same terrain. The "crack" of passing small arms fire fills the air. "What the fuck are *they* doing there?" exclaims the Lieutenant.

"Those are civilians, sir, and kids."

Grigg sees that a family is all mixed up in the middle of the firefight, and does not know which way to turn. Without reflection, the Lieutenant shucks his rifle and helmet and heads toward the civilians. He grabs two children and heads back to his platoon. The parents and the rest of the family, confused, follow, and move in among the Americans.

All day long, the Cav troopers and the NVA infantry fight it out around Hoa Hoi. By evening, the village is still in enemy hands. The 1st Brigade consolidates its position to keep the NVA from slipping away. All night long ships off the coast pound the enemy positions and light the dark with illumination rounds. The enemy soldiers are in a difficult situation. In small groups, they try to exfiltrate. Each time, they run into waiting Americans, and are forced back.

At first light the Battalion attacks. Cornered, the NVA are trapped in every trench, in each hole. Anderson searches a streambed that the enemy tried to use as an escape route. The men recover several AK47s from the water. The desperate resistance of isolated enemy soldiers constantly holds up movement into the village. The ground is cleaned up meter by meter with grenades and knives. Those enemy soldiers not killed are taken prisoner. In all, they amount to thirty-five NVA regulars, the remnant of elements of the 7th, 8th, and 18th North Vietnamese Regiments. The Americans count 231 enemy bodies in Hoi Hoa.

In spite of the sharpness of the fight, the Cav suffers only six killed and thirty-two wounded, among them Captain Frederick Mayer and Sergeant Owens. Schoendoerfer and his assistants leave Anderson's Platoon at Hoa Hoi.

Operation Irving goes on along the rest of the coast, as well as in the interior. General Norton sends units back to the Soui Ca and Kim Son areas. The Division, ubiquitous, tracks down bands of communists and keeps them from regrouping and reorganizing. Continuous reconnaissance and artillery fire exhausts the enemy, forcing them to keep constantly on the move, without a chance to catch their breath.

The operation ends at midnight on 24 October. In twenty-two days, the cumulative score including those of South Vietnamese and Korean forces adds up to 2,063 North Vietnamese killed. The number of prisoners, this time, is high: 1,930 men. It is the first First Cav operation where the number of prisoners equals the number of dead.

The Division moved the equivalent of forty-six infantry battalions and thirty-six artillery batteries: A record. With respect to recovered matériel, it uncovered a hospital in the forest in which the NVA had stocked thousands of containers of medicine. The Division also uncovered other caches. One platoon found one with five thousand canisters of film and other photographic material.

The G2 Section has all this matériel in hand for analysis. Among the various objects, a camera accompanied by a note that reads as follows: "This camera has been identified as that of Sam Castan, *Look Magazine* journalist killed in May 1966 during *Operation Crazy Horse.*"

General Norton wants to use the great amount of information

obtained from prisoners to accelerate the Division's operational rhythm and so give the enemy no time to rest. The Monsoon Season is approaching. He knows that the 18th NVA Regiment is at bay. Its rice reserves are exhausted. It will thus be obliged to replenish its stocks. This time the North Vietnamese tactic is to split up into small groups. The remnants of the Regiment break down into small and mobile light units. They move down into the lowland paddy areas to collect a tax in rice from that the peasants have already harvested and stocked themselves.

It is during these days that Norton receives a direct call from General Westmoreland, his boss. "Good show Jack! My congratulations!"

"Thanks, sir. In fact, the coordination of the two operations went very smoothly."

"Yup, I know, but I'm not calling you about that! The White House just informed me that your Division has received the *Presidential Unit Citation*.[1] Again, great going! The First Cav is the first unit serving in Vietnam to receive this *Citation*. McNamara wants to reward the courageous and offensive conduct of the First Cav during the fight at Ia Drang. A Rose Garden White House ceremony is planned for this month. I wanted to be the first to offer you congratulations. I'm going to call General Kinnard in the States too. It's a nice recognition for his work, and yours, and you are making it perfectly clear that the fine performance continues. There's also another citation in the works."

The Monsoon arrives with its leaden clouds, driving in from the Northeast. Morning fogs and afternoon storms again establish a daily rhythm for the rainy season. The pilots again are condemned to conduct prodigious feats of flight when *Operation Thayer II* kicks off on 25 October.

Under these precarious conditions the scouts and gunships of two Brigades try to track down elements of the 18th North Vietnamese Regiment. The pursuit lasts over a month. The Kim Son and An Lao Valleys are passed through a fine-tooth-comb. On 17 December, as the 1st Brigade goes to relieve the 3d, elements of the 1st of the 9th Cav make contact with two enemy companies near Thach Long village, located a bit to the east of Kim Son. At that point, the smoothly oiled machine breaks down.

Following several communications problems, the customarily excellent combat coordination fails to function at its usual standards. Platoons waste hours on standby, waiting for lift ships. When they finally arrive in the air over the scene of the fighting, it is at the same time that fighter aircraft are pounding the area. The choppers circle in the air while the battle rages on the ground.

The platoons are inserted piecemeal. Disoriented, they take a beating when they stumble onto well-camouflaged enemy positions that had not previously been identified.

Those troopers that come out alive owe it to their strong spirit and courage. The grunts, really fed up, fight in a rage. By nightfall, the NVA take advantage of their good luck to pull back. The 1st of the 12th took a hard hit. Delta Company ends the day with only a third of its men fit to fight.

To control the Kim Son Valley and deny the NVA access to it Norton decides to establish permanent fire support bases on each side of it. Batteries of 105mm and 155mm howitzers of the 16th and 19th Artillery set up on *LZs Pony* and *Bird*. From then on, they can cover the Valley with their fire.

After the unhappy contact on 17 December, activity slows down. The grunts turn their attention to the approach of Christmas. Rumor has it that there will be a truce on 24, 25, and 26 December. The isolated artillerymen are confidently serene. To them, the NVA seem incapable of taking the initiative after the losses they suffered during the preceding months.

However, at sunrise on 27 December, the yells of attacking infantry pierce the heavy fog. *My Thiet! My Thiet! Tien Len!* Seven hundred North Vietnamese regulars come out of nowhere and throw themselves in a wave on LZ Bird shouting, "Kill the Americans, kill!" Impressive mortar and heavy machine gun fire accompanies the assault. Fifty-seven millimeter recoilless rifles fire enthusiastically at the defenses of the firebase. Charlie Company, 1st of the 12th defends *Bird*. It is quickly overrun. The 22d NVA Regiment, thrashed several weeks earlier, has succeeded apparently in record time to rebuild its forces and mount this surprise attack.

As soon as they force the perimeter, the NVA rush at Charlie Battery, 6th of the 16th, and overrun five 155mm guns. At the same time, they charge toward the 105s of Bravo Battery of the 2d of the 19th. The Americans' confusion is greatest at this point. Radio communication is out. The bunkers are in flames and ammo is exploding.

The Red Legs, who up until now had never been in direct contact with the enemy, fight hand to hand this time and ferociously defend their guns.[2] The guns are the high stakes in a fight where no quarter is given. Second Lieutenant John Piper manages to slip into a 105mm gun position. He opens the breech and loads a beehive round. "Quick. Help me to get this thing pointed at C Battery," he yells at Sergeant Graham who followed him with several men. "Elevation, zero."

Before firing, Piper hesitates. He wants to warn the C battery troopers that he is going to fire a beehive round, a special munition intended to stop massive infantry assaults. The round contains 8,500 steel flechettes that spread out like shot from a sawed-off shotgun. Piper tries in vain to find some way to warn the artillerymen of the 6th of the 16th, and the Cav troopers of the 1st of the 12th. There is no practical way. The commo is out. There is no time. In desperation he shouts: "Watch out! Beehive! Beehive!"

"Damn. Fire! Fire!" Sergeant Graham, who has aimed the gun, orders. The cannon "booms." The air is filled with thousands of little flying arrows.

Liberated by action, Piper is calm. "More to the left." A soldier loads another beehive.

"Fire!"

The two loads of flying bits of metal cool the enemies' ardor, giving the ARA choppers time to arrive on scene. They pick up the action with rocket salvos. The fighting goes on all day. The NVA finish by breaking contact and disappearing into the hills around *LZ Bird*. They leave behind 266 dead soldiers. The Americans sustain fifty-eight dead and seventy-seven wounded.

The obstinate resistance of *Bird's* occupants is rewarded by a citation. The individual courage of the American soldiers deserves the honor. But Norton has a hard time figuring out how the 22d NVA Regiment was able to mount an attack on the position. "Seven hundred NVA infantrymen were able to get up within fifty meters of our positions without anyone seeing them. They brought up mortars and other crew-served weapons without drawing our attention. It's unbelievable!"

He immediately sends the two Brigades off after them. "They are going to fall back to the North. So, we'll find them again in the An Lao Valley. That's the most likely hypothesis." But the "hypothesis" does not pan out. The Americans do not reestablish contact with the 22d Regiment. The Companies return empty-handed.

Norton gets more satisfaction with the 18th Regiment. He receives confirmation that the continuous harassment by the Cav has reduced its combativeness considerably. Just about all of its leaders have been killed. The Division intercepts a message from its commander. He is reporting to his headquarters that the unit is out of action, and that his troops' morale is at rock bottom. To get away from the Cav patrols, the 18th Regiment breaks down into small teams that manage to escape to the Northwest, toward the An Lao Valley, to rest and get resupplied. *Operation Thayer II* ends after Tet, at the end of the truce of 7 to 12 February 1967.

After sixteen months in Vietnam, the Division Staff conducts an accounting of its activities and analyzes the results. The general divisional activity is characterized by relatively long and "heavy" operations with many phases of unfruitful searching and then, all of a sudden, violent confrontations.

For General Westmoreland, 1966 has enabled airmobile operations to achieve maturity. All the mobile battalions have become qualified in the use of helicopters, as much for tactical movement as for surprising and outmaneuvering the enemy. If, overall, the balance sheet for 1966 is positive, the Division Staff believes there is still progress to be made in the use of intelligence and the coordination between units, particularly in the case of joint operations.[3]

The attack on *LZ Bird* bothers Norton. He has strengthened the defenses of all support bases. Another topic with which he is preoccupied is the level of casualties sustained by the Division. From 31 January 1966 to 31 January 1967 the losses are heavy: 720 killed in combat and 3,039 wounded. To this must be added 2,304 deaths and injuries from accidents, and 13,449 casualties due to illness. The figures add up to a total of 19,512 men out of action. Norton can compare his losses to those sustained by the enemy, but he only has the body-count number: the North Vietnamese abandoned 8,835 dead in the field.

Tactically, First Cav operations have opened the way for retaking the initiative in the provinces that were, up until then, sanctuaries outside the authority of the South Vietnamese government. The Vietcong organization is profoundly destabilized. Tax collection, recruitment, medical services, and the supply system have been disorganized and thereafter are ineffective. The main communist cadres have been killed or constrained to take refuge in the forest. They have reverted to guerrilla war.

Translator's Notes

[1] The Presidential Unit Citation is the highest unit award for exceptionally courageous conduct in battle. Thereafter, all members of the unit, while assigned to the unit, wear the ribbon on their uniform. Only those personnel that were members of the unit when it earned the award are entitled always to wear the ribbon irrespective of their subsequent organizational assignments. It is a hard-earned and highly prized award and worn with particular pride.

[2] Red Legs are artillerymen.

[3] Joint operations are those involving the forces of two or more of the different armed services of the same nation. Combined operations are those involving any of the armed forces of two or more nations.

A Vietcong column of "Charlies" moving through the forest in the Central Highlands (Keystone).

A platoon of "Charlies" armed with Russian and Chinese weapons and captured US radios.

(Left) A North Vietnamese sapper armed with an AK47 and carrying a demolition charge.

(Below) 122mm artillery pieces of Soviet manufacture installed along the Laotian border.

A Vietcong Company prepares to attack a Special Forces Camp.

A "Pathfinder" in action. He guides a supply helicopter in on final approach.

The Plei Me Special Forces Camp in the mountains near the Cambodian border under attack the night of 19 October 1965.

A UH-1D Huey, the new mount of the Cavalry, coming in on final to insert a patrol (Sygma, Ph. C. Simonpiétri).

A "slick" offloads its "stick" on a "hot" LZ.

The "grunts" are ready to jump (Sygma, Ph. C. Simonpiétri).

Lieutenant Colonel Hal Moore, commanding the 1st Battalion, 7th Cavalry with his Sergeant Major, Basil Plumley, upon their return from LZ X-Ray on 17 November 1965.

Captain Tony Nadal and Captain Matt Dillon in October 1965 a few days before the battle at LZ X-Ray.

LTC Bob McDade, commanding the 2d Battalion, 7th Cavalry that came as a reinforcement to LZ X-Ray during the Battle of the Ia Drang.

Evacuation of the dead and wounded after the fighting at LZ Albany on 17 November 1965.

164

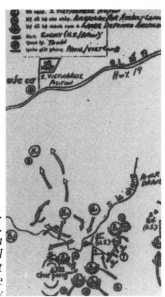

LTC Nguyen Huu An, commander of the N. Vietnamese forces during the Ia Drang Battle. His command bunker was on the slope of Chu Pong Mountain. The N. Vietnamese also call the Ia Drang Battle a victory. It is their first confrontation with an American airmobile unit. (Right) N. Vietnamese map of LZ X-Ray recovered from a prisoner in 1966.

Gen. Westmoreland, commander of American forces in Vietnam, comes to congratulate the 1st Cavalry Division for its actions in the Pleiku Campaign. The First Cav receives its first Presidential Unit Citation.

Gen. Harry Kinnard, commander of the 11th Air Assault Division (Test) in the company of Col. Tim Brown in May of 1965 at Ft. Benning, one month before its designation as the 1st Cavalry Division Airmobile.

The 1st Cavalry Division leaves Ft. Benning to embark on ships leaving from ports in Florida in August of 1965.

165

The Aircraft Carrier USS Boxer, heading for Qui Nhon, Vietnam, carries the helicopters of the First Cav in August of 1965.

The An Khe Basin chosen by General Wright as the place to establish the Base Camp of the "First Team." It is the same location as the old French base of Groupement Mobile 100.

The Command Post of the 1st Cavalry Division at An Khe in an old French Colonial House.

The "Golf Course" at An Khe, completely hand-cleared of brush using machetes.

166

Laundry Day at An Khe for Corporal Harry Clayton (Keystone).

Combing through the rice paddies near the An Khe Base in the Central Highlands.

Coming in on an LZ in Binh Dinh Province in 1966 (Sygma, Ph. C. Simonpiétri).

Elephant Grass and a 12 gauge shotgun: the daily terrain (Sygma, Ph. H. Bureau).

A platoon in the sands of a coastal province (Sygma, Ph. C. Simonpiétri).

Two "slicks" coming in on a paddy dike in Binh Dinh Province (Sygma, Ph. H. Bureau).

A 1st of the 9th Cavalry Blue Team cleaning out a cache (Sygma).

Grenadier with his M79 (Sygma, Ph. H. Bureau).

The point man, moving silently through the Elephant Grass (Sygma, Ph. H. Bureau).

A machine gunner with his M60.

A Medevac under enemy fire.

Running down the check-list before take-off in a UH-1B Huey (Sygma, Ph. C. Simonpiétri).

The interior of a "slick" with an M60 and a 12 gauge shotgun (Sygma, Ph. C. Simonpiétri).

A UH-1D Huey gunship with electrically operated machine guns, a grenade launcher, and 2.75in rocket pods, the first to be nicknamed "Cobra" (Sygma, Ph. C. Simonpiétri).

The door gunner with his M60 (Sygma, Ph. C. Simonpiétri).

A Huey shot down during Operation Pershing (Contact, Gilles Caron).

A CH-47 Chinook bringing in a sling-loaded 105mm howitzer.

A CH-47 Chinook gunship armed with 2.75in rocket pods, a grenade launcher, machine guns, and a 20mm machine gun.

AN AH-1G Cobra with a gun turret mounting a 7.62mm Gatling gun and 2.75in rocket pods (Sygma, Ph. C. Simonpiétri).

(Below) The pilot checks his 2.75in rocket pods on his AH-1G Cobra before a mission (Sygma, Ph. C. Simonpiétri).

An OH-6A Cayuse Light Observation Helicopter of the 1st of the 9th Cavalry armed with a 7.62mm Gatling gun on the left side of the aircraft beside the pilot (Sygma, Ph. C. Simonpiétri).

A Division Artillery 105mm howitzer battery (Sygma, Ph. C. Simonpiétri).

(Left) A self-propelled 175mm howitzer participates in a "prep" for a First Cav operation. The howitzer was delivered by a CH-54 Skycrane.

171

A CH-54 Skycrane resupplies a fire support base.

(Above) A B-52 Strategic Bomber based in Guam capable of providing night illumination with an Arc Light (Sygma, Ph. J. P. Laffont).

(Left) The First Cav relieves Hue after the Tet Mau Than Offensive, February 1968.

(Right) An M113 Armored Personnel Carrier of the 11th Armored Cavalry Regiment.

172

Juan Fordani of the 3d Brigade shakes the hand of a corporal of the 26th Marines following the relief of Khe Sanh.

(Below) President Richard Nixon on 1 April 1970 announcing to a television audience the incursion into Cambodia.

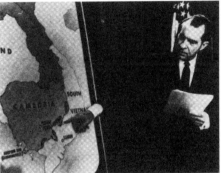

(Above Left) John Tolson, Commanding General of the 1st Cavalry Division from March 1967 to August 1968 at LZ Stud where he directs Operation Pegasus to relieve Khe Sanh (Sygma, Ph. C. Simonpiétri).

The airfield in 1970 at the Loc Ninh rubber plantation belonging to CEXO. A fixed wing observation aircraft and a cloud of helicopters from the 3d Brigade. Loc Ninh is one of the departure bases for the operation in Cambodia and the Command Post of General Shoemaker (Ph. Philippe Piechaud).

173

General Robert Shoemaker who planned the Cambodian incursion in his capacity as chief of Task Force Shoemaker. He commanded the 1st Cavalry Division from January of 1973 to February of 1975.

Cases of new SKS Carbines found in the "City" in Cambodia in April of 1970.

General E. B. Roberts, Division Commander from May of 1969 to May of 1970, congratulates Second Lieutenant Timothy Holden for discovering a cache of 1,000 tons of weapons and ammunition dubbed Rock Island East. Holden is later awarded the Silver Star.

Captain Kevin Corcoran informs his boss of the discovery of the "City," one of the North Vietnamese bases uncovered in Cambodia in April 1970.

174

General John Norton
May 1966 to March 1967.

General Harry Kinnard
July 1965 to May 1966.

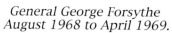

General George Forsythe
August 1968 to April 1969.

General Richard Logan Irby
August 1968

General James Smith
May 1971 to January 1973

General George Casey
May 1970 to July 1970
(killed in a helicopter accident in Vietnam)

General George Putnam
August 1970 to May 1971

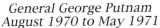

General Jonathan Burton,
Commander of the 3d
Brigade that remained in
Vietnam until 1972.

(Top and left center photos) The South Vietnamese take over from the Americans and from the Cav in particular and are able, with American logistical support, to victoriously repulse the 1972 communist offensive. They hold out until 1975.

Reconciled adversaries: Lieutenant General Hal Moore comes to Hanoi 25 years later to discuss the Battle of the Ia Drang with his North Vietnamese counterpart, Lieutenant General Nguyen Huu An.

The last salute to Major General Georges Casey. Among these six general officers five have commanded the 1st Cavalry Division in Vietnam. From the right: Lieutenant Generals Henry W. O. Kinnard, John Tolson, George Forsythe, and John Norton, and Major Generals Charles Gettys and Elvy Roberts

177

CHAPTER XIV

The United States becomes ever more deeply engaged in Vietnam and General Westmoreland continues to request more troops. He wants 550,000 men. President Johnson sends him 470,000, inasmuch as the end does not seem to be in sight. The feeble results obtained by the South Vietnamese Army astonish and worry the Pentagon and the White House. Westmoreland thus caps his request for reinforcements with a confidential document in which he defines the steps he counts on taking to improve the combat effectiveness of the South Vietnamese troops.

Subjected to numerous contradictory currents, President Johnson begins to doubt. Will a war of attrition bring the North Vietnamese and the Vietcong to their knees? During the year 1966 the Americans have lost almost six thousand men. Also, the following spring, Lyndon Johnson decides to employ another political tool along side the war of attrition. He names Robert Komer as Westmoreland's Deputy for "pacification." Fifty-five, bald, a Harvard graduate, rock solid, Komer is a civilian "General." He heads up an organization with the designation "Civil Operations and Revolutionary Development Support," commonly known as "CORDS."

Komer does not know Asia. He began his career in Italy in the intelligence service during the Second World War. After the war, he decided to stay in the Central Intelligence Agency as an analyst specializing in Eastern Europe, the Middle East, and the Soviet Union. He was appointed to the National Security Council after the election of John Kennedy. Johnson knew his scholars and was impressed by Komer's intellect. Johnson used him as his eyes on the "other war": pacification.

Komer established himself right away as one of the key people on Westmoreland's staff. To make sure there was no misunderstanding, he did not hesitate to ride about in his black Chrysler Imperial with a plate displaying four stars. But, in respect of military regulations, Komer being a civilian, the plate was also adorned with an American eagle. The tone is set. He is number three in the hierarchy of American forces in Vietnam, behind Westmoreland and his assistant, General Creighton Abrams. He has the rank of Ambassador. Neither diplomat nor military officer, Bob Komer is the man responsible for pacification.

Among the military types, some general officers are working just as diligently to reorient American strategy away from the dogma of a war of attrition. General Victor Krulak, a Marine Corps officer and Pacific War veteran, had already figured out the relationship of several factors. "The gross number of dead VC is a doubtful indicator of success," he said, because, if the killing is accompanied by the devastation of friendly areas, we'll end up doing more harm than good!" Krulak argued against the idea that the war might be won by military means. "That doesn't make any sense!" he replied to the general who was describing to him, in positive terms, the tactical situation. "You can't win this war with military force alone. You either win the whole thing, or you don't win at all." The Marines thus went on to change the nature of their missions to include a pacification dimension.

Another change was going to occur in Saigon. Ambassador Henry Cabot Lodge was retiring, and Ellsworth Bunker replaced him. General Westmoreland would very much have liked to be the single American representative in Vietnam, and have only one civilian assistant with the title of ambassador. But President Johnson did not want to relive the "MacArthur experience" and so sent a man as Ambassador accustomed to difficult situations. Bunker came to his new diplomatic post late in life. He had been a successful businessman, and later represented the United States in the Argentina of Juan Perón and the India of Nehru.

Bunker had a mission that paralleled that of Westmoreland. The military was to continue to wear out the enemy's military forces. The diplomat was to undertake the political side of the task: to put in place a constitutional South Vietnamese government and legitimize its authority. His distant air and cold look earned him the nickname of "Mr. Frigidare" from the Saigonese.

He got the opportunity to use his political talents right away. The South Vietnamese Generals had already set themselves on the path to power. General Nguyen Van Thieu announced that he would be a candidate in the presidential elections, getting into the race ahead of General Nguyen Cao Ky. Ambassador Bunker then invited for dinner Thieu, Ky, and General Cao Van Vien, Chief of the Vietnamese Joint General Staff. The Ambassador told them clearly that the United States would not tolerate any struggle for power. He demanded of the Generals that they solve the problem among themselves. At this point, Thieu revealed himself to be the fastest and strongest. Ky contented himself with the vice-presidency.

McNamara, who had been impressed by the violence of the Ia Drang Valley Battle, questions himself over the conduct of the war. After having unreservedly supported General Westmoreland in according him all the men and matériel he deemed necessary, the Secretary of Defense wanted now to put the brakes on "the unlimited escalation of the deployment of American forces" in Vietnam. McNamara met with Hal Moore upon the latter's return from Vietnam, after he had turned over command of the 3ᵈ Brigade of the First Cav.

Attached to the staff of John McNaughton, McNamara's Assistant Secretary of Defense for International Security Affairs, Moore made a case to the Secretary of Defense that the VC and the North Vietnamese deliberately threw themselves into the Ia Drang fight and that they did the same thing at Bong Son. According to him there was no doubt that the enemy intentionally courted casualties as a learning exercise. They wanted to know how the Americans maneuvered so that they in turn might outmaneuver them. The North Vietnamese General Nguyen Huu An, who directed the communist side in the Battle of the Ia Drang, confirmed this to Moore many years later.

The North Vietnamese clearly had decided to suspend their offensive intended to cut Vietnam in two. A plan that would not be taken up again and with success until 1975. At the end of 1965 they had decided to attack Plei Me to force the ARVN to move out of Pleiku. The trap was set to lead the Americans, who had just arrived in An Khe, to intervene. The General confirmed to Moore: "We wanted to attract the tiger. We had attacked the ARVN, but we were ready to fight the Americans. Our problem was that we had never fought airplanes before and had no experience against them in combat. We knew how to fight the French. We therefore wanted to draw American units into contact in order to learn how to fight them. We were looking for American combat troops without knowing which ones they might be."

In the spring of 1967 the Southeast Asia Special Bureau presented a memorandum to McNamara, an exhaustive analysis of all the combats that had taken place in the course of the campaigns of 1965 and 1966. The conclusions were disquieting. The study focused particularly on the fifty-six engagements that took place in 1966 involving units from platoon to multi-battalion size. The North Vietnamese and Vietcong had the initiative in eighty-five percent of the cases, either in attacking American forces or striking out from fortified positions. In eighty percent of the cases, the North Vietnamese had the element of surprise on their side. In only five percent of the cases did the American command element have relatively exact knowledge of the enemy's positions before the start of the attack. In eighty-eight percent of the cases, the communist forces were the first to open fire.

Compiled from a mass of statistical data, the author of the memorandum concluded that the North Vietnamese in fact determined the level of American casualties. They could increase or decrease them as a function of their willingness to sacrifice their own troops. They thus had the initiative.

"Stand Up!" The order reverberates the length of the interior of the C-130 Hercules that resembles a jam-packed metro. The men rise with difficulty, clumsy with all their gear and weapons.

"Hook Up!" The men hook their static lines to the anchor cables that run down each side along the interior of the fuselage. Instinctively, with a finger, each man verifies the position of the safety pin that secures the link. Each man checks the gear and hook up of the man to his front, then slaps him on the back. The jumpmasters issue the orders and control the preparation. The men are tightly bunched.

"Shuffle to the Door!" The line of men shuffles to the open doors on each side. General John Deane leads a stick heading for the door, his left hand extended. He is ready to jump in the first airborne assault in Vietnam. A red light over each door comes on.

"Stand in the door!" The lead man in each stick watches the light, glances out as his face is blasted by the wind. A signal sounds, the green light comes on.

"Go!" Deane exits the airplane. The air is humid three hundred meters up. The rest of his unit, the 2^d Battalion of the 503^d Infantry, airborne, belonging to the 173^d Airborne Brigade, follows him. *Operation Junction City Alternate* is underway. The 2^d Battalion jumps into Tay Ninh. It is 0925 hours, 22 February 1967, when 780 paratroopers spit from the bays of thirteen C-130s.

The 1st Battalion arrives at 1030 by chopper. The 4th Battalion is inserted on another LZ at 1420. Sixty Hueys and six Chinooks participate in the maneuver. By the middle of the afternoon 9,518 men have been air-transported, along with fifty tons of freight. The operation is marked by a few incidents. Helicopters and parachutes do not always make good neighbors. Air control can not always keep up with the pace of action. The tactical air controllers have problems mastering the ballet of jets, helicopters, and fixed-wing aircraft.

Happily, the enemy withdraws ahead of time and so does not complicate things. The airborne troops are satisfied to have been able to justify their wings, but the general staff sees in this the proof of the inadaptability of airborne operations to Vietnam. The French had tried the same thing and drawn the same conclusions. The size of the Drop Zones, their security, the logistical preparation, and the great amount of matériel that had to be mobilized made classic airborne operations uncertain or risky. This type of action was better suited to an offensive strategy rather than that

181

of the American forces in Vietnam, which had to be purely defensive.

Operation Junction City Alternate lasts until mid May and becomes an airmobile operation with most movement by helicopter and most actions initiated with air assaults. The score sheet reflects 2,700 enemy killed. The Americans recover important quantities of munitions and medicines as well as eight hundred tons of rice.

The First Cav, itself, is fighting more to the north in Binh Dinh Province. For a month now it has been conducting *Operation Pershing*. General Norton has received directives of a new type from the high command. The First Cavalry Division is to more deeply involve itself in assistance to the South Vietnamese government's efforts to reestablish its administrative control in this important rural province. It must also undertake to cooperate more closely with the South Vietnamese Army to improve the latter's operational capabilities and give it more confidence in its own capabilities. Pacification becomes the third component of the Cav mission.

Lieutenant Colonel James Oliver, a military policeman, is assigned responsibility for civic action, one of the components of psychological warfare (psywar).[1] He must combine the actions of the 545th Military Police Company, assigned to the Division with the 816th South Vietnamese National Police Field Force (NPFF). This mixed unit is born the same day as Bob Komer creates CORDS. This MP Battalion is charged with sectioning off the villages and hamlets. It seeks to obtain support from the inhabitants to find caches and tunnels, and to get them to participate in the struggle against VC terrorism and the political infrastructure. The Cav MPs working with the three Companies of the 816th NPFF identify and arrest 2,400 VC and communist cadres in the following year.

The politics of pacification can only be implemented if the area is sufficiently secure. The Division therefore establishes itself along the coast of the South China Sea. Its AO extends in the West from the Vinh Thanh Valley, Binh Dinh Province, up to Quang Ngai Province in the North and to Phu Cat in the South. Camp Radcliff at An Khe is still the rear base of the Cav. Norton, however, sets up his CP at *LZ English* near Bong Son.

Working with CORDS, the Vietnamese government launches a vast program, the *Chieu Hoi*, or *Open Arms Program* that offers amnesty to VC who turn themselves in. The government proposes to follow through and integrate them into its economic and political reconstruction effort. The security offered to the ralliers must be credible and their rights truly preserved. All the units of the allied forces participate in *Operation Open Arms*. The First Cav thus launches itself in the pacification program and the psywar effort. The Division increases its psychological operations or PSYOPS.

First Cavalry helicopters, equipped with loud speakers, cruise over the mountains, the paddies, and the jungle to disseminate messages, drop leaflets, and land Civil Affairs Teams. These teams have to convince the peasants to rally and move into areas under government control. This is a particularly difficult mission because it makes the population even more directly the objective of the conflict. Up till then the peasants ransomed themselves from the Vietcong and the North Vietnamese by paying a rice tax or money tax in piasters, and by providing recruits. Then the Americans arrived and bombed their rice caches and burned their harvests.

Both sides unleash propaganda. The North Vietnamese launch counter-pacification operations. The communist cadres organize obligatory meetings to explain that: "Saigon is in ruins," and that "the puppet government has sold out to the American imperialists and is a rotten fruit which will fall all by itself." The peasants come timidly at night to take refuge next to American support bases. They do their best to communicate with the GIs and ask them many questions. The PSYOPS teams organize excursions to Saigon for the children and adolescents to show them the city. The kids come back excited by the zoo and the markets.

The First Cav did not wait for the official pacification program before undertaking humanitarian assistance projects in its zone. Since its arrival in 1965 it had been conducting Medical Civic Action Projects, or MEDCAPs in An Thuc District, Binh Dinh Province, with a population of seventy thousand. They open a *Nha Thuong*. The two words traditionally mean "hospital." Literally, they mean, "house of love." So, in An Thuc they establish a dispensary with seventy-six beds and a maternity section with ten beds. In 1967 two thousand patients are hospitalized here, and three hundred and fifty babies are delivered. Twenty-seven thousand people will be treated here.

"We come to the assistance of all those who come here without paying any attention to their past or to their political leanings," explains Master Sergeant John Rozzell, who devotes himself to this dispensary. He has extended his tour in Vietnam to continue working there. The VC are irritated by the influence on the population of such a dispensary. Thus, in 1968, they attempt to destroy it with rocket fire. The effect is so negative that they are obliged to express their regrets.

An Tuc also has an annex. It includes a primary school for

children, classes where women receive instruction in hygiene and nutrition, and for men, instruction in agronomy. This establishment is destined to be turned over to the Vietnamese authorities. On 3 April 1969, Lieutenant Colonel Guthrie Turner, Division Surgeon and Commander of the 15th Medical Battalion officially turns over the keys of the building to the Assistant Province Chief of Binh Dinh Province.

The grunts are daily confronted with the misery of the population; the hungry children, the war wounded, and the emaciated elderly peasants. The harvest, already reduced by the severity of the Monsoon, suffers from the effects of the war. To make up for the shortage of food due to flooding, the Civil Affairs Section of the 2[d] Brigade provides eighty tons of rice to the populations of Bo Duc and Duc Phang. They provide seed to reestablish the crop.

Every unit mobilizes to help rebuild villages. The huge CH-47s enable the Cav to transport building materiel without respect to the distance or the state of the roads. DIVARTY participates directly. The Red Legs forsake their cannons to build schools and houses. Fred Rowsee, Captain of the 55th, supervises the construction, of concrete blocks and brick, of a school to replace one of wood destroyed by termites. He also determines to build a bridge so that the village will not be cut off from the road during the Monsoon.

The best way to prove that an area is secure again is to keep the roads and trails safe and maintained, day and night. The free movement of people and goods testifies to the return of government authority. The Cav works actively to open and repair the roads. The 8th Engineer Battalion, with bulldozers and graders, begins by establishing *LZ English* to accommodate the 1st Brigade and Norton's CP. It opens a landing strip and builds a huge munitions storage bunker.

Lieutenant Colonel Edwin S. Townsley is tasked with opening the route from Gia Huu to Sa Huynh, a segment of Route 1, closed to traffic since 1962. The Vietcong had blown the bridges, dug a series of trenches across the road, and emplaced other barriers. The successive Monsoons had done the rest. The 1st Platoon of Alpha Company reopens the road to traffic. In four days they move 2,500 cubic meters of dirt, level and compact it. They rebuild the roads and bridges.

Translator's Notes

[1] Civic action certainly plays a PSYWAR role, but it also fulfills a humanitarian need completely aside from its value as an active instrument of the psychological war.

CHAPTER XV

Operation Pershing will last a year, until January 1968. A mission of pacification and policing, it seems austere, with a rhythm so different than that experienced in the preceding phase where the mission was to find, fix, and destroy the enemy. The combat units are positioned to support a role of maintaining order. It seems somewhat of a lightweight mission to them. Patrol, ambush, and patrol again: minor contact with platoon-sized local VC elements. It is hardly a motivational routine, but it is effective and dangerous.

Four infantrymen from Delta Troop, 1st of the 9th Cav, in a jeep mounting an M60 machine gun slowly follow an engineer team along a road near a local VC base camp in the Bong Son area. The engineers are checking the roadway and its embankments with mine detectors. In the jeep, the men are getting impatient. "This damn road really pisses me off. If there are any Charlies around here, the thing to do is just blow them away! Don't make a big deal of it. There aren't any civilians around here anymore!"

"Yup, and a few eight inch rounds set on VT'd clear any mines off this road!"[1]

"We're never goin' to get to the coast today. I dream of wading into the ocean bare-assed, like the kids here."

"You better take a mine detector. The Charlies like to dig around in the sand. They really enjoy turning a beautiful stretch of beach into a minefield."

An engineer sergeant approaches the jeep. "The road is cut up ahead. The bridge we rebuilt has been burned out again. Watch out guys; don't go back to anyplace you've set up before. Yesterday, I set out some trip flares. When I went back to pick 'em up, the whole place was booby-trapped. Some more advice: if you were thinking of going in for a dip at Bong Son, the VC have observers on most of the hills and sand dunes overlooking the shore. Don't make that mistake! Last week an Alpha Company platoon killed four of them."

Routine operations are ongoing in Bong Son. The South Vietnamese Police and the Cav MPs conduct combined police operations. They collect information, interrogate the locals, and search for ARVN deserters. A Delta Troop jeep provides security. It is posted at the entry to the village and waits for the MPs to complete their task.

"Pass me a water can! I'm goin' to find some water for the radiator." The driver heads for the moat that surrounds the village.

As he leans down to fill up the can he spots a man crawling under the barbed wire just beyond the moat. The VC tries to hide in the grass.

"Hey, you, come here! *Lai day! Lai day!*"[2] He recovers an AK47 leaning against the wire awaiting the return of its owner. The Vietcong was simply coming to visit his family in the village. The police find a packet of photographs on him. In one of them he is posing with two of his buddies in plain day in the center of Bong Son. The two other men are carrying MAT49 submachine guns, leftover French weapons. A little while later, at the base of the An Lao hills, they will be killed and the two weapons recovered.

"Saddle up!" Blue Team grunts spill out of their tents and abandon their beers and tape players to clamber aboard a standby slick. In a few minutes they are in place and take up a position at the entrance to the village. On the ground, two dead VC are half-sunken in the mud. The Sergeant, leaning over them, has no time to check them out before a passing round cracks by his ear.

"Sarge! I saw where that came from, over there, from the trench line." The soldier emphasizes his statement with an M16 burst. The Charlie changes his target and fires at Hobbs, who refines his aim and sight picture and empties his magazine.

"I got him!"

"Cover us. We'll go find him!" The Sergeant and Hobbs extract the VC from the trench. He is dead.

A long burst of fire startles them. Just behind them a trooper is firing tracers at some haystacks. They soon burst into flame and give off intense heat. An acrid smell of burning straw joins that of grilled meat. Blackened bodies emerge from the ashes. "See that Sarge? I hit the jackpot. The VC camouflage themselves good, but I can spot 'em."

"Yeah, good!"

"Sarge. The pilot's going for reinforcements. The order is to burn this village while we wait."

The Sergeant goes to the first grass hooch and lights it off. A woman, baby in her arms, stumbles out. She takes off her shirt and tries to smother the flames. The Sergeant, surprised, lighter still in hand, restarts the fire. The young woman, now nude from the waist up, puts the fire out again, and turns on the Sergeant. She snatches the cigarette lighter from his hand and slaps him in the face. This time, exasperated, the Sergeant cuts loose with a string of curses. The woman, in an angry tone of voice, responds in a like manner. Her protests are drowned out by the noise of three helicopters bringing reinforcements.

The sky soldiers bail out and form a line to screen through the village. A voice cries out from the front of a caved-in bunker that no one had thought to check out: "*Chu Hoi! Chu Hoi!*"[3]

A young North Vietnamese regular comes out, arms over his head, and repeats the words indicating his desire to rally, or at least surrender: "*Chu Hoi, Chu Hoi.*" Minh, the interpreter, jumps on him and knocks him to the ground.

"Ask him what his unit is, Minh!" the Lieutenant, who arrived with the reinforcements tells him.

"He say he belong to Company of regular forces that go away last evening. He not want to fight any more against helicopter."

"What was he doing here with his Company?"

"They supposed to attack American base at Bong Son."

"Where's his weapon?"

"He throw it in river. He want to be prisoner."

"Put him in the chopper! We're going to finish checking this place out. Stay on line to the edge of the river. We'll hold up at the paddy field over on the right."

Scooched down on his heels, an old man in black pajamas watches the patrol move toward him on line. When it gets up to him, he stands and turns to make a getaway. "*Choi,*" Minh yells to stop him, but the old man breaks into a run.[4] Rifle fire crackles. The man disappears in the village. The patrol continues its progress. Trooper Martin, before he moves out, spots the man lying next to a hut. He finds him stretched out and losing blood quickly from a bullet wound through the wrist. The Blues' Sergeant joins him and looks at the old man who groans quietly. He covers him with a camouflaged pancho liner.[5]

"Sergeant, you can't do that! He'll bleed to death."

"Look, the patrol is leaving him behind. We've got orders to clean up this fucking village."

"But Matt, he's a human being, you can't do that."

The Sergeant looks at Martin, then turns away. He goes over to the Lieutenant who has halted the patrol for a break. "Sir, there's a wounded guy back there. I need to borrow our medic for him."

The Lieutenant knows what happened and tells him: "Sarge, the old guy shouldn't of run. He should 'a halted when Minh yelled at 'im. Right now, we've gotta link up with the infantry."

"Yes sir, I know, but you don't want the death of an old man on your conscience."

"Okay Sarge. Take Claw with you and have him check the guy out. I'll call a gunship to pick him up."

The Medic binds the wound and gives the old peasant a shot of morphine. The two of them carry him over to the chopper, which takes him back to the Aid Station.

The next day Minh charges into the Sergeant's tent.

"You hear latest news?"

"Come in. Sit."

"Old man."

"Yeah, the old man. He's Okay?"

"You save life of VC chief. He Viet Cong chief in this area. He organize training in this village for attack on Bong Son! Plan not work when helicopter have problem and have to land. When VC see more gunship come, they think we see them and try to get away. We get order to find and you know what happen. When we go through area he sit next to paddy like old farmer. S2 get him to talk. They plan attack last night. You have result of operation?"

"Yeah. We got a bunch of 'em: ninety-six NVA and VC. For once, we were lucky, but we could of really got hurt."

"I hear we lose one man from Platoon"

"Arthur got it."

"How?"

"How? By a ricochet! You know, after the village, we broke out on the river. When the Charlies saw us coming they all jumped in the water like frogs and went under, holding their breath. Whenever one of them came up for air, we shot him. The bodies floated downstream and hung up on a dam. There was a VC hiding on the other side. He had an old Mauser 98. Arthur was in a position near the rice field. The Charlie fired at us. The round hit the water in front of him, ricocheted, and hit him in the head."

To make sure of good security in its AO, the First Cav must occupy the ground, always more ground to cover. In addition to using artillery support bases, the Cav increases the size of its armored component. Tanks and armored personnel carriers give it increased tactical support and security for ground operations.

The 1st Battalion, 50th Infantry (Mechanized) is attached to the First Cavalry. The armored vehicles are used either in a conventional manner on the ground, providing heavy mobile firepower, or choppered in like artillery pieces and inserted with the Cav troopers.

Delta Troop, 1st of the 9th, securing a line along the coast, is reinforced by M42 Dusters. The M42 Duster is a lightly armored vehicle with a turret mounting twin 40mm canons and is adapted to providing convoy protection. They are employed to keep the main road, coastal Route Number 1, open.

The action is not limited to patrols and platoon-sized operations. Colonel Fred Karhohs with his 2d Brigade mounts a major operation at An Quang to the south of the Cay Giep Mountains. Once again, an innocuous event starts things going. Two pilots scouting in their H13s are amazed to see well-worked fields around An Quang and not a single farmer in sight. The area, however, appears calm and under control. The White Team calls in a Blue Team to check things out. The patrol lands just along the dirt track leading in to the village. Greeting them as they enter the village is a large banner stretched between two poles. In Vietnamese, in large black letters the greeting: "Welcome to the Vietcong and to our North Vietnamese Brothers."

The men undo the banner and head into the village. Someone fires on them. They call in a Red Team, gunships, to clean things up. The Blue Team stays just outside the village to cut off any attempt at escape to the south. Colonel Karhohs himself takes the situation in hand. He comes in overhead in his Charlie-Charlie. He sends the 1st Platoon of Bravo Company of Lieutenant Colonel Joe McDonnough's 2d of the 5th to block escape to the north of An Quang. Lieutenant Colonel R. W. Nevins, 1st of the 9th Commander, sends some of his helicopters around the Dam Tra-O Lake, to cover the west.

The enemy strength is estimated at two companies. Karhohs gives McDonnough the mission to conduct the ground assault. He employs four and a half battalions to encircle the village of An Quang. Joe thoroughly coordinates his plans. With his Operations Officer and his Fire Support Coordinator he sets up his artillery support, including ARA, as well as gunship and naval gunfire support. His S3, S3 Air, FSC and Air Force LNO integrate close air support into the plan.

The M42s of Delta Troop fire salvos of 40mm rounds. Chinooks of the 53d Aviation Detachment, armed with machine guns, canons, and grenade launchers enter the fray. Once the prep is complete Blue Teams from the 1st of the 9th and two companies of the 2d of the 5th move out in a haze of smoke. The troopers, on line, soon find themselves among the village huts. Two VC spring from a hole and toss several grenades into the American ranks. The signal given, enemy machine guns jump into action from off to the side and cut the grunts down. Hidden snipers keep the Cavalrymen from recovering their wounded. The Blues were surprised in open terrain by VC automatic weapons firing from entranceways to a network of tunnels.

Two M42s get into position. Canons level, they open fire with beehive rounds. The fusillade of flechettes scissors off the last standing coconut palms and the shooters sheltering behind them. Protected by the Dusters, the two companies evacuate their wounded before moving further into the village. During the attack, one of the M42s is hit by a 57mm recoilless rifle and takes fire.

An Quang is occupied, but not cleaned out. That night, McDonnough employs some elements of the 1ˢᵗ of the 9ᵗʰ to complete the sealing off of avenues of escape. It is clear that the NVA are going to try and take advantage of the darkness to escape from their tunnels. They are undone by a bright full moon and the continuous illumination provided by artillery flares.

The next day McDonnough is both defiant and careful. Before starting into a search of the tunnel and bunker complex, he calls back into play the artillery and close air support. Thirty-three sorties and several artillery barrages bang away at what is left of An Quang. When the 1ˢᵗ of the 9ᵗʰ moves back into the village, it only draws a few sporadic rounds of fire. Delta Troop recovers eighty-nine dead NVA, but many more must have met their end in the tunnels and bunkers all blasted to pieces by the bombs.

Lieutenant Colonel McDonnough later learns from a prisoner that the 9ᵗʰ Battalion of the 18ᵗʰ NVA Regiment had lost 150 men out of an active strength of 250. The survivors from An Quang found a refuge in the Cay Giep Mountains. They had to flee to the north of the lake hiding under water and among the reeds.

To check out Binh Dinh Province, the 1ˢᵗ Brigade, under the command of Colonel James Smith, and the 2ᵈ, under that of Colonel George Casey, search the valleys around Bong Son. They conduct search and destroy operations in this area to surprise elements of the 22ᵈ NVA Regiment. The 3ᵈ Brigade, now commanded by Colonel Johnathen Burton looks after the An Lao Valley and shares surveillance of the Soui Ca and Phu My Valleys with the 22ᵈ ARVN and Korean Tiger Divisions. He is reinforced with the 3ᵈ Brigade of the 25ᵗʰ Infantry Division.

Operation Pershing is well underway when the scheduled date for the annual rotation of Division Commanders arrives.

Translator's Notes

[1] VT or variable time fuse. This is a fuse setting on an artillery round that causes it to detonate at a set distance above the ground.

[2] " Come here! Come here!"

[3] "I surrender! I surrender!"

[4] *Choi*—stop.

[5] The pancho liner is a very light quilt-like almost square piece of materiel used with the pancho by infantrymen on operations in tropical climates as the principal means to keep warm.

CHAPTER XVI

On 1 April 1967 General Norton passed command of the 1st Cavalry Division to Major General John J. Tolson. Tolson was also one of the principal actors in the development of airmobility. He participated in all the important debates and commissions on the subject. Since 1965 General Tolson has commanded the Army Aviation School. In this capacity he was responsible for teaching all the tactical theories and for training all the pilots to prepare them in the new methods of air assault.

Originally from North Carolina, he is fifty-one when he arrives at Camp Radcliff. Shorter than Norton, less angular, he has a pleasant face and wavy hair, already gray. He graduated from West Point in the Class of 1937, at the age of twenty-two. He participated in the first large-scale airborne tactical exercises. A Colonel during the Second World War, he served as a parachutist, jumped into New Guinea, then on Corregidor during the battle in the Pacific. Finally, toward the end of the War, in the Philippines, he served with the 503d Airborne Infantry Regiment. He earned his pilot's wings in 1957 and became an ardent partisan of airmobility. He was assigned as Director of Army Aviation.

John Tolson inherits Norton's team. His two Assistant Division Commanders are Brigadier Generals George Blanchard and Edward de Saussure. The Chief of Staff is Colonel George Casey. He breaks down the command post. He leaves *English* for *Two Bits*. An Khe stays the rear-area logistical base.

The war of attrition and the different types of actions that the Cavalry Division employs have the effect of forcing the principal regiments of the 3d North Vietnamese Division to seek refuge outside of Binh Dinh Province. Since the month of October 1966, the 2d VC Regiment has withdrawn itself to a position to the north in Quang Ngai Province. In March of 1967, the 22d North Vietnamese Regiment followed suit. This enemy concentration obliges the Division General Staff to react and organize *Operation Lejeune*. It kicked off on 7 April, one week after General Tolson assumed the command of the Division.

Quang Ngai Province is just north of Binh Dinh Province. In the American breakout of military zones of action, this Province is in the I Corps area, the responsibility for which rests in the hands of the US IIId Marine Amphibious Force. Up until that time, the First Cav had never intervened outside of its assigned operational area. The Vietcong and North Vietnamese took advantage of that

191

fact to put themselves out of reach, with the Cav courteously staying in the II Corps Area, and the Marines very much occupied with the Demilitarized Zone (DMZ) that separated North and South Vietnam.

In January 1967, the 3^d Battalion of the 7th Marines, an element of *Task Force X-Ray*, is ordered from Chu Lai to Duc Pho, the southernmost town in Quang Ngai Province. General Foster La Hue, called "Frosty," commander of *Task Force X-Ray*, reinforces the 3^d of the 7th Marines with the 1st of the 4th and the 2^d of the 5th Marines. These units only have a few helicopters. They have, therefore, relatively little mobility compared to the Cav.

In March, the pressure on the DMZ increased, and the Marine General Staff wanted to call *Task Force X-Ray* back to help in the fight to stop North Vietnamese infiltration along the 17th Parallel. To enable the Marines to recall this force, General Westmoreland gives the mission of relieving Duc Pho to the First Cav. The *Operation* is baptized *Lejeune*, and the *LZ* is *Montezuma*. These are two famous names in Marine Corps History. "Lejeune" is the name of a Marine Corps general who earned renown in the Spanish-American War, and "Montezuma" comes from the Marine Corps Hymn: "From the Halls of Montezuma, to the Shores of Tripoli."

The order from MACV arrives on Tolson's desk on 6 April at 2200 hours. Lieutenant Colonel Robert Stevenson, commander of the 2^d of the 5th is immediately alerted. On standby at An Khe for another operation, Tolson changes his destination and issues new orders for Duc Pho. At 0115 hours the morning of 7 April, the 11th Aviation Group, based on *LZ Two Bits* along with Tolson's CP, receives the order to move the 2^d of the 5th and to assure its support at Duc Pho.

In place at dawn, conducting operations by 0930, the 2^d of the 5th is set up by 1700 hours. The rest of Colonel Karhohs' Black Hawk Brigade will follow. They have to build an airfield at *LZ Montezuma*. Bravo Company of the 8th Engineer Regiment arrives the morning of 7 April to recon the area and pick the best location for the landing strips. What is needed is one landing strip for the twin engine Caribou and another parallel but longer strip for the C-123 and C-130 Hercules.

In two days, twenty-nine round trips of CH-54 Skycranes and fifteen of Chinooks deliver thirty-one pieces of heavy engineer equipment. By 1800 hours on 7 April there is enough matériel in place on the ground to begin work. Lieutenant Colonel Charles Blentine gets the work underway. The engineers begin to terrace the land right away under the powerful illumination of searchlights. By midnight, that is six hours after the heavy equipment began work, a fourth of the Caribou landing strip is scraped out. The ground is sandy, which makes the work easier. On the other hand, the sand is very fine and lofts quickly in the wind stirred by rotors and propellers, creating a serious handicap for approaching and departing aircraft. The 8th Engineers spray the strip with Peneprine, an oily solution that holds the sand down and keeps it from blowing.

In a few hours, *Montezuma Base* is the subject of intense air traffic including H-13s, UH-1Bs, UH-1Ds, CH-47s, and CH-54s. As soon as the landing strips are operational, priority shifts to air traffic control. The air traffic flies low over the work crews and troops settling in on the ground. The blowing sand caused by hovering helicopters is aggravating and dangerous. Many tents and pancho half hooches are blown down by rotor wash. Some grunts, pretty much fed up the third time it happens, point their M16s at the choppers. Three air traffic controllers from the 11th General Support Aviation Company come to reinforce the Marine air traffic controllers now overwhelmed by the heavy flow of air traffic. These three men, set up on the roof of a truck in the middle of a column of blowing sand, control the come and go of more than one thousand flights per day with nothing but their radios.

By 1630 hours, 8 April, the five hundred-meter long Caribou landing strip is finished. Work continues day and night. The noise and the illumination are impressive. The Marines, who for several months have been living under a total blackout, are stupefied. The work goes on without any sign of the enemy.

To assure the security of the work site, Kahrohs organizes Night Hunter Operations every evening. They are just what the name implies. A flight of four Hueys constitutes the hunting team. The lead chopper is equipped with powerful searchlights. The three other helicopters follow at a slightly higher altitude, and just far enough back so as not to be caught in the light halo. When a target is spotted, a machine-gunner in the closest chopper fires on the objective with tracers to point it out. Then, in turn, the fourth helicopter dives on the target and neutralizes it with 2.75inch rockets. This very effective technique that Kahrohs had already tested in Binh Dinh Province discourages the North Vietnamese from coming to disturb the work in progress.

Lejeune is a joint operation that unites four distinct military entities: the Army, the Marines, the Air Force, and the Navy. The air support is significant. More than 156 sorties are employed to transport a thousand passengers and 230 tons of cargo to *Montezuma*. The Air Force drops 115 tons of bombs and 70 tons of napalm in the surrounding area during the first week. The Navy, from the *Picking* and the *Shelton*, its two ships cruising off the coast, fires 2,350 rounds from its heavy guns in support.

The Vietcong and the North Vietnamese, in the habit of being at their ease in this Province, discover the brutal capabilities of airmobility. They avoid contact and prefer to disperse and to hide. At midnight, 22 April, *Operation Lejeune* ends. The count is 176 enemy dead and 127 prisoners.

General Tolson noted that this operation had a unique character. The First Cav had demonstrated the capability of an airmobile division to move an entire airmobile brigade in a day and a half to a new theater of operations.

The 2ᵈ Brigade of the Cav leaves an important infrastructure at Duc Pho to include two landing strips, a port terminal, and a road net. Tactically, the Viet Cong organization is disorganized. The Black Horse Brigade passes the baton to the 3ᵈ Brigade of the 25ᵗʰ Infantry Division commanded by Colonel James Shanahan. This Infantry Brigade is placed under the operational control of the First Cav for several months. It subsequently becomes one of the constituent units of Task Force Oregon, attached to an element of the 23ᵈ Infantry Division. TF Oregon comes to public attention in a very poor light just a year later at Son My and My Lai. Second Lieutenant William Calley orders the extermination of all the inhabitants of the village, 347 people. William Calley will be arrested, found guilty, and imprisoned.

Since 19 April, Colonel Karhohs has been back with his Brigade in Binh Dinh Province. The 1ˢᵗ Cavalry Division is whole again in the heart of the II Corps Zone. The 2ᵈ Brigade incursion into Quang Ngai Province forced the Viet Cong and North Vietnamese to move back to their habitual hideouts in the coastal mountains, just to the far side of the coastal plain and rising up along the length of the fertile valleys.

Tolson decides to seek them out using a particular tactical offensive technique. His method is inspired by the cavalry tradition of mounting light and fast units able to strike with lightning swiftness and immediately withdraw. He has no problem adapting this confection to the airmobile sauce. He picks as objectives the An Lao and Song Re Valleys, already well known to the grunts.

The Cav maintains pressure on the enemy, destroying rice caches in the narrow valleys while looking for the headquarters of the 3ᵈ North Vietnamese Division. The first VC ralliers under the *Chu Hoi Program*, the *Hoi Chanhs*, are re-indoctrinated and trained as Kit Carson Scouts. They efficiently participate on the patrols and help in the search for information. Their detachment becomes the 191ˢᵗ Military Intelligence Detachment.

The 31st of May, to the east of Bong Son near the village of An Qui, the 9th Battalion of the 22d NVA Regiment falls afoul of the 1st of the 9th, the 1st of the 8th, and the 1st of the 12th. It loses ninety-six men.

In June, it is the 2d Viet Cong Regiment and the 18th North Vietnamese Regiment that are intercepted near Dam Tra-O Lake, while heading for the Nui Mieu Hills. The Black Knights of the 1st of the 5th and the 2d of the 5th conducting the operation count eighty-four enemy dead.

On 9 August, Alpha Company, 1st of the 8th is on a mission in the Song Re Valley. Its objective is *LZ Pat*, a narrow crest line girdled by shear drop-offs. Captain Bluhm lifts off with his hundred and twenty skytroopers. Intense antiaircraft fire suddenly erupts from the surrounding hills. Two helicopter gunships of the 1st of the 9th, an OH-13, and the Brigade Commander's Charlie Charlie, his command chopper, are shot down or badly damaged.

Bluhm and his men are nailed to the ground by face-on fire. Well protected in their positions, the NVA dominate Alpha Company. The anti-air machine guns are redirected at the ground and methodically labor over the area needed for the landing zone. The number of dead and wounded climbs quickly with no possibility of evacuation. Sergeant Stripes sets up an 81mm Mortar to neutralize the machine guns. Their muzzle blasts are visible and give away their positions. No sooner than he fires off two mortar rounds, the NVA answer with mortar salvos of their own. It is as if the Americans were in an arena. The North Vietnamese see every move they make.

The machine gunners try to find positions in which to emplace their M60s. They set up on the slopes beside the LZ, but are hit, one after the other. Air Force fighter-bombers finally burst out over the hilltops. Skyraiders bomb the NVA anti-aircraft machine guns. At the same time, and in spite of the heavy fire, Medevac choppers come in to pick up the many wounded.

Phantom jets and F-100s take the place of the Skyraiders. They cover all the surrounding hills with high explosive bombs, napalm, and cannon fire. They unload not less than 40 tons of high explosives, 14 tons of napalm, and 22,600 rounds of 20mm cannon fire to suppress the North Vietnamese flak. Alpha Company is able to withdraw before nightfall after forty-two air sorties.

LZ Pat leaves a bitter taste in Tolson's mouth. He concludes that his raid tactics are always very risky if the means employed are too light. He again concentrates his action on Binh Dinh Province with combined operations involving the police, search and destroy missions, and pacification.

On 28 September, General Tolson receives orders to again reinforce I Corps and help the III^d Marine Amphibious Force, increasingly engaged to the north at the DMZ. On 1 October, the 2^d of the 12th and the 3^d Brigade CP leave for Chu Lai. Opcon to the 3^d Brigade are the 2^d of the 12th, Bravo Troop of the 1st of the 9th, and Charlie Battery of the 1st of the 77th. *Operation Wheeler/Wallowa* kicks off in an area twenty miles southwest of Da Nang. Two times the North Vietnamese attempt to attack Brigade positions, at *LZ Ross* and *LZ Leslie*. The enemy leaves 289 dead on the field. Their losses so far during *Operation Pershing* mount to 3,188 killed.

True autonomous intervention forces, the Brigades are able to pass under the operational control of any senior headquarters to meet operational needs. That is the case with the 1st Brigade that, under the command of Colonel Donald V. Rattan, is placed under the operational control of the 4th Infantry Division at Dak To. Working with the 173^d Airborne Brigade and the 52^d Aviation Battalion, the 1st Brigade intervenes to relieve the 4th Infantry Division whose Dak To Camp is surrounded by four well-equipped North Vietnamese Infantry Regiments. Headquarters expects a massive attack on the Base. In twenty-four hours, Colonel Rattan is in place with the 1st of the 12th to relieve sorely tried units of the 4th Infantry Division on Hill 724.

Dak To led to a very large airmobile operation. Twenty-two thousand sorties are conducted to move forty thousand men and six thousand tons of freight. The North Vietnamese attack does not happen. The First Cav has only the 2^d Brigade to secure Binh Dinh Province during this time. This offers an occasion to intensify combined operations with the 22^d Division of the South Vietnamese Army. Tolson develops excellent relations with Colonel Nguyen Van Hieu.

Routine operations follow their course. Scouts from the 1st of the 9th Cav continue to overfly trails and villages looking for signs of the enemy. On 6 December an OH-13 near the village of Dai Dong spots an antenna. On the second pass, a machine-gun fires on the helicopter. At 1630, the Blues of Alpha Troop air assault near the village of Tam Quan. As the day ends, they are in contact with NVA regulars well dug in in a trench system, its bunkers concealed by crops maturing along the terraces. The terrain is strewn with hedgerows of bamboo and cactus, and with clusters of palm trees, ideal for mounting ambushes and for slowing the progress of an infantry force.

The Blues quickly ask for reinforcements, this mouthful being too big for the Blue Team to chew. Colonel Rattan, in the mean time back from Dak To, immediately dispatches a platoon from

Delta Troop by jeep, as well as the 1st Battalion of the 50th Mechanized Infantry. This time he takes pains to avoid a trap as at *LZ Pat*. He orders Bravo Company, 1st of the 8th in as reinforcement.

The North Vietnamese react strongly. Because of the topography, the fighting quickly devolves into a duel to the finish, fought around hedgerows and clumps of bamboo. The enemy leave their holes to finish off and strip the wounded.[1] The four M113 armored personnel carriers of the 50th start to bog down in the mud. One of them is hit by a B40.[2] The other three manage to pull back.

Colonel Rattan brings to bear all available tube and aerial rocket artillery. Helicopter gunships run search patterns over the village all night using their searchlights and dropping flares. Meanwhile, Colonel Rattan assigns the 40th South Vietnamese Infantry Regiment the mission encircling the village with the support of tanks and flame-throwers.

At dawn the sky is overcast and spits down an intermittent rain. Visibility, however, is still good enough for the helicopters. After making a rocket run, the gunships lay down a haze of CS gas. Four M42 Duster armored vehicles with their twin 40mm cannons take up positions in front of the village and shred all the vegetation that was blocking visibility at ground level. Eighth Engineer bulldozers scrape away the muddy top foot or so of mud on the rice paddies so that the M113s can pass over them without sinking in.

At 0900 hours, Lieutenant Colonel Dubin with the 1st of the 8th moves out toward the village with the support of the armored personnel carriers. When they reach the paddy fields they are stopped by bursts from machine guns, AK47s, and a shower of grenades. The snipers concentrate their fire on the drivers and machine gunners of the 113s. The APCs come to a halt in the middle of the field. With twenty men wounded already, Alpha Company is still caught in the open. The assault is stopped immediately. The 1st of the 8th draws back. The artillery again pounds the enemy positions to repress enemy fire and allow the dead and wounded to be collected and evacuated. Twelve Hueys are finally able to evacuate the casualties.

The Americans renew the attack at the beginning of the afternoon. This time, a flame-throwing tank precedes the M113s. One of the APCs receives a direct hit and explodes. The trooper manning the flame-thrower spots the location from where the 57mm recoilless rifle was fired. He swings his weapon around and fires a jet of napalm on the NVA position. Alpha Company, despite its spirited assault, is stopped again. It still has three APCs.

The NVA focus heavy fire on the three remaining M113s. Sud-

197

denly, the APC drivers realize that they are only fifty meters from the first enemy trench line. In a rage, they pour gasoline to their engines and accelerate toward the enemy positions. Bounding forward, they reach the trenchline and grind it under their treads, partially caving it in. The North Vietnamese, surprised by the suddenness of the armored charge, dart from their holes and crumbling trenches and attempt to climb onto the APCs, but they are either crushed or gunned down. The infantrymen follow the APCs' charge and occupy the trench line, part of more extensive North Vietnamese fortified positions.

Charlie Company, 1st of the 8th arrives the next day to relieve Alpha Company. The advance continues behind armored vehicles, bulldozers, and engineers who destroy all the fortified positions. The fighting becomes sporadic with knots of resistance within the fortified hamlets. The cleanup continues for several days.

The All the Way Brigade gathers intelligence that confirms that they had been fighting with the 7th and 8th Battalions of the 22d North Vietnamese Regiment. To bring the 1st Brigade up to strength, the 1st Battalion of the 12th Cavalry is ordered back from Dak To. The cleanup of the area around Tam Quan is conducted in depth to completely eliminate any enemy presence.

The action ends on 19 December when Brigade elements intercept a VC unit on the north bank of the Bong Son River. During these fourteen days of operations, the 1st Brigade suffers 58 killed and 250 wounded. The troops in the ruins of the trenches and the broken and tumbled bunkers count 850 dead North Vietnamese. The Battle of Tam Quan is the biggest engagement during the whole of *Operation Pershing*. The Battle demonstrated that cooperation between airmobile and mechanized forces is effective, particularly over well-defended terrain.

Operation Pershing ends on 21 January 1968. Colonel Conrad Stansberry, Division Chief of Staff, summarizes it thus:

> Although it's difficult to precisely measure the degree of success achieved in the many facets of the war as conducted in this Province, the damage inflicted on the enemy is significant, as much in the loss of human life as in combat potential. What's more, The Vietcong infrastructure has been hurt to the extent that they can't organize operations in the coastal provinces. So the local population is now aware of the presence of free world forces and their ability to wear down and destroy the enemy.

The statistics from *Operation Pershing* are not negligible: 2,049 North Vietnamese and 3,367 Vietcong killed, 236 North Vietnamese and 2,123 Vietcong captured. With its mission of reconnaissance and intervention, the 1st Squadron of the 9th Cavalry Regiment is particularly well adapted to the objectives of *Operation Pershing*. The Squadron paid a particularly heavy price for this 343-day operation. The 1st Squadron of the 9th Cavalry Regiment brought 770 men and eighty-eight helicopters into the action. It recorded 931 enemy contacts. In the course of these actions, 250 helicopters were hit by fire. One hundred and two were severely enough damaged to be withdrawn from the inventory. Fourteen were shot down and completely destroyed. The losses in human life for the same period were 55 men killed in action, one disappeared, and 264 wounded in combat. Thirty-eight percent of the Division's losses during this period, the highest for any unit, are from the 1st of the 9th, a testimony to its being in the middle of the action.

This heavy toll is understandable when you listen to Lieutenant Colonel Dean Graham define the meaning of "reconnaissance mission." "A reconnaissance mission? Well, yeah, sure! They give you ten square klicks to search through. You're supposed to find out whether or not there's bunkers and fortified villages there, and particularly if there's enemy troops. In an area that you know is hostile, you've got to fly at low altitude and in a special way. You never fly over a place twice from the same direction. You fly nap of the earth, just above the ground where it's open, and at treetop level over jungle and forest. The best altitude is three meters! At that height, you're less vulnerable. Between fifty and a thousand feet, you're an ideal target. That's the killing zone.[3]

For *Pershing*, the 1st of the 9th is credited with 513 NVA and 1,214 VC KIA and 602 prisoners. The Vietcong and the North Vietnamese in the Province take these new facts of life into account and hide from the sight of the scouts. The enemy digs himself in, excavates a labyrinth of tunnels, of hiding places. The VC and NVA create a veritable life underground to get away from the eyes of heliborne observers and bombs from B-52s. The Division is no longer able to overfly the land and then react to its observations.

The Division directly participated in 970 combined operations with the National Police Field Force, which enabled the identification of 1,600 Vietcong belonging to administrative or political organizations of the communist forces. Among them, more than two hundred were identified as playing important roles in these organizations.

Black Lists are established for use in Division police operations. The 545th Military Police Company interrogates and registers 10,407 VC suspects. Thanks to this effort at population control, the Division renders ineffective over half of the Vietcong cadres. When the government organizes elections, 96.9 percent of those registered actually voted, whereas the national average was only 80.9 percent.

The Division paid dearly for these results: 852 killed in combat, 22 missing in action, and 4,119 wounded, to which must be added 286 accidental deaths. The Infantry takes the biggest hit. Replacing trained and experienced infantrymen becomes more and more difficult.

Translator's Notes

[1] The North Vietnamese characteristically killed wounded Americans when they could, and then took not only their weapons but also their boots, uniforms, and other equipment.

[2] The B40 is a Soviet or Chinese manufactured individual anti-tank recoilless weapon that fires a shaped charge projectile. It is used against armored vehicles or bunkered positions.

[3] In fact, the chopper pilots were a bit more aggressive than that. The pilots of the observation helicopters, the small and vulnerable OH-13s, would fly right down over the tops of trees, hover, and use their rotor wash to splay the leafy branches aside, to goad the enemy into firing to give away his position. This tactic worked well, but the helicopters drew a lot of fire and were often shot down. It was the rare First Cav OH-13 observation pilot who, in country for several months, had not been shot down at least once.

CHAPTER XVII

It is 3:15 AM, 31 January 1968. Richard Stark works the control tower at Tan Son Nhut Airbase, the huge airbase near Saigon. The radio crackles. An incoming aircraft announces its approach. "Is the field secure?"

"Affirmative. It's completely secure. Call on short final."

Stark is surprised by the question and goes back to reading a comic strip.

It is 3:17 AM. "I'm on short final! I can see suspicious movement to the northwest and sporadic fire."

"The runway is clear, bring it in! Ah, yup! I see some isolated tracer fire to the northwest, probably nervous perimeter guards."

The plane lands. Shortly thereafter, a twin-engined C-47 roles down the taxiway and holds pending clearance for takeoff. Stark watches it, waiting for the pilot to request clearance. The pilot revs up each engine and checks the function of the plane's controls.

The blast of an exploding mortar round illuminates the cockpit with its flash. "You're cleared for immediate takeoff. Go," Stark shouts into the mike, as he finally realizes that the base is under attack. He alerts the 4th Platoon, Huey gunships, of the 120th Assault Helicopter Company, a unit permanently assigned to Tan Son Nhut.

The Tet Offensive begins with a panoramic attack planned long months ago by the North Vietnamese High Command. At dawn on 31 January, all across South Vietnam, tens of thousands of communist fighters begin an assault on military posts, barracks, administrative buildings, police stations, prisons, and radio stations in the cities of forty-four Provinces. Bien Hoa, like Tan Son Nhut and other large American Bases are bombarded to keep helicopters and other aircraft on the ground.

A North Vietnamese Division preceded by Viet Cong irregulars invests Hue and occupies almost the whole imperial city. The flag with the yellow star floats over Zenith Gate. In Saigon, five groups of Viet Cong sappers dressed in South Vietnamese military uniforms plan to seize the Presidential Palace, Naval Headquarters, the Joint General Staff Headquarters, and the radio station. They also attack the American Embassy to strike at American public opinion.

Fifteen sappers move up to the American Embassy next to the Presidential Palace and the hotels that house journalists. They ar-

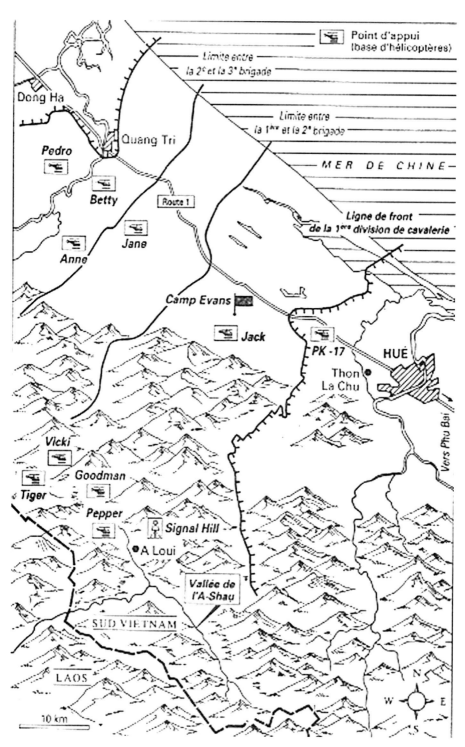

Tet and the A Shau Valley

rive in a Peugot van and an old taxi. They first breech the wall with explosives. The first two Viet Cong to penetrate into the Embassy garden are taken out by the two MP guards. The VC fire back and kill the two MPs. Two more military policemen arriving by jeep are in turn killed. A marine crawls out on a roof and, with his M16, slows down the progress of the VC suicide mission. The armored window blinds of the Chancellery are closed to block all access to the inside.

In the early light, a chopper from the 191st Helicopter Assault Company piloted by Chief Warrant Officer Richard Inskeep arrives over the Embassy. He evacuates a wounded man from the roof. At the same time a door gunner hoses down the garden. Under heavy fire, he moves out to make way for choppers bringing in a platoon of 101st Airborne Division troopers to clear the building. The fighting around the Embassy goes on for six and a half hours. There is a general offensive in all the Provinces.

It was in July of 1967 that Ho Chi Minh and General Vo Nguyen Giap decided to launch a general offensive in the South. It depended upon mobilizing the combined forces of the North Vietnamese Army and the Viet Cong in the South to prepare for a vast operation that would permit the population in the South to rise up against the Thieu regime and so end the war. They had to show the American public that the North had lost none of its offensive capability, that the North Vietnamese Army was able to surprise the American Army and inflict heavy losses on it and maybe a sharp defeat.

In this way the North Vietnamese thought to traumatize the United States where public opinion and the media were becoming more and more hostile to the war. The States was beginning an electoral year. Ho Chi Minh thus bet that the American government would come to the negotiating table and would accept any concessions to get out of the war.

For the offensive to succeed, surprise would have to be total. The North Vietnamese perfectly mastered the techniques of clandestinely moving and reassembling their troops. But the Americans had very sophisticated technical listening and surveillance means that threatened to expose their plans. The planners, searching for a successful strategy, looked for an historical precedent in the art of diversion. It was in 1789 that the montagnards of Tay Son, led by Nguyen Hue managed to defeat the Manchu forces at Dong Ha by attacking during the sacred time of Tet, the Lunar New Year. Thanks to which, they liberated Hanoi.

For Asians, and particularly for Vietnamese, Tet is the principal holiday, the most important period for those that practice ancestor worship. For several days everything comes to a halt. The population is on the move to gather in family groups and render homage, to make offerings at the shrines of their ancestors. The North Vietnamese decided to repeat the example of the montagnards of 1789 and to attack the day of Tet. They plan to hide their intentions as best they can.

For starters, the Viet Cong decree a truce from 27 January to 3 February. On the logistical side, the North Vietnamese need for the American bombing in the North to halt in order to concentrate and then move their Divisions. To this end, they start a rumor that "they might participate in negotiations if the Americans stop bombing the North." A Romanian diplomat passing through Hanoi takes upon himself the task of passing on this hint.

In mid-January the United States is ready to demonstrate its good intentions and stop the bombing around Hanoi. This decision goes along with the Tet cease fire. Finally, so that the people in North Vietnam will not have to go without the festivities associated with Tet, the Hanoi government announces that it has modified the celebratory dates. In the North, the Lunar New Year is decreed to begin on 29 January rather than on the 30th. The celebrations usually start the evening before Tet. Thus the North Vietnamese will fete Tet three days before the correct date, 31 January, the beginning of the Year of the Monkey.

The American and South Vietnamese High Commands, however, are not totally surprised. At Dak To, a document taken off an enemy informed them that that battle was just a part of the preparation for a major offensive in Kontum Province. In the Khe Sanh area the Marines next discovered new concentrations. Since the end of December 1967, intelligence reports indicated a tripling of traffic along the Ho Chi Minh Trail. By January South Vietnamese troops in Qui Nhon have also discovered tape recorded programs intended for broadcast after the seizure of government radio stations.

In light of these numerous indicators, General Weyand, IIId Corps Area Commander, concluded that enemy forces established in the Saigon area were going to come out of their sanctuaries and head for the capital. General Philip Davidson, MACV Intelligence Officer, in turn informed Westmoreland that they should expect a general offensive. General Westmoreland canceled his scheduled leave.

On 20 January 1968, Westmoreland sent a TWX to the Chiefs of Staff of the two armies: "The enemy presently threatens us in several areas with the intention of winning several victories essential to their prestige and accession to power.[1] They may initiate action before, during, or after Tet." Westmoreland insisted that General Thieu cancel the scheduled Tet Cease-Fire in the provinces of the Ist Corps Area, and limit it to twenty-four hours in the rest of the country. Thieu agreed to compromise. The Truce would last from 1800 hours 29 January to 0600 hours 31 January.

Westmoreland informed the press and, in particular, NBC Television, that the enemy was preparing an operation that was intended to produce a spectacular success for them on the eve of Tet. General Wheeler did the same, but the press gave these bits of information but scant coverage in the States. The public remained calm, reassured everywhere by the optimistic statements of the generals in their after action reports following the conclusions of large-scale operations.

The media were all focused on the last move by Hanoi: the attack on Khe Sanh just to the south of the Demilitarized Zone. On 21 January Hill 861, an outpost of the Base, had come under violent bombardment and an infantry assault. Khe Sanh Base, held by the Marines, was placed on red alert. The siege began.

Quang Tri, 31 January 1968, 0200 hours. A squad of the 10th North Vietnamese Sapper Battalion, the advance party, enters the city. Its mission is to foment confusion and panic in the city with sabotage and explosives, and to weaken its defenses and ease the way for a joint attack by the 812th North Vietnamese Regiment and two Viet Cong Battalions. The sappers destroy wire lines of communications and several other objectives. Their actions raise an immediate alert.

The two Battalions of the 1st South Vietnamese Regiment take positions to the north and north-west of the city and the 9th South Vietnamese Airborne Regiment based at Tri Buu on the outskirts of the city respond in like manner. The majority of sappers that had infiltrated the city are killed.

Just at dawn, the 812th NVA Regiment arrives alone. It is 0420 hours. The bulk of the North Vietnamese forces are at least two hours behind schedule because of weather conditions. Under heavy tropical rains, the NVA infantrymen have trouble getting oriented on unfamiliar terrain.

The 814th NVA Regiment falls on Tri Buu and immediately puts heavy pressure on the South Vietnamese paratroopers who, foot by foot, withdraw toward the center of Quang Tri. The 812th Regiment and the VC Battalions penetrate the city in several places, but are contained by the 1st ARVN Regiment. By noon, the situation is still touch-and-go.

Very worried, Robert Brewer, American Adviser to the Province Chief, calls a conference with Colonel Donald Rattan, Commander of the 1st Brigade of the 1st Cavalry Division and advisor to the 1st ARVN Regiment. Rattan has been established with his Brigade twenty kilometers west of Quang Tri since 29 January.

On 15 January, General Tolson had received an order from Saigon to move his Division north to reinforce the Ist Corps Area. At that time Tolson was in the middle of *Operation Pershing* with his 2^d Brigade in the sandy villages along the coast. During this time the Marines were building up Khe Sanh and, in the northern provinces of their area, confronting massive North Vietnamese infiltration.

Tolson thus had cranked over his logistical apparatus to move each Brigade to its newly assigned AO. The various units had transited through An Khe or *English* to replace equipment as needed and moved out quickly thereafter. The 1st Brigade headed for Quang Tri, and the 3^d for Que Son, some forty kilometers south of Da Nang, where it had already spent four months fighting the 2^d NVA Division. Colonel Rattan arrived on 25 January at *LZ Betty*, and took over the area from the Marines. Only the 2^d Brigade remained in Binh Dinh Province to assure its security.

General Tolson also moved his Command Post. He lifted out for *LZ El Paso*, a cemetery north of Phu Bai, a sinister and arid spot. Tolson had informed General Abrams that it was not such a great location, and Abrams suggested he set up his CP at Camp Evans, the Marine Base located fifteen kilometers northwest of Hue. Bravo Troop, 1st of the 9th was the first unit to set itself up there. That very evening, on the "Peoples' Armed Forces Radio," a seductive female voice welcomed the arrival of the First Cav with a particular greeting to Bravo Troop on the part of the Peoples' Army of Vietnam. A sweet voice for a radio message that concluded with these words: "I hope you have written your letters of farewell to your families and your sweethearts."

At Tolson's *El Paso* CP a message comes in on a secure line. "Sir! Colonel Rattan's got an urgent message for you."

"How goes it at *Betty*? Over."

"No problem at Betty. We've been under mortar attack since dawn, but not a problem. Where it's turned to crap is at Quang Tri. The city is partly occupied by the 812th and the 814th NVA Regiments and two VC Battalions. They're concentrated to the east of the city and are still receiving reinforcements. I've just been brought up to date by our province guy over there, Robert Brewer. He thinks our ARVN friends of the 1st and the 9th won't be able to hold out for very long. Over."

"What's your proposal? Over."

"We've really got to get into the act! *LZ Betty* is twenty klicks southwest of Quang Tri. My mission is to protect the south flank of the city. But we've got to counter-attack in the east. From a purely defensive position I can shift to the offensive. If I don't do it, Quang Tri may fall while I sit here on my butt. Over."

"It's a risky gamble Don. Be careful not to let your units get separated, particularly in light of the incoming you've been getting all morning. If you're sure you can make it work, do it! You've got a green light from me, but you'll have to depend on just your own people and your own helicopters! Happy hunting! Keep me posted. Out here."

Rattan, in the area only six days, again consults Brewer to assure himself that the NVA axes of advance really are out to the east of the city. Then he leaves to recon the LZs he will need to block the enemy's movement into Quang Tri.

"Bob, we've only got an hour to put an attack plan together. I've only got two battalions, the 1st of the 12th and the 1st of the 5th. There's only one way to relieve the defenders at Quang Tri. First, cut off the enemy's reinforcements: troops, ammo, and artillery support. Then, hit 'em from behind. What d'you think?"

"How soon can you crank it over?"

"I'll shoot for 1345, time to bring the 1st of the 9th and the ARA into the plan." He turns to his Brigade RTO. "Get the sixes of the 1st of the 12th and the 1st of the 5th on the horn, please."

Rattan outlines for Daniel French how he wants a surprise attack on the NVA artillery. His S3 follows up with a frag order to Runkle for the 1st of the 5th's part of the plan.

Charlie Company, 1st of the 12th, is the first to lift, followed by Bravo Company. After a nap of the earth flight, the two Companies air assault onto an LZ next to the village of Thon An Thai, right in the middle of the enemy position. They assault smack on top of a defensive position of the K4 Battalion, 812th NVA Regiment. The enemy soldiers, surprised and furious, try to reorient their weapons and fire on the ships coming in on final. The troopers, riding the skids, fire as they come in, leaping in clusters from their helicopters as they near the ground. They shoot their way into mortar pits, anti-aircraft machine gun positions, and 57mm recoilless rifle crews, assault rifles on fully automatic.

On the ground there is havoc. The NVA weapons crews desperately attempt to get their weapons turned around and pointed at the incoming choppers. Bravo Company lands on the other side of the NVA position. Hit on two sides, the K4 Battalion artillerymen end up by pulling out about 1900 hours, ceding the ground to the two Companies of the 1st of the 12th.

During this time, Charlie Company, 1st of the 5th air assaults to the southeast of Quang Tri, along Route 1. Alpha Company puts down on the other side of the road. The two Cav Companies take the K6 Battalion, 812th NVA Regiment in the rear, supported by gunships that strafe the enemy ranks. The K6 Battalion finds itself sandwiched between Cav units and South Vietnamese paratroopers.

Shocked by the keenness of the Americans and the strength of their counterattack, the NVA prefer to break off the engagement. They take advantage of columns of refugees to lose themselves in the crowd. By nightfall, the fighting is over. The following day, the 1st ARVN Regiment starts the clean-up operation in Quang Tri. The Cavalry takes the mission of securing the surrounding area and pursuing the dispersed NVA regulars. A group of seventy-six NVA infantrymen take refuge in one of the churches in the southern part of Quang Tri. A helicopter gunship takes them out.

The attackers of Quang Tri lose 914 killed. Eighty-six enemy soldiers are captured. They abandon 331 weapons. Five battalions had been obliged to break contact and disappear. This city, the capital of the I Corps Area and a major communications hub, had been one of the principal targets of the offensive. Apparently, the North Vietnamese were completely surprised by the fighting methods of the Air Cav. They had been used to fighting the Marines who maneuvered like classic infantry, using helicopters as a means of transport, but never as an assault vehicle.

Whenever the soldiers of the 812th NVA Regiment spot a helicopter, they throw themselves on the ground and play dead. If the chopper keeps coming toward them, they get up and fire at it. The gunship pilots do not fall for it, and unload machine gun fire and rockets on any enemy who exposes himself in the open that way.

Colonel Donald Rattan's actions, in the purest style of a cavalry charge, is the first good news Saigon gets during the grim week of Tet.

Hue, the Imperial City, is an agglomeration of 140,000 inhabitants. It is under North Vietnamese and Viet Cong control. Only the building housing American advisors escapes communist seizure. During the night of 30-31 January, the 800th, 804th, and 806th NVA Regiments attacked, as well as the K4B and K4C Battalions. Allied military authorities hesitated to damage the historic city with aerial bombardment or naval gunfire. The allies had to retake the city, then, house by house and wall by wall. The job fell on General Truong and his 1st ARVN Division, as well as upon the three Battalions of Marines.

Although the majority of 3[d] Brigade units are occupied establishing themselves at Camp Evans, some of the 1st of the 9th Blue Team lift out to block access to the west of the city and so cut off reinforcements to the North Vietnamese units in the city. In one of the lift ships the pilot, Second Lieutenant Babcock, cruises low over the suburbs of Hue. At the same time that he hears a series of explosions, his helicopter starts to vibrate, to tremble. Its engine loses power and the aircraft starts to drop.

"Heads up! We're hit," he yells. We've got to put down. I'm on autorotation. Hold on!" The Huey lands with a shock in the middle of a bunch of water buffalos and peasants working in the field. No sooner does the crew unbuckle belts and harnesses than they see some twenty VC spill out from around the nearby haystacks. There is nothing the Americans can do. They are dragged from the helicopter and led toward NVA lines.

Thomas Maerhrlein had heard the last call from Babcock. He turns his Huey sharply and heads for the downed chopper. He sees thick black smoke roiling from it. He flares to a hover just above and to its side. "Damn," he mouths into his mike, "there's nobody left! This is a pretty big field. We'll take a look over behind those trees."

The helicopter clears the top of the cluster of trees. Just on the far side, Maerhrlein breaks out over two groups of men in black pajamas. He orients his slick to align his machine guns for firing. At that moment he sees two big Americans who dive to the ground. The bursts of fire go over their heads. The pilot makes two complete turns and slows to a hover a hundred and fifty meters further into the field. Babcock and his copilot take advantage of the diversion to escape, and run like hell toward Maerhrlein's chopper which is now the target of all the VC fire.

"As soon as the two men clamber aboard, Maerhrlein instructs his door gunners to keep up a continuous heavy fire. He holds his slick in a hover. "Shit, go on. Shoot! Fuck... ." The pilot sees that one of the M60s is jammed. He turns about and lines up his other door gunner on the VC. Silence from that machine gun too. The door gunner violently racks the bolt, but without effect. The Viet Cong are no more than fifty meters away and closing.

Maerhrlein turns about, his copilot at the controls, and grabs his 12 gauge pump shotgun. He fires all eight rounds in the tube. The double-ought buck loads stop the VC charge. He puts the shotgun down and, taking over the stick, powers the helicopter out of harm's way. He leaves ten Vietcong laid out in the field. "How about that folks? A little extra firepower when the shit hits the fan!" Babcock, still out of breath, grins and comments: "It's good to be back!"

General Tolson settles in and gets his two hundred helicopters under cover. On 2 February he sends one of his Assistant Division

Commanders, Brigadier General Oscar Davis, as his representative, to the headquarters of General Ngo Quang Truong.

"Very good that Cav help us. I know when Cav reach walls at Hue, battle soon be over. What are forces that General Tolson send to relieve Hue?"

"Two Battalions of Colonel Campbell's 3^d Brigade. The weather conditions are very bad and slow down helicopter operations. For two days now the helicopters have had to fly at an altitude of under ten meters. The 1st Brigade, it's totally engaged at Quang Tri. Campbell's other battalions have got to stay put to defend Camp Evans. We just arrived in this area. So, what's your take on the situation here?"

"Ah! To be brief, and to extent that our information correct, five enemy battalions already in Hue and some forces, we don't know what, occupy Thon La Chu Village three kilometers west and also to southwest to protect enemy communications line. We sure Route 1 cut. We know enemy make ambushes on road."

General Davis moves up to the operations map to get a better idea of the local topography. "It seems to me we need to pinpoint the enemy locations in the west, fix them and finish them off. I propose to land the 2^d of the 12th here, in your troop training area, by Kilometer Marker Seventeen. That way we'll lift the threat of more communist reinforcements getting to Hue."

"When can you do that General?"

"Tomorrow. Lieutenant Colonel Richard Sweet will handle all that with his 2^d of the 12th. I'll set everything up with Colonel Campbell."

On 3 February the 2^d Battalion, 12th Cavalry Regiment moves out on foot. Starting off at Kilometer Marker Seventeen, they sweep along Route 1 toward Hue. Along about 1030 hours, just before Thon La Chu, the first enemy soldiers come into view in a large rice paddy. The village is surrounded by abundant vegetation and several lines of defense, originally prepared as a CORDS Project. A persistent drizzle and an almost nonexistent ceiling keep the lift ships on the ground. An air assault is impossible. Alpha Company, commanded by Captain Helvey, moves out in assault formation to seize a clearing located to the north of the village.

Two ARA ships of the 2^d of the 20th brave the lousy weather and cover Helvey's attack, which then makes it to the clearing. But the North Vietnamese response is fierce. They have numerous machine guns, mortars, and 57mm Recoilless Rifles. Helvey informs Battalion that he does not have enough troops, even with the available fire support, to carry the day.

The 2^d of the 12th has run head on into the base of the 7th and

9th Battalions of the 29th Regiment of the 325C NVA Division. They have just arrived from Khe Sanh to support the attack on Hue. Lieutenant Colonel Sweet decides to ease Alpha Company's situation with more artillery support.

In spite of the very poor weather, by early afternoon two Chinooks manage to bring in two 105mm howitzers of the 1st of the 77th Artillery. Set up at Kilometer Marker Seventeen, the two tubes do not provide enough additional firepower to make the difference. The 2d of the 12th reinforces its perimeter and passes a rainy night.

At 0630 hours the next day, 4 February, the North Vietnamese attack. Hundreds of mortar rounds batter the American positions. The NVA infantrymen appear determined to destroy the Americans. While the enemy mortar rounds are falling, the NVA soldiers charge. AK47 or light machine gun at the hip, the NVA, in close ranks, run at the 2d of the 12th's lines. Several of their own mortar rounds explode in their midst as they charge. Shoulder to shoulder, they continue their advance. The grunts engage and repel successive assault waves. The heavy fog still has not lifted. The fighting is at close quarters, sometimes hand-to-hand.

After six hours of contact, the 2d of the 12th finds itself in a delicate situation. They have been able to evacuate only the seriously wounded, and that thanks to an acrobatic Medevac ship. The men are exhausted. They have not slept for two days. O'Reily, one of Alpha Company's RTOs, is light headed. "Sir, we're out of water."

"Get some from the creek there and use your halazone tablets."

"That water's really shitty, and we're out of purification tablets. We're out of Cs too, and we've already used up all the sugar cane, bananas, and onions we could scrounge up around here. We're sharing smokes too."

"Well, tough shit for us. It'll get better. No sweat!"

The radio comes to life and O'Reily listens intently. "Sir, Colonel Sweet wants you at his CP in ten minutes with Top and whatever Platoon Leaders or Platoon Sergeants we can spare here.

Lieutenant Colonel Sweet gathers his officers and several noncommissioned officers from all his companies in close around him. "Gents, we're not goin' to spend another night in this place. Colonel Campbell has sent the 5th of the 7th to Marker Seventeen, but by the time they arrive, the NVA could be really deep into our shit. I've decided to get us out of here tonight. It's risky, but this time, the crappy weather's goin' to help us."

"We're goin' to break contact and move out in one long, single file column. You'll take your wounded out on stretchers. Make 'em if you have to. The objective is to reach this hill, less than three klicks behind our present position. Once there, we'll have the high ground, and the NVA'll have much more difficulty tryin' to get at us. That'll give the 5th of the 7th time to get here."

"We've got to keep the NVA from seein' what we're doin'. As you move out, keep up enough activity in your positions to make 'em think, for as long as possible, that everybody's still here. With the stuff you've got, make up some dummies that'll be visible in some of your positions. In this crappy weather they'll look real enough. Set up whatever booby traps you can. Use some of your Claymores and grenades. Short-fuse the grenades 'n set 'em up with trip wires, use up whatever C4 you've got, mix in left-over mortar charges, all that shit—use your imagination, but be God damn careful. We don't want any of that stuff to go off until the NVA stumble into it. Questions so far?"

"Start your move-out at 2000 hours. Order of march: Charlie, Battalion CP, Alpha, Weapons, and Bravo. I'll have the Battalion Mortar Platoon kick it off with some close-in H&I fires at 1945.[2] I'll switch to smoke at 2000 hours. Then our mortars'll join the column and the artillery'll pick up direct support. You'll be able to see your hand in front of your face, but not much more. Don't cough when you move through that stuff. You'll be pretty well hidden to the NVA too. Are we clear so far? Questions?"

"You've got to move real quietly through the rice paddy—no talking, no whispering, nothing. The water'll be ankle-deep. Try not to make splashing noises. Total blackout of course—no shielded lights for navigation or anything else. Make sure no one lights up. Wrap your base plates and mortar tubes so they don't make noise. Fire discipline guys—no shots fired at all. If you get fired on, everybody on the ground, dry, wet, or pig shit, and quiet—lay dog. If that happens, head count by Company when we move out. Only Company COs may order return fire. If that happens, use the M60s. Are we clear to here?"

We'll be in ranger column—real stretched out. Everybody's got to keep track of the man in front. We won't take any breaks. If somehow the column gets split up, every leader's got to be able to get his group to the hill without further help. You're clear on that?"

"Okay, you've got to really watch your fire discipline. It should be getting light as we close on the hill, but your men'll be even more tired—they'll be seeing things. Careful not to shoot at each other—watch out for possible stragglers, separated groups. This is a full-attention operation folks, all the way. Every last troop has to completely understand what we're doing, where we're going, how to get there. Don't fuck it up! Final questions? You don't have a whole lot of time. Time check. I've got 1712 hours—now. Go back and get the word out. See you on the hill! Enjoy!"

At 2000 hours Hector Comancho, walking point for Charlie Company leads out across the paddy. Thirty minutes later, underway, the column with all its attachments stretches out some fifteen hundred meters. The night is black as ink.

An M16 bolt clacks home. The troops freeze, their boots swallowed in the mud. Nothing! They move out again, very quietly. The rice paddy gives directly on the river. It is chest deep, counting six inches or more of muddy bottom. The men cross carefully, holding the wounded over the slowly moving dirty water. They make a little noise in the crossing, but the column, in pitch black, makes the other side without losing any one or drawing fire.

A muffled explosion breaks the silence, followed at irregular intervals by more of the same. The NVA are in the Battalion's old positions, tripping some of the explosive devices. The NVA wise up quickly and the explosions end after a couple of minutes.

About 0700 hours the men of the 2^d of the 12th, one by one, disheveled, exhausted, emerge from the jungle to climb the last few hundred meters to the crest of the hill. Medevac ships are on final to pick up the wounded. "Sir, Colonel Campbell on the horn." The RTO passes his handset to the Battalion Commander.

"Good show. We've got confirmation that Thon La Chu is indeed a regimental headquarters. The NVA had a lot of heavy stuff there. The Air Force is taking care of it. The weather's still so bad they're on instrument. The Navy's pounding the place too. When you get a bit of rest, I'll get you in on the final cleanup. Over."

"Roger. Thanks. Over."

"Six out."

Two days later Thon La Thu, in spite of tons of bombs and napalm, still holds. The pilots cannot always precisely locate the enemy defenses. The 2^d Brigade arrives from Bong Son. Tolson decides to commit it to the battle along side the 3^d Brigade. He plans the Thon La Chu attack for 21 February.

The 5th of the 7th attacks in the north with the 1st of the 7th on its right flank. Sweet, with the 2^d of the 12th, comes from the northeast and south. The 2^d of the 501st Infantry attacks in the west. The VC and NVA are completely dug-in in a network of bunkers and tunnels. The troops move forwards with the help of M72 Light Anti-tank Weapons. Only the LAW, among their individual weapons, has any affect on the fortifications. The OH-13s of the 1st of the 9th employ their machine guns to clean out snipers in positions hidden from ground observation.

An infantry scout from the 1st of the 9th takes prisoner an NVA soldier who emerges from a tunnel, herding him along with a .38 special. The prisoner confirms that the North Vietnamese regulars have substantial quantities of food and ammunition packed in by the Viet Cong. "The VC hole up in the tunnels while their northern 'cousins' stir up shit and bring the world down on their heads. I don't think they get along too good. There's a racial division of tasks and risks," the scout mockingly comments.

In a little village near Hue, the men of the 2^d of the 501st find a scene of slaughter of women and children. They exhume fifteen cadavers. Executed at close range, the bodies have been burned nearly beyond recognition. In Hue, the troops recover the bodies of many thousands of civilians assassinated by the VC and NVA.

On 23 February Americans reach the walls of Hue. Lieutenant Colonel Joseph E. Wasiak arrives from the north with the 1st of the 7th. His Battalion faces enemy units that are attempting to leave the city. On the 24th, the Viet Cong flag is torn from the summit of the Citadel where it had flown since the beginning of the month. On the 25th, Lieutenant Colonel Sweet reaches the western walls of the city. It remains for him to dislodge the entrenched North Vietnamese positioned on this side of Hue. All this while, in the city center, Marines and South Vietnamese forces clean the quarters of the city house by house. The Cav takes over the job of fixing and destroying enemy Regiments in the jungle and mountains as they attempt to flee the area.

The VC and NVA losses rise to five thousand killed in the city itself and to three thousand in the surrounding area. The Americans, all units included, have 120 dead and 961 wounded. The South Vietnamese lost 363 killed and 1,242 wounded. The most damaged are the civilians: 5,000 dead or missing and 116,000 without shelter.

The Tet Offensive has been defeated everywhere in a few days. Hue is the only city where the battle lasted twenty-five days. For the communist forces, the offensive is a setback. In it, they lost about 45,000 men and almost 7,000 prisoners. If the preparation for the Offensive was done with care the operational phase, on the other hand, was less well coordinated.

The communists have failed in their *coup de force* and lose face with the population for having profaned a sacred holiday and for having brutally massacred large numbers of civilians. Their conduct severely tarnished their image as "liberators." On the allied side, the good combat performance of the South Vietnamese Army is a surprise and a source of real satisfaction, as much for the government of General Thieu as for the Americans. The

214

"Vietnamization" of the conflict is now viewed with more confidence.

Translator's Notes
[1] Military telegraphically transmitted message before the era of email.

[2] Harassing and Interdiction fires.

PART THREE

1968 - 1972

MOVE TO THE SOUTH

CHAPTER XVIII

Although MACV is reassured by its defeat of the Tet Offensive, it remains preoccupied with Khe Sanh where the siege continues. Westmoreland wonders whether Khe Sanh is Giap's main objective or, on the contrary, if he is using it as a diversion. He muses: "There's no doubt the enemy hope to have a decisive victory at Khe Sanh like that at Dien Bien Phu in 1954, with the intent that it produce a major psychological shock and erode American morale."

Since 25 January General Tolson has had the mission of putting together a plan to either evacuate or reinforce Khe Sanh. He envisages three phases: relieve the forces in Khe Sanh; open Route 9 from Ca Lu to Khe Sanh; destroy enemy forces in the zone of operations. The Tet Offensive disrupted the first part of the plan, but the General picked up where he left off as soon as the situation settled down.

Khe Sanh is situated twenty-three kilometers south of the Demilitarized Zone at the 17th Parallel, and ten kilometers east of the Laotian border. The Base was set up there to overlook the Ho Chi Minh Trail and to provide support as necessary to operations along the DMZ. It also dominates Route 9, the only east-west road between Laos and the coast.

The Base is situated on a plateau of laterite and extends barely six hundred meters. It is characterized mainly by its 1,190 meter long PSP landing strip, capable of accommodating C-130 Hercules aircraft. The plateau is surrounded by four narrow valleys overlooked by mountainous terrain, mostly to the north and northwest of the Base.

During the first weeks of 1968 the North Vietnamese continued to mass their troops around Khe Sanh. At least four Divisions were identified north of the DMZ. Two of these, the 325th and the 304th, came south and took up positions to the northwest of Quang Tri Province. The 304th Division has the distinction of having "Dien Bien Phu" embroidered in its battle flag. Some NVA Companies move up to the hills that surround the base. At the same time, numerous artillery batteries dig in in the southern part of the DMZ, right next to the Laotian border.

Convinced that an attack is imminent, General Westmoreland strengthens American forces in the area. By mid-January, the garrison at Khe Sanh has been reinforced by the 1st Battalion of the 26th Marines, the 1st Battalion of the 9th Marines, and by the 37th ARVN Ranger Battalion—altogether, over six thousand men.

Operation Pegasus, April 1968.

Approximately fifteen kilometers to the west and again, about the same distance to the northwest, the US Army established two fire bases: *Camp Carol* and *Rock Pile*, respectively. From these bases sixteen 175mm howitzers can provide immediate fire support to Khe Sanh. B-52s and Phantom tactical bombers assure Khe Sanh protection by pounding without letup the infiltration routes and the surrounding hills.

On 21 January 1968, in the early morning hours, the North Vietnamese attacked Hill 861 and the Khe Sanh Base. Eighteen Americans were killed and forty wounded. The landing strip was heavily damaged. An ammunition dump of 1,390 tons of munitions along with the fuel supply sustained a direct hit and blew. One helicopter was destroyed.

General Westmoreland decides to establish a MACV forward Command Post in the I Corps Area. He assigns this task to his Deputy, General Creighton Abrams, who establishes the CP at Phu Bai on 13 February. The same day the 101st Airmobile Division moves toward the I Corps Area. The 3d Brigade of the 82d Airborne Division arrives directly from the United States and reinforces the 101st.

Tolson redistributes the missions of his Brigades. The 1st continues the cleanup around Quang Tri. The 3d, sent to Hue, is relieved by the 2d Brigade of the 101st. It is ordered to return to Camp Evans and provide security for First Cavalry Division Headquarters. The 2d Brigade, in conjunction with the 101st Airmobile Division, conducts operations in the Hai Long and My Chang area. The pressure on Khe Sanh increases daily.

On 23 February the Base is hit by 1,300 rounds of different calibers. Terrible weather conditions slow resupply and hinder the precision of counter-battery fires. North Vietnamese sappers move right up to the Marines' barbed wire barriers and breach them in several places with Bangalore Torpedoes. The Base is surrounded. The force ratio is three to one in favor of the North Vietnamese.

After the surprise of Tet, the American Press engages in impassioned coverage of the Khe Sanh drama, over-dramatizing the situation. "This will be another Dien Bien Phu!" The siege becomes a veritable duel between Giap and Westmoreland. What is at stake in this contest is who, the United States Government or Ho Chi Minh, can bring enough force to bear to carry the issue on the ground.

On 2 March 1968, at Da Nang, General Tolson reveals his plan to relieve Khe Sanh. General Abrams, MACV Deputy Commander, and General Cushman, the Marine Commander in I Corps, hear out the presentation and approve the plan. The Operation will be called *Pegasus*, the winged horse.

MACV gives Tolson carte blanche, and puts additional forces at his disposition. The 1st and 26th Marine Regiments come under his orders as well as the 3d ARVN Airmobile Regiment and the 37th ARVN Ranger Battalion. All together, Tolson now commands thirty thousand men.

General Tolson begins with a trip to Khe Sanh to meet Colonel David Lownds, check out the avenues of approach into the Base, and coordinate the Operation. To get to Khe Sanh he choppers into an LZ near Lang Vei, the Green Beret Camp overrun by the NVA in mid-January. The Khe Sanh airstrip is reserved for C130s that unload their cargoes with drag chutes as they come in just over the airstrip.

Tolson has his staff construct a sand table mock-up of the Khe Sanh Base and its surrounding terrain. Beginning the 25th of March, Tolson orders Lieutenant Colonel Richard Diller of the 1st of the 9th to reconnoiter the area, to gather as much information as possible about enemy positions, and to inflict maximum damage on enemy air defenses. Batteries of 8 inch and 155mm howitzers arrive at Ca Lu and reinforce the support already furnished by the 175s at *Rock Pile* and *Camp Carol*.

Level areas identified as desirable landing zones are cleared with *Daisy Cutter* bombs that blast away the vegetation. The surrounding areas are treated to a copious dose of all imaginable sorts of explosives.

On D-Day minus six, Tolson orders the construction of an airstrip near Ca Lu. It must be five hundred meters long and two hundred meters wide. It will be called *LZ Stud*. The 8th Engineer Battalion from the Cav works day and night with Navy Sea Bees and the 11th Marine Engineer Battalion to complete the task. *LZ Stud* will be the logistical base for *Operation Pegasus*. Munitions, fuel, and spare parts will be stocked here. It will be the location of helicopters and maintenance facilities. It will also serve as a communications hub. Lieutenant Colonel Diller sets himself up here with his Reconnaissance Squadron. It is the base for the aerial rocket artillery. *LZ Stud* also serves as the coordination center for artillery support and B-52 strikes.

General Oscar Davis, Assistant Division Commander to Tolson, supervises the final phase of installing the advance CP. Everything is ready in eleven days. On D minus one, Tolson, in turn, comes to the *LZ*. He summons the unit commanders for a final briefing before the action.

"Gentlemen, if we're going to surprise them, we'll need speed and flexibility during the attack. Everyone's got to perfectly understand his role in the plan and how everything's got to really be coordinated. This is particularly so with respect to all our firepower. The air space will be saturated with objects: bombs, rockets, artillery projectiles, helicopters, and other aircraft. We've got to be especially careful that we don't run into or through friendly fire."

"That said, I'm going to point out again the phasing of Operation Pegasus. Tomorrow, D-Day. Two Battalions of the First Marines will launch a ground attack to the west of Khe Sanh, while Campbell, with the 3[d] Brigade, conducts an air assault. On D plus one and D plus two, the attack in the west continues toward Khe Sanh. On D plus three, the 2[d] Brigade will land three Battalions to the east and attack to the north of Khe Sanh. On D plus four, airmobile forces from the 3[d] ARVN Regiment will be choppered into an area to the southwest to attack toward Lang Vei. The plan calls for wrapping things up in seven days. Any questions? Okay, that's all gents. See you at Khe Sanh."

One April 1968, D-Day. The helicopters lined up along the runway at *LZ Stud* are obscured by a heavy morning fog. The low ceiling hugs the ground. In the pale morning light, the pilots conduct their pre-flight checks and top off their choppers. Scheduled for 0700, H-Hour is set back four hours.

Noon. The sun chases away the haze. The countryside reassumes its contours. The grunts, loaded with their weapons and other gear, climb aboard the slicks. The area hums with activity. The heavy whine of Huey turbines fills the valley. The rotors pick up speed. Swirling clouds of dirt and dust cloud the air.

220

Thirteen hundred hours. The first wave of twelve Hueys rises softly in formation. The aircraft fly over the Marines who move along the road. With Colonel Stanley Hughes they head out toward the west following Route 9. The ceiling drops again, reducing visibility. This time, however, the sky is black with helicopters carrying the three Battalions of the 7th Cavalry.

The 1st Battalion heads for *LZ Mike*, mid-way out to Khe Sanh, next to Route 9. The 2d Battalion flies along the same route. The 5th Battalion turns toward *LZ Cates*, three kilometers further to the north. Thirty Hueys and Chinooks come simultaneously into view at *LZ Mike*. The pilots of the 1st of the 9th Scouts, accustomed to just about anything, are nevertheless taken aback by the sight. Tolson has a tough problem to solve: how to maintain the element of surprise when the enemy knows full well that the Americans are preparing a counter-offensive.

Tolson comments to his staff: "Our own reporters tell the whole world what they see happening here. No matter what plans we might form in confidence, something very much like them gets discussed every evening on TV in the news. Have the NVA watched all this stuff and completely sealed off Khe Sanh?"

All around the Base, the NVA have turned the hills into fire bases for rockets and mortars that block access to the area from the north and south along Route 9. Tolson still manages, however, to surprise them. The Cavalry combination of speed and overwhelming force destabilizes the communist forces. The NVA infantry, in their trenches, anticipating a classic infantry attack, are stunned by the Cav assault that arrives from every direction at the same time. The Americans attack the NVA positions from the front, side, and rear. Not a single helicopter is hit during this phase of the attack. Tolson's plan unfolds just as outlined on the sand table, even better. He must advance the schedule. Colonel McDonough's 2d Brigade will have to execute its role on one day's notice.

General Tolson impresses the journalists that cover *Operation Pegasus*. "Major General John Tolson is an officer of unusual intelligence and subtlety who acts with unbelievable speed and precision. The scope and tactics of *Pegasus* approach elegance. Stendhal would have appreciated it!" writes Michaël Herr in *Esquire*. Next, the 1st Brigade and the three ARVN Battalions attack Lang Vei. In one week, Tolson has deployed fifteen thousand men.

The enemy is now threatened from the rear, but maintains very strong pressure on Khe Sanh. The Base must hold. General Tolson orders Colonel Lownds to launch an attack in the south to retake Hill 471. This hill is a strategic objective because it dominates the Base. After a heavy artillery preparation, Lownds attacks with the equivalent of one battalion. He retakes the Hill. The same day, the 2^d Brigade assaults an old French fort located south of Khe Sanh where a Battalion of North Vietnamese is dug in.

On 5 April the NVA attempt and fail to retake Hill 471. The old fort, however, still resists. The next day, D plus five, the First Cav relieves the Marines on Hill 471. Colonel Robinson blazes through fierce resistance to clear Route 9 from the west. The North Vietnamese soldiers, fighting stubbornly, lose eighty-three men along the road.

The North Vietnamese commit their heavy artillery. From across the border in Laos, 152mm howitzers positioned in the mountains of Co Roc, just to the west of Lang Vei, join the action. It is hard to neutralize them because the Americans have constrained themselves not to cross the border, and bombing proves to have little effect.

At 1320 hours, the 84th Company of the 8th ARVN Parachute Battalion, airlifted in First Cav aircraft, offload at Khe Sanh and link up with the 37th ARVN Ranger Battalion. On 8 April at 0800 hours, the Cav closes into the Base and becomes its new proprietor. Juan Fordani, a Puerto Rican, is the first Cav Trooper to shake the hand of a Marine Corporal over the wire entanglements. There follows an uneventful change of command between Colonels Campbell and Lownds. Tolson wants no fanfare: no drums and bugles. In fact, one bugle call peals out over the base, from a bugle that Lieutenant Joe Abodeely recovered from an NVA casualty along Route 9. As the relief progresses, the Cav Troopers and Marines, in silence, pass each other by.

The Third Brigade has the task of clearing the surrounding area. The 2^d of the 7th will finish opening Route 9. The Garry Owen Troopers occupy the hills around the Base without making contact with the enemy. On the other hand, the hillsides are littered with newly abandoned materiel: rockets in their original packing, AK47s in cases, enough to equip whole battalions. The North Vietnamese Divisions have vanished into the forest, toward Laos and the DMZ. But how long have the NVA been gone?

On 10 April the 1st of the 12th, along with an ARVN unit, retake Lang Vei, which had continued resisting. In the morning an Alpha Troop scout from the 1st of the 9th spots a truck loaded with food and munitions. He destroys the vehicle, setting off several secondary explosions. The scout slips his helicopter closer to the ground to confirm the destruction. He now perceives tread marks along the path. He follows the tracks and discovers a PT76 light armored vehicle. He calls for artillery and air support. The tank is destroyed and fifteen NVA regulars along with it. The PT76s had been used in the attack on the village of Lang Vei and the Green Beret camp just before the beginning of the siege.

LZ Stud is now, after twelve days, the central nervous system that coordinates the movements of thirty thousand men and above all the control center for artillery and air strikes. The B-52s, perfectly synchronized with the artillery and the hunt on the ground, unload their bombs with surgical precision. However, the ceiling is rarely higher than five hundred feet.

"You see," comments one of the air controllers, "Giap thought he'd get our ass because of this shitty weather. The journalists forgot to tell him that today's aircraft can fly just over ground level. When I get back to the world I'm going to be a journalist—assholes." Perched on top of the FSCC bunker, he lights up, and listens to the dull thud of bombs blasting away at the hills around Khe Sanh. He continues, "I'll give you a 'scoop.' Westmoreland's on the way here."

CHAPTER XIX

A few moments later, a Huey lands next to General Tolson's chopper. "Hello John! I want to congratulate you for the excellent job you've done."

"Thanks, sir. Everything's gone well and I'm going to pick up the pace and clean up this area."

"Exactly, and with respect to that, there's some changes. It's all over at Khe Sanh. The enemy's gone. We've achieved our objective. You're to move."

"Leave? But, the NVA Divisions are in full retreat. We've got to finish them off before they can go and refit themselves in Laos."

General Westmoreland prefers to make a sudden halt and, without breaking stride, to attack in the A Shau Valley. "The Cav is the best tool to go and root out the NVA that have set themselves up in this area for going on two years. Since they overran the Special Forces Camp at A Luoi, they've occupied the Valley without resistance. It's not accessible by road. It's really a job for you, John! The price of success. What's more, it's our only chance to get them before the Monsoon and to take advantage of the psychological shock of kicking their butts at Khe Sanh. We've scoured through all the meteorological data left by the French. This month would seem to be the best time to act."

"You'll leave one Brigade at Khe Sanh to secure the Base. You'll send your two other Brigades with the Recon Squadron to the A Shau as soon as possible. You'll have OPCON the 1st Brigade of the 101st and the 3d ARVN Airborne Regiment. So, John, good hunting! Oh, I almost forgot, the name of the *Operation* is *Delaware*, like the Indians, in keeping with Cav tradition."

Tolson accompanies Westmoreland back to his command helicopter, stands by for takeoff, then returns to his CP. "Oscar, hold off on cleaning out the high ground around here. We're busting our butts for nothing."

General Davis, surprised, looks at his chief.

"Look, it took ten years to work out the airmobility concept. Now we're indispensable. Khe Sanh's done! We'll fold our tents. We're moving to the A Shau Valley, Charley's private reserve. For the time being, keep the 2d Brigade here. First and Third Brigades move ASAP. That's the plan!"

Tolson opens a packet labeled *Delaware—Lam Son 216*, and gets his staff working on maps and operations orders. Two hours later they brief him. He studies the map. The A Shau Valley is thirty kilometers to the southwest of Hue as the crow flies. It is dominated, enclosed by two high mountains of over 1,600 meters elevation with steep slopes varying from twenty-five to forty-five degrees. The Laotian frontier, some ten kilometers away, parallels the Valley. The Rao Lao River runs through the middle. In the valley, above the village of A Shau, are three abandoned airstrips, oriented in a northwest-southeast direction along the River. Route 547 crosses the mountain and links the area with Hue.

Tolson looks at the Intelligence Summary. Since March 1966 the North Vietnamese, after attacking the Green Beret Camp at A Luoi, have occupied the whole Valley. They have made it an important base on the infiltration route of troops and supplies coming from the North. The infiltrators come first through Laos, then take Route 547 to get to Thua Thien Province, in the north of the I Corps Area.

On 16 April the 1ˢᵗ of the 9ᵗʰ is ready to begin the action of locating and neutralizing the NVA antiaircraft batteries. They coordinate their plans with the Air Force, which has B-52s at the ready. But weather conditions rule out airstrikes. Tolson asks Westmoreland to delay D-Day. He suggests 19 April as the new date to kick off *Operation Delaware.*

Tolson chooses the old SF Base at A Luoi as the place to set up his CP. The 3ᵈ Brigade has the assault mission. A relatively large open area will allow the Cav to establish a good quality landing strip for air support.

But the 1ˢᵗ of the 9ᵗʰ brings back the disquieting information that they drew heavy flak flying over and between the nearby mountains. Tolson revises his initial plan. He now decides to attack in the north, but further up the Valley. The G3 identifies three *LZs*: *Tiger, Vicki,* and *Goodman.* The 3ᵈ Brigade is still tasked with the assault.

Alpha Company of the 5ᵗʰ of the 7ᵗʰ loads on the lead slicks at the Camp Evans airstrip. "Come on gents, mount up! We're the last ones to load to get this show on the road," announces Captain Taylor as he presses his troops to speed it up.

"We're on it, sir, but no one really thinks much of the A Shau. The Marines say it's got NVA crawling all over, and there'll be lots of ground fire going in."

"Hey, that's why it's so much fun! There'll be something to do when we get there. It's our job to go get 'em. As far as the ground fire's concerned, a B-52 strike's going in on our LZ right about now."

The flotilla of helicopters, in V formation, heads off to the northwest. As they near the *LZs*, the choppers hug the tree tops. The lead Hueys of the 5th of the 7th come in head high off the ground over *Tiger*, the men leaping to earth and dashing toward the edge of the *LZ* to provide security. At the same time, 1st of the 7th Troopers assault into *LZ Vicky*, a short distance to the northeast.

On the ground, enemy fire is sporadic. Captain Taylor's men relax a little and secure the arrival of a 105 Battery coming in just behind them on Chinook slingloads. "How 'bout that Sarge! You believed all that shit the Marines told us. A Shau—a piece of ... ." The kid from Brooklyn does not finish the sentence. The sky is criss-crossed with the light from thousands of tracers. Anti-aircraft fire erupts from all the neighboring hillsides. Twenty-three millimeter and thirty-seven millimeter tracers fill the sky. At the rate of 180 rounds a minute, these guns stitch a wall of steel from their positions on the mountain sides up to an altitude of seven thousand meters. In a few brief moments, thirty-three helicopters are hit, ten of them shot down.

During this time, sixteen kilometers further to the south, elements of Echo Company of the 52d Infantry accompanied by men from the 8th Engineer Battalion and volunteers from the 13th Signal Battalion rappel down from a Chinook. They occupy the highest ground in the massif, at an elevation of eighteen hundred meters. As quickly as possible they have to set up a radio relay to facilitate commo with Camp Evans. The Valley is too closed in for radio communications to the outside. A violent storm breaks out and isolates the mountaintop in a tempest of lightening and rain. Bringing in the planned reinforcements to secure the signal team has to be put off. The NVA take advantage of the night to attack the mountaintop, known thereafter as *Signal Hill*. They kill four Americans and wound three more.

In the early morning hours the ceiling clears. A Flying Crane, a CH-54, slingloads in 105s and bulldozers. *Signal Hill* becomes a support base and signal relay station. The violent tropical storm extends to the Valley and the rain falls unceasingly for several days. The grunts march, eat, and sleep in water. Everything is soaked. Strong blasts of wind accompany the rain. The drenched Americans at *LZ Vicky* are not happy. "Hey! The Marines didn't bullshit me, like you said. A Shau sucks, and it's got its own crappy fucking climate. You can't see shit. We're going to be on cold Cs for a long time."

Lieutenant Colonel Wasiak, between two downpours, tries to contact Colonel Campbell at the 3d Brigade CP. "That's it. I've got 'em," announces his RTO, struggling to hear the RTO at Brigade through the crackling caused by the electrical storm.

Wasiak takes the handset. "Rogue Six, Lancer Six. We're boxed in here on this slope. I need some lift to move to a better position."

"Roger, Lancer Six. Not right now! With this weather and terrain there's nothing we can do. I just tried to get some movement going at *LZs Tiger* and *Pepper* and the lead ship got shot down. Right now, *Tiger* is inaccessible because of the downed chopper. You're on your own for now. Move on out to *LZ Goodman.*"

Colonel Wasiak gets his men together and moves out at the head of his Battalion. *Goodman* is eight kilometers to the southeast of *Vicki*, at the entrance to the Valley. The march takes three days through broken terrain with thick, almost impenetrable vegetation. In the course of this trek, the 1st of the 7th has just one contact where they kill three North Vietnamese soldiers. On the other hand, they discover two well camouflaged Russian made bulldozers that the NVA used to maintain Route 547.

The 1st of the 7th arrives at *LZ Goodman* on 21 April. The men are numb, exhausted, and sick, but excited by their find. They use the bulldozers to open up the *LZ*.

The different units are resupplied by C-130s that offload cases of rations and munitions as they fly low over the various *LZs*. The weather conditions are so bad that all the aircraft must approach on instrument. Airplanes and helicopters circle for hours over the area waiting for the least break in the cover to dive on their targets or to land on an *LZ*.

General Tolson is impressed by the performance of the pilots. "Our young Officer and Warrant Officer pilots fly day after day in Hueys, Chinooks, and Flying Cranes. They perform well beyond expectations. This operation has become a showcase for piloting skills. From my point of view, however, it's very painful to see what my men have to go through to accomplish the mission."

On 22 April the ceiling lifts a bit. The 3d Brigade consolidates in the northern part of the Valley, poised to invest A Luoi, which must become the logistical base for the rest of the *Operation*. On 24 April the 1st Brigade moves out again in accordance with Tolson's original plan and lays siege to the airstrip at A Luoi, known thereafter as *LZ Stallion*.

The General did well to change his plan. In spite of the heavy preparation laid down by the ARA, the NVA flak is still very effective. Two Chinooks and a Huey are shot down the first day. Only three 105s can be sling-loaded in. The 1st of the 8th and the 2d of the 8th manage to occupy the terrain so that supplies, rations, and ammunition can be delivered by parachute.

The C-130 Hercules, guided by two radio stations set up on the east coast, arrive over the mountain and plunge into the thick layer of clouds. From there on, they must rely on their own instruments to avoid the mountain tops. They break out lined up over the Valley, a few hundred meters over the ground. They have ten seconds to push out their cargo and power up out of the Valley.

The C-130s of the 109th Air Support Wing based at Cam Ranh offload 2,212 tons of supplies at A Shau. On 26 April at about 1400 hours a Hercules enters the Valley. As it moves up out of the cloud layer, NVA machine guns unleash long bursts of fire. Several rounds penetrate the aircraft. It loses altitude. It crashes on the southern end of the airstrip and bursts into flame.

On 29 April, the 8th Engineer Battalion arrives with its equipment. CH-54 Skycranes land on the A Luoi airstrip and deliver the heavy engineer equipment. Two days later, at noon, the first C-7 Caribou lands, followed the next day by C-123s and C-130s.

The 1st of the 8th and the 2[d] of the 8th enlarge the security perimeter around *LZ Stallion* and move their reconnaissance patrols all the way out to the next terrain feature of Ta Bat, further to the south. They discover numerous caches of weapons, ammunition, and other materiel. They recover thousands of rounds of 23mm and 37mm ammo. At the same time, further to the south, the 3[d] ARVN Regiment begins its move up into the Valley. Colonel Hoa is tasked with providing security for *LZ Suzy*. On the way there he passes by the Rao Lao River on the south-east. He too uncovers major stocks of spare parts, ammo, and commo equipment.

To the east, the 1st Brigade of the 101st Airmobile Division comes in to support two other Bases: *Bastogne* and *Veghel*. One of its Battalions occupies the crossroads of Routes 547 and 458 on D plus One.

On 3 May, the 2[d] Battalion of the 3[d] ARVN Regiment spots a six truck convoy seven kilometers southeast of *LZ Lucy*. Colonel Hoa immediately intercepts the vehicles. He destroys two, unleashing secondary explosions. The rest of the convoy manages to disappear into the night.

In the days that follow each unit continues to uncover considerable quantities of materiel. Delta Company, 1st of the 8th, discovers a corduroy road over a kilometer and a half long stretching through a shallow basin.[1] Along its length the men find large storage bunkers. The road and bunkers are defended by an NVA Company supported by tanks.

Delta Company kicks off the assault. The Company Commander decides to use CS grenades. The grunts put on their gas masks and charge. Sergeant Hallery Craig spots a tank. Like a hunter stalking his prey, he crawls toward his target. He extends a LAW and fires away. It is a hit. "Pass up another one. I'm going to make sure." He fires a second rocket. The PT-76 burns. The enemy infantrymen react quickly, and try to isolate the Company. Delta Company withdraws to avoid encirclement.

The 1st of the 8th Commander, Lieutenant Colonel George C. Horton, brings in more support for his Company, and calls for reinforcements to surround the enemy defending the area. On 3 May, the 1st of the 8th Jumping Mustangs close in. They find that the NVA troops had been defending a logistical and medical center. It is the Headquarters of the 559th NVA Transportation Group. For the next two days the Americans continue the treasure hunt. The men are enthused by the game, and play it with the same feverish energy that children expend searching for Easter Eggs.

The Pentagon takes advantage of this event to send a small team of experts from Washington with a new model acoustic sensor. The electronic specialists seed a certain number of them in the Valley to test their effectiveness to monitor North Vietnamese movement through the area. They will be particularly useful when the Cav leaves the Valley.

The North Vietnamese try to take back the initiative and launch a counterattack with artillery. They employ massive fire from 122mm rockets, mortars, and recoilless rifles. The Laotian border offers them sheltered positions, secure from a Cavalry reaction.

Meteorological forecasts for the period beginning 7 April are alarming. They project the rapid arrival of a tropical front. Tolson decides to break contact within three days. The Monsoon hits on 11 May. Walls of water batter the Valley. The flooded paths are rapidly rendered unusable. Most of the units are lifted out by chopper, the only way to escape from the mud and unrelenting downpour. *Operation Delaware-Lam Son 216* officially ends on 17 May.

General Westmoreland describes the *Operation* as audacious and well executed. "The exceptional results obtained by the team of combined forces reflect the confidence of their leadership, their professionalism, and an unequaled zeal for combat." The General is effectively impressed by the by the results: one PT76 tank, four tracked vehicles, two bulldozers, 137,757 small caliber cartridges, 34,140 12.7mm rounds, 34,332 23mm rounds, 5,850 37mm rounds, 975 57mm rounds, 127 75mm rounds, 229 76mm rounds, 698 122mm rockets, 1,580 hand grenades, 2,500 individual weapons, ninety-three crew served weapons, thirty-one flamethrowers, eighty-five tons of food, and sixty-seven vehicle tires.

For the 1st Cavalry Division, the A Shau Valley Battle will have been the first operation where it confronted a strong anti-aircraft defense. Until now the pilots had never endured such dense fire.

The Division lost twenty-one helicopters in this *Operation*. But the pilots had more to fight against than the NVA tracers. The worst adversaries were the wind, the rain, the fog and cloud cover, and the storms. The pilots, because of the terrain relief and the weather hazards, had to always follow the same axes of arrival and departure. This made easy the job of the NVA gunners who could set up narrow zones of fire ahead of time.

For General Tolson, the Cav, during the course of *Operation Delaware*, along with allied forces, destroyed another notion once and for all. A Shau had been an inviolate North Vietnamese fiefdom for two years. The notion of a sanctuary no longer existed. The 1st Cavalry Division paid a price for that: 86 killed, 47 missing, and 530 wounded. They inflicted 739 KIA on the North Vietnamese.

In four months, the flexibility, fire power, and fighting spirit of the First Cav led the High Command to use it in all the decisive battles: Quang Tri, Hue, Khe Sanh, and A Shau. From 22 January to 17 May, the Cav was credited with a total of 5,900 enemy kills.

From that time on, the Vietnam War is branded by the Cav's style. Images of its helicopters highlighted against a background of rice paddies illustrate the news on television. The viewing public is witness to these assault helicopters spitting rockets and machine gun fire. Psychological Warfare specialists print millions of leaflets showing ARA ships opening fire. It is the most persuasive argument to use to encourage the VC to rally and the NVA soldiers to desert.

The Cavalry, however, remains true to its history, to its flashing charges, and to its vocabulary impregnated with images of the past. It is not by chance that its operations are called *Crazy Horse* or *Delaware*; or that all its helicopters have names such as Sioux, Iroquois, Chinook, Apache, or Kiowa; that its Brigades are called Black Horse or Garry Owen. The song Garry Owen highlights the attachment of the Skytroopers to their link with the Army Blue uniforms of the traditional cavalry troopers and the saga of the Indian Wars and of the Far West.

Garry Owen[2]

Let Bacchus' sons be not dismayed
But join with me each jovial blade
Come, drink and sing and lend your aid
To help me with the chorus:

Chorus:
Instead of spa, we'll drink brown ale
And pay the reckoning on the nail;
No man for debt shall go to jail
From Garry Owen in glory

We'll beat the bailiffs out of fun,
We'll make the mayor and sheriffs run
We are the boys no man dares dun
If he regards a whole skin.

Our hearts so stout have got no fame
For soon 'tis known from whence we came
Where'er we go they fear the name
Of Garryowen in glory.

Translator's Notes

[1] A road made of lengths of log placed in the roadway at right angles to the direction of travel. This type of crude roadway improvement enables road movement over wet and swampy terrain.

[2] Garry Owen (or Garryowen) was an Irish drinking song made famous by a group of hard-drinking, hard-playing Irish roughnecks in an area known as Garryowen in Gaelic, or Owen's garden, near Limerick in Ireland. Irish Regiments sang it as a drinking song. Apparently General Custer heard one of his soldiers, many of whom were of Irish origin, singing the song. Custer liked it. In 1867 the 7th Cavalry Regiment adopted it as its official song. Seventh Cavalry Troopers salute each other with the greeting: "Garry Owen." Verses one, four, and five of the original version appear above.

CHAPTER XX

One hundred and thirteen years earlier one of McNamara's predecessors, Jefferson Davis, as Secretary of War, was himself interested in a well armed mobile unit. Thus it was that on 3 March 1855, Congress authorized the formation of a new troop unit that took the name of "Cavalry." A General Order specified the organization and its armament. At its origin, this Cavalry was distinguished from dragoons and mounted soldiers only by the color of the piping on the men's trousers.[1] They adopted yellow in place of the orange and the green that characterized the two other mounted formations.

The Cavalry adopted a very simple organization. A Regiment of Cavalry consisted of three Squadrons, each composed of four Troops. The Regiment was commanded by a Colonel with a Lieutenant Colonel as Executive Officer. The Squadrons were numbered 1 to 3 and the Troops A to M, leaving out the letter "J," to avoid any possible confusion with "I." Because of these letter Troop designations the 3[d] Squadron was often called "MILK," taking the four letter Troop designations out of order.

Jefferson Davis named Colonel Edwin V. Sumner to the head of the 1st Regiment of Cavalry with Lieutenant Colonel Joseph E. Johnston as his XO. In the summer of 1855 Colonel Sumner and his troopers took their quarters at Fort Leavenworth and began immediately to conduct training.

To constitute these Regiments, men were enlisted in Alabama, Virginia, Pennsylvania, Maryland, Missouri, Kentucky, Indiana, and Ohio. Initially, the 1st and 2[d] Regiments of Cavalry were to be equipped with available matériel recovered from the Mexican war. However, a board of officers ordered that these units be equipped with experimental arms and equipment. They were looking for the most suitable equipment and arms for the light cavalry missions whose tactical function was reconnaissance along the Western Frontier. Thus they inherited quite an irregular mixture of gear.

There were muzzle-loading Model 1842 .69 caliber Springfield percussion rifles, .54 caliber Merrill folding-stock carbines. They also had Breech-loading Model 1833 .53 caliber Hall carbines, the first breech-loading rifles issued by the American Army. They also distributed Harper's Ferry rifles as well as a few flintlocks such as the Model 1828 Hall rifle. The officers were issued Colt Navy six-shot revolvers or the Model 1847 .44 caliber Colt revolver nicknamed the "2ᵈ Dragoon" after a unit that conducted an expedition against the Seminoles. The Prussian Saber was part of the armament of every trooper.

Two years later, during the course of the winter of 1856, Robert Peck embarked on an old steamer with three hundred other recruits, volunteers like himself. The stern-wheeler mounted slowly upstream, its destination Fort Leavenworth. The recruits pushed down along the gangway, watching their new horizon unfold before them. The village was dusty. Scattered here and there were a few commercial houses, small banks and, along the river, wharfs. Peck and his comrades looked in vain for some sign of military construction. "Where the hell's the Fort!" Peck, puzzled, asked aloud. A soldier on guard moved out of the shelter of a warehouse, his bayonet gleaming in the winter sun. He pointed a finger toward a starred flag floating halfway up the hill. "A mile from here," he announced.

The three hundred new soldiers moved out in a disorderly manner and climbed the hill, packing their gear over their shoulders. They arrived at the foot of the Fort, an edifice of stone, bricks, and logs, built in the frontier fashion. The men had no time to stare. A pair of Corporals took them immediately in charge, issued brisk orders, and formed the men in ranks.

Peck was assigned to E Company of the 1ˢᵗ Cavalry Regiment. Along with his fellow enlistees he was marched in formation to the supply building. The young recruit received his blue campaign hat with its crossed sabers, the regimental numeral affixed just above and between the point where the sabers cross. He also was issued a blue campaign jacket and a pair of blue trousers with a yellow stripe sewn down the outer side of each trouser leg. Thereafter they were part of the frontier military known as "Yellow Legs."

Weighed down with uniforms and other issued gear, Peck returned to the barracks to drop off his load. He went right back to the quartermaster to pick up his saddle, a Grimsley. He would make his stop at the armory later. Robert Peck and the other recruits quickly became aware of the personality of the Fort's Commander, Colonel Edwin Sumner. He was nicknamed "Devil," "Old Sumner," or "the Gauntlet." Silver haired, with a will of iron, Sumner enjoyed the full confidence of Jefferson Davis. He devoted all his energy to organizing punitive expeditions against the *Cheyenne*.

He decided in April 1857 to launch a new expedition. The objective: follow the Santa Fe Trail and reach the source of the Kansas River while searching for the *Cheyenne* in the Foothills of the Rockies. Major James Sedgwick was to command four

Troops of the 1st Cavalry Regiment and rejoin the forces commanded by Colonel Sumner along the Platte River. The Colonel had two Cavalry Troops and four Companies of the 6th Infantry.

On 18 May Captain Sturgis, followed by E Troop, departed Fort Leavenworth in Major Sedgwick's column. The cavalrymen were in the lead, followed by the Infantry Companies, and by the wagons. They moved out on the plain. Little by little, with the passing days, the countryside became increasingly austere. In the hills, trees were few and far between. There was scarcely enough wood for fires. The men would soon resort to buffalo chips for fuel and to Prairie Chickens to augment their rations.

At Cottonwood Creek the column saw its first buffaloes. At first, just a scattered few, then small bands, and finally, large herds as they got closer to Grove. They were impressive animals, powerful, large, and prehistoric in appearance. The men had to overcome their apprehension in the middle of these herds that moved all about them.

In the wagons, it was harder to calm the oxen and mules. The panic was contagious. The Buffaloes bolted, stampeded, and charged. Two or three kilometers from the column they began a great charge, surging toward them like an avalanche. With a hollow Rumbling the animals formed a huge brown mass that moved toward them at a rapid pace. The men were frozen with fear. Sedgwick did not know what to do, having no experience with this sort of thing. The unfolding scene seemed to disarm him, as the animals stampeded toward his column. He turned to face Sturgis. "Sturgis! What now?"

"I haven't got time to explain. Let me take it from here and I'll get us out of this, sir!"

"Okay Captain. It's your show. You give the orders!"

Sturgis had already spurred his horse over to the bugler. "Move out and inform the unit commanders that I'll be giving the commands. Then, go to the tail of the column and pass the order to the quartermasters to circle the wagons as tight together as they can, facing to the center with the oxen in the middle."

The buffaloes roll down from the north. Sturgis halts the column and orders the men to dismount. "Dismount and take up firing positions." Designated men in each Troop take the reins of the now riderless mounts. "Form in two ranks!" The rest of the men take up firing positions. The buffaloes rumble closer at full gallop. The men form a "V" with the point directed at the approaching mass of animals. The horses and wagons are inside the "V."

Robert Peck and his fellow troopers are confounded by the spectacle of such an avalanche of horns and hooves rushing down on them. "Crap! They'll stomp us to shit!" Sturgis leaves them no time to worry. "Commence firing!" The order liberates their energies. The first rank in the kneeling position and the second standing behind them shoulder their carbines and open fire. The salvos cut like a scythe through the leading rank of buffaloes. Under the impacts of the heavy projectiles the animals waver. Behind them, the bison, running hard, collide with each other, entangling themselves in the confusion.

Peck fires as rapidly he can with his carbine. After each round, he feverishly opens the breech of his weapon and reloads. The hot barrel burns his fingers. In spite of the continuous fire, the charge of the buffaloes seemed unstoppable. The dust they raised and the smoke from the carbines burned the men's eyes, obscuring their vision. Would they be submerged in the living wave?

The opaque cloud of dust and smoke and the powerful odor of black powder also disoriented the buffaloes that, in spite of everything, continued to close on the troops. Without slowing their fire, the men pulled back, step by step, under pressure from the huge herd. They soon found themselves backed against their wagons. The brown mass of beasts appeared suddenly to split, thinning as they shied away from and around the circled supply train. The soldiers could not believe it. "Cease fire!" yelled Sturgis.

They did not return. The hurricane of bison charged off into the distance, deterred by the sang-froid of the cavalrymen, Sturgis's know-how, and the constant fire from the Sharps carbines. A Lieutenant who had weathered the stampede next to Robert Peck took out his pocket watch. The rolling fire had lasted thirty minutes! Dust and silence reclaimed the prairie. Before moving out, supply details butchered some of the just killed animals for fresh meat. They left the rest for hungry wolves. They set up camp at Big Bend on a sand bank in the middle of the river

They moved out again at dawn the next day. The way was dreary, only punctuated by the appearance along the way of grave sites marked by wooden crosses. Quite often the cross bar was not at right angles to the vertical post. Peck would not have noticed if a scout had not pointed them out to him. "You see, friend, if the straight across part 'a the cross ain't horizontal, if it sort 'a slants, that means he died with his boots on, you follow? A violent goin', huh! Killed by the Indians. When the cross is squared away: a natural dyin', or took by sickness—usually by prairie fever." The scout let out an explosive laugh and spit out a wad of tobacco.

After it passed Cherry Creek, the column overtook half a dozen or so ragged travelers preceded by a wagon drawn by two emaciated oxen. One of the old men was stretched out in the wagon, in very bad shape. One of his traveling companions told how he had hurt himself when he grabbed his loaded rifle by the muzzle. It fired through his hand, breaking it. Two days later he had gangrene. The Regimental Surgeon examined him and decided to move him to the column's infirmary.

During the halt, the other members of the party told their story. They were prospectors. They came from the Cherry Creek region where they had discovered a fantastic vein of gold. To back up their story, they emptied their pockets of bottles and purses filled with gold dust. They wanted to keep their discovery secret, but Indians attacked their encampment and made off with their supplies and most of their gold. The thieves left them with just the two oxen yoked to the empty wagon.

Out of everything, they had decided to return to Missouri, to announce their discovery there, and to get an expedition together to settle accounts with the Indians. They were fanatically determined to recover their gold. A few days after the encounter with the gold seekers, however, two men deserted. The officers were worried. Would there be a contagion of gold fever? Captain Sturgis decided to start a rumor that the gold strike was a sham. In exchange for a payoff, the injured prospector denied the existence of important veins of gold.

Sedgwick and his men arrived in Denver on 29 June 1857, forty days after their departure from Fort Leavenworth. The only human beings they had encountered were the prospectors. Five days later Sedgwick installed his men on a sand bank along the Platte River. It was the 4th of July. At the raising of the colors, the men were particularly well turned out. Two howitzers fired a thirty-two gun salute to honor the American national holiday, Independence Day.

The boom of the guns echoed and reverberated in the mountains on the other side of the River. A few moments later, the men heard similar noises responding: one "boom," then two, then three. The men counted thirty-two. "It's Colonel Sumner's column greeting the Fourth," concluded Sedgwick.

"Captain. Send two *Delaware* guides on a recon across the River." The guides came back two days later. Colonel Sumner's camp was about forty kilometers downstream near Crow Creek. The two forces linked up without incident on six July.

On 13 July 1857, the men were ordered to get ready for a mission. They would go light. They packed twenty days' of rations in their saddle bags and as much ammunition as they could carry. Everything else was loaded on the supply wagons which then left for Fort Laramie. Sumner wanted his men to campaign as lightly equipped as possible and so to be completely mobile. Tents, blankets, and changes of clothing and overcoats were all consigned to the wagons. They kept only their saddle blankets. As far as wheels were concerned, they took only the ambulance, which followed the column, and four mountain howitzers, reunited as a Battery commanded by Second Lieutenant George Bayard from G Troop.

The unit moved out, with Indian scouts up front leading the way. For three or four days they headed east, and then angled off to the south-east. The only visible signs of life were the remains of a *Cheyenne* camp, some several months old. Fifteen days later, the *Delaware* scouts found fresh signs less than twenty kilometers ahead of the column. Immediately, the Colonel ordered the unit into a formation of three echelons, stepped back in a manner to ward off any attack. The mules were regrouped and brought up the rear.

The following day at ten in the morning, Old Dead Leaf, the chief *Delaware* guide sent a messenger to Colonel Sumner with the following word: "Spotted party of *Cheyenne* far off." Sumner believed the *Cheyenne* were in full retreat and he was worried that they would escape. He decided to attack and force them to fight, even if that meant leaving his infantry and artillery behind.

He ordered a halt and assembled his four Squadron commanders. "Gentlemen. Inspect your men. Get ready for immediate action."

The cavalrymen dismounted. Hustled along by their sergeants, the men inspected their weapons and cinched their saddles tighter. Ready to fight, they remounted and lined up. "Ready troop," the Captains commanded. The Old Man then spurred his horse to review the line.[2] Alone, upright on his mount, he stood highlighted against the sky. Robert Peck thought that Colonel Sumner deserved his nicknames, "the Gauntlet, Bull of the Woods," and others. In a powerful and loud voice that resonated over the prairie the Colonel said: "We've finally found the enemy. I don't know how many *Cheyenne* we're going to fight, but I do know that if my officers and men follow orders promptly and if we work together, we can sweep up the whole tribe. I have total confidence in you."

"Column, foorwaad—hah!"

The Colonel's orders had their effect. The bugler blew the call and the sound electrified the men who had not heard its music for several days. The Colonel had forbad its use so as not to alert the Indians. These precautions, however, were no longer useful. The Colonel then ordered the column into a trot. The bugler blew the command. The Captain repeated the order verbally and the horses picked up the pace.

The rhythm of the whole column was transformed. The mules trotted along in the rear. The infantry had already been left behind. Lieutenant Bayard's Battery bogged down attempting to cross a muddy creek, the mules miring down in the process. The caissons were stuck in place, prisoners of the mud.

Unaccompanied by either infantry or artillery, the three hundred cavalry troopers continued their advance at a rapid pace, in groups of fifty. They debouched in the bed of the Solomon River, passing around a meander enclosed by steep banks on both sides, and finally moving out of the river bed on the north side. Here the land opened into a flat and open valley.

The view to the horizon was interrupted here and there by thin and scraggly bushes. The officers called a halt and, using field telescopes, peered into the distance, carefully scrutinizing the areas around the bushes and brush. They spotted some movement, and supposed it to be a herd of buffalo. Captain Sturgis was skeptical. The scouts had told them that the buffalo herds were more than two days' march to the west. He wiped clean the lenses and looked even more attentively through the spy glass. "For sure, it's Indians. There's a bunch of 'em. There's no camp. I can't see any teepees. Yeah, there's movement alright."

"Look, something flashed over there." The sun had reflected off a rifle barrel or a lance point. The troop moved ahead once more. Now, visible against the horizon, the Indians advanced to encounter the cavalrymen. The Americans now discovered that the *Cheyenne* warriors greatly outnumbered them. Advancing in fighting formation, the Indians were echeloned in several ranks, each rank at some distance from the others, and free to maneuver as needed. Their war cries were loud and clear as they advanced toward the troopers.

When the cavalrymen and the Indians were no more than five hundred meters from each other, a mounted rider moved out at full gallop from the right wing of the cavalry formation. Peck recognized Old Dead Leaf, the old *Delaware* Scout. He moved out alone, positioned himself to face the line of advancing *Cheyenne*, reared his mount, raised his carbine, fired one round, turned about and, with loosened reins spurred his horse back toward the formation. The Indians' rifle fire whistled and snapped all about him, but he quickly returned to his post.

Sumner, who was watching the scene, turned quickly to Lieutenant Stanley. "You will note," he told him, "that an Indian fired the first shot." The old scout had well known what was necessary to satisfy the powers that be in Washington. The instructions were: "Seek out all possible means of conciliation with the Indians before engaging in hostilities."[3]

So it was that it was an Indian who fired the first shot, no mat-

238

ter if it was a scout or a *Cheyenne*. It was necessary to avoid a "pow wow" with the *Cheyenne* just to please the East Coast "doves."

The two camps faced each other. The *Cheyenne* then spread to either side so as to overlap the cavalry's flanks. The Indians on the right front advanced along the bank of the creek and crossed it to outflank the cavalrymen and form up again to the rear of the column. On the left flank the Indians executed a similar and symmetric movement to the sound of their war cries. Sumner ordered Captain Beall, commanding the left wing, to deploy his Troop.

"Draw, Sabers!" commanded the Colonel. The men, surprised, suddenly realized that their Colonel wanted to mount a charge with cold steel. In perfect order three hundred steel blades, drawn from their scabbards, gleamed together in the sun. Surprised by this unusual spectacle, the *Cheyenne*, for the moment disconcerted, slowed down their maneuver to envelop the cavalrymen. His left wing deployed, Captain Beall took advantage of the Indians' uncertainty to reverse the tactical situation and turn the Indians' flank. Those who had crossed the river hesitated to cross back.

One warrior loped forward of the ranks, lance in hand. He approached the line of soldiers at full gallop, long hair dressed for battle streaming behind him in the wind. He shouted rudely at his comrades, sensing some hesitation among them that might turn to panic. The cavalrymen, in a neat line, moved forward at a sustained trot.

The *Cheyenne* apparently were fascinated by their Chief's harangue as he galloped back and forth to their front, brandishing his lance to emphasize the salient points of his address. The war cries died off. The Indians slowed their mounts to a walk, facing the troopers. The only sound on the prairie was the pounding of hooves and the clatter of scabbards and stirrups against saddles. Old Sumner's stentorian voice again demanded action. "At the gallop, Hah!" then "Charge!"

With this commanding call to action, the cavalrymen themselves unleashed their own savage war cries and shouts of battle. Twelve hundred shod hooves pounded the ground, as if beating on an unseen drum, accompanied by the haunting notes blown by the bugler sounding "Charge." The troopers, sabers pointed toward the foe, prepared for the first clash.

The *Cheyenne* vacillated and then panicked. By reflex, however, before they fled they unleashed their arrows. A hail of arrows fell among the Blue Coats. The Redskins dispersed every which way, some recrossing the river. Encouraged by the Indians' apparent disorganization, the cavalrymen tried to close with them. The *Cheyenne's* horses, fresh and fast, avoided the seemingly forced charge of the comparatively heavily mounted cavalry.[4] A running pursuit, sometimes one on one, stretched over several kilometers.

The ponies of those Indians that attempted to recross the river came almost to a standstill in the mucky bottom. Their riders leaped down into the water and dashed for the shore, scrambling up the bank and up the slope of a hill. Cornered by the cavalrymen, they fought with wild abandon. The idea that they might surrender never seemed to cross their minds.

The bugle sounded "Recall." The Colonel ordered the men to reassemble along the Solomon River. He received their reports. Thirty Indians had been killed, a dozen as they fought desperately to defend themselves on the hill across the River. The rest had been killed as they fled. There was one prisoner, a large and solid type who finally gave himself up after attempting everything he could to get away. The Indians, having the custom of horribly torturing their prisoners, thought a similar fate awaited them at the hands of their enemy and so they fought pugnaciously.

Then the three Companies of the 6th Infantry arrived on the scene along with Lieutenant Bayard's Artillery Battery. The men cursed their bad luck at missing out on the action. However, in the hastily erected medical tent, two bodies were laid out side by side on a saddle blanket and covered with another. Robert Peck recognized his friend George Cade of G Troop and, beside him, trooper Lynch from A Troop. Cade had been struck in the chest by an arrow that pierced his heart. Lynch had been hit several times by arrows. He had also been shot twice with his own revolver. His scalp had a long gash in it. The Indians had not had time to finish scalping him.

Lynch had spent the day leading the mule train. As they crossed the river he asked his Sergeant to be relieved of that duty so he could take his place in the line. "There's no time to get a replacement for you now. Get back to the pack train." Annoyed, Lynch went back to his mules at the back of the column and took the lead line back in hand. When he heard the bugler sound "Charge," the blood raced to his head. "Damn, I haven't come all this way just to lead pack animals while everyone else's charging."

He threw down the lead and, with his hands now free, drew his saber. He moved off at a gallop into the river to catch up with his Troop. As they came out on the far side his horse, caught up in the excitement and urgency, picked up its pace to a run. Unable to restrain the charging mount, he overtook his comrades and charged alone into the Indian lines. There he was taken by a volley of arrows. He faltered and slipped slowly from the saddle. A *Cheyenne* jumped on him, seized his Colt from its holster, and shot him twice.

Another, knife in hand, began to scalp him. The Troop arrived too late. They found the revolver in the hand of a dead Indian. Lynch's horse had followed the fleeing Indians.

To these two dead were added twelve wounded. Among them Lieutenant James Stuart, with a pistol ball in the shoulder fired by a *Cheyenne* whom he was attempting to spare. The Red Skin had probably misinterpreted his gestures.

Colonel Sumner estimated the number of Indians at nine hundred or a thousand. Among the Cavalry's Indian auxiliaries Old Dead Leaf and his *Delawares* had actively participated in the fight after providing the Colonel with the alibi regarding who fired the first shot. On the other hand, the *Pawnees* who had accompanied the units from Fort Kearny contented themselves with scalping dead Indians and catching their mounts. A good harvest, almost sixty horses, which the Colonel let them keep.

But when the *Pawnees* learned that there was a *Cheyenne* prisoner, they tried to bargain for him, prepared to trade their sixty horses and even to give up their reward. They only thought of the "scalp dance," of torture, and of putting the captive to death. Fed up, Sumner ordered them to immediately return to their encampment and sent them on their way the next day to Fort Kearny.

Thus, thanks to the Cavalry, calm returned to the prairie. There were only a few skirmishes in 1858 and 1859. In 1861 the Americans began their Civil War: the War of Secession. In the West, most regiments were torn apart, each man choosing a side depending on his native land and political leaning. Lieutenant Colonel Robert E. Lee, 2^d Cavalry, submitted his resignation to take his place in the service of the Confederacy. On the opposing side, George Armstrong Custer, freshly graduated from West Point, went to build a legend as a General at the head of the Brigade of Volunteers from Michigan. He was at the Battle of Gettysburg in July of 1863.

At war's end the Volunteer Corps were dissolved. Custer reverted to his permanent rank of Captain. To his men, however, he was still "General." At the beginning of hostilities, President Lincoln decided to designate as regular cavalry all mounted troops. The 1st Dragoons became the 1st Cavalry Regiment; the 2^n Dragoons, the 2^d Cavalry Regiment; the Mounted Rifles, the 3^d Cavalry Regiment. The original 1st Cavalry Regiment became the 4th, the 2^d was renamed the 5th, and the 3^d became the 6th.

Following the end of the War of Secession, in July of 1866, the Congress authorized the formation of four additional Cavalry Regiments: the 7th, 8th, 9th, and 10th. The 9th and 10th Cavalry were open to enlisted blacks, cadred by white officers. Custer was promoted to Lieutenant Colonel and assigned to command the 7th Cavalry.

In 1867 he was criticized for his part in operations against the Indians. A military Court suspended him from command for one year. General Phil Sheridan, however, commanding the Department of the Missouri, needed a fighting unit to confront turbulence on the Indian frontier. He wanted Custer, and gave him back his 7th Cavalry.

Custer was the man of the hour. Without delay he transformed his Regiment into an elite arm, motivated and sustained by a powerful esprit de corps. He committed his troopers and their mounts to intensive training with forced marches, strict orders, and daily firing exercises. A great fan of military music, Custer formed a mounted band to accompany his troopers on campaign. The old Irish song of the 5th Royal Lancers, "Garry Owen," became the haunting air of the Regiment.

The 7th was quartered at Fort Hays, Kansas. General Sheridan moved out of Fort Leavenworth and installed his headquarters in this same place in 1868. Custer was in complete agreement with Sherman's doctrine: offensive operations. He also believed that the best time to harass the Indians was the winter, because their horses were also short of forage during the cold season. He followed his logic through with action.

On 4 November 1868, as had Sumner ten years earlier, Lieutenant Colonel Custer ordered the charge sounded. The bugle launched the assault at two AM while the band played "Garry Owen." The music did not last long. It was freezing. The charge was devastating and the encampment of the great *Cheyenne* Chief Black Kettle at Washita was raised. One hundred and three *Cheyenne* were killed; fifty-three women and children were captured. On its side, the 7th Cavalry lamented twenty-two killed and brought home fourteen wounded.

This victory ended the Indian revolt for a while. It contributed to Custer's entry into the legends of the West. Just eight years later, in June of 1876, the saga of Lieutenant Colonel George Armstrong Custer came to its abrupt end at the Little Big Horn.

On 17 May 1876, at Fort Abraham Lincoln, in Dakota Territory, General Terry had reunited twelve Battalions to launch an expedition against the Indians who at that time were regrouping. Custer commanded the six hundred men of the 7th Cavalry. Before their departure, the "General" could not resist the pleasure of organizing a review.

Custer wore his buckskin shirt with its long tassels, a large sombrero, and a red scarf around his neck. He led the formation, with his men in regulation blue uniforms, a yellow band down each trouser leg. But they wore no sabers. Custer had ordered them racked and stored. Their rattling and clacking was a giveaway and made any surprise attack impossible. He had mounted his saber on the wall in his office. He had, however, had the blade engraved: "Never draw me without cause, never sheath me without victory."

The cavalrymen of the 7th were armed with the carbine version of the .45 caliber, Model 1873, single shot Springfield Rifle. This was a weapon with an opening breech, modified by what was known as the "Allin Conversion" to accept cartridges with a metallic case. The breech of this carbine had the disadvantage of rapidly becoming fouled with a mixture of black powder residue and grease when employed with sustained fire. The residue gummed up the extractor.[5] Some veterans missed the saber, because in close combat it was more effective against an enemy armed with lances and tomahawks than a rifle with fixed bayonet.

As was the custom, after a thunderous rendition of "Garry Owen," the mounted band played "The Girl I Left Behind Me." The Battalions moved out under the command of General Terry. The watching civilians from the fort were moved by the scene.

On 17 June, one month after their departure, Major Marcus A. Reno of the 7th Cavalry found an Indian trail heading west, toward the Little Big Horn Mountains. On 21 June General Terry convened Custer and Gibbon to define his plan of action. "Custer, you will follow the trail that Reno located. At the same time Gibbon and I will move around the flanks so as to arrive at the Little Big Horn at the same time and attack together."

General Terry proposed to Custer to reinforce the 7th with Major Brisben and his four Companies as well as with a Gatling Gun mounted on wheels. Custer turned the offer down. "I don't need them! All of that would slow me down. That old Major has rheumatism. He isn't up to hard riding. I don't need anybody, just the 7th."

He moved out after the Indians at a pace of fifty kilometers a day. This was a normal pace for his old troopers, but very hard on the recruits. The trail got fresher as he followed it leading him to believe that they were near a large group of Indians making their seasonal migration. After three days of march, Custer was certain they were heading for the Little Big Horn River.

He had a simple choice. Either respect his orders and wait for the two columns to catch up with him, or continue hot on the trail, disobeying those orders. He did not struggle much or long over a decision. He chose to move on, day and night, in a forced march.

On 24 June his scouts led him to the top of a crest from where they had observed the Indian gathering. Custer could not discern the village, but it reportedly contained an immense mass of Indians, about ten thousand. There were more than 3,500 *Sioux* and

Cheyenne warriors, allied by the shaman Sitting Bull and Chief Crazy Horse. The scouts were sure that the Indians had spotted the 7th Cavalry. Custer was thus isolated. He had gone too fast. He was more than a day ahead of Terry's and Gibbon's columns. He had to attack the Indians now. Custer believed his fate was charmed. It would be Washita all over again.

Custer assembled his commanders. He divided his command into three parts: he would directly command an element consisting of five Troops; Major Reno and Captain Frederick W. Benteen would each lead three Troops. Another Troop would guard the pack train. Custer discounted any objections regarding the relative strength of the Indians.

Benteen and his three Troops split off to the left, or south. Custer and Reno continued on toward the Little Big Horn River. When they came upon a small group of Indians, apparently a rear guard moving back to the village, Custer ordered Reno to move up rapidly and attack, promising support if needed. The Indians, however, turned on the Cavalry Troopers, who had to retreat while fighting for their lives. Custer, rather than moving to Reno's support, was apparently attempting a flanking movement to the north, parallel to the river and masked by some bluffs, intent on assuring that the that the Indians not escape. He sent his orderly back to Benteen with a note instructing Benteen to send up the ammunition packs. Benteen hurried back toward the battle, but held up with Reno's forces, cut to half their strength in a running battle with the Indians. Some men and units from this force tried to come to Custer's aid, but could not make out the details of the fighting through the dust and smoke. When they tried to join the fight, they were halted by warriors well out to the flanks of the main battle.

Custer, happy to have finally caught his foe, and in the still living tradition of the 7th Cavalry, engaged the vastly superior indigenous force. This time, his luck was not sufficient to the challenge. Encircled, Custer's men, conscious of their inferior strength, halted their horses and dismounted. They shot their mounts and took position behind them. The *Sioux* and *Cheyenne* warriors submerged the Cavalrymen in a hail of bullets, arrows, and flailing tomahawks. A small square of survivors fought to the end from the shelter of their downed mounts.

Crazy Horse, Gall, and Rain in the Face exhorted their warriors to make an end of the Blue Coats. The Indians rushed to assault the few remaining 7th Cavalry Troopers, Custer among them. His final act as a soldier was to empty his revolver at the wildly shouting Red Skins. Then it was over. The battle did not last long, an hour perhaps. Terry and Gibbon arrived the next day, 27 June 1876, and discovered the carnage.

They located Custer, dead, his body intact, neither mutilated nor scalped. He was surrounded by 211 7th Cavalrymen. There were no survivors in his column. Even Mark Kellog, the journalist who accompanied him on this expedition, was killed, unable to report the battle. It is by gathering the various accounts told by the Indians who participated in the battle that the story of Custer's fate has been, in part, reconstructed.

Custer's aggressiveness was not appreciated by everyone. President Grant wrote: "I consider the massacre at the Little Big Horn as an unnecessary sacrifice, Custer's fault. He should not have attacked." The Battle of the Little Big Horn was a shock to Americans. Thereafter, the Army had but one driving goal: avenge Custer and reestablish order on the frontier.

But following the trail was not easy. Colonel Crook's scouts fell into an ambush near the Rosebud River. Colonel Meritt went to their aid with the 5th Cavalry. After a thirty hour forced march, he ambushed War Bonnet in the extreme southeast of what is now South Dakota. This time the Indians were caught in a trap. William Cody, the famous Buffalo Bill, was part of the ambush. In the fight, he fought Yellow Hand, one of the Indian Chiefs, in single combat. Buffalo Bill unhorsed him with a shot from his revolver, and then killed him on the ground, stabbing him in the heart with a knife.

The survivors of the 7th Cavalry of Reno and Gibbon took their revenge in the Black Hills. They cornered Crazy Horse and his men in a cave. The psychological advantage gained by the *Cheyenne* and the *Sioux* at the Little Big Horn was erased.

But the real revenge of the 7th Cavalry would not be had until much later, 27 December 1890, at Wounded Knee. Colonel Forsyth was ordered to obtain the surrender of the *Sioux* who, again, were in revolt. After making believe to surrender their weapons, the Indians drew repeating carbines hidden under the skirts of their women. The troopers immediately opened fire. The 7th Cavalrymen, still armed with their old single shot Springfields had the advantage of numbers this time. They nailed the Indians in place with their field guns. The *Sioux* lost 145 killed and 33 wounded.

The 7th returned to Pine Creek with its wounded and the Indian women and children. The *Sioux*, reacting to the noise of the previous evening's gunfire, regrouped and attacked the cavalrymen. Troopers from the 9th Cavalry happily charged to the rescue. Major Harry and his Buffalo Soldiers crushed the *Sioux*, thanks to the artillery that the Cavalry now employed in all its battles.

That is the source and history of the songs and traditions of the grunts of the First Cav. Those traditions are directly linked to the saga of the Indian fighting cavalry. The American Cavalry is the direct issue of this period of Indian fighting and the conquest of the West. In these battles one can find certain similarities with the fighting in Vietnam: the vicious violence of ambushes, torture, and the unfriendly climate where hot and cold alternate. Other similarities include the presence on the American side of Indian auxiliaries, the importance of public opinion, the attitude of the press with respect to the army, the refuge that the Indians could take in Mexico, and finally the hostility of eastern intellectuals toward the army, as many easterners viewed these operations as repression and a stain on the American ideal of justice. One must keep in mind that this climate of insecurity and periodic Indian revolts lasted almost fifty years in the Western states and territories and profoundly marked the spirit of the pioneers as well as the traditions of the Cavalry.

The weight of this past is directly inscribed in the insignia of the 7th Cavalry. It is composed of a gold horseshoe with seven visible nail holes surmounted with a blue banner on which appear the words "Garry Owen" in gold letters. A gloved fist in white with a right arm in blue grasps a raised saber with a white blade and a gold guard. If one goes further back in the heraldry of the Regiment, on the shield are seven gold horseshoes on a blue chevron that divides the shield. On the top left is a Phoenix rising from its ashes. On the top right is the head of an Indian Chief wearing a war bonnet. A green yucca plant appears under the chevron. A banner under the shield reads "The Seventh First." A similar arm and saber surmount the shield.

The symbolism of this supercharged heraldry is significant. The background is gold or yellow, color of the Cavalry. The principal motif is the chevron which represents a spur. The number of holes in the horseshoe corresponds to the numerical designation of the Regiment. The Phoenix symbolizes the resurrection of the Regiment after its virtual extermination in the Battle of the Little Big Horn in 1876. The Indian head and the yucca commemorate the Indian campaigns and the 1916 punitive expedition into Mexico. The unsheathed saber recalls that in 1873 the saber was still part of the uniform. The spirit of the 7th Cavalry and of the First Cavalry Division itself is very marked by the tradition of "Garry Owen."

The 3[d] Brigade of the First Cavalry Division was known as the Garry Owen Brigade. Although the brigade organization is flexible, and any infantry unit may be attached to any brigade, in Vietnam the 3[d] Brigade initially consisted the 1st and 2[d] Battalions of the 7th Cavalry that arrived in Vietnam with the Division in September of

1965. Nearly a year later the 5th Battalion of the 7th Cavalry arrived in country in August and joined the Brigade. The 7th Cavalry has a prestigious history. Among other campaigns, in the Second World War its battalions fought along the Rhine and in the Battle of the Ardennes.[6]

"Garry Owen," the old Irish song immortalized by Custer, became popular again at the start of the 19th Century. It was part of the repertoire of the Irish Regiments and particularly of the 5th Royal Lancers. In 1981, while the First Cavalry Division was at Fort Hood, it was made the official song of the Division. The patch that the Sky Soldiers wear on their shoulder was designed in 1921 by Mrs. Dorcy, the wife of the Lieutenant Colonel who at that time commanded the 1st of the 7th. The design symbolizes the shield of a knight. The diagonal stripe represents a ladder used to assault fortifications. The horse's head represents the cavalry. Mrs. Dorcy chose the traditional army blue, and yellow, the color of the cavalry, for the original patch. With the passage of time, the blue of the horse's head and the stripe were changed to black. Beginning in Vietnam and continuing today, subdued colors are used in the patches worn on combat uniforms. On the Battle Dress Uniform, the First Cavalry Division Patch yellow gives way to olive drab. The patch worn on the left shoulder indicates the unit to which one belongs. On the right shoulder it identifies a unit or organization in which one served in combat.

Translator's Notes

[1] Dragoons employed horses for mobility but fought dismounted.

[2] Common title of respect used by soldiers for any commander.

[3] In fact, on the frontier during this period, the military was more inclined to deal fairly with the Indians than were the settlers.

[4] Still today the American soldier is so heavily burdened with gear compared to most of his foemen that the latter generally retain the option of avoiding contact at all or of flight when the situation turns against them, as it usually does.

[5] When this happens, you must pry or force the expended cartridge case from the breach. The early version of the M16 Rifle had an analogous problem in Vietnam. See translator's note 10, Chapter 3.

[6] The 3[d] of the 7th, the Reconnaissance Squadron of the 3[d] Infantry Division, recently performed in its traditionally audacious cavalry fashion as it led the 3[d] Infantry Division attack in southern Iraq in 2003.

CHAPTER XXI

"Westy is being promoted and transferred," explains Ambassador Ellsworth Bunker when President Johnson announces, on 22 March 1968, that he has selected General Westmoreland to be Chief of Staff of the Army in Washington DC. The command of MACV will pass to General Abrams on 11 June. The nomination will not be official until 3 July.

The climate began to change after the Tet Offensive. On 26 March in a meeting with President Johnson Cyrus Vance had declared, "If we don't do something pretty quickly, public opinion's going to force us to pull the troops out."

On 31 March Lyndon Johnson, in a televised speech, announces to the nation the suspension of bombing in the North and his withdrawal from the presidential campaign. He will not be a candidate to succeed himself.

On 1 April, D Day of *Operation Pagasus*, McNamara, who got himself transferred to the World Bank, is replaced by Clark Clifford as Secretary of Defense.

The electoral campaign is already underway. In the New Hampshire primaries Senator Eugene McCarthy, a pacifist leader, almost beats Johnson in the Democratic camp. When the President announces his withdrawal from the race, Robert Kennedy announces his own candidature and takes a position for the withdrawal of American forces from Vietnam. Opinion polls show thirty percent of the American people favor such a withdrawal.

Back at Camp Evans the Cav Troopers quickly recover from the terrible combat conditions they had confronted in the A Shau Valley, a veritable baptism of fire with lots and lots of water. Tolson does not give them much of a break. The Brigades go back to their pre-Tet hunting grounds. Those involved in *Operation Jeb Stuart* go back to Hue and Quang Tri. The mission, once again, is to keep the Viet Cong from getting to the rice fields along the coast and to force them out of their sanctuaries.

On 27 June a Black Horse patrol air assaults six kilometers north of Quang Tri on a beach near Binh Anh. The grunts march in column in the fine white sand. Movement is difficult. The men's boots sink in the soft, hot sand. Geysers of sand rise in front of them, barring the route. They are followed by the sound of automatic weapons fire coming from the village. The Lieutenant takes the handset his RTO passes him, gives his position and requests ARA. Ten minutes later the ARA choppers come in behind the grunts

just over the beach and rake the village with fire. The sound of a long and modulated explosion accompanies their strafing. "I'm not used to the sound of miniguns. I was expecting the slower fire from M60s. The effects sure are different." The helicopters break out over the ocean and come right back on their target, coming in to fire like fighter aircraft. "The Cobras, they'll blow your ass away! I wouldn't want to be a Charlie when the pilots use those miniguns."

For several months the First Cavalry has been replacing its Huey UH-1B gun and ARA ships with Cobra AH-1G choppers, the first helicopter conceived for attack. Six Cobras were delivered to Vietnam in September 1967 for evaluation. The new attack helicopter demonstrated its effectiveness very quickly. Used during the Tet Offensive, the 334th Assault Helicopter Company routed the NVA and Viet Cong in Saigon, Long Binh, and Bien Hoa and contributed to repulsing the communist assault.

Flying at 280 kilometers an hour the Cobra is much faster and more maneuverable than the Huey. It is also less vulnerable because it is smaller, with a better profile, and has only a pilot and copilot for crew. The cockpit, hermetically sealed, soundproofed, and armored better protects the crew and the vital centers of the machine. Under its nose, at the feet of the pilot, the aircraft is equipped with a turret TAT102 with an electronically operated M134 machine gun with six rotating barrels. The rate of fire is variable from two thousand to four thousand rounds per minute. The pilot controls the rate of fire with the trigger. The stubby wings on each side of the cockpit give the pilot better stability and also serve as anchor points for the rocket pods. The designer baptized it "Cobra." The grunts call it the "snake."

"They still have some problems with the Cobra. The cockpit is so soundproof that the pilot and copilot can't hear it when they're fired on. Also, since there's a crew of two instead of four, they have fewer people observing so they've got to fly higher up."

"Who told you all that?" surprised, the Lieutenant asks his RTO.

"A mechanic buddy who works in aircraft maintenance."

Binh Anh is now covered with a thick layer of smoke and rocked by explosions. The ARA Cobras work over what the 1st of the 9th gunships missed. As the Cobras move aside, naval guns unload on the enemy. The Battalion encircles the village and blocks the escape routes. The NVA are trapped in Binh Anh. They wait for night to attempt flight. This time, however, the Black Horse net is tight. In the morning, the Battalion moves in preceded by bulldozers that crush the bunkers and other fortified positions. They take 44 prisoners and count 233 NVA dead.

For no particular reason, Pacific Command issued an order in June of 1968 designating the First Cavalry Division as the "1st Cavalry Division (airmobile)" and the 101st Airborne Division as the "101st Division (airmobile)." These designations produced no little indignation. The First Cav Division, in its Vietnam role, had come to designate itself the "First Air Cavalry Division," a title that it merited and that distinguished it from all other units in Vietnam. The 101st always considered itself as an elite airborne outfit. Each unit was very attached to its name and heritage and came aggressively to its defense. The opposition was sufficiently intense that on 26 August the directive was revoked and the two Divisions recovered their original names.

During this period the command of the Division changes. Major General Tolsen comes to the end of his tour. He leaves the Division on 15 July, and command devolves temporarily on his assistant, Brigadier General Dick Irby. Irby, however, enjoys command only briefly. Before Westmoreland left the country, he had picked as Tolson's successor Major General George I. Forsythe. Fifty years old with an MBA dating to 1939, he completed jump school in 1959. Forsythe participated in campaigns in the Pacific and Europe. Since June of 1967 he has been the Deputy CORDS Commander assigned to MACV. He has already completed one tour in Vietnam in 1958 as an advisor to the operations section of the general staff of the South Vietnamese Army.

"George, I have a command for you!" Westmoreland tells him.

"Which one, sir? I thought all the Infantry Divisions were taken... ."

"The First Cav," Westmoreland responds with a smile.

At first, Forsythe is speechless, because the Cav represents, especially after its recent exploits, the elite of the US Army.

"That's great news, sir! But, you know I'm not a pilot. So, George Forsythe finds himself at Fort Rucker, Alabama, to earn his wings. On 19 August, with his brand new flight wings, he is back in Vietnam. He goes to Camp Evans and takes command of the First Team.

Before leaving, Tolson rendered homage to his men, not with an official address, but in his notes:

> To conclude, I cannot leave without once again recalling the role that men play in the equation, 'the man-machine' of airmobility. During this period, I have had many opportunities to have exceptional officers and non-commissioned officers under my command. The Division itself was particularly endowed with courageous young men, volunteers and draftees. I have every confidence in your ability to train the non-commissioned officers we need. These men are the most intelligent that I have seen since the Second World War. They are just as good, just as courageous.

At the end of its stay in the I Corps tactical zone, the Division must replace 23,200 men, without counting replacements for the killed, wounded, and ill. In American universities pacifist movements are more and more active. They conduct large demonstrations as an integral part of their mobilization. This activity evidently has a direct influence on the behavior and recruitment of young men.

When the veterans, volunteers for a second tour in Vietnam, debark at Tan Son Nhut following an absence of several months, they get a shock. The Base has become the biggest airport in the world. At Camp Alpha, the reception area for the troops, the barracks are no longer canvas or wood, but metal, and air conditioned. But the American soldiers there wear mustaches and sideburns, and wear pacifist medals on chains around their necks.[1] Six months earlier, the "thumbs up" sign meant "okay," or "good luck." Now, truck and bus drivers greeted new arrivals with the "V" sign. This is not the "V" for victory sign of Winston Churchill, but that of the campus, now a "peace" sign.

There is some indefinable something in the air, something in the discipline and demeanor of the troops the veterans sense right away. In Saigon, the ambiance has changed since Tet. The veterans do not stay in the capital long. A hurried massage and blow job just outside Tan Son Nhut and, as quickly as they can they find a flight to An Khe. The climate in the rear seems unhealthy to them.

An Khe, the village of scattered huts next to the "Golf Course" that had been cleared by machete-wielding grunts offloaded there in September 1965 has become a prosperous village with laundry and cleaning shops. The children are clean and wear clothes. The souvenir shops are next to massage parlors, bars, and restaurants. There is electricity, fans, air-conditioners, neon lights, and type-writers.

The Fucking New Guys do not have to sleep in the elephant grass any more, but in bunks inside a steel bunker with a rein-forced roof layered over with sandbags. After a day in Base Camp to take care of administrative chores, the replacements depart for Camp Evans. An Khe is no longer the heart of the First Cav. For a long time it was the rear area for the Division, assuring all classes of resupply and Third Echelon maintenance for the helicopters. Since the beginning of the year, just after the Tet Offensive, logistical bases were established at *Red Beach* in Hue and at Phu Bai. At that time, each Brigade became autonomous with its own mainte-nance facilities. An Khe dozed.

At Camp Evans the veteran relocates the tents and the odor of C-rations being heated with C4, the plastic explosive with the side benefit of serving as readily available fuel. "Hello Doc!"

"I was sure you'd come back, Sarge. It's good to see you."

"Hey, except for you Doc, I don't recognize anyone from the Platoon."

"Yeah, you're right. There's a bunch that've finished their tour and gone home. Some were killed in an ambush on 31 May."

"So, what's new?"

"Well, shit, since you left, we've been busy. First Khe Sanh where we bailed out the Marines—a real piece of shit. They were really worn down by two and a half months under siege. Our company was the first to get to them at Lang Vei."

"Yeah, then they sent us to the A Shau Valley. That was like something I'd never seen before. There, the NVA were waiting with anti-aircraft guns aimed with radar tracking. Luckily, the pilots had some kind of detector that told them when they were being tracked, but they had to react fast. On the third 'bleep,' the guns were locked on and your ass was grass."

"Finally, we shut down the air strip at A Luoi which gave us the chance to check out their 130s fired from over the border in Laos. So Sarge, that's what you missed. But what you're going to find is a bunch of pussies: NCOs that made their rank in seven months. We call them "instant" NCOs, like coffee."

"Fuck! It took me eighteen months to make SP4. I didn't make E5 until after my first tour"

"Right, Sarge, but now the Non-Coms like you or the officers that volunteer for a tour, there aren't any more. They've either finished their tour or they're dead."[2]

"You're not giving me a warm and fuzzy feeling!"

"The men coming in now really don't want to tangle with the NVA. They want to get home alive. Go find yourself an interesting job. Every outfit's looking for guys like you, with your experience."

On 26 October 1968, General Forsythe's telephone at Camp Evans wakes him in the middle of the night. "MACV here, General Abrams for General Forsythe."

"Yes, it's me."

"Good evening, George. I've decided to move the First Cav down to the III Corps Tactical Zone. I'm certain that four NVA Divisions are forming across the Cambodian border to launch an offensive. An attack is immanent. All our intelligence sources come together on this."

"But the First and Twenty-Fifth Divisions already cover the area between Saigon and the border."

"Yes, but they've begun major pacification programs in some very populous regions and I don't want to unhorse a program that promises relative stability in the area. I want the Cav to take up positions along the border and to be ready to intervene if the North Vietnamese show signs of crossing into South Vietnam. It will be your mission to destroy them before they can attack into a populated area. If some of them manage to get through, they need to be so chewed up that they don't pose a threat. You may move out right away."

"That's a move of over nine hundred kilometers," notes Forsythe.

"Yes, I know, and you've got carte blanche for whatever support you need."

"I think that the operation should remain secret. I'll have the unit patches and insignias removed so that the movement of the Division will be more discrete."

"Negative! I want to show the NVA that we can move a Division over nine hundred klicks from one day to the next. Above all, leave the unit markings on the nose of your helicopters. The name of the operation is *Liberty Canyon*. Here is an opportunity to conduct the largest movement from one theater of operations to another in the war in Indochina."

"Good! Understood sir!"

At dawn Forsythe convenes his staff to plan the operation. *Liberty Canyon* kicks off on 28 October and should have one Brigade operational in its new AO by 2 November. The first to leave are the Mountain Boys of the 2ᵈ of the 8ᵗʰ. Lieutenant Colonel Frank Henry has them ready to move out by the evening of the 27ᵗʰ.

All the matériel is packed away in containers. The men move out and wait on the tarmac at Quang Tri with only their combat gear. Two four-motor C-130s deposit them the next day at Quan Loi where they prepare their assault on *LZ Joe*, planned for 31 October.

General Irby planned to move one Battalion per day. He organized a joint staff to provide fuel and control the air movement of the units with their logistical support. The aircraft carrier *Princeton* transported aircraft and associated equipment from Da Nang. The Marine Corps furnished three ships to move more men and equipment. Light vehicles and equipment were shipped out by air from LZs and airstrips at Camp Evans, Quang Tri, and Phu Bai.

It took 437 C-130 flights to move 11,550 men and 3,400 tons of freight. Four hundred and fifteen of the Division's aircraft took off and headed south. The remainder of the Division went by sea with a fleet of thirty-seven ships plus an aircraft carrier which itself carried 30 aircraft, 4,100 men, and 16,500 tons of freight.

In twelve days the Division had closed on its new location. Four days after General Abrams' call, the 2ᵈ of the 8ᵗʰ mounted its first assault in the III Corps Zone. On 1 November the 2ᵈ of the 7ᵗʰ, coming from Quan Loi, landed on *LZ Billy* and occupied the terrain. They have one priority: dig and build and do it fast.

The site is cleared, the trees felled, and trenches outlined, all with the help of the 2ᵈ Battalion of the 19ᵗʰ Artillery and teams of engineers. Bunkers, mortar pits, stocks of ammunition ... . The forest and the laterite are molded according to the wishes of the new arrivals. To announce their presence, the grunts continuously pound the forest with eight inch artillery.

In two days, the helicopters make 181 round trips to bring in the rest of the ammunition, rations, and other remaining supplies. The 3ᵈ Brigade is now installed. The 1ˢᵗ arrives just behind it to cover the southeast flank. Forsythe adjusts his dispositions to conform to the most recent intelligence. He is thus set up to profit from the extreme flexibility of his Division. The 5ᵗʰ of the 7ᵗʰ, which was to have taken a position at Phuoc Vinh, is diverted at the last minute. Forsythe assigns it to the *Hook* area to surround the enemy. The 2ᵈ Brigade, finishing up *Operation Comanche Falls* in the north, is the last to leave, and is in its new location and ready to go on 7 November.

The Division Base sets up at Phuoc Vinh, the General Staff at Bien Hoa. Forsythe and his CP set up for two weeks at Long Binh, the main communications hub for US Forces in Southeast Asia. The new Operational Area of the First Cav extends over 7,700 square kilometers along the length of the Cambodian border.

The old practice of securing an area with a belt of strong points, a proven technique with a long history, including the Indian Wars, is employed with up to date means. From Fire Support Bases all the approaches to Saigon are covered. Surveillance is organized to spot the movement of the NVA or Vietcong along these routes.

The nine battalions trace a perimeter that stretches from the *Hook* north to the Plain of Jars up to the *Angel's Wing* and south to the *Parrot's Beak*. The infantry mission is simple: continuous day and night patrols. The scout helicopters have the same mission. General Forsythe summarizes their task. "We have great latitude of action and complete freedom of maneuver. What's more, neither the Division nor its assets are tasked for other missions. We have therefore all of our means available to find the enemy and fight him, wherever we find him. It's clear now that the total combat power available to an Airmobile Division functioning as a whole is much superior to the sum of combat power of elements of the Division operating independently."

The Division distinguishes two distinct areas in its AO and baptizes them in pure Cav style. The largest is designated *Sheridan Saber* and extends from the south of Tay Ninh to the border of the II Corps Zone, including the *Hook* area. The other is called *Navajo Warhorse*, and extends from the *Parrot's Beak* to the *Angel's Wing*.

The pilots who regularly overfly this frontier zone quickly discover that the place is very bad news. The North Vietnamese have concentrated an enormous density of anti-aircraft weapons here. Gunships must accompany reconnaissance missions. Cobras fly behind and above the scouts as cover. At any sign of the enemy, the snakes dive on targets unmasked by the scout ships.

While the UH-1B gunships and ARA helicopters have been replaced by the Cobra, the light reconnaissance choppers have also evolved. The tiny bubble H-13 Sioux has given place to the OH-6A Cayuse as the standard Light Observation Helicopter or LOH. On the ground they call it the Loach. It is shaped like a peanut. This Scout chopper is armed. It has an electrically powered 7.62mm machine gun with six rotating barrels in a small, streamlined turret located to the pilot's left. It fires at a rate of two thousand to four thousand rounds per minute. A machine gunner, armed with an M60 suspended on a nylon sling, sits behind the pilot.

The army scoutship pilots such as those of the 1st of the 9th are true aerial artists. They are not only virtuoso pilots, but demonstrate incredible sangfroid and courage. They pay for their impetuousness with a high casualty rate. These pilots are very young, rarely over twenty-one.

Flying their Loach as if it were a "bronco," they use any means available to expose the enemy. They know that there is a Cobra above them on permanent overwatch. The scouts carry an arsenal with them because the risk of being shot down in the middle of the NVA or VC is very real. The helicopter, as a part of its on board equipment, has an AR15 assault rifle, the shortened version of the M16, with three thirty-round magazines. The pilot is issued a Colt .45 caliber semiautomatic pistol that he carries in a shoulder holster. This he wears loaded, with a round in the chamber. He usually has four or five clips in ammo pouches on his belt.[3]

In Vietnam, however, experience taught the pilots to double-up on personal arms. The scoutship pilot adds to his belt a caliber .38 Special Smith and Wesson revolver with two-inch barrel. In the cockpit, next to his seat, he places a twelve gauge pump shotgun and an M16 assault rifle with a pack containing another ten magazines of 5.56mm ammunition. Behind him his machine gunner carries an M79 grenade launcher in addition to the sling-mounted M60. At his side are cases of fragmentation and white phosphorous grenades. This "bronco" is a real dragon.

Practice soon adds a third man to the cockpit, the observer, seated to the right of the pilot. It was essential to improve the observational capacity of the scout ship and, above all, teach the observer the rudiments of flying so he could bring the chopper safely to earth if the pilot was killed, something that, unfortunately, becomes more and more common.

At the end of December, a scout from the 1st of the 9th is checking along a part of the Cambodian border, Cobra flying overwatch. As the Loach comes up on a clearing, the crew spots a group of NVA infantrymen seated in a semi-circle shadowed by heavy clusters of bamboo. An officer standing on a box conducts a meeting.

Before the NVA can react, the pilot makes a tight turn and fires his minigun. The "Gatling" machine gun wipes out the whole class. The snake, whose pilot has been observing from on high, dives down to check out the results. The pilot counts forty-one dead North Vietnamese sprawled out in the bamboo amphitheater. The scouts refine their excellent senses of perception and sharp reflexes that allow them to confront any situation with professional aplomb.

Near Chu Lai a Loach pilot spots a white patch on a low hill very near a village. The machine gunner is already taking aim with his M60. The chopper breaks out just behind a Viet Cong, black pajamas down around his feet. The white of his buttocks reflected in the pilot's sunglasses. Surprised and scared the VC jumped up yelling, pajamas still around his ankles, hands covering his eyes. The whine of the turbine engine fades in the distance with no burst from the M60. The VC removes his hands from his eyes to see the machine gunner wave "goodbye" from the Loach that has regained altitude. The American had the time to observe that the VC was a young woman, and to take his finger off the trigger.

Translator's Notes

[1] Many officers and men in the Seventh Cavalry cultivated mustaches, many of them handlebar moustaches. They were recognized as part and parcel of the old horse cavalry tradition and not a sign of indiscipline. Despite this tradition, sometime in 1966 officers and men were ordered to shave their mustaches if the mustache did not appear in the photograph on their Military Identification Card. This order was often overlooked which was facilitated by the fact that the Battalions of the Seventh Cavalry were almost always in the field. Some orders are destined to be ignored!

[2] Second tours were automatic for Infantry Officers. The time between tours was twelve months for Captains, eighteen for Majors.

[3] Although the magazine for the .45 caliber pistol is commonly called a "clip," it is really a spring-loaded "magazine."

CHAPTER XXII

In its new Area of Operations, the Cav has not only to control the sky and the ground. The *Parrot's Beak* area is crossed by numerous waterways that greatly facilitate infiltration toward Saigon no more than fifty kilometers distant. The Airmobile Division decides to become equally "water mobile." The Division forms a "Navcav" with landing craft and patrol boats provided by the Navy. The craft are armed and armored, and some of them decked to accept helicopters. The patrol boats complete the coverage of the AO. They daily patrol the Vam Co Dong and Vam Co Try rice plantations. The landing craft serve equally well as troop carriers and freight transporters.

The Jumping Mustangs of the 1st of the 8th are charged with conducting this new strike force which operates in cooperation with the Navy. Together they organize operations in the Delta, coordinating them with units from the IVth Corps area.

On the ground, the Infantry work gets harder and more dangerous. The forest is more exuberant and luxurious here than in the high plateau country. It offers the NVA and VC, masters of camouflage and booby traps, a terrain that compliments their creativity. Every patrol becomes a nightmare. It is not just the punji stakes, but grenades, Claymore mines, machine guns rigged to fire with nearly invisible trip-wire. The Chinese Claymores are even more fearsome than the American ones: packed with all sorts of scrap metal they create atrocious wounds. One step too far and a booby-trapped machine gun shoots up the patrol or shrapnel from a mine tears into bodies.

The Viet Cong, already gifted with fertile and pernicious imaginations, profit from their hunter instincts and twenty years of guerrilla warfare. The young American draftees, freshly arrived from the United States, are easy targets for the professionals in black pajamas. Their apprenticeship in the jungle is murderous and traumatic.

The Cav sinks into a routine of border patrol with an attitude more defensive than offensive. Under the pressure of media attention and public opinion, the Generals become obsessed with casualties. From now on, every patrol, every troop movement employs an excess of resources. It is the tactic of stacking forces. The war is fought with an excess of means, with helicopters, artillery, and B-52 strikes.

Sergeant Matt Brennan, veteran of the campaign in 1965 that

The 1st Cavalry Division in III Corps, 1969

ZCT - Zone du Corps Tactique

Sheridan Sabre
Navajo Warhorse

CAMBODGE

Kratié

Mekong

Piste Jolley

Route Adams

II ZCT

Autoroute de la Jungle

ZONE D

Route des Caches X

Carolyn

Dot

Quan Loi

Eleanor

ZONE C

Grant

Corridor de Saigon

Phuoc Vinh

III ZCT

Dong Naï

Tay Ninh

Plantation Michelin

SUD VIETNAM

Aile de l'Ange

Bec de Perroquet

Rivière de Saigon

Bien Hoa

Long Binh

Xuan Loc

Bear Cat

SAIGON

Long Thanh

IV ZCT

Mekong

Vung Tau

MER DE CHINE

50 km

cleared the "Golf Course" at An Khe, back for a second tour, wonders what happened. "The war has become something impersonal," he says. "The NVA are killed by scouts and Snakes, by artillery or by B-52s. Our guys get killed by rockets, infantry attacks, or by sappers that figure on getting killed themselves. The fighting happens in defensive positions at the Cav bases. We don't go deep into the jungle where we used to chase and attack the bastards. An army on the defense's got some big problems. The discipline starts to go to shit. The new troops, already unhappy to be here, feel impotent under the constant mortar attacks. They're reduced to turning on each other, racial bullshit I haven't seen for a long time. Some of these assholes threaten their officers and NCOs. The officers aren't exactly doing their part either. On top of all that shit, the fucking drug problem makes everything worse."

This change in attitude, which had reached the rear areas of the American Army during the course of 1968, begins to spread into areas closer to the action in 1969. The Marines are hit by it. The Cav is the least affected.

Along the border the patrols go out one after another in a jungle without leaves. The defoliant Agent Orange kills the vegetation of all three levels of the triple canopy. The countryside has the aspect of a lunarscape: water-filled bomb craters, and tree trunks standing straight and bare.

In December 1969 the allies are convinced that the North Vietnamese are preparing an offensive, the objective of which will be to launch several divisions on Saigon during the upcoming 1969 Tet. The 5th Vietcong Division infiltrates all the way in to Bien Hoa and Long Binh with the objective of neutralizing the strategic bases of the allied command. For their part, the 1st, 7th, and 9th North Vietnamese Divisions get their logistical affairs in order and hold themselves ready to support the 5th VC Division. The 1st NVA Division also has the mission to conduct a diversion in the Tay Ninh area to draw the American forces and so open the way to Saigon.

Black Virgin Mountain, 986 meters at the summit, dominates the Tay Ninh Plain. There are many pagodas at this important Cao Dai religious site.[1] The spiritual nature of the mountain serves as a reason to forbid regular helicopter overflights and surveillance. It is, however, the location of a radio relay site.

During this time the 7th NVA Division is supposed to attack Saigon from the north and the 9th NVA Division is to do the same from the west, coming directly from the *Angel's Wing*. All this requires a long preparation by the North Vietnamese who multiply their arms and ammunition caches as well as improving their trail network in the jungle.

Colonel Karl R. Morton, who has just taken over the 3ᵈ Brigade, concentrates his attention against all attempts at infiltration. The 2ᵈ Battalion, 7ᵗʰ Cavalry along with Brigade Headquarters, sets up at Quan Loi, on the airstrip of the main plantation of the Terres-Rouges, just a little to the east of the tiny village of An Loc. The 3ᵈ Brigade takes over the site from the Big Red One, the 1ˢᵗ Infantry Division that had transformed the area into a military camp. The French planters had established excellent relations with the Brigade of the Big Red One, whose men had fallen in love with the plantation's French nurse.

"I've never seen trees planted like that! Where the hell are we," asks Pete, the jeep's machine gunner, a "rat" from Dusty Delta, the jeep-mounted Recon Platoon of the 1ˢᵗ of the 9ᵗʰ.

"I told you, in a rubber plantation," the Lieutenant chimes in: "the *rubber jungle*, even more dangerous than the natural forest."

"This trail is something else, just like at home, straight as an arrow, no curves," adds the driver.

"It's real comfortable here in the shade, a real change from the elephant grass, the rice paddies, and the jungle."

"Yeah! But we've been warned to be real careful because it's easy to hide behind groups of trees and set up an ambush or trigger a mine. The guys in the 1ˢᵗ Division told me never to drive on the trails."

"Seen from here, the trees are lined up like on parade. You could even say they're in uniform with their brown trunks, cup at the side, and white net at a slant around their waists."

"You must be a farmer if the rubber trees inspire you like that!"

"These plantations, they look good, but working here can wear you out."

"Uh! Look, there's somebody up ahead dressed all in white."

"Don't shoot. It's one of the Frenchmen who works on the plantation. I know him."

"He's goin' to play tennis?"

"No! The planters dress in white—an old colonial tradition. Drive up by him. Maybe he'll ask us to stop by for a beer. Don't treat these guys like French VC right away," the Lieutenant counsels the machine gunner.

"Hello sir!"

"*Bonjour messieurs! Vous êtes nos nouveaux voisins? Bienvenue sur les plantations des Terres-Rouges!*"

"*Terres-Rouges!* Sounds like an Indian name," Pete comments.

"*Si vous avez cinq minutes, venez au cercle*, the club, *boire une 33. Vous me suivez*—to follow." He gets into his little white car.

"Great!" The two jeeps follow the planter.

Astonished, the Americans look at this calm universe, everything so orderly and clean. The gardens, surrounded by plots of Bougainvilleas, Anamandas, and Crotons are perfectly maintained.[2] The lawns of Kikouyou grass are razor cut by machete and the fragrance of Frangipani fills the air. The American helicopters, however, have covered everything with a thin coat of red laterite dust.

"We come out of hell and here, you'd think you're in paradise."

The planter leads them to the terrace that dominates the garden and the rubber trees.

"It's beautiful, but you live in the middle of a combat zone."

"*Ah oui, bon*—here, *vous savez*, on the plantation, *on vit dans la guerre*, we live in war for more than twenty years. I show you in the main office the wall with the names of all our dead. *Les planteurs des Terres-Rouges*, of CEXO, of SIPH, and of Michelin, *ont payé un lourd tribut*, a heavy price in the war. Those plantations that defended themselves with partisans paid a particularly high price... . From here you have a good view of the plantation, not from a helicopter, *mais presque*."

"Is the plantation big?"

"About seven thousand hectares for Quan Loi. There is Xa Track to the southeast with two thousand hectares and Xa Cam to the north with three thousand hectares. You have to, to *convertir* to acres."

"It's big!"

"*Ti Nam, apporte-nous quatre Ba Muoi Ba!*" The bare-foot servant disappears and returns silently with the bottles of beer and ice.

"*Cam on.*"[3]

"It's incredible! You'd think there was no war here. Everything seems so organized."

"*En fait*, we are so used to the war that we live with it. That has also to do with the form of this war. *Vous le savez bien*. There are no front lines. So while we are not occupied *militairement, eh, on continue à saigner*, to bleed the trees and produce rubber."

After a large gulp of beer, the driver can no longer hold his tongue. "What do you have to do to keep working here? The VC don't mess with your operation?"

"Ah. You want to know if I am a French VC? I know, you are sure that we, *les Français*, that we wish that you lose this war, because we were not able, *pas été capables de gagner la nôtre*, to win our own. That's a bar joke, like if you want to know whether a cognac-soda is better than a whisky! More anticommunist than the planters you have a hard time to find. Here, we are in Asia and nothing is simple. You follow me?"

"Go on!"

"My job is uh, *de faire 'pisser' les hévéas*, to bleed the rubber trees and to export the rubber. For the South Vietnamese Government, we are a major source of money and *recettes d'exportation*, of foreign exchange. We employ thousands of workers and supervisors whom we pay a diverse range of salaries and social benefits. In addition to all the technicians we have our own doctors, clerics, architects, teachers, communications specialists, and pilots. *En fait*, we operate much as you. *On est autonome*, autonomous. We have no helicopters, but we do have airplanes."

"On the communist side the plantations are just as indispensable, but for different reasons. *D'abord*, first, they hide here. Then, *d'ailleurs*, they forbid us to clean up certain lots. But they let us produce rubber. Then they can extract taxes in piastres and rice from our workers, and stay in contact with the population."

"Above all, the Vietnamese are not choirboys." In each family they have one boy with the VC and one in the Army, *pour préserver l'avenir*, to protect their future. They get together peacefully on the holidays. So, what will you do? Defoliate everything and 'zap' everyone with slant eyes—*gooks* as you call them?"

"It's not easy," the Lieutenant responds in a conciliatory manner.

"Today the French are neutral in the war, and everybody has an interest in the plantations continuing to produce. The VC blow hot and cold but pretty much let us work. We can sometimes go into areas where they would shoot at you, or set off a mine. *Mais*— the North Vietnamese do not necessarily share the attitude of the local VC. The local VC, known around here as '*cousins*,' do not see things the same as the Northerners. A little like you, the NVA regulars more closely comply with military and tactical imperatives— *eux aussi*. Here, there are many wars, one of them here at home using locally crafted munitions and between the local VC and the popular and regional forces. And then there is your war against the NVA using sophisticated and modern weapons."

"*Merci pour la bière*. We've got to go to An Loc. We'll see you. We'll talk about this again. I'll come back with the Public Information Officer, the PIO. He'll be interested in knowing your point of view for a press release."

"If you come back, do it in the afternoon. The girls working in the fields are much cuter than the ones on the morning shift, *et surtout*, they do not smell like rubber."

On 3 December Delta Company of the 2^d of the 7th lands with 116 men in a large clearing to secure a new landing zone, *LZ Eleanor*. The slicks land in a semicircle while the door gunners hose down the edge of the jungle with a continuous fire. There is no reaction.

"The Lima Zulu is green!"

The Captain decides the area is clear. "Cease fire!"

The M60s cease firing. The men offload the choppers and move out nonchalantly to establish the perimeter. Captain Fitzsimmons sends out his XO to verify that the perimeter is secure, and moves into the center of the LZ to greet Lieutenant Colonel George D. Hardesty, the Battalion Commander of the 2^d of the 7th, who gets off his command chopper and sends it back to base. As Colonel Hardesty's Charlie-Charlie climbs away to tree top level, the edge of the jungle erupts with fire: automatic weapons, mortars, and B40s. Four hundred North Vietnamese hidden behind the trees were patiently awaiting the order of their officers to open fire.

The first B40 rockets set fire to the dry grass in the clearing. The fire and smoke increase the panic of the grunts, surprised by the attack. Many are wounded and killed trying to put out the fire with their ponchos or poncho liners. The wounded are burned and asphyxiated. Their ammunition explodes in the furnace.

Sergeant Allison, an old trooper, attempts to reassemble his men and get them out of the brazier. Three men are killed while trying to raise the Fire Direction Center on the radio. Buzz, the Captain's RTO, takes off and lays aside his radio to grab a machine gun and fire back at the NVA. He moves off and out of sight through the charred remains of high elephant grass. "Buzz, get your ass back here with the radio, goddamn it!"

Allison, furious, recovers the radio and reestablishes commo on the battalion push. The reception is poor. Complicating the problem, incoming mortar rounds are landing all around him while he is trying to transmit. Moreover, the radio antenna sticks up just over the grass, and a sniper works diligently at putting a round in its operator. Allison hugs the ground with his nose in the dirt. "This is Six Mike, Six Mike. We need reinforcements here. We can't hold out for long, over."

"Roger Six Mike, clear copy, reinforcements on the way, water, and Medevac, over."

"Roger. Thanks. Out."

A Huey emblazoned with a red cross is the first sign of support to come in view. The pilot, copilot, and medics are all wounded. The pilot just manages to get his chopper out of the zone of fire. Just behind him, other slicks attempt to offload crates of ammo.

Shoved out in haste, they fall too far away. Several men are killed trying to recover them. All about the wounded call for help and ask for water. Three medics have already been killed trying to get to the wounded.

After five hours of fighting the intensity of fire weakens. "Pay attention now people! Keep your ammo and grenades handy! They're gonna charge." But the North Vietnamese, fearing the arrival of massive American reinforcements, break contact.

The Battalion Commander lands in the clearing, a disaster area. "Is that you Six Mike? You've done a great job!"

Sergeant Allison does not answer; preoccupied as he is by the surrounding devastation and taking stock of what is left of Delta Company, 2^d of the 7th.

Fortunately, not all the contacts with the NVA take place under such unfavorable conditions. The mobility of the Cav enables it to fix the NVA forces and keep them from getting close to Saigon. As in a soccer game, the 1st Brigade covers the 9th NVA Division as soon as it moves out of the *Angel's Wing*. From the 15th of December 1968 on, Colonel Robert J. Baer, 1st Brigade CO orders a careful, low-flying recon of the *Navajo Warhorse* AO, scrutinizing it with the effect of a fine tooth comb. He has to prevent the NVA from restocking their caches and building up their logistical infrastructure. The 2^d Brigade, which remained south of the Fishhook to block the route into Saigon, has uncovered caches of weapons all set to equip a battalion-sized unit.

Under the pressure of First Cav operations the NVA have to split up their forces to infiltrate the tight American net. The new enemy offensive begins on 23 January 1969, just after the Tet Truce. As planned, the 5th VC Division attacks the outskirts of Saigon. The 199th Infantry Brigade reacts rapidly and pushes the VC regiments to the edge of the Michelin Plantation.

At the same time the 1st NVA Division attacks *Fire Support Base Grant*, defended by the 2^d of the 12th commanded by Lieutenant Colonel Peter L. Gorvad. On 8 March 1969 *Grant* is bludgeoned by a violent mortar and 122mm rocket attack. The Battalion CP takes a direct hit. A rocket pierces the fortified command post and explodes on the inside. Gorvad, seated before the operations map, is killed on the spot. One of the radio operators is wounded. The S2 is knocked flat on his stomach by the blast.

The 95th NVA Regiment launches an assault on the bunkers protecting *FSB Grant*. Captain Bill Capshaw of the 1st of the 77th Artillery takes the situation in hand. He points a 105mm howitzer at the assault wave. Out of flechettes, he loads the gun with nails, bolts, and scraps of metal, like a bombard.[4] The 2^d of the 12th

returns the NVA fire with its M60s, slaughtering the NVA tangled in the concertina. They repulse several assaults. After two days of being pounded, *Grant* is still secure. The NVA want to finish the job. They reinforce the 95th Regiment with two battalions of the 101st Regiment.

At dawn on 11 March, the 1st of the 9th's Snakes loosen the vise. The communists break contact having failed to take their objective. From prisoners the Americans learn that the NVA had assaulted, believing they were attacking a poorly defended logistical base. The NVA officers thought that in mounting a successful attack they might reduce the fear their men had of attacking a First Cav support base.

Later that morning General Forsythe lands at *Grant*. He orders Colonel Robert C. Kingston, 3d Brigade CO, who had arrived earlier that morning to take his men and pursue the NVA so as to maintain contact.

"Hold on sir! These men have been fighting without rest for four hours. They're exhausted. If you really want them to move out you'll have to lead them yourself because I won't do it!"

Forsythe bites his tongue not to call down Kingston for insubordination, but he lets it pass and gives the defenders of *FSB Grant* some breathing space. The following day a scout ship overflies the Support Base. The pilot counts 154 dead NVA. The 2d of the 12th and the 1st of the 77th had ten men killed, thirty wounded, and one 155mm howitzer destroyed.

The contest continues. Colonel Baer intercepts elements of the 9th NVA Division which is trying to come down out of the hills to move on Saigon from the east. Men from the 11th Mechanized Cavalry in their M113 APCs chase down the regiments from the 7th NVA Division that had taken refuge in the Michelin Plantation.

By the end of March the communist threat to Saigon seems to have been averted. The North Vietnamese and the Vietcong, out of breath, have had to return to their refuges. The four NVA Divisions that have been ceaselessly harassed by the First Cav have not been able to maneuver freely enough to accomplish their original plan. But for all that, the North Vietnamese do not renounce their plan to lay siege to Saigon. In May the 9th NVA Division again attacks Tay Ninh and the 7th NVA Division attempts to gain control of the corridor toward the capital.

On 5 May General Forsythe's command tour ends. Major General Elvy Benton Roberts takes command of the Division. He is a product of the First Cav. He had already commanded the 1st Brigade in December of 1965 in the high plateau area, just after the battles in the Ia Drang Valley. Fifty-two years old, from Kentucky,

West Point Class of 1943, a paratrooper and explosive demolitions expert, as a Lieutenant he had joined the 501st Airborne Regiment of the 101st Airborne Division. On 6 June 1944 he jumped into Normandy and fought in the great battles on the European Front. He jumped into Holland, participated in the Battle of the Ardennes, and fought at Bastogne.

After the war, he was stationed in Germany, then Iran. He commanded the 1st Airborne Combat Group of the 506th Infantry Regiment. In January 1963 he was assigned to General Kinnard's staff in the 11th Air Assault Division. He thus figures among the pioneers of the airmobile concept and of the First Team.

When his tour as Commander of the 1st Brigade ended in December of 1965 he was promoted to Brigadier General and assigned to MACV Headquarters. In June 1968 he came back to Vietnam as Assistant Division Commander of the 3d Infantry Division. Roberts has a perfect understanding of the First Cavalry Division and takes command without hesitation or doubts.

Beginning the next day, 6 May, he gets right down into the action. *LZ Carolyn*, established a few days earlier by the 2d of the 8th is transformed into a support base with B Battery, 1st of the 30th Artillery, a 155mm Howitzer Battery, and A Battery, 2d of the 19th Artillery, a 105mm Howitzer Battery. *Carolyn*, as predicted, is very much in the way of the NVA and VC because it dominates a resupply route extending from the Cambodian border to the west of the *Fishhook*. The resupply corridor comes out in the Michelin Plantation, and then continues on toward Saigon. The Americans have named it the *Caches X Trail*. Its trace on the intelligence map is marked with Caches denominated X1, X2, X3, etc.

At dawn on 6 May the 95th NVA Regiment attacks the perimeter of *Carolyn* on the north and west in a pincher movement. There were fewer troops in the base at that time since many platoons were out on patrol. The NVA infantrymen lay siege to six bunkers of the defense network. Charlie and Echo Companies cannot hold back the flood of NVA soldiers who make off with several howitzers.

Lieutenant Colonel Richard Wood organizes a counter attack employing all the forces on *LZ Carolyn*. Artillerymen, radio operators, engineers, cooks—all mount the defenses to repulse the attack on two fronts. The 155mm howitzers become the centerpiece of the extremely brutal fighting. The artillery pieces change hands several times. The troopers fight it out hand to hand with knives, bayonets, entrenching tools, and machetes. Wood advises Brigade of the situation and requests help.

The Cobras surge into view at treetop level and hit the North

Vietnamese from the rear. They disperse the enemy with rockets and fire from their Gatling guns. The Air Force is also called into play, and sends up Spooky, a C-47 armed with an electrically operated 20mm canon, and an AC-119 aircraft, called Shadow to assist with air control. Jets arrive and treat the perimeter to a feast of high explosives and napalm.

LZ Carolyn is soon no more than a vast crater on fire. To keep the NVA from attacking from the west, Lieutenant Colonel Wood sets fire to his reserves of fuel. The flaming barrier forms a continuous front with the napalm laid down by the jets. Stocks of artillery rounds are touched off by direct hits. As they explode they light up the night. Six hundred 105mm rounds blow in the course of a few minutes, filling the *LZ* with crashing explosions.

The situation for the defenders on *LZ Carolyn* becomes untenable. Since the beginning of the attack, the 155mm Battery has not had an operational Fire Direction Center. The gun crews aim the huge gun tubes by hand and load them with Beehive rounds that riddle the bunched up ranks of the NVA soldiers with millions of flechettes. The mortar FDC was spared. The Mortar Platoon keeps four tubes in action. It fires 1,500 rounds. White Phosphorous rounds illuminate the base and give the defenders a clear view of enemy movements. Getting mortar ammunition up to the tubes gets more and more difficult. The survivors, prone on the ground, arms full of mortar rounds, form a chain to pass the ammo from man to man and to the guns.

"Watch out! Get down. They're on the flank. There's a machine gun there!"

"Yeah, but how're we gonna get at 'em. If we try to move on 'em snipers'll get us." The 155mm Howitzer gun crews see the problem of the Mortar Platoon.

They direct their tubes at the NVA and pulverize the enemy machine gunners and riflemen. After an uninterrupted day of combat, the NVA, disheartened by so much resistance, prefer to withdraw from the perimeter, leaving 287 dead behind. On the 12th and 14th of May *Grant*, *Jamie*, and *Phyllis*, bases similar to *Carolyn*, are themselves subjected to rocket and mortar attacks.

General Roberts is not pleased. "Okay, that's one way to do it, but the Cav is not a border guard, we aren't police. We don't sit around in holes until the NVA decide to attack us. That kind of crap is for somebody else! We've got to get back into an offensive mode and take back the initiative."

Operation Liberty Canyon ends on 23 June. In seven months, the Division has lost 567 men killed and 3,555 wounded, but it has stopped the four NVA Divisions from getting into Saigon again.

For the grunts, life in the southern part of South Vietnam is not much fun. In isolated, hastily set up bases, they pass their time digging holes and burying containers under sand bags. They pull guard duty in bunkers or mount night patrols. With the monsoon, the holes fill with water: everything gets soaked. When it is not raining, the containers are stiflingly hot. It is impossible to sleep. Outside, one is always at the mercy of a rocket or a sniper.

Since 1965 the Skytroopers were always the attackers, the hunters. They now have the disagreeable impression of becoming stationary targets. The only advantage is the proximity of Saigon for those rare occasions when they can get a few days off. The bars and massage parlors are cleaner than the ones in An Khe or Camp Evans. The PX is like a supermarket, a real feast of stuff. Before leaving on pass, the men exchange the names and addresses of the "girls." Saigon has become the biggest bordello in the world, with an Asian exoticism.

"Well, FNG, this your first visit to Saigon? You wanna get a little; indulge your wildest dreams to hold you over till your next pass?"

"Unhuh, they told me you know where to go."

"Affirmative! I've been here long enough to scout out just about anything the city's got to offer. So's not to waste time, and to get you horny, go eat at '149.' That's a restaurant where the girls are topless by noon. You'll have their little tits bobbing under your nose while you eat."

"Um, yeah! But they're not real, they're silicon. You'll bounce off 'em if you touch 'em."

"Hey guy, do you see 'dumbass' on my nametag? No! So, listen! That evening you go back to the same joint and, now, pay attention! Don't be surprised. The girls are all dressed up, long skirts, split along the hip, classy! But you remember the ones you saw topless at noon. You remember what they look like underneath. Always very ladylike they'll turn gracefully around you while you munch on ginger chicken. About 2300 hours watch out! You could screw it up. There'll be some older troopers there and some Frogs on their time off from the plantations. They're just as horny as you, they speak the language, and they've got it all together. They take their pick fast and leave!"

"So: then what?"

"So: if you're not stupid, you can find one you like and check her out for silicon yourself! But don't go wandering around just anyplace like a new troop, you could get hurt."

"What the hell do I do for the afternoon?"

"After dining at the '149,' if eating chicken and thinking about nookie put you in the mood, get a massage to set your head straight for what comes later."

"You think so? Is that better than shopping on the Black Market?"

"For sure! The massage is obligatory when you're on pass! Take a cyclo, but bargain down the price first or you'll get screwed. Don't forget, the guys peddling those things claim not to know street names or numbers. You've got to tell them which way to go. I've got a great place to go on the road out to Tan Son Nhut."

"Well, I'll just get laid and that's enough!"

"Bullshit! The massage. It's an art! Take your time. Ask the Mamasan to pick you out a real friendly girl who knows what to do."

"Ah, so. I don't get to choose which one I want?"

"It's not a help yourself kind of thing. Besides, just relax, Max. They'll take care of you. She'll wash you, very gently. Don't get up to go when she takes you to the wooden steam cabinet and motions for you to get in. It's got a hole where your head sticks out. Inside it's hot, steam, your private steam bath."

"What the fuck's that for?"

"You spend twenty minutes there, sweating like a hog at a pig roast. She'll help you out and rinse you off with cold water."

"A public bath, shit!"

"If you want, go suck on an ice cream cone at the PX. That's what kids your age do in the world."

"Okay! But just don't give me any crap. Tell me what I need to know. I'm not into all this subtle Asian playboy shit. I come from Minnesota and now for three months I've been rotting away in this goddamn container."

"All right. Just keep cool. The girl will take you to a bed in a curtained off alcove. She'll take her clothes off, except for her panties. Once she gets her hands oiled up she'll begin."

"Begin what?"

"To give you a massage, dummy! But she'll start with your feet, with your toes. If you've got a good one, she'll suck them, and work her tongue around your big toe! Then, a shiver will take you and climb from your tail to the roots of the hair on your head, just like someone stuck an electric wire up your ass."

"And after that?"

"Saddle up! Take your posts! Mortars, incoming!"

"The address. Give me the address of the massage parlor."

"'Le Darling!' Watch your ass guy. That's incoming. I hope Charlie doesn't fuck up your R&R. Follow through on what I told you, and ask for girl number six. When you leave, you'll have a hard time walking. You'll be pussy whipped and all pooped out. Now put your fucking helmet on!"

Translator's Notes
[1] One of several religions practiced in Vietnam.
[2] Various tropical decorative shrubbery.
[3] "Thanks."
[4] A cannon employed in the middle ages and loaded with a large stone.

CHAPTER XXIII

A helicopter approaches the "Plantation," the name given to the Headquarters of the Second Operations Force at Bien Hoa. The Huey lands gently with General Creighton Abrams. There is hurried activity on the ground. This is the first visit of the MACV Commander to Lieutenant General Michael S. Davison, who had arrived in Bien Hoa just nine days earlier.

Heels click, officers and men salute, and shake hands with "Abe" who, followed by Davison, heads for the latter's office. Abrams takes a seat and carefully takes a cigar from a pocket. He strikes a match and draws the flame to the Havana, a cigar made in Virginia. After several puffs, settled deep in Davison's chair, he starts the conversation in a jocular tone.

"Mike, I would like you to go into Cambodia and clean out all the enemy sanctuaries for me. I'd like you to be able to do that within seventy-two hours after I give the word. Tell me when you're ready."

Davison takes the hit right in the gut. He is just beginning his first tour in Vietnam. He glances at the map to pinpoint the notorious sanctuaries. Abrams joins him and points out the area around the Fishhook. "Mike. The First Cav is already in this area and Roberts is the man for the job. Check it out with him."

Davison takes two days and a half to work on a plan with his staff and get it ready for Abram's approval. The proposed operation then goes to Washington for approval and a final review by Kissinger and his staff and by President Nixon and the Cabinet. On 26 April 1970, Davison calls General Roberts to his Headquarters to issue the now approved order from General Abrams.

"The operation is called *Total Victory, Toan Thang* in Vietnamese. The preparation for this mission must be completely secret. You are not to tell more than five members of your staff about it."

"That's going to be tough, sir. General Casey, who's going to replace me in ten days, is in the States getting his second star. He won't be back before the 5th of May. My G2 and G3 are both on leave in Hawaii."

In fact, Roberts is not surprised by the mission, in any case, much less than Davison himself. In effect, during April, General Abrams had taken Roberts into his confidence regarding the deterioration of the situation in Cambodia. Roberts had even suggested ways to prepare for an eventual raid.

In Washington, the principal decision makers discuss the situation. The North Vietnamese offensive against the Cambodian troops of Lon Nol, who had just overthrown Sihanouk, reinforced the logic of American intervention. Kissinger and Nixon, not receiving any precise advice from presidential advisors and members of the Cabinet, turn to the Ambassador in Saigon, Ellsworth Bunker, and to the military commander, General Creighton Abrams. Both of these men are strongly in favor of military intervention in the zones of the *Parrot's Beak* and the *Angel's Wing*.

Richard Helms, the CIA Chief, advises expanding the operation so as to cut the Ho Chi Minh Trail to Laos. "If you conduct one or two operations, you will pay the same political price, but the strategic advantage you will get from two attacks will be much greater."

At Bien Hoa Davison works on the details of his plan. He tells Roberts: "So that you can conduct the *Operation* in the very near future, and under the most favorable conditions, you may bring your Brigade Commanders into the loop. You will be ready to move out within forty eight hours of receiving the order."

Roberts immediately places a land line call to his Assistant Division Commander, Brigadier General Robert M. Shoemaker, an Officer with the reputation of being the best "pro" in the Cav. Bob Shoemaker has exceptional references. In 1963 he joined the 11th Air Assault Division. As a Lieutenant Colonel he commanded successively the 1st of the 12th and the 1st of the 8th. Next, at General Kinnard's insistence, he took command of the 1st Squadron, 9th Cavalry in December of 1965, in the Central Highlands. In May of 1966, as a Colonel, he became Division Chief of Staff. Promoted to Brigadier General, since October 1969 he has been the Assistant Division Commander and right hand man of General Elvy Roberts.

"Hello Bob! We're cooking up something pretty serious here. Put together a small but top notch staff and come to Quan Loi. Set up your operation in one of Kingston's offices at the 3d Brigade and get ready to do some serious planning. If this comes off, we'll have to move within forty-eight hours."

Shoemaker selects specialists in intelligence, plans and operations, fire support, logistics, and communications. They get to work with no one in the 3d Brigade, Colonel Kingston included, aware of the nature of their project. Shoemaker estimates the strength of the North Vietnamese forces stationed on the other side of the border at twelve regiments. He is not well informed of their specific locations or of their air defense capabilities.

"I have two questions that I need an answer to," he tells Roberts. "One: Are there Cambodian civilians in the area? Two: Just exactly what is the AO?"

"I understand perfectly the importance of your questions. All I can do is give you a partial answer to the second," Roberts answers. "It's an area some forty kilometers beyond the border. I don't how long the operation is to last."

"That helps a lot. I'll take as a hypothesis that it will be a raid into the *Fishhook*, and of short duration."

"Okay!"

Shoemaker and Colonel Morris J. Brady, DIVARTY Commander, get together one on one. The most difficult problem concerns working out the final plans for artillery support. They do not have an up to date map of Cambodia, and MACV refuses to provide aerial photos, citing security concerns. Roberts gets into the act and manages to get access to the most recent aerial photos taken by the Air Force over the Quan Loi area. He notes that, on the far side of the border, the land is pocked by huge craters left over from B-52 bomb strikes, which explains why MACV was unwilling to release the photos.

Thanks to these aerial photos, Shoemaker observes that the relief and vegetation are identical to a depth of several kilometers on each side of the border. He easily picks out Route Number 7 that crosses the region from west to east, and then turns toward the north. "Good, the area is just the same as Military Zone II," Shoemaker concludes, reassured. He will be able to establish the necessary fire bases.

From the pieces of information they have, Roberts and Shoemaker draw the conclusion that the mission will probably be to neutralize COSVN, one of the command centers of the North Vietnamese for operations in South Vietnam, also known as the B3 Front, with a staff that controls the operations in this one of the four operational fronts established by the North Vietnamese High Command. Shoemaker shows his plan to Roberts.

"We can move on this in less than forty-eight hours. First, six B-52s are set to make thirty-six strikes. The details are classified. At 0600, D-Day, we'll be informed of additional support. We'll concentrate one hundred tubes of 105s, 155s, and 175s. Most of them are already in position in various fire support bases established by the Cav and attached units."

"The prep will go on for one hour, from 0600 to 0700. The targets will be the LZs we've picked out and what we've been able to identify of air defenses. My problem at this stage is to be sure of completely neutralizing the NVA anti-air batteries so as not to receive the same bad surprise that we got at A Shau. The NVA have, in addition to 37mm anti-aircraft batteries, some very respectable double-barreled 14.5mm guns."

274

"After the artillery prep, Air Force fighter-bombers will pick up the action. We're doubling up the stuff we're using for the prep to be sure that we take out their air defenses as well as their fortified positions on the ground."

"The 1st of the 9th is going to move in just in front of the infantry. They are the best folks to get us an estimate of the situation just before our troopers make their air assaults. There will be no air recons before the attack so as to not tip off our hand to the NVA."

"Just behind the 1st of the 9th recon flight, I'm sending Major Pokorny from DIVARTY into the area to confirm, or modify if necessary, the disposition of our artillery. He'll transmit whatever info he uncovers to all the artillery batteries."

"On the ground, everything will be ready to go. Three airmobile ARVN battalions will assault into LZs to the north of the *Fishhook* to block the NVA. Two Squadrons of the 11th Armored Cavalry Regiment will arrive to the south of the *Fishhook* and link up with two ARVN battalions near *LZs East* and *Center*. Two other ARVN battalions will move to positions to the west of the Mimot Rubber Plantation. I count six thousand American troops and three thousand South Vietnamese."

"That sounds good to me but, now that everything is ready, Washington is gong to stall! We'll never get the green light to cross the damn border," notes Roberts, who adds, "Bob, you know that we're the only ones working with the hypothesis that COSVN is the target.[1] Neither Davison nor Abrams has given us the least indication that this is so."

On Tuesday, 28 April 1970, General Shoemaker is still finalizing the plan. The map in his plans section reflects the light from an overhead neon lamp. It is already late. The telephone on his table rings, a special secure line. "Bob, Edward here. I've just been ordered to have my Brigade ready to move out on Thursday, but I don't know what time."

"H-Hour is 0730 hours. Don't ask me any more. That's the time set for you to move. They're going to fill us in on what's up little by little."

On 30 April MACV calls with an urgent message. D-Day has been set back twenty-four hours. President Nixon has decided to address the nation. The chosen date and time for the address is Thursday, 30 April, at 2100 hours. In Saigon, with the time differential, that corresponds to 1000 hours, Friday morning, the 1st of May.

At Robert's CP at Camp Govard, the First Cav Base, everything is organized to give the impression of everyday normal activity.

The journalists harry the public information officers, puzzled over why the ARVN needs so many helicopters and why they, themselves, are no longer being permitted to go along on operations in the Hueys as has normally been the case. They demand to speak with more senior officers. CBS directly requests of General Roberts that he receive their correspondent, Jack Laurence.

Roberts organizes a breakfast at the Officers Mess at Phuoc Vinh for Wednesday, 29 April. At this gathering, Roberts and Meyer brief the press on the general situation, focusing on the interdiction activities mounted by the Cav that use so many helicopters. It is a very pedagogical presentation, supported by several maps and visual aids.

"Questions?"

"Yes General! Jack Laurence, CBS. Can you tell us if you are getting ready to cross the Cambodian border?"

Roberts answers expressionlessly. "You know very well that we can't do that!"

Another journalist poses a question that directly concerns his colleagues. "Why can't we move about freely in the units any more? Are you hiding something?"

"Do not think that the First Cav isn't still open to your queries. I have the pleasure to invite Mr. Laurence to accompany Charlie Company, 2^d of the 7th, on operations as often as he wishes. You, gentlemen, you may without any problem go with Air Force aircraft to Bien Hoa, Tan Son Nhut, or to the First Cav support bases. If you want to go somewhere by chopper, no problem. Get in touch with my PIO."

For Roberts, Meyer, Shoemaker, Brady and the few others in on the plan, the facts are about to come out. The South Vietnamese are the first to announce that they are going to invade Cambodia. Then President Nixon appears on television. He stands erect in front of a large map of Indochina, calm, his notes in hand. He points with his finger to North Vietnam on the map.

"The North Vietnamese have just launched a large-scale offensive against Cambodia. We, the Americans, we announce the imminent withdrawal of 150,000 men from Vietnam at the very moment that Cambodia is going to fall into the hands of North Vietnam. Hanoi is going to use Cambodia to set up bases along the border with South Vietnam and directly threaten our soldiers, those who will still be over there."

Then, abruptly, his tone of voice rises. He announces to his countrymen: "I reject all political considerations. I will be a one-term President and do that which I believe to be my duty rather than be reelected at the cost of seeing America become a second rate power and accept that the nation suffer its first defeat in ninety years of history ... . The time for action has come!"

Leaving the White House Oval Office Nixon goes to the Pentagon for a conference with his military chiefs to whom he says: "I want to get rid of all these enemy sanctuaries in Cambodia. Come up with a good plan and let's get on with it! Destroy them so that they can't be used against us—ever!"

In fact, the plans are already made and in the process of execution. At Quan Loi Bob Shoemaker awaits the dawn to unleash the first phase of the operation. Six B-52s unload their tons of bombs on the *Fishhook* at the place supposed to be the base area designated "353." The last bombs explode at 0545 hours. A quarter of an hour later the ninety-four tubes of artillery commence a bombardment that goes on for an hour, in accordance with the plan. They fire exactly 2,436 shells. Bronco OV-10 sends out three reconnaissance flights to see how much enemy flak they can expect. The enemy anti-air guns remain relatively quiet.

At 0630 hours the Regiments of the 1st South Vietnamese Army move toward the northwest of An Loc to cross the frontier and take up positions on *LZ East.* Before their arrival, aircraft drop five and seven ton bombs set to detonate two and one half meters above the ground. Their blast clears the ground and creates an instant LZ, from which its designation: *Instant LZ.* Fifteen minutes later, the same procedure creates *LZ Center.*

At 0740 hours the 1st of the 9th Reconnaissance Squadron makes first contact with the enemy. Five North Vietnamese and a two and one half ton truck become the first victims of a Pink Team on Route Number 7, near Mimot.

At 0800 hours, the 1st of the 9th recons to the east of *LZ East.* A quarter of an hour later, six 105s and three 155s crewed by South Vietnamese are landed and immediately go into battery. The 11th Armored Cavalry Regiment crosses the border.

At 0945 hours Charlie Company, 2d Battalion, 47th Mechanized Infantry crosses the frontier in its turn.

At 1005 hours forty-two Hueys of the 227th Assault Helicopter Battalion air assault into *LZ Center.* They sew panic among the North Vietnamese who are completely surprised. The NVA disappear into the forest, dispersed by rocket salvos and streams of minigun fire from the Cobras.

Further to the west, Lieutenant Colonel Patton and the 2d of the 7th assault into *LZ X-Ray,* courtesy of the 229th AHB. The *LZ* is named in honor of the Ia Drang fight. The lead slicks are loaded with Charlie Company of the 2d of the 7th, with Bravo Company following just to the rear. These troops must clear and secure the

LZ for the arrival of the 2^d of the 5th, coming in by Chinook. As soon as they land, the 2^d of the 5th is tasked with linking up with the 9th South Vietnamese Airborne Brigade. During this time the two companies of the 2^d of the 7th are to link up with the 3^d Brigade at support base *Bruiser* near Sre Khtum.

The enemy reaction is confused. Surprise is complete. The operation is a tactical success.[2] Shoemaker and his team are satisfied. There had been no response from NVA anti-air guns, just isolated resistance with individual arms. The score for the first day, however, is modest. The activities of the 1st of the 9th account for 157 NVA killed by helicopter. Other aircraft identify 109 NVA KIA. ARVN forces report twenty-seven enemy killed and eight taken prisoner from the 7th NVA Division. The 11th Armored Cavalry Regiment that, after crossing into Cambodia, overran a base area occupied by the equivalent of a regiment killed fifty NVA. Losses on the American side are two killed, both from the 11th ACR.

The 3^d Company of the 3^d South Vietnamese Airborne Regiment, at about 1730 hours, makes an interesting discovery: a cache containing three tons of medicine and a surgical suite in kit form that came from Western Europe and that had been delivered by Air France.[3]

If, militarily, everything went along very well, the management of the public information aspect left something to be desired. Media coverage was mediocre. *Time* magazine published an article conjured from a few words spoken by a soldier: "We didn't find anybody wearing a COSVN tee-shirt." The operation is presented as a joke. On 2 May General Roberts evidently endures the jibes of journalists he had invited to dine with him the previous evening.

Jack Laurence, however well disposed he might have been after having rejoined Charlie Company of the 2^d of the 7th, could not restrain himself from writing: "This sophisticated military trap having failed, the mission has changed to one of looking for enemy supplies."

In Washington, Nixon is briefed by the military chiefs on the progress of the operation. In the course of the military presentation he points out that the North Vietnamese sanctuaries he had designated on the map during his televised presentation to the American people are not the same ones as those that were attacked. "If we can significantly reduce the threat to our forces by cleaning out the rest of the enemy safe areas, we've got to do it now," he contends.

The operation takes on a new dimension. General Shoemaker agrees with President Nixon's decision to extend the scope of the operation. He is shocked, however, when he learns that the cleanup will extend the operation to 30 June: sixty days. He immediately returns to Quan Loi. Among the correspondence waiting for him he finds a note that, for the first time, specifies that the operation has no specific limit, neither in its objectives, nor in length. The same morning, General Davison had informed him that the 11th ACR was to go to Snoul. "I had never heard that name before," contended a surprised Shoemaker.

Bob Shoemaker realizes right away that his plan, envisioned as a week-long raid, has, within twenty-four hours been transformed into a vast two-month long operation. He calls Sky Meyer right away, then Elvy Roberts. The Cav Commander reassures him.

"The operation that you organized, Bob, corresponds to Phase I of the plan, and it's going well. For Phase II, I want you to send an infantry battalion with artillery support up Route Number 7 and occupy Snoul, located in the middle of an area where there are lots of rubber plantations. By doing that, you'll keep the NVA from evacuating their matériel by road and from getting back onto the Ho Chi Minh Trail to hide up north. Since the President laid the cards on the table when he announced that we'd stay in Cambodia just until 30 June, the NVA are going to try and get out of our way and wait us out."

Shoemaker asks Roberts to assign the 2d Brigade to him. The 2d Brigade had just been placed under the operational control of Lieutenant Colonel James Anderson, commanding officer of the 1st of the 5th. Colonel Clark, the 2d Brigade Commander, had gone back to Loc Ninh. Anderson, a few months earlier, was on General Abrams' staff. General Abrams had given him a battalion command in the Cav in January. He took over an operation in progress, very exposed to eventual criticism from his peers and superiors. Just a short while earlier he had had to resolve some racial incidents in his unit. Thanks to his careful leadership, his Battalion was soon calm and combat ready.

On 2 May Shoemaker and Anderson plan the assault on the *Flat Iron*, a narrow region situated twenty kilometers across the border in Cambodia. Regiments of the 7th NVA Division were presumed to have withdrawn into that location after their incursion into Binh Long Province. Shoemaker extracts every possible bit of intelligence from the reports coming from this area. One of them catches his attention, a report from Chief Warrant Officer James Cyrus, LOH pilot, Bravo Troop, 1st of the 9th Cavalry.

"In a densely vegetated area to the northwest of our axis of advance, I spotted a well camouflaged hooch while flying at treetop level. It was almost invisible, even though I was flying so low. I could see bamboo paths going from hut to hut. The huts seemed to be marked with some kind of panels. There were some pole bridges crossing a stream, and they had rope hand rails. It looked like a forestry workshop area. I also saw some antennas."

"That looks like something that may be significant!" exults Shoemaker.

"Anderson, you wanted a tough mission. You've got one. First, you're going to keep the lines of support open to the 11th ACR as it continues northeast on Route Number 7 to block any eventual NVA movement to the north and east of the *Fishhook*. Second, you're going to follow up on the loach pilot's observation. You'll be covered in the south by the 1st of the 12th. Norman Moffett has just taken command. Kick off tomorrow at 1000 hours."

Translator's Notes

[1] Central Office for South Vietnam. The second highest level of Vietcong political organization directly below the Politburo/Secretariat.

[2] This is an operation that, in today's terminology, was conducted at the *operational level* and was thus more correctly an "operational success."

[3] Properly speaking, medical supplies are not legitimate matériel for destruction. If the supplies are abandoned by the enemy, they are fair game. If, however, the area us to be bypassed, and if the enemy is expected to return to and reoccupy the area, the medical supplies and equipment, if not needed by the occupying force, should be left in place. War is sufficiently deadly and cruel without destroying medical supplies. It should go without saying that patients should never be intentionally harmed unless they resist with deadly force.

CHAPTER XXIV

Before daybreak, Anderson rejoins his Battalion at Loc Ninh, the 2ᵈ Brigade base. His men have been up and about since 0500, checking their gear and weapons and packing away three days' rations. At 1000 hours the 1ˢᵗ of the 5ᵗʰ lifts off. The Battalion flies over Route Number 7 and lands at *LZ Terry Lynn*, destined shortly to become base area *North*.

Anderson sends Charlie Company into the jungle to recon and clear in depth the area in front of the perimeter and so avoid any unpleasant surprises. The jungle undergrowth is almost impassable. Captain Corcoran forces his Company almost a kilometer deep into the entangling hell of green. Bursts of AK47 fire lash out from two dug-in bunkers. Corcoran issues orders to his Platoon Leaders. Soon, several fire teams maneuver into position and neutralize the NVA gunners.

It is about 1500 hours when Charlie Company discovers a large base area complete with straw huts and wooden barracks. They have stumbled upon a permanent base camp some three kilometers long by two kilometers wide. The camp seems empty. The grunts are astonished. They move in as into a village of the dead, convinced that the fires of hell will burst upon them one second or the next. Sergeant Dean Sharp hesitates to sling his M16 to take pictures. The size of the place almost compels them to designate it "*The City.*"

At first, Corcoran's men find only a few old SKS carbines. Troopers help themselves to them as souvenirs. When Corcoran finds stacked crates of the latest model carbines in factory packaging, he begins to appreciate the importance of his discovery.

On 5 May the 1ˢᵗ Cavalry Division assumes command of *Operation Total Victory*. The *Operation* includes thirteen allied Battalions. Snoul is taken after a few skirmishes by the 11ᵗʰ Cav. The 2ᵈ Brigade with two Battalions establishes a base on 6 May at Bu Dop. During this time, Anderson and the 1ˢᵗ of the 5ᵗʰ feverishly search through *The City*.

The discovery made, the initial search complete, the 1ˢᵗ of the 5ᵗʰ and the 1ˢᵗ of the 12ᵗʰ leave the chore of a more in depth exploration of *The City* to the 1ˢᵗ Brigade. It takes them a whole week to complete the search and inventory of all the bunkers and their contents. The camp has a surface area of many square kilometers and has 182 separate storage bunkers, each of which measures about five meters long, three wide, and two high. It has eighteen

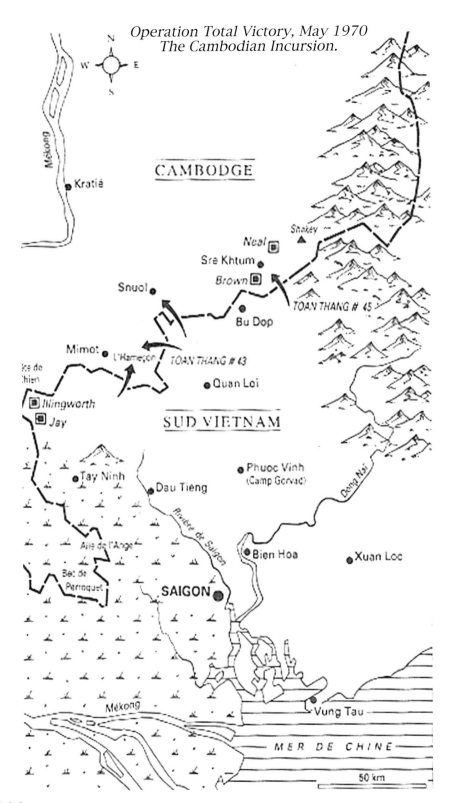

Operation Total Victory, May 1970
The Cambodian Incursion.

CAMBODGE

Kratié

Mékong

Neal

Shakey

Sre Khtum

Brown

Snuol

TOAN THANG # 45

Bu Dop

Mimot

L'Hameçon

TOAN THANG # 43

te de
hien

Quan Loi

Illingworth

Jay

SUD VIETNAM

Tay Ninh

Dau Tieng

Phuoc Vinh
(Camp Gorvad)

Aile de l'Ange

Dong Nai

Bec de
Perroquet

Rivière de Saigon

Bien Hoa

Xuan Loc

SAIGON

Mékong

Vung Tau

MER DE CHINE

50 km

282

buildings for mess facilities, fourteen with bunks, an athletic field, and a farm for raising chickens and hogs.

It appears that the North Vietnamese quit the area in haste, abandoning clothing, military gear, food, medicine, ammunition, and weapons. In addition to serving as a logistical base, *The City* was also an educational, training, and rest area for NVA troops coming from the north. Despite its size, this base area had never been spotted, either by the Air Force or by allied intelligence agencies. The *Flat Iron* area showed no indication of occupation. Even the veteran troopers were impressed by the complexity of the base and the organizational effort that it represented.

Set up in a very nice area, it is not a haphazard arrangement hidden in the forest and constructed of logs and thatch. The Americans find well-constructed wooden buildings that give evidence of good carpentry. They are fitted out with high quality furnishings. On the best barracks building there is a sign that, in Vietnamese, reads: "VIPs and Officers." On another the sign reads: "Troop Dayroom." The communist army has yet to institutionalize "equality" if you go by the placards on the camp buildings.

"Hey, guys! Come and look at this. Here's a swimming pool. My travel agency never told me about this place in its brochure!"

It was quite plausible that *The City* could have sheltered the famous COSVN. Colonel Ken Mertel, Aviation Group Commander, is sent to *The City* to assure the evacuation of the captured matériel. There is so much of it that it cannot all be hauled out by chopper. Engineering earth moving equipment is brought in by helicopter to open up a road that will link *The City* with Route Number 13 leading to Loc Ninh. Truck convoys haul away the goods that the helicopters cannot transport.

The list of military matériel and foodstuffs is impressive: 1,282 individual weapons, 202 crew served weapons, 319,000 12.7mm rounds, 25,200 14.5mm rounds, 1,559,000 7.62mm cartridges, 2,110 grenades, twenty-nine tons of explosives, 16,920 120mm mortar rounds, thirty tons of rice, eight tons of wheat, and five hundred kilograms of salt.

On 5 May, Task Force Shoemaker is dissolved. Command passes to a new operational headquarters organized to handle a larger scale operation. While the 1st Brigade moves all the captured matériel out of *The City*, the other Cav Companies actively search the Cambodian side of the border. From an *LZ* named *Myron*, Lieutenant Colonel Ianni, commander of the 2d of the 12th, sends Captain Johnson with Delta Company four kilometers east of the *LZ* to check out a report from a Pink Team.

Johnson moves with difficulty through the heavy, thorny forest undergrowth. The point man comes in contact with an element of NVA. Johnson sends up a Platoon to engage the enemy. The NVA infantrymen, after some light resistance, break contact. Delta Company conducts a search of the area around the bunkers that the NVA had occupied. They find palm-trunk shelters, caches containing crates full of small arms ammunition.

Johnson maintains radio contact with Lieutenant Colonel Ianni because his precarious perimeter is assailed on all sides. The NVA went to get reinforcements and now try to annihilate the Company. Daylight wanes. It gets darker and darker under the forest canopy. Delta Company's Platoons counterattack to avoid encirclement. Ianni decides to send his Reconnaissance Platoon in to reinforce Delta Company. Lieutenant Jimmy Hudnall, the Platoon Leader, in constant radio contact with Johnson, finally reaches the Company perimeter, but several of his men are wounded.

Ianni sends in another Company as reinforcements. The movement takes place in the black of night. In the darkness the troopers cannot see a thing. Every noise indicates a probable enemy presence. The two Companies spend a frightening night next to each other expecting an NVA assault. In fact, the North Vietnamese have broken contact, leaving a few snipers behind until dawn as a rear guard to cover their withdrawal.

With the arrival of dawn and the enemy gone, the 2^d of the 12th inventories the contents of the various caches without interference. The men are as excited as children as little by little they realize the amount of matériel they are uncovering. However, they are very careful because the NVA usually booby trap their caches.

"Shit! It's *Rock Island East*!" notes Lieutenant Timothy Holden, Charlie Company, 2^d of the 12th who, after thirty-six hours of combat with his Platoon uncovers a mountain of crates. Called that because the sheer magnitude of "stuff" recalled Rock Island Arsenal in Illinois, the name stuck.

General Roberts choppers in and proposes Holden for a Silver Star.[1] This time the journalists rain down on the area to see the extent of the booty for themselves. The place is not as sophisticated as *The City*. The matériel is just piled into crates sheltered under coconut palms. A large pit one thousand meters long and five hundred meters wide is located inside the immediate perimeter formed by the straw huts. The untidiness of the area testifies to the NVA haste to move their stocks out once the extent of the American threat on Phuoc Lang Province became clear. Just as in the case of *The City*, it was necessary to open up a road to move out the 325 tons of weapons and ammunition. Among the crates of weapons this time they find the component parts of 85mm mortars "made in USSR." These were new models never yet employed in Vietnam.

MACV decides to extend General Roberts' command tour for nine days so he can finalize plans for the redeployment of the allied forces to the NVA sanctuaries further north. On 12 May Roberts passes command to George Casey, fifty-two years old, originally from Maine, West Point Class of 1945. He was a paratrooper with the 11th Airborne Division where he served until 1948. He fought in Korea where he was awarded the Silver Star. He had a command in the 7th Infantry Division. But Casey is above all a Cavalry Trooper. He had been the "Old Man" of the Black Horse Brigade in 1967 for six months, and then he was assigned to Division Staff until 1968. He had been General Norton's and then General Tolson's Deputy.

The only thing missing in his background as an aspiring Cavalry Commander was his flight wings. As with General Forsyth, the Army sent him to Fort Rucker for an accelerated flight training program. He returned with his pilot's wings. In his Command Helicopter he distinguishes himself from his predecessors because, although he takes the right hand seat beside the pilot, he uses it as his working command area, and is seldom tempted to play the role of copilot. He prefers to study his maps and follow the progress of the artillery rather than handle the control stick.

The harvest of military supplies and foodstuffs continues, each unit contributing to the effort. The area of the *Dog's Head* where NVA Base 707 had been uncovered is surrounded in its turn. The maneuver is consigned to the 25th Infantry Division. All the supplies for a major headquarters are uncovered here including a printing capability, typewriters, telex facilities, and generators. Nearby the men uncover a cache of four hundred tons of rice.

On 25 May Alpha Company of the 2d of the 8th has a lucky day. It penetrates into a vast automotive work shop area including a garage. The men count 305 vehicles in working order and a few light vehicles, among the latter a Porsche, a Mercedes, and a few jeeps. This is but a tiny part of the fleet of trucks that the North Vietnamese have in Cambodia to fulfill all the logistical needs of their army. From the first days of *Total Victory* the Air Force and the Intelligence Services have noted a strong increase in road traffic leaving the area under US attack.

President Nixon had fixed the duration of the Cambodian intervention at sixty days. The 29th of June was the limit. With the violent pacifist campaign that was developing in the States it was not a question of his extending the *Operation* for even one day longer. Politicians were visiting the troop units in the field, accompanied by the press. They were attempting to find out if the military really had enough time to tactically exploit the results of what they were finding.

"Haven't the constraints of time and distance imposed by the President himself ruined the efficiency of your operations?"

"No, not at all," responded General Davison. "All the important caches have been located in our area of operations. On the other hand the rainy season will also soon be on us. In any event, our actions would have been interrupted by the monsoon. All the important caches were found in May—few in June. To stay longer would not pay dividends. What's more, the North Vietnamese know our schedule and have relocated accordingly."

General Shoemaker had succeeded very well in getting the Cavalry into Cambodia. The next task was to get back out smoothly. This was not an easy thing because the maneuver had to be conducted with equal emphasis on speed and efficiency. It would be necessary to mobilize all the airlift available to withdraw the infantry, the artillery, and the considerable other matériel deployed during the course of these two months. Again, the weather did not favor the Cav. With a very low ceiling the Chinooks of the 228th Assault Helicopter Battalion begin to move on 24 June. They evacuate *Support Base Bronco*. The Chinooks fly at tree top level, the 105s and 155s suspended beneath them on slings.

The North Vietnamese did not all move out. Some of them remained in the area, hiding out, waiting for the Cav to leave. They open fire on the helicopters. They hit six of them, one of which they down. The Snakes have to get into the act to silence the NVA machine guns.

The CH54 Flying Cranes and the 273d Aviation Company, OPCON to the Cav for the whole of *Operation Total Victory*, take on the task of backhauling the 272 bulldozers, fifty-four forklifts, and forty-one graders, in addition to sections of engineer bridging. The 273d carried out 2,486 sorties in the two-month period. The support bases are evacuated, one after the other, as well as each artillery and infantry unit.

On 29 June, at 1728 hours, a Pink Team from Bravo Troop brings up the rear. The two helicopters are the last American aircraft to leave the sky over Cambodia. At dawn on the first of July, the thirty thousand American soldiers are all back in Vietnam. Only the South Vietnamese, who are not particularly worried by Nixon's promise, stay put in Cambodia. General Do Cao Tri, called the Patton of the *Parrot's Beak*, continues his mission with his armored and mechanized forces.

President Nixon and his Administration are the subject of constant attacks by the Democrats and the focus of student agitation on college campuses. It is very difficult for him to exploit the concrete results of *Operation Total Victory*. The only positive point on which the observers are in agreement is that the South Vietnamese troops conducted themselves very well in the fighting. All the experts admit that vietnamization is a success. The American Administration prematurely concludes from this that the ARVN is just about ready to take on the major burden of the war effort. The fact that the southern forces owe their efficiency on the ground to the massive American air support and to the US helicopters is modestly overlooked.

The press does not pay much attention to the results of the incursion into Cambodia. It is, however, far from being negligible. The matériel recovered would have been sufficient to equip thirty-five battalions of 250 men each and the rice that was seized would have fed them for a year!

The losses inflicted on the North Vietnamese during these two months come up to a total of 11,369 killed and 2,328 prisoners. These are principally the result of bomb strikes and of the constant harassment of the armed helicopters. Then too, an exact accounting is difficult to establish. On its side, the First Cavalry counts 123 killed, 966 wounded, and 16 missing, among whom 10 were captured.

Since the beginning of its blocking campaign begun in February 1969 up to its return from Cambodia, the Division is credited with 16,143 enemies killed. It has recovered 3,240 individual weapons, 726 crew-served weapons, more than 1,700,000 rounds of ammunition, and 1,500 tons of rice.

In the afternoon of 6 July George Casey, who has commanded the Division for three months, puts the final touches on a letter that he has decided to personally address to every soldier, non-commissioned officer, and officer of his Division. He rereads it attentively before signing it.

> As you know, the 1st Air Cavalry Division was involved in operations against enemy sanctuaries in Cambodia during the last two months. The results of these operations surpassed by far our expectations. It was the most successful operation in the history of the 1st Cavalry Division.
>
> All the members of the First Team had a part in it. Each one of you, by your hard work and professional skill, contributed to the team effort. The mechanics who enabled the helicopters to fly. The pi-

lots who so audaciously put in more hours of flight time than ever before. The engineers who accomplished such great projects, the support units that worked without a break to keep the supplies coming, even as the front got bigger. The artillerymen who daily rained tons of steel down upon the enemy everywhere and above all, the infantrymen who grappled with an obstinate adversary and uncovered his hidden supplies. Altogether you have made this success possible and deserve the recognition of the First Team.

The results are impressive. You have put the equivalent of three enemy regiments out of action, captured or destroyed enough individual and crew-served weapons to equip two of his divisions and you have taken from him the equivalent of one year's supply of rice. You have captured more rockets, mortar rounds, and recoilless rifles than the enemy brought down into the III Corps Zone during the twelve months preceding our intervention in Cambodia.

Without doubt and most importantly, intervening as an airmobile force, you have destroyed the enemy's entire logistics network, sewing chaos in his rear areas, killing or dispersing his personnel. Only time will tell how long it will take the North Vietnamese to rebuild it, but you may be certain that you did enough damage to stop the enemy in his tracks. In so doing you have opened the way to go forward successfully with President Nixon's plans for redeployment so that our Vietnamese allies can defend their own freedom. That is your contribution.

This is another demonstration that you, members of the First Team, have richly earned the praise of your nation. It is an honor for me to have served by your side during this critical and historic period.

The next day at 0700 hours Casey plans to chopper over to Cam Ranh Bay to talk to the wounded and give them some encouragement as they are being prepared for evacuation to Japan and the United States. Colonel Edward Meyer, a veteran of the Ia Drang Campaign, comes to see him in the early morning hours.

"General, the weather is very bad. You should postpone your departure."

"Ed, I've got to go congratulate and thank these men who are now leaving Vietnam and the Division. After what they have lived through it's my duty. Their air evacuation won't hold off for me, and then, my pilot is quite used to this kind of weather."

"Yes, but you'll have to pass over the mountains of the Central Highlands. It's a very risky thing."

"It'll be a good checkout for the DECCA system. Wilhem will get some more practice instrument flying."

At 1010 hours George Casey's Huey is seen for the last time. The remains of the helicopter are discovered in the mountains three days later. There are no survivors. The cause of the accident was never officially determined. The pilot, Wilhelm Michel, as he neared the mountains, must have flown into heavy cloud cover. Suddenly, with zero visibility, he may have suffered vertigo. Casey, as copilot, but preoccupied with other work, and not observing the instruments, was not able to react fast enough to stabilize the helicopter. Six men died in the crash.

The death of General Casey upset the whole Division as well as the military higher-ups. He was considered to be one of the most brilliant superior officers of his generation. ABC News describes his disappearance. Frank Reynolds declares: "General Casey was a man for whom the responsibilities of high command mostly exceeded its privileges. He accepted all of the former and abused none of the latter. General Casey knew war and hated it. He was a splendid example of a military man who wasn't really a militarist."

With the military honors due his rank, he was interred at Arlington National Cemetery. His casket resting on an artillery caisson was accompanied by six general officers, five of whom had commanded the First Team: Harry Kinnard, John Norton, John Tolson, George Forsythe, and Elvy Roberts.

The 1st Cavalry Division is proposed for the Presidential Unit Citation. It is the second, after that earned in 1965 for the Pleiku and Ia Drang Campaigns.[2]

Translator's Notes

[1] Such a recommendation for a Silver Star or for any award for valor would have to be for some specific act of heroism, not for simply discovering an enemy cache, no matter how significant.

[2] It may have been the second at that time. In 1973 the 2d Battalion, 7th Cavalry and attached units were awarded the Presidential Unit Citation for extraordinary heroism for services performed from 25 August 1966 to 13 February 1967. As every fighting soldier who served in the First Air Cavalry Division in Vietnam knows, countless instances of self sacrifice and heroism went un-

recorded. The witnesses who might have recommended formal recognition were either killed on the spot, wounded and evacuated, or just too caught up in the rush of events and responsibilities that the times demanded to record what at that time seemed to be normal behavior.

CHAPTER XXV

In the back of the Cayuse, his feet hanging out half in the open, Roger Palomino watches the contrasting colors of the ground. At three thousand feet the view is panoramic, well adapted for an observation mission. Leaning down on his M60 he is rocked by the movement of the machine gun suspended on its sling. He is isolated from the world by his large flight helmet that muffles the whistling of the wind and the noise of the turbine engine.

A blowing rain begins to lash the ground below. The curtain of water, illuminated by the setting sun, makes waves of vapor rise from the hot and humid forest. The "click" from the intercom brings him out of his daydreams.

"Roger! Look over toward three o'clock. There's a buck down there. Hang on; I'm goin' to dive down on it so you can zap it. The venison'll be a welcome addition to the usual."

"Okay sir."

The helicopter leaves its flight path and plunges earthward. It eats up the three thousand feet and finds itself at ground level. The animal is chased by a series of rounds that impact the ground as they catch up with it. Hit in mid-bound, it collapses in a heap.

The pilot puts the chopper down next to the fallen animal. The machine gunner dismounts, unsheathes his knife, and addresses the deer. He wipes the blade on the hide and, as an experienced hunter, cuts the young buck's musk glands away to protect the venison. With the animal across his shoulders he carries it to the helicopter and places it among the ammunition cases. He does not have time to buckle into his harness before the Loach leaps into the air, the ground falling away at full speed under his feet. He replugs his helmet into the intercom.

"Where're we goin' in such a rush sir?"

"A Blue Team is into a fight close by. We gotta get over there."

The radio crackles, but this time the voice is coming from the ground. "We've got a *line one*. We can't move around carrying his body. If you can evacuate him, it'll be easier for us to break contact. Be careful! The Charlies are very close to us!"

The pilot lands next to two grunts that are carrying their dead comrade. The machine gunner reaches out and grips the dead soldier's web gear with one hand and pulls him into the chopper to his side. At the same time, with his other hand he continues to fire at the jungle's edge where the VC are positioned.

The fire comes from all directions and tracers converge toward the cockpit. No sooner is the body aboard than the Cayuse quickly lifts from the *LZ*. The crew is surprised to get away unhurt. Up and out of the zone of fire, the machine gunner pulls the body closer to his side. He has some trouble doing this because the body is that of a big man, almost six feet tall. It is headless.

Roger Palomino looks at the decapitated body, astonished, but with no sign of disgust. The KIA is an unknown, faceless. While outside the aircraft the storm rages violently and the rain drums against the chopper's skin, Roger's mind is somewhere else. He tries to remember if he has seen the man the day before, or some other time. He recreates for him a life, a family. He decides to write the man's wife and tell her that he was the last person to take care of him.

The helicopter comes in on final and lands at the helipad of the field hospital. Standing just outside the tangle of wire and concertina, the crew waits for two medics coming to pick up the casualty. The two men, bare-chested and without helmets, take hold of the cadaver's legs and arms and pull it from the helicopter. Surprised by the weight, they drop it. It lies in the mud. Without even bending down, they role it over with their feet like a bucket.

"Hey, assholes! Do it right! Treat him with respect!," Roger snarls at them.

"Don't get all bent out of shape. He's dead. He doesn't feel anything anymore!"

Roger takes his machine gun, arms it, and aims it at the two men. "You'll carry the body correctly or you'll be the ones rolling in the mud! I don't want to know if he feels anything or not! Carry him into the perimeter. You've got two seconds to do it."

The two men stand dumbstruck. The pilot, watching them, motions to them to obey. Roger keeps the machine gun on them until they reach the doorway to the container that serves as a hospital. Palomino returns to base, still white with rage, and tries to find out the name of the dead soldier, but no one seems to have known him. He had just arrived in the unit.

A few days later Palomino learns that the Blue Team the man belonged to was still out in the field, and in a state of rebellion. They had gone out on patrol under the command of a young, newly arrived-in-country Lieutenant. When he gave the order to return to base they refused to obey. He wanted to head home by the same route they had taken going out. As everyone well knows, the first thing you learn in Vietnam is to never take the same route twice. The Lieutenant gets upset, and stubbornly refuses to change his orders. He is sure the same route home is safe. His platoon stands fast in place and refuses to budge. The night ends the debate. It is no longer a question of moving at all.

The next morning just renews the impasse. The Lieutenant re-states his order. The men refuse to move. They will not return by the same route. Headquarters is informed of the problem. The men make a demand of their own: transfer the Lieutenant to an-other unit. They will not budge until their demands are satisfied!

A Major General comes to negotiate. He sends helicopters out to bring the Blue Team back to its base. The men refuse to board the choppers. The grunts stay in place for thirty days. Their defi-ance is the main topic of discussion in the Division. After the pas-sage of a month, they win their case. The Lieutenant is transferred and they are amnestied, thus escaping a Court Martial. This type of incident would have been inconceivable before.

But, for several months now, a new epidemic has been at work in American units: *fragging*. The word comes from the fragmenta-tion grenade, the standard hand grenade used by American forces. During the course of the year 1970, the number of officers and non-commissioned officers killed or wounded by a shot fired from behind, or from the explosion of a grenade, both from a "friendly" hand is on a steep upward incline.

The First Cavalry Division is not entirely spared. During the six final months of 1970, five instances of fragging were recorded to which may be added twenty-two incidents of shootings. These figures should be compared with thirty-eight cases of fragging and ninety-seven shooting incidents for other American Divisions.

"Listen up, trooper," Roger Palomino tells an FNG, "this kind of shit doesn't happen to a LRRP Lieutenant.[1] In those units, the platoons of Echo Company of the 52d Infantry, given the most dangerous reconnaissance missions way deep into NVA areas, there's no chickenshit bullshit like that. The Lieutenant who com-mands the patrol has eight teams of six men each, all volunteers. Each team is led by a senior noncom with another NCO as assis-tant team leader. They put a point man up front and a man out as rear guard. They've got an RTO and a medic. They're all airborne. It's not a question of voting on what to do. Everybody knows his job by heart: navigation, commo, demo, killing quietly."

"When they go out on a two-day patrol, they don't load up with rations and other unnecessary crap. They stuff whatever they need in pouches on their web gear and take a poncho and poncho liner. Their main concern is to go quiet and light."

"But, they don't take any rations at all?" the green troop wants to know.

"Each man packs two LRRP rations, dehydrated stuff, and a

canteen of water. They cover up completely with skin camo and wear camouflaged patrol caps, no helmets or other useless heavy noisy shit."

"But what do they do that the Blue Teams don't do?"

"Infiltration, sabotage, radio interception, like navy Seals, the Navy commando guys. But nobody talks about them much, and you hardly ever see 'em! Their job, they do it in secret. They don't talk about what they do. With VC ears listening everywhere they know it's in their own interest to be quiet. With them, I promise, there's never any fragging or other fucking disciplinary problems."

To replace General Casey, accidentally killed on 7 July 1970, the high command designates Major General George Putnam. They had to find a person with the right credentials to fill the position. General Putnam was at the time the commander of the 1st Aviation Brigade. He had just supported the entire South Vietnamese Army during the operation in Cambodia.

Putnam is just fifty. He was born in Maine at Fort Fairfield in 1920. Commissioned in the artillery at twenty-two, he served as an instructor, then as Operations Officer in a Battalion. He arrived in Europe at the beginning of 1945, and elected to remain on active duty following the War. In 1946 he went to Japan as a member of the occupation forces. In 1956 he earned his flight wings and then was assigned to the Howze Board. He participated directly in elaborating the concept of airmobility, working without a break in the shadow of the principal actors on the Board.

He was subsequently promoted as the Deputy Commander of the Army Flight Training Center at Fort Rucker. His next assignment takes him to Vietnam as he leaves with the 1st Cavalry Division for his first tour in country. He is initially Chief of Staff to General Norton and then is DIVARTY Commander from March to September of 1967. In 1968 he is promoted to Brigadier General and assigned to the Pentagon as Director of Personnel. He returns for a second Vietnam tour in January of 1970, this time as the 1st Aviation Brigade Commander and Officer in Charge of US Army Aviation in Vietnam. George Putnam thus has a double competence: that of knowing perfectly the First Cav, and that of having collaborated intimately with the South Vietnamese. He is ordered to participate in the effort to Vietnamize the War in order to allow for the rapid withdrawal of American forces. The government in Washington wants to maintain a rhythm of 12,500 men per month.

The Nixon Administration decides to support the operations conducted by the South Vietnamese with growing American air support. At the same time, the Americans withdraw their troops and negotiate a cease fire with North Vietnam. They plan to leave a residual force of fifty thousand men to support the ARVN which is to take on the largest part of the confrontation with the communist adversary.

The mission of the Division thus evolves into one of support and training. The First Cav contributes to the growing offensive capability of the ARVN and improves the training of the South Vietnamese militias: the Regional and Popular Forces. These actions earn the Division new awards: the Vietnamese Civic Action Medal and the Vietnamese Gallantry Cross with Palm. These awards henceforth may be worn by all soldiers assigned to the Division, and at all times, wherever they serve, by soldiers that were assigned to the Division when it received the decoration.

The High Command assigns the Division an Area of Operations that extends from just to the east of Saigon over to the Cambodian border, and from Zone D to the South China Sea. The extent of this new AO obliges Putnam to rethink the way the Division will operate. In August 1970 he completes a study on the effectiveness of the different types and configurations of helicopters and their organization as employed by the First Cavalry Division. In light of his findings, he combines the Delta Troops of the 227th and 229th Assault Helicopter Battalions and assigns them to the 1st Squadron, 9th Cavalry. Thus reinforced the 1st of the 9th with five Troops becomes a search and destroy squadron.

By doing this Putnam confirms one of the predictions of the Howze Board that, in its report of 21 January 1962, foresaw the creation of an Air Cavalry Combat Brigade (ACCB), designed to seek out and destroy the enemy, and to carry out all the classic cavalry missions. For budgetary reasons and because of the escalation of the War in Vietnam, the First Cavalry division had never been authorized to organize such a Brigade. This new Brigade, the heart of which is the 1st of the 9th, has its capabilities increased by the attachment of several other organizations: H Ranger Company of the 75th Infantry, the 62^{d} Scout Dog Platoon with Black Labradors specialized in seeking out tunnels and caches of supplies, and the 2^{d} of the 20th Blue Max ARA Battalion with its heavily armed Cobras for direct fire support. The 9th Cavalry Brigade is officially recognized on 5 December 1970.

Along with the increase in fire power, the Brigade improves its capabilities with the deployment of seismic intrusion detection devices. These improve its information collection capabilities and the resulting intelligence. Deployed by Hueys flying above the forest and jungle canopy along the axes of movement of the North Vietnamese, the very sensitive detection devices give early warning of the movement of even very small numbers of enemy soldiers. Exposed in such a manner they are destroyed by artillery or by platoons on alert status that move after them in Eagle Flights.

But, in its new configuration the Brigade has hardly any chance to operate as a unit. It gives priority to its support for the ARVN. It is in this role that it is going to return to Cambodia. On 22 February 1971, it lifts four companies of South Vietnamese airborne troopers to Snoul. They will be reinforced two days later by M113 Armored Personnel Carriers of the ARVN 11th Armored Cavalry Regiment.

As a part of the Vietnamization program, the American "Blue Teams" are replaced by South Vietnamese "Brown Teams." The language barrier and above all the lack of training in airmobile tactics prevents the Brown Teams from achieving the same effectiveness as the American Blue Teams.

On 8 February 1971, the 1st Airborne Division of the 1st South Vietnamese Army crosses the Laotian border. At 1000 hours ARVN Rangers penetrate ten kilometers deep into the interior of Laos along Route Number 9, just beyond Khe Sanh. *Operation Lam Son 719* begins. This time the South Vietnamese make up the point of the lance for the action on the ground, the Americans having orders not to intervene in the ground fighting. The mission, as it was in the invasion of Cambodia, is to clean out major communist refuges and logistics bases.

The First Cav does not participate in this major offensive. It assures the security of the III Corps Area. This time air and tactical support is provided by four Troops of the 2[d] Squadron of the 17th Cavalry Regiment of the 101st Aviation Group. The helicopters come from the 1st Aviation Brigade, as well as a Squadron of helicopters from the US Marines. *Lam Son 719* lasts until 9 April 1971 and extends to a depth of about sixty kilometers almost to the town of Tchepone, the logistical center of the North Vietnamese in Laos.

The amount of matériel captured in Laos is at least as much as that recovered in Cambodia. The ARVN attack and destroy five supply depots. They capture four thousand individual weapons, 106 tanks and 405 trucks, as well as twenty thousand tons of munitions. The fighting costs the enemy 13,914 dead and sixty-nine men captured.

On the other side, the communist resistance was violent and the North Vietnamese anti-aircraft flak was very heavy. The density of fire from 12.7mm, 23mm, and 37mm machine gun fire made the sky unhealthy for helicopters and drew the attention of headquarters to their vulnerability. One hundred and seven are shot down.

Operation Lam Son 719 marks a turning point in the evolution of airmobile combat tactics and techniques. The most vulnerable helicopters are the Hueys that must descend on final approach and hover to offload their infantry troops. On the other hand the Cobras, though sometimes hit by 12.7mm rounds, are able more easily to escape, thanks to their handling characteristics and speed. Above all they can shoot back with their very considerable fire power. After the Laos operation, the Cobras, equipped with TOW missiles, are recognized as the best tank killers.

On 26 March 1971, at the Base at Bien Hoa, General Creighton Abrams, Commander in Chief of the American troops in Vietnam listens, moved, as the First Team's band plays *Garry Owen*. He is there for the ceremony where command passes from Major General Putnam to Major General James Smith.

"No other Division has fought as much in South Vietnam, or created such an image of combat efficiency, such a rapid reaction capability, or such professionalism as has the 1st Cavalry Division," exclaims General Abrams.

Three days later the Division folds its Colors, furls its battle streamers, packs away its guidons, and returns to the world, to Fort Hood, Texas. But, right up until the last minute, the units of the First Cavalry remain active and operational. The 1st of the 5th engaged in fifteen firefights during the final nine days of its presence on the ground. The 2^{d} Brigade turns over its fire bases to the South Vietnamese on 11 March.

Although the Division leaves Vietnam on 29 March, it only goes with two Brigades. The 3^{d} Brigade, organized as an independent force stays in country. On 15 March Brigadier General Jonathan Burton took command of the Garry Owen Brigade which became an autonomous unit.

The Brigade strength is augmented. It is brought up to four Infantry Battalions: the 2^{d} of the 5th, the 1st of the 7th, the 2^{d} of the 8th, and the 1st of the 12th. It has one Battalion of artillery as well as the 229th Assault Helicopter Battalion and the 215th Support Battalion. To that, add sixteen other company and platoon-sized units of artillery, infantry, communications, engineers, reconnaissance, and aviation.

The Garry Owen Brigade becomes a miniature Division with a strength of 7,600 men, equipped to carry out all the functions of an airmobile unit. It still has a many-sided mission. It must assure the security of a zone located around Saigon and Long Binh, and at the same time establish a cordon to protect the capital area from rockets or other unpleasant surprises. It still has the mission of searching out and destroying the enemy and his bases. Now, however, this role is mostly done using air power.

White Teams run armed reconnaissance patrols with the Cayuse. Red Teams of Cobras provide the destructive power. Working together they constitute the famous Pink Teams. They rack up about fifty percent of the kills and damage attributed to the 3^d Brigade during the last nine months of 1971.

On the ground, the Brigade uses its force in a more discrete manner but no less effectively. The Rangers of Hotel Company of the 75th Infantry work the terrain. General Burton trains them intensively and recruits for them from volunteers from the Brigade. The selection is strict. Only one man in four passes muster. Their specialty: penetration operations into enemy territory, special reconnaissance missions, and conducting ambushes. During the final nine months of 1971, thirty percent of enemy casualties are attributed to them.

The Brigade thus accomplishes a very large majority of its missions either through its air power, or thanks to its Rangers, who work under a cover of secrecy. The Infantry, ordered to intervene as little as possible on the ground, is thus quartered in its base areas and fire support bases.

General Burton must manage an enormous "factory" of 7,600 men whose occupation is not combat. The last draftees arrive weakened by campus propaganda and pacifist agitation. The lack of enemy action and boredom makes the troops an easy target for the Chinese drug dealers in Saigon. These entrepreneurs operate with the complicity of the Vietcong and the North Vietnamese who participate in the drug trafficking. And so this is where General Burton must wage his most difficult war.

He launches a major intervention program against drug abuse. He calls upon the services of his military intelligence specialists who work in close collaboration with South Vietnamese counterespionage personnel to ferret out the infrastructure of the drug trafficking hierarchy. General Burton has his Military Security Detachment assign women to the Brigade. It is the first time that special security personnel have been ordered to intervene in the affairs of a combat unit in Vietnam.

Along with the steps taken to repress drug use and drug trafficking, Burton sets up a detoxification and treatment center. This center tracks down drug users, detoxifies them, and follows through with administrative and judicial procedures. In six months, it treats three hundred cases.

Jonathan Burton, fifty-two years old, is a veteran of the War in the Pacific and of the fighting at Leyte and Luzon. A horseman of Olympic caliber, he trained the military equestrian team for the United States for the 1948 Games in London and participated himself in the 1965 Games. He is also a helicopter pilot and has completed two Vietnam tours in the First Cav. He is not the type of man to permit a tiny minority to distract the unit from its duty or to besmirch the image of the Garry Owen Brigade. He is fully determined to stop any risk of gangrene.

"Morale crises; they must be solved in some other way than by drugs and hospitalization. The only way to get control of this kind of moral depression and the foolishness it engenders is to get the men out in the field. Except for basic security, get everybody out of the base areas and the forward support and fire bases."

Burton puts into practice a system of unit rotation. From then on, every platoon and every company, in turn, spends fifteen days in the field. Inserted with arms, ammo, and rations, the grunts must again get active and search out the enemy. The FNGs go through a very tough training session at Long Binh before they conform to the mold of the Garry Owen Brigade.

Choppers bring in hot meals and clean uniforms, but the new troops are out in the field.[2] They stand watch from their fighting positions or nap an hour or two in turn. The time spent in base areas and support bases is limited to five days, and this time is completely devoted to maintenance and cleaning details as well as improving the defensive perimeter and conducting patrols.

Every forty-five days, the reconnaissance platoons and companies are sent on a brief R and R at a rest center in Vung Tau operated by the First Cav that they had set up in 1971. Known in the Colonial Era as Cap-Saint-Jacques, this ocean-front resort had already been used as a rest center by the French Army in Indochina. The grunts get a three-day break here after six weeks in the field. In this way, Burton restores the morale of his Brigade to good health, and gets it, less touched than other units, through the "Vietnam Syndrome" that accompanied the final months of the War. On 14 December 1971, General Burton, in his turn, passes command of the Gary Owen Brigade to General James Hamlet.

As the result of the redistribution and transfer of American units, the 3[d] Brigade absorbs a portion of the effectives from the 101st Airborne Division. They join the Garry Owen Brigade at a rhythm of five hundred men a week. The security of Saigon and the training of Vietnamese Regional Forces remains the major preoccupation of the Brigade.

The Brigade often has occasion to intervene near Xuan Loc in Long Khanh Province. There are several contacts with elements of the NVA 33[d] Division. The Brigade uncovers important caches of flour and rice in the area. The Americans receive for distribution a part of the food aid destined for Vietnam as participants in *Op-*

eration Joined Hands. The Brigade establishes an airfield and a POL dump at Xuan Loc to facilitate its operations in the Province.

On 30 March 1972, at 0515 hours, General Vo Nguyen Giap launches the North Vietnamese Army in a major offensive. It begins with an attack in the Demilitarized Zone then, starting on 3 April, forty-eight thousand North Vietnamese and Vietcong from the *Fishhook* in Cambodia fall on Loc Ninh, then lay siege to An Loc. Radio Hanoi proclaims An Loc the new capital of the South. The 9th VC Division is designated to have the honor of marching in review at this inauguration.

Fighting around Loc Ninh and An Loc last until 15 May. B-52 Bombers unload thousands of tons of bombs. Third Brigade Cobras strafe the waves of enemy infantrymen that attack, elbow to elbow, as if indifferent to the deluge of fire. But the anti-air artillery, employing 82mm guns and SAM7 Missiles, make providing fire support much more risky. On 12 May, in less than a half hour, five Cobras are shot down by the missiles. The 3[d] Brigade lifts and supports the South Vietnamese troops who counterattack.

In forty days, the Garry Owen Cobras destroy more than one hundred T54 Tanks, as well as many armored troop carriers and several anti-air batteries around An Loc. The 1972 North Vietnamese offensive ends with a decisiveness that reassures the Americans that the South Vietnamese are quite able to accept responsibility for their own defense. By 31 March, just after the beginning of the offensive, the Americans had only ninety-six thousand troops remaining in country. Now, they accelerate the repatriation of their forces.

After their defeat at An Loc, the communists seem to be winded, whereas the South Vietnamese show themselves to be more determined and confident than ever. The Americans prepare to send the Garry Owen Brigade home. First, reduced to a smaller Task Force, the last units leave Vietnam in June to return to Fort Hood where the 1st Cavalry Division has been for the past year.

During this time, the First Cav has already turned over a new page in its history. It is in the process of an organizational mutation to address the demands of potentially different operational environments. Since 5 May 1971 the 1st Cavalry Division, Airmobile, has become the 1st Cavalry Division, Tricap. This designation indicates a division with a triple capability. Under the influence of Generals Westmoreland and Kinnard, the Division combines an Armored Brigade, an Airmobile Brigade, and an Air Cavalry Brigade. The Division goes to Germany to work out the details of this new organization. The European Theater of Operations is again the first priority for the Americans.

On 23 June 1973, the Nixon Administration, in the middle of the Watergate Scandal, signs a cease fire with Hanoi. The process of withdrawal of American forces enters its final phase.

For two years the South Vietnamese were able to defend themselves, but Saigon will fall on 29 April 1975. For lack of support, they will not be able to stop the North Vietnamese offensive launched from the mountains and highlands. The North Vietnamese strategy is the same as in 1965, just before the bloody fighting in the Ia Drang Valley, the battle related at the beginning of this story.[3] This time, however, Hal Moore and his Garry Owen Troopers are no longer there to stop the flood of invading North Vietnamese soldiers. The North Vietnamese make themselves masters of the highlands before falling upon Saigon, which they rename Ho Chi Minh City.

Translator's Notes
[1] Long Range Reconnaissance Patrol.

[2] Clean uniforms and hot meals were not always the rule, at least during the early years in Vietnam in the First Cav. After a week or ten days on the move: climbing, digging, pushing oneself to the limit, hungry, exhausted, an infantry soldier and his uniform become incredibly filthy. The uniform is often in tatters, and even combat boots begin to wear out and become unserviceable. You cannot get clean, and you are always a little bit hungry. Most men, young and lean to begin with, lose ten to twenty pounds and are down to skin, bones, sinew, and muscle. They are in the best shape they have ever been in their lives. The crud, discomfort, and hunger pangs are an inconvenience, but one to which the soldier quickly adapts. Quality of life issues pale next to survival issues. There is, however, another and more important aspect to these conditions. First, the unwashed soldier stinks. His odor gives him away to the enemy out to a distance of several hundred meters, depending on the direction of the wind. Second, the American soldier on operation is the hardest working living creature known to man. He literally burns up all the calories he consumes, and then begins to consume himself. I issued four rations per man per day, and we were still hungry. It is not just a matter of hot meals for morale purposes; it is a matter of food energy that must be provided to sustain the pace of operations. The folks that design the rations have an incomplete concept of the energy consumption of a soldier operating in the field.

[3] For the professional soldiers of my generation, who were young men at the time, who understood duty but had no hand in politics, who served one or two or several years defending the

liberty of others, that America abandoned the Vietnamese is to this day an embarrassment. We were not quitters, and would have fought on to victory. We wish the courageous and hardworking people of Vietnam well. May they one day soon enjoy a greater measure of individual liberty and political freedom.

FINAL ACCOUNT

The First Cavalry Division conducted operations in Vietnam from September 1965 to June 1972

In eighty-two months more than 150,000 men served under the emblem of the chevron and the horse's head.

In this service, 4,469 American soldiers were killed;
25 are missing;
20,070 were wounded in combat.

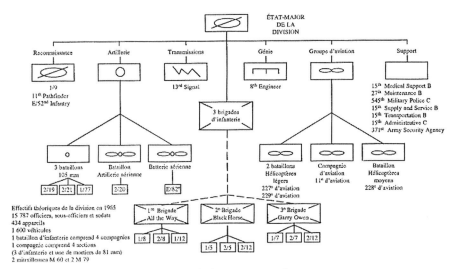

Organization of the 1ˢᵗ Cavalry Division.

CHRONOLOGY OF THE AMERICAN ENGAGEMENT IN VIETNAM

1950
7 February: The United States recognizes the legitimacy of Bao-Dai as Emperor. The Americans establish diplomatic representation in Saigon.

1954
7 May: The Viet Minh surround Dien Bien Phu.

24 October: President Dwight Eisenhower notifies South Vietnamese President Ngo Dinh Diem that the United States would henceforth provide its assistance directly to South Vietnam and not through the intermediary of French authorities.

1956
28 April: An American Military Assistance and Advisory Group (MAAG) takes charge of training the South Vietnamese Forces. French forces leave Vietnam.

1959
May: The Headquarters of the American Pacific Theater begins to send American military advisors to Vietnam.

1960
5 May: The strength of the MAAG goes from 327 to 685 men.

1961
11 – 13 May: Vice President Lyndon Johnson visits South Vietnam.

16 November: President Kennedy decides to step up military assistance to South Vietnam. He increases the number of military advisors.

1962
8 February: The MAAG becomes the Military Assistance Command Vietnam (MACV). It consists of four thousand men and is commanded by General Paul Harkins.

27 February: Two South Vietnamese aircraft attack the Palace of President Diem.

1963

April: The beginning of the *Chieu Hoi (Open Arms) Program* to rally the Viet Cong.

1-2 November: A military coup, with American participation, overthrows Diem. He and his brother are assassinated.

15 November: The American government announces the withdrawal of one thousand of the fifteen thousand American advisors; McNamara predicts the end of the conflict by 1965.

22 November: President Kennedy is assassinated in Dallas, Texas. Lyndon Johnson becomes President of the United States.

1964

7 March: The first American combat units (3,500 Marines) debark at Da Nang.

20 June: General William Westmoreland replaces General Harkins at the head of MACV.

2 August: Gulf of Tonkin incident. Shooting incident between North Vietnamese Patrol-Torpedo boats and the American Destroyer *Maddox*.

4 August: The Destroyer *Turner Joy* reports being attacked in a similar manner.

5 August: Aircraft from the American VIIth Fleet reply to the attacks with bombs.

7 August: The United States Congress adopts the Tonkin Gulf Resolution that grants war powers to the President.

1 November: Viet Cong Artillery bombards Bien Hoa killing two Americans.

November: Lyndon Johnson is elected President of the United States. The number of American service personnel stationed in Vietnam rises to twenty-three thousand.

1965

2 March: *Operation Rolling Thunder* begins aerial bombardments over North Vietnam.

8 March: The 9th Marine Brigade, commanded by General Frederick Karch, debarks at Da Nang.

3 May: The American Army's 173^d Airborne Brigade arrives in South Vietnam.

24 July: The first bombing of the Haiphong and Hanoi areas.

28 July: President Johnson announces on television that he will order the First Cavalry Division to Vietnam.

13 September: Arrival of the First Cav at Qui Nhon. American forces reach a strength of 181,000 men during the autumn.

15 November: Battle at the Drang River Valley.

1966

31 January: Resumption of bombing of targets in North Vietnam.

February: The 1st Cavalry Division deploys along the coast of Binh Dinh Province. *Operation Masher/White Wing.*

March: The communists overrun an American Special Forces Camp in the A Shau Valley.

2 March: The Secretary of Defense, Robert McNamara, announces that there are now 215,000 American soldiers in Vietnam with another 20,000 on the way.

12 April: For the first time, B-52s bomb objectives in North Vietnam.

1 September: General Charles de Gaulle gives an address in Phnom Penh against the American military intervention in Vietnam.

December: Establishment of the "McNamara Line," employing electronic surveillance devices and intended to slow down infiltrators from the North. It is installed just to the south of the Demilitarized Zone.

1967

11 February: Beginning of *Operation Pershing* that will last a year in Binh Dinh Province. Development of the politics of pacification.

22 February: *Operation Junction City*, the biggest operation of the War, begins in Tay Ninh Province. American strength reaches 436,000 men.[1]

15 April: At the request of the South Vietnamese Government, the American Marines are assigned responsibility for the frontier between the two Vietnams.

19 April: *Operation Lejeune* begins. The First Cav sends a Brigade to relieve the Marines at Duc Pho.

3 September: General Nguyen Van Thieu is elected President of South Vietnam.

13 September: North Vietnamese assault against the Con Thien Fire Support Base. Beginning of the siege of *Angels' Hill.*

1968

20 January: Beginning of the siege of Khe Sanh.

27 January: General Tolson, First Cav Division Commander, sets up his headquarters near Quang Tri at Camp Evans, in the I Corps Zone.

30 January: The North Vietnamese and Viet Cong begin the Tet Offensive. The 3^d Brigade goes to clear out the Quang Tri area.

<u>31 January:</u> The communists take Hue.

<u>1 February:</u> The 1st Brigade intervenes in the Hue area.

<u>24 February:</u> Hue is retaken from the communists in its entirety after twenty-five hours of fighting.

<u>31 March:</u> Televised speech by President Johnson who announces a halt to bombing raids north of the 20th parallel, the improved capabilities of the South Vietnamese Army, and that he will not run for reelection.

<u>1 April:</u> Clark Clifford replaces Robert McNamara as Secretary of Defense. General Tolson begins *Operation Pegasus* with thirty thousand men.

<u>8 April:</u> Relief of Khe Sanh.

<u>19 April:</u> *Operation Delaware.* The First Cav Division moves out to clean up the A Shau Valley.

<u>3 May:</u> President Lyndon Johnson accepts the North Vietnamese offer to hold preliminary peace talks in Paris.

<u>3 – 5 May:</u> A wave of communist attacks.

<u>13 May:</u> American and North Vietnamese delegations hold their first official meeting in Paris.

<u>27 October:</u> *Operation Liberty Canyon.* The First Cav crosses the 17th parallel near Saigon, executing a movement of nine hundred kilometers.

<u>31 October:</u> President Johnson announces the end of the bombing of North Vietnam.

<u>November:</u> Election of Richard Nixon as President of the United States.

1969

<u>25 January:</u> Official opening in Paris of negotiations for a cease fire.

<u>23 – 24 February:</u> Communist attacks in South Vietnam.

<u>5 June:</u> New American air raids on North Vietnam in reprisal for the downing of a reconnaissance plane.

<u>8 June:</u> In the course of his meeting at Midway with Thieu, Nixon announces an initial withdrawal of 25,000 American soldiers.

<u>4 September:</u> Ho Chi Minh dies.

<u>16 September:</u> President Nixon repatriates an additional 35,000 men. There are still 474,000 in country.

1970

<u>29 April:</u> Nixon, in a televised address, announces an imminent invasion of Cambodia in response to North Vietnamese activities with the objective of cleaning out their sanctuaries.

<u>1 May:</u> The First Cav enters Cambodia with South Vietnamese Army units on *Operation Total Victory*.

<u>29 June:</u> The First Cav leaves Cambodia. The score for the Operation: 22,892 individual weapons, 2,509 crew-served weapons, 16,762,167 rounds of small arms ammunition, 199,552 anti-aircraft machine-gun rounds, 68,593 mortar rounds, 43,160 B40 Rockets, 29,185 recoilless rifle rounds, 62,022 hand grenades, 40 tons of explosives, 2,133 22mm rockets, 435 vehicles of various types, 55 tons of medicine, and 7,000 tons of rice.

<u>15 October:</u> The Americans withdraw another 40,000 men from South Vietnam, leaving 335,000 still in country.

<u>31 December:</u> Congress repeals the Gulf of Tonkin Resolution.

1971

<u>8 February:</u> *Operation Lam Son 719*, an incursion into Laos by South Vietnamese Rangers.

<u>9 April:</u> End of *Operation Lam Son 719*. The accounting: 4,000 individual weapons, 1,500 crew-served weapons, 20,000 tons of ammunition, 12,000 tons of rice, 106 tanks, 76 artillery pieces, and 405 trucks.

<u>24 April:</u> Massive anti-war demonstration of some 500,000 pacifists in Washington, DC. A similar demonstration in San Francisco.

<u>29 April:</u> Two Brigades of the First Cav Division leave Vietnam and return to the United States, to Fort Hood, Texas. The Third Garry Owen Brigade remains in the Long Binh area near Saigon.

<u>13 June:</u> The *New York Times* begins to publish the "Secret" Pentagon Papers about the American involvement in Vietnam.

<u>October:</u> Thieu is reelected President of South Vietnam.

<u>26 – 30 December:</u> In response to North Vietnamese reinforcements in South Vietnam, American aircraft attack airfields and other military objectives in North Vietnam.

1972

<u>13 January:</u> Richard Nixon announces that American strength in South Vietnam will be brought down to 69,000 men by the 1st of May.

<u>30 March:</u> Communist general offensive.

<u>3 April:</u> In response, the Aircraft Carrier *Kitty Hawk* links up with two other fighting ships already in position off the Vietnamese coast.

<u>5 April:</u> The US Air Force reinforces its units based in Thailand.

<u>6 April:</u> Marine Aviation lands at Da Nang. Admiral Thomas Moorer, Chairman of the Joint Chiefs of Staff, prepares to resume shelling and bombing of North Vietnam.

1 May: Quang Tri falls into communist hands.

8 May: Richard Nixon, in an address, announces the mining of North Vietnamese ports.

22 May: Moscow: A Nixon-Brejnev Summit on strategic relations between the United States and the Soviet Union.

12 June: South Vietnamese troops break the siege of An Loc begun on 5 April.

26 June: The 3^d Brigade in its turn returns to Fort Hood.

12 August: The last American ground combat troops leave South Vietnam. Remaining are only 43,000 pilots and ground support personnel.

16 September: The South Vietnamese retake Quang Tri.

18 December: Following North Vietnamese provocation, President Nixon orders the renewal of bombing north of the 20th parallel on Hanoi and Haiphong. The Paris Peace Talks are suspended until 8 January.

30 December: Bombing north of the 20th parallel ends after the North Vietnamese agreed to negotiate a cease fire.

1973

23 January: Henry Kissinger and Le Duc Tho initial the Paris Peace Agreement putting an end to the fighting and prescribing the release of prisoners of war.

27 January: Henry Kissinger, Le Duc Tho, and representatives of Saigon and of the Viet Cong officially sign the peace accords in Paris.

29 March: The last American troops leave South Vietnam. All that remain are those in the Office of the Defense Attaché.

1 April: The last American prisoners from North Vietnam arrive at Clark Air Force Base in the Philippines.

1974

4 January: Thieu affirms that the war has started up again in South Vietnam. Fifty-five government soldiers are killed in two confrontations with communist troops.

5 August: The American Congress limits to one billion dollars the amount of assistance to South Vietnam for the fiscal year ending on 30 June 1975.

9 August: Richard Nixon resigns from the Presidency as a result of the Watergate Affair.

24 September: The American Congress reduces by half the amount of funds programmed for South Vietnam.

1975

1 January: The North Vietnamese take Phuoc Long Province.

5 March: The North Vietnamese attack in the Central Highlands.

10 – 15 April: The North Vietnamese take Xuan Loc.

17 April: Phnom Penh falls into the hands of insurgents.

20 April: Da Nang falls.

21 April: Thieu resigns.

28 April: Duong Van Minh, a participant in the overthrow of Diem in 1963, takes up the reins of the South Vietnamese Government.

30 April: North Vietnamese troops enter Saigon while the last Americans and a large number of their South Vietnamese allies are evacuated. Minh announces the unconditional surrender of South Vietnam.

Translator's Notes

[1] All references to American strength, personnel, troops, and men include, of course, the gallant women who served there in uniform or some other capacity alongside their brothers. Not to be overlooked are the men and women that came to entertain the troops.

BIBLIOGRAPHY

Printed Material

Bernier, Jean-Pierre. *GM100: Combats d'Indochine après Diên Biên Phu.* Paris: Presses de la Cité, 1977.

Brennan, Mathew. *Brennan's War:, Vietnam 1965-1969.* Novato, California: Presidio Press, 1985.

Brennan, Mathew. *Stories from the 1st Squadron, 9th Cavalry in Vietnam.* Novato, California: Presidio Press, 1987.

Colby, William. Vietnam: *Histoire secrète d'une victoire perdue.* Perrin, 1992.

Coleman, Major J. D., ed. *First Air Cavalry Division Vietnam 1965-1969.* Tokyo: Dia Nippon Printing Company, Ltd., 1970.

Coleman, Major J. D. *Incursion.* New York: St. Martin Press, 1991.

Coleman, Major J. D. *Pleiku: The Dawn of Helicopter Warfare in Vietnam.* New York: St. Martin Press, 1988.

Downey, Fairfax. *Indian Fighting Army.* Scribner's edition, 1941.

Hasford, Gustav. *The Short-Timers.* New York: Bantam Books, 1979.

Herr, Michael. *Dispatches.* Alfred A. Knopf, Inc., 1968.

Kelly, Colonel Francis J. *US Army Special Forces 1961-1971.* Department of the Army, 1985.

Lanning, Michael Lee and Cragg, Dan. *Inside the VC and the NVA: the Real Story of North Vietnam's Armed Forces.* New York: Ballantine Books, 1992. (Source used by translator.)

Manley, Perry. *UH-1 Huey in Action.* Squadron Signal Publications.

Mason, Robert. *Chickenhawk.* Corgi Books, 1984.

Merill, James M. *Spurs to Glory: The Story of the United States Cavalry.* New York: Rand McNally & Co., 1966.

Myerson, Joel D. *Images of a Lengthy War.* Center of Military History, 1986.

Moore, Lieutenant General Harold G. and Galloway, Joseph L. *We Were Soldiers Once ... and Young.* New York: Random House, 1992.

Mutza, Wayne. *CH-47: Chinook in Action.* Squadron Signal Publications.

Orcival, François d' and Chaunac, Jacques de. *Les Marines à Khé Sanh.* Paris: Presses de la Cité, 1979.

Pearson, Lieutenant General Willard. *The War in the Northern Provinces 1966-1968.* Department of the Army, 1991.